Journal of the American Revolution

JOURNAL

OF THE

AMERICAN

REVOLUTION

ANNUAL VOLUME 2018

WESTHOLME
Yardley

Westholme Publishing, LLC
904 Edgewood Road
Yardley, Pennsylvania 19067
Visit our Web site at www.westholmepublishing.com

ISBN: 978–1–59416–304-3

Printed in the United States of America.

CONTENTS

EDITOR'S INTRODUCTION

Life is full of surprises. So is the editor's desk at *Journal of the American Revolution*. Completion of our fifth year means that we've published over 1000 articles, and this is our fifth annual volume showcasing a diverse sample of articles from the previous twelve months. Having come so far may be a surprise in itself, but the real surprise is the range of content that our contributors continue to provide.

Wool was an important consideration to the founders of the United States—we didn't know that. An American ambassador made overtures to Russia during the American Revolution—that was a new one to us. Benjamin Franklin played a key role in the treatment of American prisoners of war held in Great Britain—is there anything that man didn't do? Privateering vessels played a role in the slave trade—we'd never thought about that before. The Knights of Malta lobbied to establish themselves in the new United States—we had no idea. And these are just a few of the topics addressed in articles in this latest annual volume, only a small sample of the broad range of articles published in *Journal of the American Revolution* this past year.

The more we learn, the more we realize that we're only scratching the surface. There are more perspectives to consider, more primary sources to present, more events to chronicle, more personalities to analyze. That's a good thing. It means that *Journal of the American Revolution* will continue to provide fresh, insightful material for years to come—and that countless surprises will cross the editor's desk.

Country Crowds in Revolutionary Massachusetts: Mobs and Militia

❀❧ RAY RAPHAEL ❦❀

Peter Oliver, the Crown-appointed Chief Justice of provincial Massachusetts, knew how to discredit popular protest. Mindless and incapable of acting on their own, crowds that opposed British imperial policies "were like the Mobility of all Countries, perfect Machines, wound up by any Hand who might first take the Winch." They needed a director who could "fabricate the Structure of Rebellion from a single straw."[1] Without ringleaders or rabble-rousers, the masses would remain inert.

To this day, country crowds in Revolutionary Massachusetts are often viewed this way. One recent account of the 1774 popular actions in rural Massachusetts puts it this way: "Radical leaders drew forth the mobs. In the nether parts of the province, armed mobs utterly refused to allow the courts to open."[2] Unwittingly, this reflects the old Tory view of revolutionary dynamics: so-called "mobs" do not act on their own volition but must be aroused by politically astute leaders.

Such portrayals skew our narratives of the American Revolution. Rebellious colonies were overwhelmingly rural—in Massachusetts, ninety-five percent of the people lived outside of Boston. To understand how that province cast off British rule, we need to take a closer look at crowd actions in the hinterlands. Who *were* those people whom leaders supposedly "drew forth"? How did they organize, and what, exactly, did they do?

MILITIA

Let's start with the largest gatherings, which closed the courts in the shiretowns, or county seats, throughout Massachusetts. On September

1. Peter Oliver, *Origin and Progress of the American Rebellion,* eds. Douglass Adair and John A. Schutz (Stanford: Stanford University Press, 1961), 65, 75.
2. Derek Beck, *Igniting the American Revolution* (Naperville, IL: Sourcebooks, 2015), 40-41.

6, 1774, in the town of Worcester, 4,622 militiamen from 37 companies throughout the county closed the Court of Common Pleas and the Court of General Sessions.[3] That was the date these courts were first slated to convene under the newly enacted Massachusetts Government Act, which overturned democratic safeguards guaranteed by the 1691 Massachusetts Charter.

A broad range of citizens, not just a handful of "radical leaders," had been planning for this event. First, they armed. On July 4, 1774, in the town of Worcester, the American Political Society, which included about one-quarter of the enfranchised citizenry, declared "that each, and every, member of our Society, be forth with provided, with two pounds of gun powder each 12 flints and led answerable thereunto."[4] Then, on August 9, fifty-one members of the Committees of Correspondence from twenty-two towns in Worcester County met for two days to discuss "wise, prudent, and spirited measures ... to prevent the execution of those most alarming acts of parliament, respecting our constitution."[5]

One week later, citizens from Berkshire County closed their county courts, setting a precedent that Worcester and other counties would soon follow. On August 30, when the Worcester County Committees of Correspondence convened once again, 130 delegates attended. This assemblage "recommended to the inhabitants of this county to attend, in person," the forthcoming court sessions "in order to prevent the execution of the late act of parliament." Further, it recommended that each attendee "purchase at least two pounds of powder in addition to any he may have on hand" and to "use all his exertions to supply his neighbors fully."[6] Word had spread that Thomas Gage, military governor of the province, was planning to send troops to Worcester to protect the courts. An armed confrontation seemed possible, even likely.

With stakes this high, delegates to the convention worried that some stray shot might set off a conflagration. "It is recommended to the several towns, that they choose proper and suitable officers, and a sufficient

3. Ebenezer Parkman, Diary, September 6 and 7, 1774, American Antiquarian Society. The diary can be accessed at: rayraphael.com/documents_2/parkman_diary.htm
4. American Political Society, Minutes, American Antiquarian Society. This can be accessed at gigi.mwa.org/netpub/server.np?quickfind=271132&sorton=filename&catalog=catalog&site=manuscripts&template=results.np
5. *The Journals of Each Provincial Congress of Massachusetts in 1774 and 1775, and of the Committee of Safety, with an Appendix, containing the Proceedings of the County Conventions,* ed. William Lincoln (Boston: Dutton and Wentworth, 1838), 628, 631. This can be accessed at archive.org/details/journalsofeachprma00mass
6. Lincoln, *Proceedings of the County Conventions,* 632, 634.

number, to regulate the movements of each town, and prevent any disorder which might otherwise happen; and that it is enjoined on the inhabitants of each respective town, that they adhere strictly to the orders and directions of the officers."[7] People were to act as soldiers, not as an unwieldy mob.

But on September 2, as tens of thousands mustered in response to rumors that British soldiers had set Boston ablaze, Governor Gage had a change of heart. He instructed Lord Dartmouth, secretary of state for the colonies, that although he had intended "to send a Body of Troops to Worcester, to protect the Courts there," he would not in fact dispatch any troops. "Disturbance being so general, and not confined to any particular Spot," he did not know "where to send them to be of Use." Sending soldiers to quell every "disturbance" would require "dividing them in small Detachments, and tempt Numbers to fall upon them, which was reported to be the Scheme of the Directors of these Operations."[8] (Note the Tory perspective: "Directors" had a "Scheme," while the people themselves were mere pawns.)

When the American Political Society learned that Gage would not be sending troops, it resolved "not to bring our fire-arms into town the 6 day of Sept."[9] Guns were no longer necessary, and a chance firing could taint the day's events. Only a few companies, coming from afar and ignorant of the new policy, arrived with weapons.

The militiamen's mood, formerly tense, turned festive and triumphant. Attention turned to staging the court closure in a dramatic fashion that colonials favored. But who would write the script and direct the action? A few ringleaders or the "body of the people," as they said in those days?

In Boston, "the body of the people" assembled in a one sizeable, group. Here "the body" was a composite of thirty-seven discrete militia companies, the military embodiments of each town's citizenry. This arrangement complicated the proceedings. Each company chose a special representative, distinct from the military captain it had already elected, "to wait on the judges." This ad hoc committee then met with the court officials, who had retreated to Daniel Heywood's tavern after being barred from the courthouse. The committee and the officials

7. Lincoln, *Proceedings of the County Conventions*, 632-3.
8. Gage to Dartmouth, September 2, 1774, *The Correspondence of General Thomas Gage, 1763-1775*, Clarence E. Carter, ed. (New Haven: Yale University Press, 1931-3), 1: 370.
9. American Political Society, Minutes; Parkman, Diary. Parkman reported that "a few companys had arms," and according to a second-hand account from an anonymous Tory, "about one thousand of them had fire-arms." Boston's *Weekly News-Letter*, February 23, 1775, and New York's *Rivington's Gazette*, March 9, 1775.

hammered out the terms of surrender: a formal statement that Breck Parkman, a participant, characterized as "a paper . . . signifying that they would endeavor &c." The draft was then taken back to the separate companies, to be approved or rejected. As it turned out, militiamen determined that the judges' statement was no more than an empty promise—in Parkman's words, it "was not satisfying." Representatives then returned to Heywood's tavern to devise a stringent, binding contract. The process was democratic but cumbersome and time-consuming, and when some militiamen grew impatient, the Committees of Correspondence appointed three men to inquire about the delay.[10]

Finally, in the mid-afternoon, militia companies formed along both sides of Main Street. The lines stretched for a quarter-mile, Uxbridge in front of the courthouse, Westborough next, and so on, down to Upton and Templeton, stationed outside Heywood's tavern.[11] When all were in place, two dozen court officials—judges, justices of the peace, court attorneys, and any whose power had been sanctioned by the Crown—emerged from the tavern. Hat in hand to signal deference, each official recited his formal recantation to the first militia company. But other militiamen could not hear, so each official then made his way through the gauntlet, repeating his recantation over thirty times. They all pledged "that all judicial proceeding be stayed . . . on account of the unconstitutional act of Parliament . . . which, if effected, will reduce the inhabitants to mere arbitrary power."[12]

MOBS

In addition to closing the courts, the Massachusetts citizenry went after the thirty-six men whom the Crown had just appointed to the Council, taking the place of elected council members. One-by-one, each councilor was confronted by inhabitants of his town and told to resign. Those who refused, faced with their neighbors' wrath, were forced to leave home.

Returning home to Plymouth after taking his oath for the Council, George Watson unsuspectingly attended church. The *Boston Evening-Post* reported what happened there:

> When he came into the House of publick Worship, a great number of the principal Inhabitants of that Town left the Meeting-House im-

---

10. Parkman, Diary; Lincoln, *Proceedings of the County Conventions*, 635–637.
11. The order of formation comes from Parkman's diary.
12. Parkman, Diary; Lincoln, *Proceedings of the County Conventions*, 637. A detailed narrative of the day's proceedings appears in Ray Raphael, *The First American Revolution: Before Lexington and Concord* (New York: The New Press, 2002), 130–38.

mediately upon his entering it; "being determined not to worship in fellowship with one, who has sworn to support that change of our constitution, which professedly establishes despotism among us."[13]

Watson got the message and agreed to resign. He presented his reasons in a letter to Governor Gage:

By my accepting of this Appointment, I find that I have rendered myself very obnoxious, not only to the inhabitants of this place, but also to those of the neighboring towns. On my business as a Merchant I depend, for the support of myself and Family, and of this I must be intirely deprived, in short, I am reduced to the alternative of resigning my Seat at the Council Board, or quitting this, the place of my Nativity, which will be attended with the most fatal Consequences to myself, and family.[14]

When Josiah Edson, another councilor, went to church after taking his oath, his fellow parishioners in Bridgewater did not "even deign to sing ye psalm after his reading it, being deacon of the parish." That was ultimatum enough, and Edson, refusing to resign, departed for the protection of British troops in Boston, a safe haven for those who no longer dared to live among their own townsmen.[15]

Those who neither resigned nor departed were treated harshly. Joshua Loring of Roxbury was awakened at midnight by "five men disguised, their faces black'd, hatts flap'd, and with cutlasses in their hands."[16] Timothy Ruggles of Hardwick, fearing what might happen if he returned home after taking his oath, sought refuge with a friend in Dartmouth, one hundred miles away—but he could not escape so easily. There, his prize horse "had his Mane and Tail cut off, and his Body painted all over."[17]

After taking his oath, Abijah Willard of Lancaster journeyed to Union, Connecticut, to avoid his angry neighbors. Yet Union's patriots seized him, tossed him in jail for a night, and then returned him to Brim-

13. *Boston Evening-Post,* August 29, 1774.

14. George Watson to Gage, August 30, 1774, in L. Kinvin Wroth, ed., *Province in Rebellion: A Documentary History of the Founding of the Commonwealth of Massachusetts, 1774-1775* (Cambridge: Harvard University Press, 1975), 533. Watson's public resignation appears in the *Massachusetts Spy,* September 22, 1774.

15. Andrews to Barrell, August 31, 1774, in "Letters of John Andrews of Boston, 1772-1776," Massachusetts Historical Society, *Proceedings,* 8 (1864-1865), 349–350; see also *Boston Evening-Post,* August 29.

16. Joshua Loring to Thomas Gage, August 31, 1774, in Wroth, *Province in Rebellion,* 537–538.

17. *Boston Evening-Post,* August 29, 1774.

field, Massachusetts, just over the border. He was placed in the hands of four hundred local citizens who "called a Council of themselves, and Condemned Colonel Willard to Newgate Prison, in Symsbury; and a number set off and carried him six miles on the way thither."[18] Finally, once he agreed to resign, Willard was set free.

Yes, these were "mobs," but like the militia companies in Worcester, they were not under the command of alleged leaders. Willard's tormentors "called a Council of themselves" to determine his fate, and this was common. When Berkshire County's David Ingersoll was seized by a mob, participants took "Several votes one way or another" before deciding in the end to release him.[19] In Braintree, Abigail Adams witnessed an out-of-doors "council" from her window. A troupe of about two hundred men, having forced the sheriff to burn two warrants he was attempting to deliver, wanted to shout "huzzah"—but alas, it was the Lord's Day. Should they or should they not disturb the Sabbath? "They call'd a vote," Abigail reported to her husband John, and "it being Sunday evening it passed in the negative."[20]

Such behavior should come as no surprise. Democratic principles served as a foundation for communitarian life in New England, even in times of heated protest. But the Massachusetts Revolution of 1774, although truly democratic, did not resemble the liberal democracy we think of today, in which rights of unpopular minorities are legally protected. It was a less refined majoritarian form of democracy, in which crowds had their way in any manner. When Jesse Dunbar purchased some "fat Cattle" for resale from Nathaniel Ray Thomas, a Crown-appointed councilor from Marshfield, a crowd skinned and gutted one of the carcasses, placed Dunbar inside the belly, and carted him from one town to the next as local citizens hurled mud or tripe at his face.[21] Shaming was the name of the game. Outright violence was rare, although the threat of violence was omnipresent. Few Tories were actually tarred and feathered—but only because the mere presence of a bucket of tar generally sufficed to produce submission.

More often than not, even acts of intimidation were considered affairs. A crowd deliberated before an event and during it, holding what

18. Dispatch from New London, September 2, 1774, in St. Clair Clarke and Peter Force, *American Archives,* 4th series, 1:731; Declaration of Abijah Willard, August 25, 1774, in Wroth, *Province in Rebellion,* 527–528.
19. Clarke and Force, *American Archives,* 4th series, 1:731; Declaration of David Ingersoll, in Wroth, *Province in Rebellion,* 606–609.
20. Abigail Adams to John Adams, September 14, 1774, *Adams Family Correspondence,* L. H. Butterfield, ed. (Cambridge: Belknap Press, 1963), 1:152.
21. Clarke and Force, *American Archives,* 4th series, 1:1260–61.

was in effect a mobile town meeting. Why is it so difficult to imagine that people in the hinterlands of Massachusetts, rehearsed in the practice of democracy for over a century, might rise up on their own when disenfranchised by Parliament—without being under the command of a few alleged ringleaders?

The problem stems, in part, from the implicit acceptance of an urban-centered model for revolutionary dynamics. In Boston, forceful individuals pushed their agendas through the press and public oratory. Witness John Adams's iconic remark: "The evening spent in preparing for the next day's newspaper,—a curious employment, cooking up paragraphs, articles, occurrences, &c., working the political engine!"[22] Even at mass meetings, prominent speakers commanded the podium while ordinary folks huzzahed or hooted them down. Conveniently, such venues have allowed historians to trace revolutionary politics through detailed newspaper accounts and the extant writings of "key" individuals who spoke at crowd gatherings.

In Massachusetts townships outside of Boston, the venues of political life were quite different: regularly scheduled town meetings, militia training days, and quarterly sessions of the courts, as well as informal encounters in public houses or other community hubs such as blacksmiths shops.[23] Many political interactions transpired orally, leaving historians out of the loop, but we do have some records. To understand the "engines" of revolution in rural Massachusetts, we look not only at the scanty press reports in Boston papers but also at the minutes of town meetings, often buried in basements of town halls; the journals of the Committees of Correspondence county conventions; and of course personal accounts of the multifarious confrontations that comprised this ubiquitous uprising. The sweeping social movement that transformed the political landscape in the fall of 1774—and set the stage for military conflict the following spring—was truly a group effort. We struggle with how to narrate this people's revolution, which was to a large extent anonymous. Traditional trickle-down narratives, in which a few alleged leaders drive the agenda, or dismissive accounts of mindless "mobs," will never suffice.

22. John Adams, Diary, September 2, 1769, *The Works of John Adams*, ed. Charles Francis Adams (Boston: Charles C. Little and James Brown, 1850), 2:219.
23. For the blacksmith shops as political hubs, see Ray Raphael, "Blacksmith Timothy Bigelow and the Massachusetts Revolution of 1774," in *Revolutionary Founders: Rebels, Radicals, and Reformers in the Making of the Nation*, eds. Alfred F. Young, Gary B. Nash, and Ray Raphael (New York: Alfred A, Knopf, 211), 35-52.

"The Man Unmasked": Henry Laurens, Egerton Leigh, and the Making of a Revolutionary

AARON J. PALMER

Henry Laurens, one of colonial South Carolina's wealthiest and most politically powerful planter-merchants, was a conservative by nature.[1] When the imperial crisis began to drive Britain and its colonies apart, Laurens moved cautiously even when he disliked British policy. When Laurens refused to join the Sons of Liberty in protest of the Stamp Act, a mob accosted him at his home, suspecting that he was hiding stamped paper for the British.[2] The Sons of Liberty remained suspicious of Laurens throughout the imperial crisis, and Laurens even suspected that they had sometimes intercepted and searched his private mail.[3] Henry

---

1. There is no modern, full-length biography devoted entirely to Henry Laurens. The most recent work is a dual study of Laurens and his rival Christopher Gadsden: David McDonough, *Christopher Gadsden and Henry Laurens: The Parallel Lives of Two American Patriots* (Selinsgrove, PA: Susquehanna University Press, 2000). The only biography entirely focused on Laurens remains David Duncan Wallace, *The Life of Henry Laurens With a Sketch of the Life of Lieutenant-Colonel John Laurens* (New York and London: G.P. Putnam's Sons, 1915). For a study of Henry's son John that often touches upon the father's life, see Gregory D. Massey, *John Laurens and the American Revolution* (Columbia: University of South Carolina Press, 2000). For in-depth political context related to the Laurens-Leigh duel, see Aaron J. Palmer, *A Rule of Law: Elite Political Authority and the Coming of the Revolution in the South Carolina Lowcountry, 1763-1776* (Leiden: Brill, 2014).
2. "Henry Laurens to Joseph Brown, October 11, 1765," in *The Papers of Henry Laurens*, ed. Philip Hammer and George C. Rogers (Columbia: University of South Carolina Press, 1968-), 5:24.
3. "Henry Laurens to James Grant, November 1, 1765," *ibid.*, 35. For a study of the artisans and their increased politicization during the imperial crisis, see Richard Walsh, *Charleston's Sons of Liberty: A Study of the Artisans, 1763-1789* (Columbia: University of South Carolina Press, 1959). For a detailed study of the committee structure of the re-

Laurens certainly believed in the ideals of English liberty. He certainly opposed British policies like the Stamp Act and Townshend Duties. Nevertheless, he believed in the rule of law and opposed the mob and those who led it just as strongly. Laurens even once described the leader of Charles Town's Sons of Liberty—Christopher Gadsden—as "a very Grand Simpleton."[4] What then pushed this conservative elite to become a leader of the American Revolution—eventually serving as the president of the Continental Congress? It was a slow transformation that has its roots in the nature of the eighteenth-century British Empire and its governance.

Henry Laurens experienced a series of personal conflicts with British placemen (i.e. political patronage appointees) as part of his business dealings in the 1760s. These incidents, especially with Vice Admiralty judge Egerton Leigh, slowly pushed Laurens closer to the break with Britain. These personal conflicts are complex, often revolving around delicate legal, business, and family affairs. They often seem petty and perhaps even not particularly important to the overall story of the coming of the American Revolution. However, Laurens's battles, especially with Leigh, demonstrate a problem that greatly contributed to the break between Britain and its colonies and one that long pre-existed the well-known events of the imperial crisis of the 1760s and 1770s. The problem of placemen, and particularly their lack of accountability to provincial leaders and monopolization of important political offices, led to explosive political conflicts in nearly every colony but was especially fierce in South Carolina, where the provincial elite held especially great power over colonial governing institutions and jealously guarded its control of these tools of political power.[5]

---

sistance government, see Eva Bayne Poythress, "Revolution by Committee: An Administrative History of the Extralegal Committees in South Carolina, 1774-1776" (PhD diss., University of North Carolina, Chapel Hill, 1975). Two studies focus on the course and consequences of mob violence; see Pauline Maier, *From Resistance to Revolution: Colonial Radicals and the Development of American Opposition to Britain, 1765-1776* (New York: Alfred A. Knopf, 1972) and Benjamin Carp, *Rebels Rising: Cities and the American Revolution* (Oxford: Oxford University Press, 2007).

4. "Henry Laurens to James Grant, October 1, 1768," in *The Papers of Henry Laurens,* 6:117. On Gadsden, see E. Stanley Godbold, Jr. and Robert H. Woody, *Christopher Gadsden and the American Revolution* (Knoxville: University of Tennessee Press, 1982).

5. The placemen or placeholder issue is extensively covered in chapter five of Palmer, *A Rule of Law.* Many of the most important pre-imperial crisis conflicts are detailed in Jonathan Mercantini, *Who Shall Rule at Home? The Evolution of South Carolina Political Culture, 1748-1776* (Columbia: University of South Carolina Press, 2007). See also Robert M. Weir, *"The Last of American Freemen:" Studies in the Political Culture of the Colonial and Revolutionary South* (Macon, GA: Mercer University Press, 1986).

Despite their extensive control over almost every branch of colonial government, the lowcountry elite had no authority over many offices filled by British appointees and had no direct way to hold these men accountable. The South Carolina elite often found themselves excluded from high office—increasingly so in the 1750s and beyond. No provincial, for example, ever held the post of royal governor. Placemen who did not share provincial agendas and priorities often held these top positions. Powerful (and often corrupt) placemen in the executive and judicial branches of government could intervene, block and frustrate the assembly's efforts to manage provincial society, and maintain centralized political authority. The situation could become especially explosive if a placeman's behavior seriously challenged the elite's control over government institutions that the colonial legislative assembly had come to dominate and that the elite relied on to govern the colony. An examination of Henry Laurens's battle with the most notorious South Carolina placeman of them all demonstrates the philosophical underpinnings of the colonial elite's vision of government and the tactics they used to combat perhaps the gravest threat to their control of South Carolina's political system—British placeholders.

Henry Laurens and Egerton Leigh had once been friends. Both enjoyed elite status in South Carolina, though Laurens's derived from his great wealth as a planter and merchant and Leigh's from his English political connections. Leigh came to South Carolina from England in 1753 along with his father Peter Leigh. Peter, former High Baliff of Westminster and another blatant placeman, took the family across the Atlantic upon his appointment as Chief Justice of South Carolina. Peter Leigh quickly proceeded to work for his son's advancement, despite Egerton's lack of legal education or qualifications. Egerton thus became clerk of the Court of Common Pleas in 1754. He received an appointment as Surveyor General in 1755. Leigh became judge of the Court of Vice Admiralty in 1761 and Attorney General in 1765. He held these last two offices to the end of the colonial period.[6]

Despite his unusually rapid advance in politics, Egerton Leigh enjoyed friendly relations with the lowcountry elite at the beginning of his tenure. He even gained a seat on the colony's Royal Council. His multiplicity of offices, abuse of those offices, and defense of royal power eventually ended his friendly relations with lowcountry elite. Leigh married a niece of Henry Laurens, though Laurens was always critical of Leigh's holding of multiple offices or places. Egerton Leigh even re-

---

6. Walter Edgar and Louise Bailey, eds., *Biographical Directory of the South Carolina House of Representatives* (Columbia: University of South Carolina Press, 1977), 2:396-397.

Henry Laurens from a painting by John Singleton Copley, 1782.

ferred to himself as a placeman in 1773.[7] Thomas Lynch, a Commons House member and signer of the Declaration of Independence, described Leigh as a "rascal." The terms were synonymous with the Leighs in colonial South Carolina.[8]

Leigh's troubles all began over a dispute between Henry Laurens and the customs service during the Townshend Duties crisis. The case is long and complicated, but it boils down to Laurens battling with two placeholders—George Roupell (customs inspector) and Egerton Leigh (attorney general and vice-admiralty court judge)—again over regulations stemming from the new Townshend acts.[9]

7. Ibid., 2:397-398.
8. Robert M. Calhoon and Robert Weir, "The Scandalous History of Sir Egerton Leigh," *William and Mary Quarterly* 26.1 (January, 1969): 1.
9. The Townsend acts required that bonds had to be given before goods bound for outside the colony were even loaded onto a ship. The question of what constituted ships going outside the colony caused much confusion and trouble, as coastal schooners (never intended to leave the colony) became the targets imperial officials. If a ship were seized for violating the new regulations, the owner had to go before the Vice Admiralty Court, where he was essentially guilty until proven innocent. Regardless of verdict, the ship owner also had to pay all court costs. Robert Middlekauf, *The Glorious Cause: The American Revolution, 1763-1789*, Rev. Exp. Edition (Oxford: Oxford University Press, 2007), 194-198.

Laurens's ship *Ann* arrived from Bristol on May 24, 1768, loaded only with enumerated goods (those specific goods subject to customs duties). George Roupell searched the ship after its arrival and while it was being re-loaded on the dock. Quite shockingly to Henry Laurens, the customs inspector then had the ship seized on June 4. Roupell claimed the ship had been loaded with non-enumerated goods without having bond issued prior to loading. Laurens, who had just returned from Georgia, was unaware of the situation, and had not been able to get the appropriate paperwork before the ship was re-loaded. He actually arrived at the site with the proper paperwork while the ship was being loaded, but Roupell would not accept the bond, saying it had to be issued *before* any cargo could be put on the ship. Laurens had experienced problems with Roupell in the past and even took him to court on one occasion, so it appeared to Laurens that a royal official was out to settle an old score with him by manipulating regulations.[10] At this time, Henry Laurens was still friendly with Egerton Leigh, and Leigh cleared the charges against the *Ann* in the Court of Vice Admiralty when the case came before the court.

Unfortunately, Leigh's ruling included technicalities that he hoped would placate Laurens while still protecting his fellow placeman Roupell. In the process, Leigh infuriated Laurens, offended his honor, and caused Laurens to launch an all-out assault on him personally and the entire British customs service in general. Leigh's ruling did severely admonish Roupell, who clearly had manipulated the byzantine customs regulations of the British Empire in order to accumulate a fortune for himself in fees and fines.[11] Leigh wrote that customs regulations regarding loading enumerated and non-enumerated goods had been inconsistently enforced. Sometimes officials said bonds had to be issued before loading, and sometimes they allowed bonds to be given while the ship was being loaded, which Roupell did not allow in this case. Such behavior, Leigh said, could be used to "draw unwary persons into snares, and involve the most innocent in ruin." In other words, officers like Roupell could set traps to collect more fees and fines, and Roupell was not the first customs collector in South Carolina to face this accu-

10. "Henry Laurens to Peter Timothy, July 6, 1768," *Papers of Henry Laurens*, 5:730-733.
11. Henry Laurens to William Fisher, July 11, 1768," ibid., 735. British customs regulations were becoming increasingly complex in this period. An excellent overview of this complex topic can be found in Thomas Barrow, *Trade and Empire: The British Customs Service in Colonial America, 1660-1775* (Cambridge, MA: Harvard University Press, 1999).

sation.[12] Moreover, Laurens had actually listed the non-enumerated goods on the ship's manifest and just failed to obtain the bond in time for loading. According to the fine letter of the law, Laruens simply had not delivered his paperwork at the proper time. Leigh wrote that "matters were so artfully conducted, that the claimant was unable to conform . . . before an actual seizure was made." Judge Leigh suspected some "private design" on Roupell's part.[13]

Leigh was already becoming an unpopular figure at this point, especially because of his ever-increasing multiplicity of offices. As Attorney General, Leigh was the sole government prosecutor in South Carolina and had power to decide which cases came to trial. As the lone Vice-Admiralty judge, Leigh had complete control of adjudicating imperial maritime law. Leigh's service on the Royal Council often put him on the wrong side of conflicts with the assembly over tax and spending issues. Laurens claimed that he once advised Leigh to "shake off his pluralities" of office, and the South Carolina assembly itself complained to London about Leigh holding too many offices in 1766.[14]

South Carolina's provincial leaders resented placemen, but Leigh's multiple offices made him particularly offensive. However, as long as he did not directly challenge provincial authority, there were no overt conflicts. The Laurens case proved to be the incident that led to Leigh's undoing. How could a friendship have fallen apart so dramatically, and how could Leigh, who seemed to be on Laurens's side in this case, have faced such scorn? Leigh simply prevented Henry Laurens from launch-

12. Another customs collector and placeman named Daniel Moore became embroiled in a heated controversy with Charles Town's merchants (led by Henry Laurens). The merchants accused Moore of charging high and arbitrary fees and not posting any official list of fees. Moore apparently even threatened those who challenged his practices with violence. Egerton Leigh, the vice-admiralty judge, refused to hear a case about Moore's abuse of the fee structure, and he threatened, as attorney general, to prosecute any group of merchants who would attempt to bring any suit against Moore in civil court. The merchants took their case to London through the colonial agent and eventually drove Moore from the province. A detailed narrative of this case can be found in Palmer, *A Rule of Law*, chapter 5, "All Matters and Things." The basic facts, from the merchant's point of view, were published in a pamphlet that did great damage to Moore's reputation: *A representation of facts, relative to the conduct of Daniel Moore, esquire, collector of His Majesty's customs at Charles Town in South Carolina* (Charles Town: Charles Crouch, 1767).

13. "Extract from the *South Carolina Gazette*, July 11, 1768," *Papers of Henry Laurens*, 742.

14. "Henry Laurens to William Fisher, August 1, 1768," in *Papers of Henry Laurens*, 6:3.

ing a full political attack upon the hated Roupell in the courts. Hence, he attempted to stop the familiar political tactics used to remove an offensive—and in this case corrupt—placeman. Leigh chided Roupell for his inconsistent customs practices, but he allowed Roupell to clear his name and retain his place. The sole Vice-Admiralty judge refused to hold an obviously corrupt British official accountable.

Even though Leigh cleared Laurens of all charges and ordered restitution paid for the *Ann*'s seizure, Leigh ruled that the *Ann* was still technically liable for seizure under the law. Roupell, thus, had done nothing illegal. Leigh thus had Roupell swear an oath of calumny that his actions were not motivated by personal malice or revenge. Because Leigh ruled this way and issued a certificate of probable cause and seizure, Laurens could not sue Roupell in civil court and recover damages. Leigh, therefore, faced Laurens's scorn.[15] He did not just want his ship cleared, he wanted the offending placeholder punished and humiliated. With legal action out of the question, Laurens used all his influence to bring pressure on Leigh through public shame, leading eventually to vicious back-and-forth attacks on both men's reputations and honor.

Laurens, having been in his mind denied justice, printed a detailed attack pamphlet that effectively destroyed Leigh's already shaky reputation. By the fall of 1768, Leigh resigned from the Court of Vice-Admiralty. Laurens explained his resignation by writing:

> He felt the weight of public, almost universal contempt confirmed by his own consciousness of improper conduct too heavy for him to bear . . . his late misconduct should not pass without such public reprehension as may legally and with propriety be applied to it, as a caution to his successor. If the ministry knew how much injury is wrought to the true interest of Great Britain by the tyrannical oppression and misconduct of ministerial officers in America and the difficulty and almost impossibility of retaining redress upon complaints against them, they would certainly be more circumspect in their appointments.[16]

Even after the resignation, Laurens was not finished with Leigh. He wanted to punish him and drive him from South Carolina politics by permanently destroying his reputation. Moreover, destroying the reputation of one placeman would call the general and increasingly difficult issue of placemen into question.

15. Henry Laurens, *Extracts from the Proceedings of the Court of Vice Admiralty, Second Edition* (Charles Town, David Bruce, 1769).
16. "Henry Laurens to William Cowles and Co., October 15, 1768," *Papers of Henry Laurens*, 6:136.

Laurens launched his assault on Leigh's character by publishing *Extracts from the Proceedings of the Court of Vice Admiralty*, which explained the details of his case and showed Leigh's corruption. This pamphlet, published by William Fisher of Philadelphia and reprinted throughout the colonies in several editions, tied the issues of placemen and the imperial crisis together:

> At a time when the powers of commissioners and other officers of the Customs in America are so greatly increased, and to render them still more formidable, the jurisdiction of vice-admiralty courts extended beyond its ancient limits—when too many men are employed in those offices, whose sole view seems to be amassing and acquiring fortunes at the expense of their honor, conscience, and almost ruined country . . . attacks of this nature concern every merchant on this continent.[17]

Clearly, Lauren's personal feud with Leigh had led him to embrace the fight against imperial taxation and policy in a way that had never previously occurred to him. The pamphlet painted a damning picture of Leigh and of British colonial government in general.

Going into every detail of his and other similar cases, Laurens portrayed Leigh as a deceitful man who held office only for his own profit and who was entirely unfit as a judge.[18] In a letter to friend James Habersham, Laurens explained that the purpose of *Extracts* was to show the danger of giving one man too much power. He worried about placemen such as Leigh having "unlimited and uncontrollable powers over the property and reputations of us poor Americans."[19] In general, Laurens concluded that imperial government itself was to blame. The customs laws were "numerous and intricate . . . a great science which requires a great deal of time and application to comprehend." They were snares, designed to trap innocent, law-abiding merchants like himself so that placemen could extract their fees. The only recourse when one violated these laws was the vice-admiralty court, where one's "property is at the disposal of a single judge, whom it is possible to suppose is a weak, unqualified person or corrupt trucking knave."[20]

---

17. Laurens, *Extracts from the Proceedings of the Court of Vice Admiralty.*
18. "Henry Laurens to William Fisher, September 12, 1768," *Papers of Henry Laurens,* 6:92.
19. "Henry Laurens to James Habersham, August 15, 1769," *Papers of Henry Laurens,* 7:124-125.
20. Laurens, *Extracts from the Proceedings of the Court of Vice Admiralty.*

Leigh would not stand idly by and allow his reputation to be destroyed, so he responded with a pamphlet of his own entitled *The Man Unmasked.* Leigh began by stating the problem: "This is a hard and cruel case: to be stigmatized in print, and either to remain silent in which event the world will take every charge *pro confesso* or (bitter alternative!) to set myself up as a candidate for literary fame."[21] *The Man Unmasked* went on to accuse Laurens of flaunting the legal system when it no longer met his needs. When the system ruled against him, Laurens decided to abandon the constitution and resort to his extra-legal means to get his way. Laurens, in other words, had utterly no respect for the rule of law. For his part, Leigh insisted that his role as judge was to interpret and uphold the law, which is exactly what he had done in the Laurens case.

He also stressed that "where the stream of justice" was interrupted by a corrupt judge, appeal to the king—"the fountain of justice"—was always available. Instead, Laurens chose to appeal to the people and attack the motives and character of a man who was only doing his duty to king and country. Leigh argued that Laurens was a man who only followed the law when it suited his personal and political purposes. Laurens's attack upon Leigh was thus an attack on justice itself:

> Nothing can be more idle and absurd, than for a party in a cause, to fly in the face of that judge, whom he has so lately and humbly implored for relief, to desert his constitutional remedy, and to set himself up as a Lord Paramount, to arraign his justice, load him with reproaches, vilify his resume, and blast . . . his reputation . . . to try him too by his own unlettered judgment, without color of law, against law, in defiance of the King's authority, in exclusion of a superior jurisdiction clothed by the law of the land.[22]

It was then unjust in Leigh's view for Laurens to, on the one hand, seek his aid as judge to resolve his case, only to turn around when the law did not fully support him and attack him as a man and an official. Laurens set himself up as a judge, and was a hypocrite for at first trusting the imperial system to resolve his problem and then attacking the same system when he did not get his way. Thus, Leigh's approach was to defend his role as a judge and defend the imperial system, while attacking Laurens's judgment, honor, and motives. Naturally, Leigh did not have the last word in this dispute.

21. "The Man Unmasked," *Papers of Henry Laurens*, vol. 6, 455.
22. *Ibid.*

Laurens was always very defensive in matters of honor and reputation. He was no stranger to dueling. He seems to have thus challenged Leigh to a duel over *The Man Unmasked*. Leigh, however, called off the duel, which left Laurens free to continue his attacks on Leigh's character.[23] Laurens thus had another edition of his *Extracts* printed in Charles Town, but the conflict became much more personal. When the two had been friends, Leigh married Henry Laurens's niece. Now, Laurens (in England at the time) got word that Leigh had impregnated his wife's sister and had abandoned the poor woman on a ship, where she died alone. Furious, Laurens accused Leigh of adultery and murder, promising to take his case directly to the King.[24] Since Laurens was in England at the time, he had his son James carry on the attack at home. James Laurens wrote that his efforts had met with success, saying "he is almost universally condemned, despised, and shunned." James hoped that Leigh would be driven from the colony, but he wanted Leigh to first confess his quilt.[25]

Leigh never did so, but his reputation in South Carolina was all but destroyed, and he became a social pariah. Nevertheless, he received a baronetcy from the crown and became Sir Egerton Leigh in 1772 and served as president of the South Carolina council from 1773 to 1775. His appointment and controversial tenure as president did permanent damage to that body's already fragile reputation. In the end, Leigh resigned when he again faced public ridicule and attack for his role in the Wilkes Fund Controversy, which pitted the council against the assembly.[26] Laurens never succeeded in driving Leigh from the colony until the royal government fell, but he had utterly shamed him and destroyed his honor.

Egerton Leigh had hoped to unmask his former friend Laurens as a dishonorable man with no real sense of justice or regard for the law.

23. "Egerton Leigh to Henry Laurens, May 29, 1769," *Papers of Henry Laurens*, 6:580,
24. "Henry Laurens to Egerton Leigh, January 30, 1773," *Papers of Henry Laurens*, 8:556.
25. "James Laurens to Henry Laurens, October 19, 1773," *Papers of Henry Laurens*, 8:125.
26. Edgar and Bailey, *Biographical Directory of the South Carolina House of Representatives*, 2:397-398. A detailed account of Leigh's troubles with the council is found in Calhoon and Weir, "The Scandalous History of Sir Egerton Leigh," 67-74. Leigh's involvement in the Wilkes Fund Controversy (a major dispute between the South Carolina assembly and the royal governor) also helped lead to his downfall in the colony. That dispute, along with a pamphlet on the case by Leigh, is detailed in Jack P. Greene, *The Nature of Colony Constitutions: Two Pamphlets on the Wilkes Fund Controversy in South Carolina by Sir Egerton Leigh and Arthur Lee* (Columbia: University of South Carolina Press, 1970).

The affair did unmask Laurens. It forced him to confront the deep flaws in the system of imperial government in a very personal way, and that confrontation led him ultimately to conclude that rule of law was more important than attachment to the British Empire and that British government itself would only continue to subvert the rule of law. The fight with Leigh did not cause Laurens to dramatically break with Britain. However, this incident and many others like it eroded his faith in a system that had made him rich and politically powerful. When that system seemed to increasingly threaten practical things like wealth and power (along with idealistic elements like English liberty), men like Laurens gradually awakened to the possibility of a colonial world that was no longer colonial.

It is hard to see much truly revolutionary activity in the Leigh episode, and there is little evidence that Henry Laurens became revolutionary (e.g. an advocate for independence or a republican) as a result of it.[27] Laurens never attacked the empire, George III or Parliament. He expressed no disloyalty or radical sentiment. He remained cautious and conservative (and suspected by more radical elements within the revolutionary movement as late as 1775) throughout the imperial crisis. This incident though strained Laurens's attachments to Britain and the Empire, but there is nothing revolutionary about the incident itself. It is not directly connected to the imperial crisis or colonial resistance efforts to the Townshend acts, but it was one in a long series of provincial battles to make British placemen accountable to provincial authority. Nevertheless, those local battles—inherent to the politics of the British Empire—in this period must be understood to see how and why conservative elites like Laurens eventually came to embrace radical ideas like republicanism and separation from Great Britain.

27. Mercantini, *Who Shall Rule at Home*, 235.

John Adams: Portrait of the Founder as a Young Schoolmaster

GEOFF SMOCK

Before ever he was a president, vice president, ambassador, Continental Congressmen, or Massachusetts lawyer, John Adams was a schoolmaster in a rural hamlet in Colonial Massachusetts.

And he was in a state of torment. "I find myself very much inclined to an unreasonable absence of mind, and to a morose and unsociable disposition," he lamented.[1]

Suddenly gone was the constant intellectual stimulation and community of high-minded peers and faculty he had enjoyed at Harvard. "At Colledge gay, gorgeous, prospects, danc'd before my Eyes, and Hope, sanguine Hope, invigorated my Body, and exhilerated my soul," he wrote. "But now hope has left me, my organ's rust and my Faculty's decay."[2] Classrooms replete with Latin discourses, philosophical debates, and dramatic readings were replaced by a schoolhouse full of young boys struggling with the rudiments of reading, writing, and arithmetic. To Adams it was "a school of affliction", full of "little runtlings, just capable of lisping A.B.C. and troubling the Master." If he was stuck there for long, it "would make a base weed and ignoble shrub" of him.[3]

For a man known throughout his life for the inner, convulsive passions roiling just below the surface (and which oftentimes erupted far

---

1. John Adams, "Diary & Autobiography," in *The Portable John Adams*, edited by John Patrick Diggins (New York, NY: Penguin Books, 2004), 4.
2. John Adams to Nathan Webb, September 1, 1755, *Founders Online*, National Archives, founders.archives.gov/documents/Adams/06-01-02-0001 (original source: *The Adams Papers*, Papers of John Adams, vol. 1, *September 1755–October 1773*, ed. Robert J. Taylor (Cambridge, MA: Harvard University Press, 1977), 1–2).
3. Adams to Richard Cranch, September 2, 1755, *Founders Online*, National Archives, founders.archives.gov/documents/Adams/06-01-02-0002 (original source: *The Adams Papers*, 3–4).

above), Adams's two years at the head of Worcester's grammar school were an epoch of anguish. His soul was a tempest churned and wrought by conflicting fears, ambitions, responsibilities, and senses of guilt. More than anything, he was haunted by questions of what was next in his life. Should he follow his father's wishes and become a minister (or even his mother's to become a medic), or should he follow his own inclination to become a lawyer? If he chose the latter, did he have it in him to be successful, or would he be undone by his own indolence? Would he make an enduring name for himself, or would he remain in the "common Herd of Mankind," destined to "be born and eat and sleep and die, and be forgotten"?[4] Did he even deserve a better fate, or was he too prone to passion, vice, and vanity?

Perhaps of the greatest aggravation to Schoolmaster Adams was his realization that he lived in a momentous age. Great Britain and France were embroiled in the Seven Years' War, which would reshape the fate of North America and, ultimately, global history. The Age of Enlightenment was also redefining human knowledge of the natural and supernatural worlds. Much to his seething frustration, all Adams could do was observe all of this from the periphery, a mere spectator in a play he wanted a leading role in. Just entering the prime of his life, he was terrified by the suspicion that he was watching life pass him by.

Yet for all of the angst and uncertainty Adams had about his own destiny, he possessed a remarkable serenity of mind about the destiny of Great Britain's American colonies. Fresh out of his teenage years, and having not yet served in any type of political role, John Adams nevertheless had a preternatural understanding of where history was going years, if not decades, before it went there. It was an emerging aspect of what Joseph J. Ellis describes as the "Adams pattern" – an ability to foresee history's trajectory and then "make decisions that positioned America to be carried forward on those currents."[5]

The first evidence of this "pattern" comes from Adams's stay in Worcester. In October of 1755, only a few months into his time as schoolmaster, Adams penned a remarkable letter to childhood friend and former Harvard classmate Nathan Webb. "All that part of creation that lies within our observation is liable to Change," he began. "If we look into History we shall find some nations rising from contemptible beginnings, and spreading their influence, 'till the whole Globe is sub-

---

4. John Adams to Jonathan Sewall, February 1760, in Gordon S. Wood, ed. *John Adams: Revolutionary Writings 1755-1775* (New York, NY: Library of America, 2011), 51.
5. Joseph J. Ellis, *Passionate Sage: The Character and Legacy of John Adams*, 2nd ed. (New York: Norton, 2001), 26.

jected to their sway." Adams was writing in general, grandiloquent terms, but he had a specific nation in mind. "Soon after the Reformation a few people came over into this new world for Concience sake. Perhaps this (apparently) trivial incident, may transfer the great seat of Empire into America. It looks likely to me."

He continued that if and when the French were expelled from the continent, "our People, according to the exactest Computations, will in another Century, become more numerous than England itself. Should this be the Case, since we have . all the naval Stores of the Nation in our hands, it will be easy to obtain the mastery of the seas, and then the united force of all Europe, will not be able to subdue us."[6]

On the cusp of Great Britain's absolute victory over the French in the Seven Years' War, and the confirmation of its global hegemony, the teenage John Adams was blithely prognosticating its downfall in North America and the advent of an American empire. Demography and the continent's bounteous natural resources would upend the global balance in an independent America's favor. The writing was on the wall.

The dichotomy between Adams's certainty towards America's destiny and the uncertainty towards his own is as startling as it is instructive, for it was that certainty that would ultimately provide Adams the means of escaping the relentless ambiguities he harbored over his own fate. The desire to participate in America's rise "from contemptible beginnings" would not only confirm his desire to become a lawyer, but give him the emotional and psychological means he needed to channel all of the cacophonous energies raging inside of him into a career path that, within twenty years, would see him not only at the top of his profession in Boston, but as one of the foremost leaders of colonial opposition to British imperial policy.

Accordingly, a study of Adams's time in Worcester allows us to not only acquire an uncommon glimpse into the personality of one of America's central "Founding Fathers" at the time of his own founding, so to speak, but it also explains so much of the John Adams best known to history—Adams the "Atlas of Independence."

Nearly twenty years to the day after writing his letter to Nathan Webb, Great Britain and her American colonies were in crisis. Years of frustration had boiled over into bloodshed at Lexington, Concord, and Bunker Hill, and the word "independence" was no longer being whispered in private only. Representing Massachusetts at the Second Continental Congress, Adams put pen to paper in another letter, this time

---

6. Adams to Webb, October 12, 1755, in Wood, ed. *Adams: Revolutionary Writings*, 3.

to his wife Abigail, reflecting upon the themes he had touched upon in his epistle to Webb. "From my earliest Entrance into Life," he wrote, "I have been engaged in the public Cause of America: and from first to last I have had upon my Mind, a strong Impression, that Things would be wrought up to their present Crisis. I saw from the Beginning that the Controversy was of such a Nature that it never would be settled, and every day convinces me more and more."[7]

What he had prognosticated in 1755 was coming to fruition in 1775. As a result, Adams was uniquely prepared for his first, and maybe most important national role: de facto floor leader for the independence faction in the Second Continental Congress.

Personally resolved that America was predestined to separating from Great Britain, he patiently shepherded a gradualist approach that set the stage for a formal declaration while allowing events on the battlefield and across the sea in London to make independence a reality in all but legal declaration. This method allowed moderates time to see that there was no alternative and isolated those voices in Congress who still held out hope of reconciliation. By sponsoring measures that called on the colonies to create their own constitutions and that institutionalized Washington's Continental Army, he was also responsible for America *functioning* as an independent state even if it was not yet declared as such. For this and more, Thomas Jefferson would later describe him as the independence faction's "Colossus on the floor." Other colleagues would give him the infamous sobriquet: "Atlas of Independence."[8]

It was this role for which Adams's days as schoolmaster, his own personal time in the wilderness, had prepared him. The genesis of the John Adams who became the "Atlas of Independence" is found in the John Adams of Worcester two decades before. To understand the former requires a portrait examination of the latter, for in determining his individual destiny, John Adams ultimately positioned himself to lead America in determining its own.

---

7. Adams to Abigail Adams, October 7, 1775, in John P. Kaminski, ed. *The Founders on the Founders: Word Portraits from the American Revolutionary Era* (Charlottesville: University of Virginia Press, 2008), 22.

8. Jefferson's quote is taken from Daniel Webster's eulogy of him and Adams, as quoted in John H. Hazelton, *The Declaration of independence: Its History* (New York: Da Capo Press, 1970), 162. For a more detailed narrative of Congress' road to declaring independence, John Ferling's *Independence: The Struggle to Set America Free* (New York: Bloomsbury Press, 2011) and Richard Beeman's *Our lives, Our Fortunes and Our Sacred Honor: The Forging of American Independence, 1774-1776* (New York: Basic Books, 2013) are exemplary.

Reflecting upon his childhood in the twilight years of his life, John Adams wrote that before he was ever born "my father had destined his first born . . . to a public Education."[9] The Adams's had a family tradition of upward mobility, rising from illiterate farmers to (in the case of Adams's father) property-owner, shoemaker, and town deacon, to (as Adams's father hoped for his first-born son) Congregationalist minister. It was for this reason that Deacon Adams patiently but firmly guided his son away from outdoor pursuits and towards his books and tutors.[10]

It was also with this expectation that *pater* Adams committed to the significant expense of sending his eldest son to Harvard. Once there, Adams *filium* developed a "growing Curiosity, a Love of Books and a fondness for Study."

This affinity did not extend to theology though, and he quickly lost patience with the "Spirit of Dogmatism and Bigotry in Clergy and Laity." Adams realized "very clearly" that "the study of Theology, and the pursuit of it as a Profession would . . . make my life miserable, without any prospect of doing any good to my fellow Men."

Instead, his interests were attracted towards another vocation. Adams was making a name for himself in the Harvard community for his eloquence in public discussions and his flair in dramatic readings. In short time peers began to whisper in his ear that he would "make a better Lawyer than Divine." This only reinforced his own ideas, and his "Inclination was soon fixed upon the Law."

He was not yet ready to admit it though – to himself and certainly not to his father. "I therefore gave out that I would take a School," he wrote of his indecision at the time, "and took my Degree at Colledge undetermined whether I should study Divinity, Law, or Physick."[11]

Thus Adams soon found himself in Worcester, dogged by the age-old conundrum of sons who yearn for one thing in their life while their fathers expect another.

From all appearances, it was a conundrum that did not take long to resolve—if anything because of Adams's deepening disenchantment with religious offices and dogma more than his determination to study the law. The early entries in his Worcester diary brim with disgust at the hypocrisies he perceived. "Very often," he wrote in February of 1756,

9. John Adams, "Autobiography," begun October 5, 1802, in Wood, ed., *Revolutionary Writings*, 617.
10. John E. Ferling, *Setting the world ablaze: Washington, Adams, Jefferson, and the American Revolution* (Oxford: Oxford University Press, 2000), 5-6.
11. Adams, "Autobiography," in Wood, ed., *Revolutionary Writings*, 621-623.

"shepherds that are hired to take care of their masters' sheep go about their own concerns and leave the flock to the care of their dog. So bishops, who are appointed to oversee the flock of Christ, take the fees themselves but leave the drudgery to their dogs." The very next day he complained that the "Church of Rome has made it an article of faith that no man can be saved out of their church, and all other sects approach to this dreadful opinion in proportion to their ignorance."

Reflecting his annoyance with tedious theological disputes, he questioned the very need for most church infrastructures and canon law. "Where do we find a precept in the Gospel requiring Ecclesiastical Synods? Convocations? Councils? Decrees? Creeds? Confessions?"[12]

The notion of a life within all of this was one Adams could no longer pretend to entertain, no matter how much it might disappoint his father. "The frightful Engines of Ecclesiastical Councils, of diabolical Malice and Calvinistical good nature never failed to terrify me exceedingly whenever I thought of preaching," he concluded to a former classmate.[13] The conclusion was no longer avoidable: a lawyer he would be.

One great certainty in his life was thus resolved, but through the remainder of his time in Worcester Adams would grapple with an ambiguity that was greater still. He burned, in the words of John Ferling, "with a fever for recognition and fame."[14] This ambition created two problems in Adams's mind: overcoming a youthful penchant for idleness and harnessing his ambition before it metastasized into vanity and vice. Wrestling with these would consume a majority of Adams's emotional energies in Worcester, and the pages of his diary would be saturated by anguished doubts and self-criticism. These convulsions were some of the most intense struggles of his life, "directed not outward to a hostile environment," as Bernard Bailyn writes, "but inward, into the ambiguities and tensions of his own nature."[15]

Throughout his youth and early manhood, Adams was easily impressed by his surroundings. As a boy in the country, his interest in outdoor pursuits amongst thickets and streams—"and Inattention to Books"—had consistently alarmed his father. Once among a community of scholars and inquiry at Harvard, his intellect spurred into action,

12. Adams, "Diary and Autobiography," in Diggins, ed., *Portable John Adams*, 1-3. For a more ordered and expansive window into Adams's views on religious authority, see his *Dissertation on the Canon and Feudal Law* (Numbers I, II, and III), in Wood, ed., *Revolutionary Writings*, 110-125.

13. Adams to Cranch. August 29, 1756, in Wood, ed., *Revolutionary Writings*, 26.

14. Ferling, *Ablaze*, 20.

15. Bernard Bailyn, *Faces of Revolution: Personalities and Themes in the Struggle for American Independence* (New York: Vintage Books, 1990), 5.

and he "soon perceived a growing Curiosity, a Love of Books and fondness for Study which dissipated all my Inclination for Sports, and even for the Society of Ladies."[16]

This cognitive energy would itself dissipate in Worcester. Adams was a man alone with his thoughts, gripped in the clutches of ennui. Struggling to establish the same drive he had gained a reputation for at Harvard, he implored former Harvard classmates to write to him regularly, hoping to reignite, through their correspondence, embers within himself that their contact had first ignited in Cambridge. "I shall think myself happy if in your turn," he wrote to Nathan Webb, "you communicate your Lucubrations [sic] to me." He was deeply "sorry that fortune has thrown me at such a distance from those of my Friends who have the highest place in my affections."[17] To another he pleaded, "Pray write me, the first time you are at Leisure. A Letter from you sir would ballance the inquietude of schoolkeeping."[18]

When Adams was not searching for motivation to develop his legal knowledge, he was being distracted by the attractions of nature. "The weather and the season are, beyond expression, delightful," he wrote in May 1756, and "the fields are covered with a bright and lively verdure; the trees are all in bloom, and the atmosphere is filed with a ravishing fragrance." Overwhelmed by a vernal ecstasy, he spent the next day rambling about the countryside, "gaping and gazing."[19]

Such natural revelry led Adams's mind towards philosophy, and the pages of his diary were soon filled with theoretical speculations on the universe and human existence. "But man, although the powers of his body are small but contemptible," he philosophized in one entry, "by the exercise of his own reason can invent engines and instruments, to take advantage of the powers in nature, and accomplish the most astonishing designs." Gazing towards the heavens in another, he opined that "when we consider that space is absolutely infinite and boundless, that the power of the Deity is strictly omnipotent, and his goodness without limitation, who can come to a stop in his thoughts and say, hither does the universe extend and no further?" A few entries later he wrote that, when considering the magnificence of so many "planets,

16. Adams, "Autobiography," in Wood, ed., *Revolutionary Writings*, 618-621.

17. Adams to Webb, October 12, 1755, in Wood, ed., *Revolutionary Writings*, 4.

18. Adams to Cranch, September 2, 1755, *Founders Online*, National Archives, founders.archives.gov/documents/Adams/06-01-02-0002 (original source: *The Adams Papers*, 3–4).

19. Adams, "Diary and Autobiography," in Diggins, ed., *Portable John Adams*, 8-9.

and satellites, and comets," one could not help but be overwhelmed. "Our imaginations, after a few faint efforts, sink down into a profound admiration of what they cannot comprehend."[20]

Adams had allowed his mind to drift into the clouds and beyond, and as he approached the one-year anniversary of his arrival in Worcester he became palpably displeased with himself. "I know not by what fatality it happens, but I seem to have a necessity upon me of trifling away my time." In his next entry, all he could record was, "I know not what became of these days."

He had determined that he would pursue the law, but the pursuit itself had yet to begin and his self-regard was reaching its nadir. "I seem to have lost sight of the object that I resolved to pursue. Dreams and slumbers, sloth and negligence, will be the ruin of my schemes. However I seem to be awake now; why can't I keep awake?"[21] The young schoolmaster was trapped in a MacBeth-ian state of paralysis and loathing, lacking the "spur . . . To prick the sides" of his intent, full only of "Vaulting ambition, which o'erleaps itself . . ."[22] Instead of dedicating himself to reaching his professional aspirations, he was whiling away his time in physical and intellectual frivolity.

This could not continue, and a week later Adams informed his diary that he had contracted with Worcester attorney James Putnam to live in his home and to "study Law under his Inspection for two years."[23] The agreement stipulated that Worcester would pay for his board while he continued as schoolmaster. He would later pay Putnam a fee of one-hundred dollars "when I should find it convenient." His life would soon become "Reading Law in the night and keeping School in the day," following Putnam on his court circuits when the opportunity allowed.[24]

The novitiate lawyer had won his battle against indolence, but concurrent to this had been a battle with his own ambitions, passion, and the deep sense of guilt these enflamed inside of him. "Oh! that I could wear out of my mind every mean and base affectation," Adams anguished in one entry, and "subdue every unworthy passion."[25] Months

20. Ibid., 10-11.

21. Ibid., 17.

22. William Shakespeare, *Macbeth*, ed. Jesse M. Lander (New York: Barnes & Noble, 2007), 1.7.25-27.

23. "22 Sunday," *Founders Online*, National Archives, founders.archives.gov/documents/Adams/01-01-02-0002-0008-0009 (original source: *The Adams Papers*, Diary and Autobiography of John Adams, vol. 1, *1755–1770*, ed. L. H. Butterfield. Cambridge, MA: Harvard University Press, 1961, 42–44).

24. Adams, "Autobiography," in Wood, ed., *Revolutionary Writings*, 623-624.

25. Adams, "Diary and Autobiography," in Diggins, ed., *Portable John Adams*, 2.

later he confessed, "Vanity . . . is my cardinal vice and cardinal folly; and I am in continual danger . . . of being led [on] an *ignis fatuus* chase by it, without the strictest caution and watchfulness over myself."[26]

Combined with the scattered entries on his idleness, the self-remonstrations of Adams's diary against his own passions—most notably his desperation for fame—depict a young man seeking to purify himself through self-accusation. The aspiring lawyer was essentially prosecuting himself, and we can imagine Adams alone in his boarding room on many a night, a tight grip on his pen, admonishing himself by the light of a guttering candle as a medieval monk scourging himself in penitential confession of his sins would.

For Adams this was psychologically necessary. If overcoming his own idleness could make it possible for him to attain the fame he yearned for, he still had to make himself worthy of that fame. "The love of fame naturally betrays a man into several weaknesses and fopperies that tend very much to diminish his reputation, and so defeat itself."[27] It was one thing to achieve fame, it was quite another to trust himself with it.

The bitter, occasionally melodramatic self-criticism he engaged in in his Worcester diary can thus be interpreted as a process of harsh, but necessary preparation of himself. As Peter Shaw writes, Adams conditioned himself for fame "not by stimulating his desire but by damping it. In his Worcester diary he launched a lifelong, secret struggle with pride calculated to make him worthy of success."[28]

If he was to trust himself with fame, he had to first find the peace of mind not to crave it. "He is not a wise man, and is unfit to fill any important station in society, that has left one passion in his soul unsubdued," he would advise himself. The violence with which these passions convulsed inside of him led Adams to view them as wild beasts in need of strict subjugation. "Untamed, they are lawless bulls; they roar and bluster, defy all control, and sometimes murder their proper owner." If he could accomplish this, not only would he be able to suppress his passions, but channel them in a productive direction. "But, properly, inured to obedience, [passions] take their places under the yoke without noise, and labor vigorously in their master's service."[29]

26. Ibid., 7.
27. Ibid.
28. Peter Shaw, *The Character of John Adams* (New York: University of North Carolina Press, 1976), 19.
29. Adams, "Diary and Autobiography," in Diggins, ed., *Portable John Adams*, 14.

Adams's solution to this conundrum—how he would make himself
fit to fill an "important station in society"—was not to seek fame for its
own sake, but to seek it at a personal cost. It would become the second
half of Ellis's aforementioned "Adams Pattern:" to gain a reputation for
laboring more than others in public service, to succeed, "but to do so
in a way that assured his own alienation from success."[30] His pursuit of
fame, begun in the obscurity of Worcester, would be a lifelong repetition
of building his public recognition while making implicit, but indis-
putable gestures towards the contempt he felt he must have for fame
and the popular acclamations of others.[31] It was an internal bargain he
made with himself: rise to elevated heights, but in so doing isolate himself from widespread love and affection. This helps explain his unpopular decision to represent the British soldiers involved in the Boston
Massacre, "hazarding" at the time "a [personal] Popularity very general
and very hardly earned."[32] So too, after personally undertaking so much
of the political legwork in Congress to make independence possible,
did he insist that Thomas Jefferson take the fateful lead in drafting the
Declaration thereof—and to take the short- and long-term credit for
independence.[33]

Adams would never quite be at peace with this bargain, and spent
much of his adult life vituperating at the mythologized history of the
Revolution he had taken a large share in leading. "The History of our
Revolution will be one continued [lie] from one End to the other," he
would lament in the closing years of his life. "The Essence of the whole
will be that Dr Franklins electrical Rod, Smote the Earth and out Spring
General Washington. That Franklin electrified him with his Rod—and
thence forward these two conducted all the Policy Negotiations Legislation and War."[34]

Yet it was this self-bargain—made as a schoolmaster in Worcester,
Massachusetts—that allowed Adams to internally dedicate himself to
the personal quest of becoming a renowned lawyer in Boston, and in
turn a renowned political leader of the soon-to-be United States.[35]

---

30. Ellis, *Passionate Sage*, 26.
31. Shaw, *The Character of John Adams*, 25-40.
32. Adams, "Autobiography," 639.
33. As he would recall telling Jefferson at the time, "I am obnoxious, suspected and unpopular." Adams to Timothy Pickering, August 6, 1822," *Founders Online*, National
Archives, http://founders.archives.gov/documents/Adams/99-02-02-7674.
34. Adams to Benjamin Rush, April 4, 1790," *Founders Online*, National Archives,
http://founders.archives.gov/documents/Adams/99-02-02-0903.
35. Ferling, *World Ablaze*, 21.

Adams left Worcester in 1758 and was sworn into the province's bar in 1759, the same year as Great Britain's victory over the French in the Seven Years' War. "This event," as he remembered years later, "which was so joyfull to Us, and so important to England if she had seen her true Interest, inspired her with jealousy, which ultimately lost her thirteen colonies and made many of Us at the time regret that Canada had ever been conquered."[36]

Finally freed from the obscurity of Worcester, the fates began to align for the schoolteacher-turned-lawyer, and John Adams embarked upon a personal and professional ascent that would mirror America's own climb from thirteen isolated British colonies to one independent republic. He had seen this fate coming, and now that he had resolved his own trajectory in life he would play a seminal role in realizing it. Due in no small part to his own efforts, what Schoolmaster Adams had fore-ordained as America's destiny would soon become history—America's and his own.

36. Adams, "Autobiography," 626.

Cornwallis and the Autumn Campaign of 1780: His Advance from Camden to Charlotte

❦ IAN SABERTON ❦

As events would prove, the autumn campaign was a very risky venture indeed, yet despite the operational difficulties attending it Cornwallis saw no option but to go on to the offensive after his victory at the Battle of Camden, South Carolina, on August 16, 1780. As he had explained to Clinton, "It may be doubted by some whether the invasion of North Carolina may be a prudent measure, but I am convinced it is a necessary one and that, if we do not attack that province, we must give up both South Carolina and Georgia and retire within the walls of Charlestown."[1]

Throughout the campaign a pressing concern would be the sickliness of the troops, whether they were those who marched with Cornwallis or those who were intended to join him later from Camden.

An immediate problem, which delayed the march, was the formation of supply trains. Waggons there were aplenty, what with those taken in recent engagements and others pressed from Orangeburg and Ninety Six, but sadly horses, gear, conductors and drivers were wanting.

Another cause of delay was the severe lack of provision at Camden, exacerbated by additional mouths to feed after the recent battle. On

---

1. Ian Saberton ed., *The Cornwallis Papers: The Campaigns of 1780 and 1781 in the Southern Theatre of the American Revolutionary War,* 6 vols (Uckfield: The Naval & Military Press Ltd, 2010) ("CP"), 1, 177. Cornwallis's dispatches to Germain and Clinton have for the most part been long in the public domain and have been relied on by historians to provide a broad outline of Cornwallis's advance to Charlotte. As in this article, those accounts may now be supplemented with much more detailed information based on the CP.

August 31 Cornwallis remarked to Lt. Col. Nisbet Balfour,[2] "Hitherto, so far from being able to get a few days' [*provision*] beforehand, which is absolutely necessary for our march, we are this day without either flour or meal and Tarleton's horses have had no forage since the action."[3]

Against all the odds Cornwallis managed to assemble a proviant train of thirty-eight waggons by September 7, twenty of which were loaded with a puncheon of rum in each and the rest with flour and salt. At daybreak, accompanied by two 3-pounders, he marched towards Charlotte with the 23rd Regiment (Royal Welch Fusiliers), 33rd Regiment and Volunteers of Ireland, leaving behind material numbers of their dead, sick and wounded. Two days later he reached the border settlement at the Waxhaws and was joined by Col. Samuel Bryan's North Carolina militia. The troops soon set up camp on Waxhaw Creek, living on wheat collected and ground from the plantations in the neighborhood, most of which were owned by Scotch-Irish revolutionaries who had fled.

On September 8 Lt. Col. Banastre Tarleton crossed the Wateree at Camden Ferry and advanced with the British Legion and a detachment of the 71st Regiment's light troops towards White's Mill on Fishing Creek. While there on the 17th, he fell ill of a violent attack of yellow fever. His entire command was now needed to protect him and it was not until the 23rd that he became well enough to be moved to Blair's Mill on the eastern side of the Catawba. Crossing on the same day at the ford there, which was six hundred yards wide and three and a half feet deep, the Legion joined Cornwallis. All in all, Tarleton's illness was one of the main reasons for setting back the entry into Charlotte. It took place on the 26th.

By then Cornwallis had been reinforced by the 71st, but both battalions were much depleted, not only by their dead and wounded in the Battle of Camden, but also by their sick who had fallen down earlier at Cheraw Hill. Many, who were recovering, had relapsed before their march and returned to the hospital at Camden. Accompanied by a detachment of artillery with two 6-pounders, a few pioneers, the convalescents of the 33rd, and two supply trains, one of rum and salt, and the other of artillery stores, arms and ammunition, the remains of the 71st arrived at the Waxhaws on the 21st, but they too were in poor shape, adding considerably to the sick of the other regiments there, who by

2. Biographical information on Balfour and other persons mentioned in this article may be found in the CP.
3. CP: 2, 66.

that date amounted to above 120 and were daily increasing. When Cornwallis advanced to Charlotte, the debris of the 71st was left at Waxhaw Creek to form a staging post.

Meanwhile Lt. Col. James Wemyss[4] and Major James Moncrief had been engaged on their two expeditions designed to pacify the vast expanse of territory east of the Wateree and Santee that was no longer under British control. They failed miserably and both returned to Camden by early October.[5]

Like Wemyss and Moncrief, Major Patrick Ferguson, the Inspector General of Militia, had been busy too. In compliance with Cornwallis's instructions he left Sugar Creek for Camden on August 23 to discuss the part to be played by his corps and the backcountry militia in forthcoming operations. He rejoined his corps on September 1 near Fair Forest Creek, having obtained Cornwallis's approval to his making a rather hazardous advance into Tryon County, North Carolina, the purpose of which was to secure the left of Cornwallis's march. He was then to join the troops at Charlotte so that his corps and the militia might accompany the onward advance. Having crossed the frontier on the 7th, he proceeded to pass some time in and around Gilbert Town, defeating Col. Charles McDowell at Cane Creek on the 12th. He then attempted to settle the county by disarming the disaffected and putting their arms into the hands of loyalists who came in. On the 14th he had some 650 militia with him, but they were old and infirm and part neither armed nor trained. By the 28th, when he was seeking to intercept Lt. Col. Elijah Clark, his militia had increased to under 800, but of what quality he does not say. In the meantime he had mustered 500 loyalists within twenty-five miles of Gilbert Town, "half of whom are of the first class and arm'd," while another body nearly as numerous had been formed on the Catawba from its head forty miles downwards. Aware by now of the revolutionary parties gathering to oppose him, he was confident that, centrical as he was, he would prevent a general junction and remain master of the field. He could have not been more egregiously mistaken.

As Cornwallis lingered at the Waxhaws, Clark, who had returned with about 200 men to the Ceded Lands in Georgia, incited some 500 more to join him and on September 14 made a surprise attack on Lt. Col. Thomas Brown's post at Augusta. It was a close-run thing. Brown

---

4. Pronounced "Weems."

5. For an account of the expeditions and a justification for them, see Ian Saberton, "The Revolutionary War in the South: Re-evaluations of certain Revolutionary Actors and Events," *Journal of the American Revolution*, December 6, 2016.

held out courageously but was saved only by the spirited and active conduct of Lt. Col. John Harris Cruger, who came promptly from Ninety Six to his relief. Clark with many of his party fled across the Savannah River and crossed some two weeks later into North Carolina, going off at the head of Saluda at a gap beyond Ferguson's reach. After the attack severe measures were taken to pacify the Ceded Lands.[6]

Of the 2nd division intended to reinforce Cornwallis at Charlotte, only the 7th Regiment (Royal Fusiliers) came up, much depleted by 106 sick left behind at Camden. Accompanying it were 150 convalescents—some for the 23rd, some for the 33rd, and the rest for the 71st—and a supply train of ten puncheons of rum and fifty-six bushels of salt. On October 5 they all arrived at the Waxhaws, and two days later the 7th, but not the convalescents, advanced to Charlotte. The rest of the 2nd division consisting of the 63rd Regiment and the Royal North Carolina Regiment never came up. Of the 71st, which had been posted at the Waxhaws, the 2nd Battalion was ordered forward on the October 1, whereas the 1st Battalion, which had initially been intended to meet Ferguson at Armour's Ford,[7] was given its marching orders on the 8th. Together, they would have brought to Charlotte the numerous sick and convalescents left behind with them.

On October 7 Cornwallis explained his plan of campaign to Wemyss:

> The object of marching into North Carolina is only to raise men, which, from every account I have received of the number of our friends, there is great reason to hope may be done to a very considerable amount. For this purpose I shall move in about ten or twelve days to Salisbury and from thence invite all loyalists of the neighbouring countys to repair to our standard to be formed into Provincial corps and armed, clothed and appointed as soon as we can do it. From thence I mean to move my whole force down to Cross Creek [to raise the Highlanders]. As it will then be about the middle of November, I hope the lower country will be healthy. I shall then be in full communication with our shipping and shall receive all the arms and clothing that Charlestown can afford.[8]

6. The Ceded Lands" was an expression commonly used to refer to part of the territory ceded to Georgia by the Cherokees and Creeks in 1773. It was located in the up country above Augusta, extending from the headwaters of the Oconee downwards and between that river and the Savannah.

7. he ford lay near the mouth of the south fork of the Catawba. It was deep and crossing was at times dangerous.

8. CP: 2, 222.

Wemyss, who had been intended to command an intermediate post at Charlotte, now to be abandoned due to the inveteracy of the locality, was instructed to operate again east of Camden before joining Cornwallis at Cross Creek, but his orders were almost immediately countermanded.

For Cornwallis, overstretched as he was, it was now that the chickens came home to roost.

Of the risks he was running, some would have been apparent to him at the start of the campaign, aware as he was that it might be an imprudent measure. Among the greatest risks was that of losing control of much of South Carolina and Georgia, so few were the troops that he left behind. Charlestown and Savannah were safe, but what about the rest of the country? If we leave aside the relative backwater of Georgetown, there were only two principal posts in South Carolina outside Charlestown at Camden and the village of Ninety Six. Left to garrison Camden were the New York Volunteers and the South Carolina Royalist Regiment under the overall command of Lt. Col. George Turnbull, who, in the words of Cornwallis, "tho'. . . not a great genius, . . . is a plain rightheaded man." According to Turnbull, the South Carolina Royalists, who did not arrive until September 17, made a very sorry appearance and on the 22nd did duty for no more than 160 rank and file. By October 2 only 91 of them were fit for duty, as some had fallen down with the small pox and others presumably with the other illnesses prevalent there. Two days later those fit for duty in both corps came to a total of 247. Admittedly, part of the Royal North Carolina Regiment was also at Camden in September, as was the debris of the 63rd, and both were augmented by the arrival of Wemyss' party at the beginning of October. Yet neither corps formed part of the garrison, for both were awaiting orders (which never came) to reinforce Cornwallis. On October 20, as Wemyss and the remains of the 63rd were about to depart next day for Ninety Six, the three British American regiments afforded no more than 300 men fit for duty. All in all, given the need to maintain the post of Camden itself, the garrison had precious few troops for exerting control over the vast expanse of territory dependent on it or for supporting the royal militia to this end. Alone, the royal militia were in Turnbull's eyes a busted flush. As he would soon observe, ". . . our officers of militia in general are not near so active as the rebels, and great numbers of their privates are ready to turn against us when an opportunity offers . . . Depend on it, militia will never do any good without regular troops."[9] With so few troops in the garrison to support them,

9. CP: 2, 250.

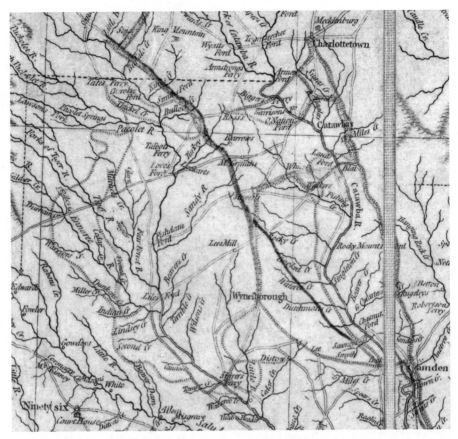

"The marches of Lord Cornwallis in the Southern Provinces," William Faden, 1787. Camden is at the lower right, Ninety Six is lower left, and Charlottetown is at the top right.

the militia were, if attacked, an edifice waiting to crumble, far beyond the reach of Cornwallis to sustain them if he had penetrated deeper into North Carolina, taking Ferguson and Hamilton with him. That was the risk. Nor would it have been markedly lessened if an intermediate post under Wemyss had been established at Charlotte, so composed would it have been of convalescents. The risk was in fact low for only so long as Cornwallis remained within reach, Wemyss and Hamilton were not brought up to reinforce him, and Ferguson continued to protect the northern border against incursions. Even so, control of the area east of Camden had long been lost, and despite Wemyss' and Moncrief's expeditions, nothing could be done to reassert it. Cornwallis desperately sought to scrape the barrel at Camden for a further foray there, but it was all to no avail. Nothing really effective could be done but to advance Col. Samuel Tynes's militia to the forks of Black River, where they were promptly routed by Lt. Col. Francis Marion, and to await Tarleton's punitive but brief incursion in November.

The situation at Ninety Six was pretty parlous too. Garrisoning the village were the 1st Battalion, De Lancey's Brigade, and the 3rd Battalion, New Jersey Volunteers, under the overall command of Cruger. He had with him near 300 men fit for duty. As with Camden, the problem was not so much the post itself as the vast hinterland. Split as it was into tracts of loyalists and revolutionaries, the most worrying parts were the Long Canes settlement and the tract contiguous to it, being the catchment areas of Col. Richard King's and Lt. Col. Moses Kirkland's regiments. There the inhabitants were preponderantly disaffected and the bulk of the two regiments was not to be relied on. Of almost equal concern was a rebellious tract of fifty miles about the Tyger and Enoree, where the inhabitants had mostly fled and were waiting for Cornwallis and Ferguson to move on before they returned and commenced hostilities. In general the royal militia left behind by Ferguson were reluctant to turn out, and in any event Cruger was exceedingly short of men to support them. With Ferguson on the northern border and on his march to join Cornwallis, Cruger was of opinion that, if a tenuous hold on the district was to be maintained, a body of regular or British American troops was essential to occupy the area between the Broad and Saluda Rivers vacated by Ferguson. Unfortunately, none was available, and so there was a high risk that the district would be overrun. An intermediate post, if established at Charlotte, would have been too remote to have any effect.

Despite the defeat of Clark, the British hold on the back parts of Georgia remained tenuous. We have no record of the casualties sustained at Augusta, but at the time of Clark's attack Brown's garrison consisted of 199 men of the King's Rangers fit for duty, 35 members of the Indian Department, 100 convalescents of the King's Rangers and New Jersey Volunteers, and 500 native Americans who happened to be visiting the village. After the attack Cruger left upwards of 200 militia to complete the work of scouring the Ceded Lands. With so remarkably few troops and militia to maintain control of Augusta and the hinterland, the door remained open to enemy incursions.

Overall, the situation was most precarious and ripe for disaster. What transpired next, and its knock-on effect, are, however, matters for another day.

James Abercrombie, Much Lamented Victim of Friendly Fire at Bunker Hill

❀❀ DON N. HAGIST ❀❀

Bunker Hill is one of the best-known battles of the American Revolution, recognized by name even among those who know little about the war.[1] In spite of this recognition, many important facts of the battle are overshadowed by misconceptions and romantic images. Undeniably, it was a British victory won at a cost so great that it improved the American cause and diminished that of the British. This fact has caused popular history to present the battle as an example of British ineptitude and American prowess. Among the misconceptions are that the British made an overconfident frontal assault on a fortified position, that their soldiers marched into fire encumbered by heavy knapsacks, that superior American marksmanship greatly influenced the flow of the battle, and even that an African American named Salem Poor personally killed the senior British officer to fall in the fight. Like much popular history of the war, many of these perceptions change or evaporate completely when weighed against first-hand accounts.

That the British made a frontal assault on a fortified position cannot be disputed. Widely overlooked, however, is that this frontal assault was more an accident of war than an intentional tactical blunder. Understanding this is critical for appreciating British tactical doctrine throughout the war. The commander of the attack, Gen. Sir William Howe, won repeated victories later in the war with bold and decisive flanking movements. Often this is seen as a response to the massive casualties taken at Bunker Hill. In fact, the Bunker Hill redoubt was also intended to be taken by a flanking maneuver, the first and last of Howe's to go awry.

1. This article refers to the scene of the action as Bunker Hill. The American redoubt was actually on a secondary eminence on the slope of Bunker Hill facing Boston, called Breed's Hill. Although semantically accurate, the battle was not referred to as Breed's Hill in contemporary accounts nor in most modern histories.

The fortifications on Bunker Hill were erected hastily on the night of June 16–17, 1775 by an American army that had encircled the British garrison in Boston since hostilities began openly in April. When dawn brought the American redoubt into view, British commanders knew that swift action was necessary. Besides the threat the redoubt posed to Boston, it was also an aggressive display of American initiative requiring a decisive response. There was little doubt that the position could be taken. In spite of having been roughly handled during the retreat from Concord on April 19, British officers and soldiers had little regard for American military capability. While the state of training of the Boston garrison is debatable, the British military system was sufficiently refined and the personnel sufficiently experienced to constitute a formidable fighting force. They were keenly aware that their opponents were haphazardly brought together, poorly supplied and just learning how to establish their own organization. Regardless of any deficiencies in the British army, there was no reason to doubt its superiority.

The speed with which the redoubt was constructed may have emboldened the attackers. Although well-positioned, it was not yet strong enough to be impenetrable. Digging a wide, deep ditch and piling the earth behind it to form a rampart created a formidable obstacle, but it was far from a refined military fortification. It could be stormed, albeit at a cost. The system of rail fencing extending from the left side of the redoubt down to the shore was even more feeble but nonetheless provided some shelter for its defenders. Howe, a cost-conscious commander, saw the best approach as getting behind the fortifications to compromise their strength and prevent reinforcement. Because Bunker Hill was the summit of a peninsula connected to the mainland by a narrow neck of land, the works should have been easy to isolate and then reduce either by siege or by storm depending on the defenders' fortitude.

That the fort had to be flanked and enveloped was obvious; the problem was how to get men behind it. At a council of war, senior British officers discussed options of which two came to the forefront. The most tactically effective approach was to land men behind the redoubt to secure the neck. The logistical drawback was that this required a lengthy trip in rowboats from Boston. After a first wave of troops landed, they would have to stand their ground with no support or avenue of retreat for a long time before the boats could return with a second wave. This made the venture risky, but certainly not impossible. The alternative was to ferry the troops the shortest distance from Boston to Charlestown neck. This put the assault force in front of the

American fortifications, but out of musket range. It also allowed them to be reinforced quickly.

Among those who favored the plan of landing behind the redoubt, in spite of the dangers, was Lt.-Col. James Abercrombie. He was an officer in the 22nd Regiment of Foot, Lt.-Gen. Thomas Gage's own regiment. The 22nd had only recently been ordered to America and was still at sea on June 17, but Abercrombie had arrived early to work on Gage's staff. Gage wanted his experience with the people and warfighting conditions in America. Abercrombie was the same age as George Washington and had served in the French and Indian war on the staff of his "friend and relation" Gen. James Abercromby at the abortive assault on Fort Ticonderoga in 1757.[2] The following year he was appointed aide-de-camp to Gen. Jeffrey Amherst. This service gave him invaluable experience with warfare in America and brought him into contact with many men who by 1775 held positions of influence on both sides of the conflict.

Abercrombie had been following the rising tensions in America closely while serving with his regiment in Great Britain, and he made many comments in his letters. On March 14, 1774 he wrote from Dublin, "I dare say the Americans behaviour give Administration much uneasiness, it requires mature Deliberation to determine what is best to be done."[3] On March 21, "the most probable conjecture is to Block up the Ports untill they pay for the Tea & acknowledge the Right the British Parliament . . . Pray how did the six American apples Eat there were so many on the tree."[4] On March 26, "I am vastly pleased to find by a Pamphlet sent me from the Admiralty, that Wedderbourn has painted Mr Franklin in true Colours. if he was hanged it would be doing Justice to both Countrys, & had I the power, none of his breed should have any imployment under the Crown."[5] On April 3, "You arrived in good time to lend the bostonians a Cat with nine tails, & to hear the D of Richmond argue in their favor, its said they have Committed greater

---

2. Lt. Col. James Abercrombie's parentage is not clear. He was certainly related to several other Abercrombies in the military. His will cites the general to whom most of his estate was bequeathed as his "friend and relation" without specifying the relationship. Some sources incorrectly state that the general and the lieutenant-colonel were the same man.

3. James Abercrombie to the Earl of Loudoun, March 14, 1774, Mount Stuart, Rothsay, Isle of Bute, Scotland.

4. Abercrombie to Loudoun, March 21, 1774, Mount Stuart, Rothsay, Isle of Bute, Scotland.

5. Abercrombie to Loudoun, March 26, 1774, Mount Stuart, Rothsay, Isle of Bute, Scotland.

Outrages if so inflict a double punishment for if they are spared the more insolent they will be."[6] A letter the following week commented on the military buildup in Boston, including several regiments sent that spring from Great Britain, and that General Gage, the 22nd Regiment's colonel, having been appointed military governor of the Massachusetts colony, would arrive before them:

> By the Orders issued there is to be a Jubilee Camp at Boston Consisting of eight Regts, & all Officers to attend, tis a pitty they sent of my Colonel so soon, as he might have made a Triumphal entry to His Govt at the head of such a chosen Band the General at their Head and Earl Percy in the Rear, By the appointment of such chosen Men, they surely only intend making Game of the Bostonians
> It is reported here that Our Acquaintance Lt Col Charles Lee set out [fast?] for Boston the moment he heard there was a probability of an insurrection there. As Gage and he are intimately acquainted they possibly may settle every thing Amicably.[7]

Another letter four days later indicated doubt in Gage's suitability for the command: "If the Bostonians are to be Chastized, why the Deuce did they send out my Colonel, if there is any disturbance He will abdicate His Government, but I forgot the Gallant Percy is his Second."[8] Some months later, he wrote directly to Gage, expressing sympathy for his having been appointed to an untenable situation:

> Of all the troublesome employments, that could possibly have been thought of, they could not have desired a more disagreable One than the present you are engaged in, tho' I have not the ear of a Minister or the Correspondance of the Great, yet I am pleased to hear your Conduct hitherto is verry agreable to Administration. The Colonies are in Such a ferment that I am afraid their frenzy will carry them too far. I am extreamly sorry that you are so situated, for little honor or Credit is to be got, but your All is at Stake. If you succeed in bringing about a reconciliation the Cockpit plume themselves; if force to force is necessary it may rediculously be called a Massacre and tho' you have done duty in both Capacitys as Civil & Military Commander, yet your Name may be unjustly execrated.[9]

6. Abercrombie to Loudoun, April 4, 1774, Mount Stuart, Rothsay, Isle of Bute, Scotland.
7. Abercrombie to Loudoun, April 10, 1774, Mount Stuart, Rothsay, Isle of Bute, Scotland.
8. Abercrombie to Loudoun, April 14, 1774, Mount Stuart, Rothsay, Isle of Bute, Scotland.
9. Abercrombie to Thomas Gage, September 21, 1774, Thomas Gage Mss., W. L. Clements Library, Ann Arbor, MI.

Abercrombie arrived in Boston on April 23, just four days after hostilities had broken out. With armed Americans flocking to the towns surrounding Boston, the situation was fluid and the future unclear. Abercrombie set to work establishing defenses for Boston. In a matter of days he was confident that he had put the town "in perfect security." Being nonetheless prevailed upon to erect artillery batteries that he considered "contra la luna," he "resignd [his] charge as Engineer not choosing to be laugh'd at."[10] The following day he noted in a letter to a friend in New York, "Parties run as high as ever they did in Cromwels time, & was there not a Red Coat in the Country they would Cut one anothers throats."[11]

On May 3 Abercrombie was appointed adjutant general and began gathering intelligence, among other military matters. A few days later he shared some thoughts with Gen. Sir Jeffrey Amherst, under whom he had served in the previous war:

> to tell the truth I have never advised a General Sortie as I really detest the thoughts of a Civil War, and am satisfied the Country within Six miles of this will suffer as much from the ravages of their own people, as if we had laid it waste, another reason, Connecticut & Providence have sent Deputies from their Assemblies to intreat the General to suspend hostilities hoping all matters may be accommodated ... the Deputies and many of the Principal people have waited on me. If I do not flatter myself too much, I imagine I have done more good with my tongue than I could have perform'd with my Sword, yet if the Phrenzy of the people still continue they will find it is not rusty in the Scabbard.
>
> Words cannot express the animosity that subsists between the Whigs and the Tories, the latter are but few, yet they reciprocally wish the ruin of each other.
>
> You must remember the kind of Arms the Provincials had last War. I have seen some thousands of those they have now, as bright as ours & Bayonets fixt, yet I am certain We shall never come to les Armes blanche.
>
> I dare say Fools will exhibit this Seige on the Stage.[12]

10. James Abercrombie to Sir Jeffrey Amherst, May 7. 1775. Amherst Mss, U1350 080/1, Center for Kentish Studies, Maidstone, Kent, England.
11. Abercrombie to Cadwallader Colden, May 2, 1775, Library of Congress.
12. Abercrombie to Amherst, May 7. 1775.

On May 18 he was fired upon while taking soundings from a boat in one of the rivers adjacent to Boston, prompting an officer in the garrison to write that "I don't hear that he has been as found of reconnoitring since."[13] Other intelligence gathering activities were more traditional: "Our intelligence is bad, but one of the fair Sex told me some days since, that Seven of their heaviest Cannon she saw at Dedham nine miles from this on their way back to Providence. & that the Men begin to refuse to take paper money in lieu of pay. I am sure the Damsel does not deceive me for I pay her in Sterling."[14] On May 28 he brought a couple of artillery pieces to reinforce a detachment on Noddles Island. After driving some American troops off this small island in Boston harbor the British force withdrew, leaving the cattle grazing there to be seized by the Americans on the 29th.[15] In spite of Abercrombie's prior staff experience in America, General Gage decided that Abercrombie's "talents were mistaken" in the role of Adjutant General; Abercrombie was a fighter. On June 4 he was given an appointment that was "more to his wishes, and in a way more adapted to his genius:" command of a battalion of grenadiers.[16]

At this time in the war, the established strength of a British regiment was about 440 non-commissioned officers and private men, divided equally into ten companies. Two of these companies were composed of experienced and reliable men, one called the light infantry and one called the grenadiers. In very general terms, light infantry were intended for rapid movement and skirmishing while grenadiers were intended for shock and assault; in practice, both were employed for rapid movements to gain tactical advantage. Although grenadiers had ceased to throw hand grenades decades earlier, their uniforms retained some of the trappings of this specialty, while those of the light infantry were adapted for fast movement. The common practice was to detach each of these companies from their regiments and form them into grenadier and light infantry battalions, typically of eight to twelve companies each, which would be first into battle. Each regiment's remaining eight companies, called battalion companies, continued to operate as an entity.

13. *The British in Boston: the Diary of Lt. John Barker*, Elizabeth Ellery Dana, ed. (Cambridge, MA: Harvard University Press, 1924), 48.
14. Abercrombie to Amherst, June 7, 1775. Amherst Mss, U1350 080/2, Center for Kentish Studies, Maidstone, Kent, England.
15. Ibid.
16. Thomas Gage to Secretary at War Barrington, September 28, 1775, in "Private Correspondence of Barrington and Gage," *Sources of American Independence: Selected Manuscripts from the William L. Clements Library* , Howard H. Peckham, ed. (Chicago: The University of Chicago Press, 1978), 139.

This methodology led to the grenadiers and light infantry being employed on the expedition to Lexington and Concord in April. They were roughly handled that day, but the casualties were quickly replaced by drafting qualified men with at least a year's experience from the battalion companies into the grenadiers and light infantry; wounded grenadiers and light infantry men were sent to battalion companies.[17] When Lieutenant Colonel Abercombie took command of the grenadier battalion, he took responsibility for an organization of men who were capable but who had only recently begun working together. Prior to the formation of the battalion on June 4, the grenadiers had formed together only once for the April 19 expedition. Since then the companies were adapting to the new men appointed to replace casualties; as late as June 12 transfers were still being made.[18] The light infantry battalion was in a similar state. In spite of these challenges, Abercrombie had sufficient confidence to favor landing on Charleston Neck behind the American redoubt. This was the type of duty that grenadiers and light infantry were designed for, and Abercrombie must have believed that his new charges were equal to the task. He wrote to a colleague, "If the War was with Spain or France I should have been proud of the Command, but I do not like such fine fellows should be Shott at by such Rascals."[19]

The British general staff chose to take the more conservative approach, one which used the grenadiers in a more traditional manner. All the troops would take the shortest route to the peninsula and form in front of, but out of range of, the American works. The grenadiers would advance on the American works while the light infantry rapidly made their way around the flank, to the right of the grenadiers. The grenadiers would not assault the works immediately, but occupy the defenders while the light infantry invested their rear, attacking only when the enemy was thrown into confusion. It was a sound plan based on good military principles.[20]

With the plan in place, embarkation orders were given at 10 AM on June 17 that were characteristic of almost every tactical movement of the war:

17. Muster rolls, 23rd Regiment of Foot, WO 12/3960 and 38th Regiment of Foot, WO 12/5171, The National Archives, Kew, Richmond, Surrey.

18. General Orders, America, WO 36/1, 106; muster rolls, 38th Regiment of Foot, WO 12/5171, The National Archives.

19. Abercrombie to the Earl of Eglinton, June 5, 1775, GD3/5/1101, National Library of Scotland.

20. Harold Murdock, *Bunker Hill Notes and Queries* (Boston: Houghton Mifflin Company, 1927), 22-25. Although deficient in many points of detail, this is one of the first histories to accurately present the British strategy based on primary sources.

The ten oldest companies of Grenadiers and the ten oldest companies of light Infantry, (exclusive of the Regiments lately landed) the
5th and 38th Regiments, to parade half after eleven o'Clock, with
their Arms, Ammunition, Blankets, and provisions ordered to be
cooked this morning, they will march by files to the long wharf.[21]

The mistaken image of British soldiers marching up Bunker Hill
laden with knapsacks seems to have begun with one of the first British
histories of the war, published in 1794. Charles Stedman, who served
in America but was not at Bunker Hill, wrote that the troops were "encumbered with three days provisions, their knapsacks on their backs"
and estimated their total burden at 125 pounds.[22] Even if knapsacks had
been carried, other contemporary accounts estimate the British soldier's
full load of knapsack, blanket, provisions, and arms at about sixty
pounds,[23] and the embarkation order makes it clear that knapsacks
weren't carried. A later author who expressly intended to rectify misconceptions about the battle repeated the error, going so far as to present the embarkation order but also suggest that the British troops were
"in heavy marching order, each man encumbered with a superfluous
weight estimated at nearly one hundred pounds."[24] Stedman's error has
been reinforced by historians who have taken descriptions of especially
harsh campaigns to be representative of the typical mode of operation.[25]
Troops from the Boston garrison had indeed gone on marches into the
countryside in "heavy marching order" on occasion, but these excur-
sions were to develop the fitness of the soldiers, not achieve military
objectives.[26]

The grenadiers and light infantry were the first to land on
Charlestown Neck at a point out of American musketry range. Here

21. General Orders, America. WO 36/1, 108-109.
22. Charles Stedman, *The History of the Origin, Progress and Termination of the American War* (London, 1794), 128.
23. John Burgoyne, *A State of The Expedition From Canada, as Laid Before The House of Commons, by Lieutenant-general Burgoyne, and Verified by Evidence; with a Collection of Authentic Documents, And Additions Of Many Circumstances Which Were Prevented From Appearing Before The House By The Prorogation Of Parliament...* (London, 1780), 148.
24. Murdock, *Bunker Hill Notes and Queries*, 27. The embarkation orders are given on page 14 of the same source.
25. For example, in the last stages of Burgoyne's 1777 campaign soldiers were forced to carry their knapsacks, adding to the overall hardship, but a contemporary account of this presents it as a contrast to conditions earlier in the campaign when wagons or boats transported the knapsacks. Don N. Hagist, *A British Soldier's Story: Roger Lamb's Narrative of the American Revolution* (Baraboo, WI: Ballindalloch Press, 2005), xxxv, 42.
26. Frederick Mackenzie, *The Diary of Frederick Mackenzie* (Cambridge, MA: Harvard University Press, 1930), 13.

Detail from an 1834 engraving of *The Death of General Warren at the Battle of Bunker's Hill, June 17, 1775* by John Trumbull. The body of James Abercrombie is to the right of the mortally wounded Warren.

they formed, the grenadiers into a line facing the rail-fence breastwork that extended from the redoubt down to the shore, the light infantry into a column for their advance along the beach to the right. Two regiments formed on the left facing the redoubt. While the grenadiers advanced with deliberate slowness as a distraction, the light infantry trotted along the beach. It was expected that the narrow beach would provide an avenue around the end of the breastwork. Unknown to the attackers, the Americans had constructed a barrier across the beach and manned it. The British navy had no ships or floating batteries positioned to bear on this location, leaving the defenders unmolested as the light infantry approached. The hail of fire from the barricade inflicted heavy casualties on the head of the British column, and the confines of the beach with water on the right and an embankment on the left afforded no alternative to retreat. This check was the undoing of British plans and the remainder of the action was conducted extemporaneously.

It is not clear exactly when the grenadiers became aware of the failure of the flanking movement, but they fatefully continued their advance towards the breastworks. Progress was perilously slow, not because of "superfluous weight" or rigid marching, but because of a series of fences, brick kilns, enclosures and other obstructions. The fences could not be quickly broken down, so the grenadiers had to climb over each one. This prevented the rapid advance they would normally have maintained in the face of an enemy. But the slow and irregular advance brought about a danger even greater than hostile fire. The battered light infantry battalion, having withdrawn from the barricade on the beach, reformed into a line near their initial staging area. The shape of the coastline put them behind the advancing grenadier battalion. From this disadvantageous position they opened fire. The distance was too great to have any material effect on the enemy, but the impact on the grenadier battalion was disastrous.

This friendly fire incident is occasionally mentioned by historians, but the importance of it is largely overlooked. It calls into question not only British discipline at this early stage of the war, but also American marksmanship. The disproportionate casualties in this battle are some-times used as evidence of the effectiveness of American firepower. That some of the casualties were inflicted by friendly fire means that Amer-ican musketry was that much less lethal. In a letter dated three days after the battle, Abercrombie indicated that "our Light Infantry killed many of the Grends." After ordering them to desist, the friendly fire abated for eight or ten minutes, but then the light infantry "gave me a plumper & killed two officers & 3 private."[27] He used the vernacular "plumper" to refer to a volley of lead.[28] We have no precise figures on the total number of friendly fire casualties. Looking only at Abercrom-bie's description of the volley that killed five men, we can estimate the proportion of wounded at around twenty based on the overall casualty figures for the battle of 226 dead and 828 wounded. Abercrombie im-plies that more were struck previously, and there may have been other casualties of which he was not aware. Of particular importance was that the grenadiers' commander, Abercrombie himself, was among the wounded.

There are several possible explanations for the light infantry firing into their own men. While the light infantry was composed of trusted and experienced men, several years of peace may have diminished their discipline and operational readiness. Certainly some of the men were not completely familiar with their officers or comrades, having been re-cently transferred into the light infantry to recruit losses sustained on

27. Abercrombie to Amherst, June 20, 1775, Amherst Mss, U1350 080/3, Center for Kentish Studies, Maidstone, Kent, England.
28. "To plump; to strike or shoot. He pulled out his pops and plumped him; he drew out his pistols and shot him." Francis Gross, *A Classical Dictionary of the Vulgar Tongue*, Eric Partridge, ed. (New York: Dorset Press, 1992), 265.

April 19. The withering fire that they'd received from the barricade threw them into confusion and inflicted significant casualties, further diminishing their organization. Perhaps some of the soldiers were overly determined to inflict punishment on the rebels that had handled them so roughly in April and again this day. One officer wrote that although they rallied after being pushed back from the barricade they were "in such consternation that they fired at random, and unfortunately killed several of their officers."[29] Regardless of the reason, their fire may have been more instrumental than that of the Americans in breaking the assault by the grenadiers. After the action Abercrombie wrote that "Our men must be drilled before they are Carryed to action again."[30]

The muddled assault on the American works was repulsed with heavy losses caused by the confluence of several factors: the favorable high-ground position of the defenders that afforded both protection and an open field of fire, the obstructions that prevented a rapid British advance, the friendly fire that added to British casualties and confusion, the inability of the British to bring significant artillery fire on the fort. Deficiencies in British battle readiness and overconfidence that the defense would be weak may have also contributed. A final British assault, better organized and more suited to the situation, overwhelmed the defenders who were by this time low on ammunition. Given the difficulties that they'd faced, the British military regarded it as a triumph of arms. But if the concept of a pyrrhic victory had not already been known, it would have been established by the battle of Bunker Hill. About half of the British officers and soldiers who landed at the foot of the hill that afternoon were killed or wounded.[31]

Lt.-Col. James Abercrombie had been shot through the middle of the right thigh and was out of the action. No account of his removal from the battlefield has been found, and we do not know if he was there to see the British forces finally carry the day. He was keenly aware of the cost, however, and echoed the sentiments of many of his fellow officers when he wrote that "a few of such Victories would Ruin the army."[32] His wound did not appear fatal; General Howe went so far as to call it "only a flesh wound."[33] But there was a complication. The shot that came from behind had hit Abercombie "with such power from its

29. *Edinburgh Advertiser*, August 11, 1775.

30. Abercrombie to Amherst, June 20, 1775.

31. The British officially reported 226 killed and 828 wounded out of some 2200 troops engaged.

32. Abercrombie to Amherst, June 20, 1775.

33. *Correspondence of King George III*, Vol. 3, John Fortescue, ed. (New York: McMillan & Co., 1927), 223.

proximity, as to force a pen case which he had in his side pocket, along with it into his thigh, from the lodgment of the ball it could readily be extracted—but part of the pen case being got so far it baffled the art of the surgeons."[34] In addition, he was "said to have been in a very bad habit of body."[35] Three days after the battle he wrote that "all the Doctrs agree that wound Looks well but it has not Begun to desist yet," but he was nonetheless in such a state of convalescence that he dictated the letter to his servant.[36] In spite of the good prognosis, the wound proved fatal.

On June 22 James Abercrombie died. Because the official casualty list sent to the War Office and subsequently widely published included the regiment to which each officer belonged, the 22nd Regiment is often presented as having been in the battle. The regiment, dispersed in several transport ships, actually arrived piecemeal during the next four weeks.[37] In keeping with army tradition, Abercrombie's military effects were sold at auction in the encampment on Boston Common on August 11, where a junior officer in the regiment whose baggage had been captured purchased some of the goods.[38] Abercrombie's servant, a soldier named James Grant, was discharged from the army and carried a trunk containing personal effects back to Great Britain.[39] Abercrombie's will was proved in London on October 17.[40] He was the highest-ranking officer to die as a result of the battle. Although he was "much lamented" at the time,[41] memory of his loss has been eclipsed by the death of Maj. John Pitcairn, probably because of that officer's role in the events of April 19.

34. *Edinburgh Advertiser*, August 18, 1775.
35. *Correspondence of King George III*, 223.
36. Abercrombie to Amherst, June 20, 1775.
37. The first of ten transports carrying the 22nd, 40th, 44th and 45th Regiments arrived in Boston on June 28, the last on July 19. "Stephen Kemble's Journals," *Collections of the New York Historical Society for the year 1883* (New York: New York Historical Society, 1884), 45-49.
38. Baggage belonging to Lt. Arthur French was captured when a ship inadvertently put into Philadelphia after hostilities began. Minutes of the Pennsylvania Committee of Safety, August 12, 1775, in *Naval Documents of the American Revolution*, Vol. 1. William Bell Clark, ed. (Washington, DC: US Government Printing Office, 1964), 1125-1126; *General Sir William Howe's Orderly Book*, B. F. Stevens, ed. (Port Washington, NY: Kennikat Press, 1970), 65; Agent's ledgers, 22nd Regiment of Foot, Lloyds Bank Archives, London.
39. Earl of Loudon to James Robertson, August 5, 1775, GD172/2576, National Archive of Scotland.
40. Agent's ledgers, 22nd Regiment of Foot.
41. *Edinburgh Advertiser*, August 11, 1775.

The battle of Bunker Hill influenced subsequent actions, at least during the 1776 campaign, but not in the ways that are often described. Bunker Hill was a failure of execution, not of planning, and subsequent successful British flanking movements were the result of better execution rather than changed doctrine. The heavy casualties gave the neophyte American army a tremendous morale boost but also caused them to rely on fixed positions at several engagements, a reliance that proved fatal at Brooklyn in August 1776, Kipp's Bay in September 1776, and other actions early in the war. The slow British advance up the slopes was not due to staid discipline and unnecessary burdens, and the signature of British infantry movements for the rest of the war was rapidity. The battle that is often used to characterize the tactical aspects of the war was in fact an anomaly that was not intended and not repeated.

Displaced: The Donation People of 1775

KATIE TURNER GETTY

In late November 1775, just as the bone-chilling New England winter started to settle upon Massachusetts, British General Howe loaded three hundred poor, sick inhabitants of Boston onto transport ships with no provisions or firewood.[1] They were landed on windswept Point Shirley peninsula, a narrow, beachy finger of land situated in between the gentle waves of Boston Harbor and the vast expanse of the Atlantic. Lacking in food, fuel and warmth, the Bostonians were destitute.

Among the hundreds of townspeople unceremoniously deposited on the point by General Howe were a wide cross-section of Boston's poorest residents—married couples, widows (such as "aged widow" Martha Tompson), and men whose occupations included shoemaker, laborer, butcher, and brazier. Numerous children arrived on the point with their parents—Israel Cowing and his wife had seven children with them. Both Edward Edwards and his wife and Lewis Channel and his wife had four. The widowed Sarah Brown had four children. Henry Harris, a peddler, had three. Dozens of other adults were accompanied on the point by at least one child. Other children such as "Elizabeth Orr, orphan girl of fourteen" and "Jacob Tuckerman, Orphan Boy, 12 years old" were on the point alone.[2]

These individuals are just a few of the thousands of inhabitants of Boston and Charlestown, largely forgotten by history, who were displaced by the Siege of Boston in 1775. Sometimes called "donation peo-

---

1. *Boston-Gazette and Country Journal*, November 27, 1775, page 3, 3rd col., John Adams Library at Boston Public Library, Internet Archive, archive.org/stream/bostongazette-orc269bost#page/n81/mode/2up.
2. Henry J. Cadbury, "Quaker Relief During the Siege of Boston," *Transactions of the Colonial Society of Massachusetts*, Vol. 34 (1937-1942): 39-179, www.colonialsociety.org/node/616#ah1002.

ple" or "the Boston poor," they numbered among the most vulnerable of Boston's residents—many were widowed, orphaned, elderly, or suffering with smallpox. These donation people were removed from Boston during the siege and subsequently relocated to various towns in the Massachusetts countryside, enduring significant hardships and uncertainty along the way.

The three hundred Boston poor on Point Shirley suffered exceptional privation. As Lt. Col. Loammi Baldwin informed Gen. George Washington, "The people that came out of Boston now at the Point are in a most Shocking Condition yesterday in the afternoon there was one dead and another Just Dieing upon the Beach Sevral other very Sick no bread believe that they have had some of pulling Point Sheep killed & carved them."[3] General Washington likewise observed that, "the whole [were] in the most miserable & piteous condition."[4]

A most miserable and piteous condition, indeed—some of the Bostonians on Point Shirley were infected with the dreaded smallpox.[5] At least three women were widowed on the point. Elizabeth Manwaring's husband died upon their arrival at Point Shirley. The husband of Sarah Usher, too, "died the day he landed on the point." Rebeckah Spears' husband also died, leaving her alone with one child.[6]

Thomas Francis, a young Boston apprentice, was suffering from smallpox due to having been inoculated. He claimed that his master forced him to board a second transport ship to Point Shirley despite his illness. He ended up surviving his battle with the disease and lived to later testify in a deposition that his condition had so alarmed the other passengers that they tried to keep him off the ship and refused to stay below deck with him, for fear of contracting the illness. Francis also claimed that a man named Morrison threatened the passengers that if they continued to protest against the presence of the ailing boy, then he would turn them back on shore again. Desperate to leave Boston, the passengers must have acquiesced to Morrison's demands and resigned themselves to exposure to smallpox. Francis added that "a Number of said Passengers that came down with me have since Broke out with that Distemper at Point Shirley."[7]

3. Loammi Baldwin to George Washington, November 26, 1775, *Founders Online*, National Archives, founders.archives.gov/documents/Washington/03-02-02-0393.
4. Washington to Joseph Reed, November 27, 1775," *Founders Online*, founders.archives.gov/documents/Washington/03-02-02-0401.
5. Ibid.
6. Cadbury, "Quaker Relief."
7. *Boston-Gazette*, February 12, 1776, page 4, 1st col., John Adams Library at Boston Public Library, Internet Archive.

In addition to some of their number suffering with smallpox and having no firewood, the Bostonians had been robbed of their possessions by the British troops while on board the ships to Point Shirley.[8] The Provincial Congress and General Washington scrambled to supply them with wood and other necessary provisions. The congress resolved that "any old decayed stores, barns, or fish-houses" on the point could be ripped down and used as "fuel for the relief of the sick and distressed." And, "Public buildings were authorized to be torn down for firewood, if necessary."[9]

Though General Washington wasted no time in ordering supplies for the displaced townspeople, he greatly feared them transmitting smallpox to the Continental Army camp in nearby Cambridge. "I have order'd Provision to them till they can be remov'd, but am under dreadful apprehension's of their communicating the small Pox as it is Rief in Boston."[10] A committee dispatched to the area reported that they had directed local selectmen to "take care of and provide for the Indigent, and guard and secure the Country against the Small Pox."[11]

THE REMOVAL PROCESS

After the British staggered back into Boston from Lexington and Concord, the Americans closed in and bottled up the British on the Boston peninsula. Thus commenced the Siege of Boston, which lasted until March 1776 when the British evacuated.

During the siege, many thousands of people both within and without Boston desired relocation. Thousands of townspeople wanted to leave British-occupied Boston and enter the friendlier territory of the surrounding countryside. Likewise, many loyalists out in the country wanted to gain the protection of the British by seeking refuge in Boston. Even prior to the siege, life in Boston had been difficult. Some inhabitants had already left due to the food shortages and other privations resulting from the Port Bill's stranglehold on Boston.[12]

The removal of Bostonians to the countryside was plagued with many stops and starts. Negotiations between General Gage, the senior British officer in Boston, and the Boston Selectmen to allow the inhabitants to leave town started shortly after the Battles of Lexington and

---

8. Peter Force, ed., *American Archives* (Washington, DC, 1843), Ser. 4, 4:1329.
9. Ibid., 1333.
10. Washington to Reed, November 27, 1775.
11. John Henry Clifford, *The Acts and Resolves, Public and Private, of the Province of Massachusetts Bay* (Boston: Wright & Potter Printing Co., 1918), 17.
12. *The Journals of Each Provincial Congress of Massachusetts in 1774 and 1775* (Boston: Dutton and Wentworth, 1838), 143.

Concord on April 19. At first, General Gage permitted people to leave "with their familys & their Effects" as long as they left behind any arms they possessed.[13] A common sight in Boston were "parents that are lucky enough to procure papers, with bundles in one hand & a string of children in the other, wandering out of the town (with only a Sufferance of one days provision) not knowing whither they'll go."[14] But General Gage's policy was subject to change without warning and some Bostonians who tried to leave town encountered "numerous delays and embarrassments."[15] Whether passes would be granted or precisely which items townspeople were permitted to carry out with them remained unpredictable.

One group of fleeing townspeople managed to surprise part of the main guard of the Continental Army in July 1775. Having somehow gained permission from General Gage to leave Boston, they approached the Chelsea shoreline by boat. According to Lt. Col. Loammi Baldwin, "we wase all allarm'd by the approach of a Boat to Winnisimmit Ferry & by a Signal Soon found them to be friends who Landed with their Houshold good: there ware Several of my Intimate acequaintance."[16] The overwhelming relief felt by the townspeople when they found themselves not only among friends again, but welcomed ashore by the Continental Army, is easy to imagine.

The Provincial Congress had begun the process of coordinating the removal of many of the poorest inhabitants of Boston who could not leave of their own accord. The congress estimated that "about five thousand of said inhabitants are indigent, and unable to be at the expense of removing themselves . . . and it is hereby recommended to all the good people of this Colony . . . that they aid and assist such poor inhabitants with teams, wagons, etc."[17]

Boston Selectman John Scollay intimated in a letter to the congress that "the state of the inhabitants is really distressing" and "many of these poor unhappy people are not in a condition to be removed by land carriage, therefore, we should think that the place of their destination might be as near water carriage as may be convenient . . . we would

13. Boston town meeting minutes, April 22, 1775, Miscellaneous Bound Manuscripts, Massachusetts Historical Society, Boston, Massachusetts.
14. John Andrews to William Barrell, May 6, 1775, Massachusetts Historical Society.
15. *The Journals of Each Provincial Congress*, 213.
16. Baldwin to Washington, July 29, 1775, *Founders Online*, National Archives, founders.archives.gov/documents/Washington/03-01-02-0120.
17. Peter Force, ed., *American Archives*, Ser. 4, 2:777, Digital Collections, Northern Illinois University.

beg leave to suggest the towns of Salem or Marblehead, as the proper place."[18]

Transporting the Boston poor to the north shore of Massachusetts by water would serve to lessen the chance of spreading smallpox through the countryside. The congress also promised to provide a hospital and lodging for the Bostonians, as well as "cleansing" to help prevent the spread of the disease.[19] The congress ordered that boats "shall convey the inhabitants of the town of Boston to Salem . . . that beds, beding, necessary Stores & Medicines be sent out with the Poor.[20]

MOSES BROWN AND THE QUAKER RELIEF EFFORT

Moses Brown, a Quaker from Providence, Rhode Island, spearheaded a mission to donate money to as many of the suffering Boston poor as possible. Leaving Providence in December 1775, Brown and some fellow Friends traveled to Boston in order to distribute donations. Upon their arrival in Cambridge, they met with General Washington and requested permission to enter Boston and provide relief. Although the General received them "kindly," he did not permit the Quakers to enter the town.[21]

Brown then went to Watertown where the Provincial Congress was sitting and discussed the needs of the poor with some of the members. Returning to Cambridge, he and his companions rented a room for the night. No beds were available so three men shared one straw mat and blanket. One man slept on the floor and another on a bench, "without any covering but our great coats."[22]

That evening, as he lay sleepless on the shared straw mat, Brown "thought it was a preparation of us to a suitable sympathy for the poor where we were to Vissit and I observed to my companions it was Necessary for us to partake of the Sufferings of the Times . . . We were much better off than thousands around in the Camps and Else Where."[23]

The Quakers never gained access to Boston. But instead of heading back to Providence without having distributed any of the donations, Brown decided to travel approximately sixteen miles northeast of Boston to the north shore areas of Marblehead and Salem to relieve the Bostonians that had been relocated there.

18. *The Journals of Each Provincial Congress*, 477.
19. Clifford, *The Acts and Resolves*, 9.
20. Ibid., 10.
21. Mack E. Thompson, "Moses Brown's 'Account of Journey to Distribute Donations 12th Month 1775,'" *Rhode Island History* Vol. 15, No. 4 (October 1956): 97-121, 112, www.rihs.org/assetts/files/publications/1956_Oct.pdf.
22. Ibid., 115.
23. Ibid.

Though Brown had planned to be away from Providence for only a few days, his journey lasted almost three weeks. Thinking they wouldn't be in Massachusetts for very long, the Quakers did not pack any blankets or extra clothing for themselves despite the wintry grasp of December.[24] As they traveled through the north shore, Brown found the weather to be "Extreem Cold yet the Necessitys of the Poor were such as prompted us to go through much sufferings on that Account without complaint."[25]

The Friends were shocked by the extreme poverty they encountered in Marblehead. Almost immediately, Brown met a "Number of Poor children out Begging Saying Master give me a Copper to buy a Biskett, etc."[26] The Friends provided donations to between sixty and seventy families in Marblehead, mostly widows and children. Brown later commented in a letter to a friend that "Such Scenes of Poverty I had before been a strainger two."[27]

The Quakers traveled further up the coast and entered Gloucester. Food and firewood were scarce. "We . . . have very little idea of their poverty, yet their children seemed healthy, crawling even into the ashes to keep them warm . . . they could keep but little fires for want of wood."[28] Brown recalled that "Some families [had] no other bread but potatoes . . . which with Checkerberry tea was seen the only food for a woman with a sucking child at her Breast."[29]

Displaced Bostonians were not the only people whom the Friends encountered in their travels. They also met people from the coastal area who had been rendered destitute by the closings of local fisheries by which they had previously been able to eke out a meager existence.[30] "We found great poverty to abound; numbers of widows and fatherless, wood and provisions greatly wanting among them."[31] In an effort to obtain firewood, many women had to venture at least two miles from their homes and then carry back the wood. Brown noted one woman in particular "a widow woman with five children . . . [who] looked to lie in with [give birth to] another, had been out in a cold day more than that distance . . . and had no bread in the house."[32]

24. Mack E. Thompson, *Moses Brown: Reluctant Reformer* (Chapel Hill: University of North Carolina Press, 1962), 120.
25. Thompson, "Journey to Distribute Donations," 118.
26. Ibid., 117.
27. Ibid.
28. Cadbury, "Quaker Relief," 56.
29. Ibid., 56-57.
30. Ibid., 56.
31. Ibid.
32. Ibid.

Brown and his companions continued their travels and headed down the Massachusetts coast. They ended up in Point Shirley, where the three hundred poor, ill Bostonians had been deposited by General Howe, General Gage's replacement. By this time about a month had passed since the townspeople had been landed, but Brown managed to find thirty to forty families to relieve as well as fifty other people in nearby Chelsea.[33] Before the Bostonians were permitted to leave the point, they were quarantined for twenty-one days to ensure that they were clear of the smallpox. According to Brown, they were then "transported into the Country as fast as Teams could be got. This was a very Unpleasant scene to see people going from the place of their Birth, where they knew not depending on the Benevolence of the publick and Unknown Individuals."[34]

TRANSPORTED INTO THE COUNTRYSIDE

The desperate Bostonians who were landed on Point Shirley represented a mere fraction of the people who were displaced during the siege. Thousands of people were transported to various corners of the Massachusetts countryside by teams, the congress having authorized carriages to be impressed into service.[35] The congress had also established a quota system where towns were required to take in certain numbers of the poor, thereby providing shelter to over 4900 individuals.[36] Later, however, the congress loosened the quotas, resolving that "such suffering poor shall be allowed to remove into any town or district in the colony."[37]

Dozens of the Boston and Charlestown poor arrived in Reading, Massachusetts, a country town twelve miles north of Boston. On November 27, 1775, the Reading Town Meeting considered "what measures the Town will take in order to support the Donation People from Boston and Charlestown."[38] The town voted to "choose a comecary to provide necessaries for all such donation persons."[39] Some of these donation people included Margaret Bodge, aged thirty-five, of Charlestown and her three young sons, Samuel, aged six, Henry, aged four, and David, aged two. Ebenezer Leman, described as "a cripple,"

33. Ibid., 57.
34. Thompson, "Journey to Distribute Donations," 120.
35. Clifford, *The Acts and Resolves*, 418.
36. Peter Force, ed., *American Archives*, Ser. 4, 2:778, Digital Collections, Northern Illinois University.
37. *Journals of Each Provincial Congress*, 302.
38. Records of the Town of Reading, 1632-1812, Volume II, Local History Room, Reading Public Library, Reading, Massachusetts.
39. Ibid.

aged forty-four, of Charlestown, arrived in Reading with his thirty-six-year-old wife and four of their children, aged eight, six, four, and two. Thirty-three-year-old Ann Shepard was accompanied by her children Thomas, aged nine, Anna, aged five, and Asa, aged three.[40]

In a letter to the Committee of Supplies in June 1775, the town of Reading explained why they were unable to provide blankets and provisions to the army. "We are as ready to assist in the defense of our country as any town in the province, but the great flow of the inhabitants of Boston, Charlestown . . . Salem and Marblehead daily flocking into this town, must, we think, be an excuse."[41] In addition, Reading had just fully outfitted 100 of her own men who had enlisted into the Continental Army.[42]

Many Massachusetts towns sheltered dozens of donation people which, no doubt, strained local resources. The Selectmen of Newburyport (forty miles north of Boston) wrote the Provincial Congress to inform them that:

> a number of the poor inhabitants of the Town of Boston have taken residence in this Town, viz: thirty-five adults and forty-three children, the greater part of whom have been here for the last three months . . . as little or no provisions are raised in this Town but brought from the country, and as wood, a necessary article the approaching season, must be scarce and dear . . . and in the winter season provisions of all kinds will be dearer, the expense of maintenance will be nearly double.

The Newburyport selectmen delicately suggested that the Boston poor "would be as well accommodated, and at less expense, in some of the farming Towns back of the seacoast.[43]

In response, the Provincial Congress ordered that some of the Boston poor who had found lodging in Newburyport were to be "distributed" to other locations in the province further inland. Some of the donation people who were to be removed included, among many others, the prolific Piper family—Walter Piper, his wife, and their five children, and Walter Piper Jr., his wife and mother-in-law, and their seven children, who were directed to Lunenburg.[44]

40. Names of Some of the Persons Belonging to Boston and Charlestown Who Were Relieved and Assisted at Reading, By the Town 1775, in Hon. Lilley Eaton, *Genealogical History of the Town of Reading, Mass.* (Boston: Alfred Mudge & Son, 1874), 715.
41. Eaton, *Genealogical History of the Town of Reading*, 181.
42. Ibid.
43. Peter Force, ed., *American Archives*, Ser. 4, 3:1498, Digital Collections, Northern Illinois University.
44. Ibid.

The Selectmen of Abington, a town south of Boston (whose original quota was for twenty-two persons), wrote to the congress stating that

> there are now forty persons got into the Town of Abington, who were partakers of the donations while they resided in the Town of Boston, and are in want of support. Bread corn is an article that is very scarce and dear among us; and as your petitioners are credibly informed there is a large quantity of corn, bread, flour, etc., sent to the Town of Dartmouth . . . being a donation for the poor of Boston, your petitioners therefore humbly pray this honourable Congress would please to give orders that we draw our proportion out of said donation.[45]

The donation people appear to have had little agency in determining to which town they were distributed. If they had "relations and connections in other towns" then they could be moved there.[46] But otherwise, Bostonians were shuffled to whichever town had the best ability to feed and shelter them. Sometimes that meant traveling further and further away from Boston, the distance between the donation people and their home growing ever greater.

Finally, in March 1776 after almost a year of tremendous hardship and upheaval, the British evacuated Boston. On April 25, the Provincial Congress passed a resolve that any indigent former residents of Boston and Charlestown who had been removed to towns in the countryside could be assisted with carriages and provisions in their return to Boston and Charlestown.[47]

It is difficult to know with certainty what happened to the thousands of men, women, and children who were displaced during the Siege of Boston. History has failed to remember their sacrifices; the details of their daily lives and the personal hardships that they endured have been forgotten. Their stories of the siege are scattered and largely unknown—much like the donation people themselves.

45. Peter Force, ed., *American Archives,* Ser. 4, 2:1477, Digital Collections, Northern Illinois University.
46. *Journals of Each Provincial Congress,* 283.
47. Clifford, *The Acts and Resolves,* 353.

Anxiety and Distress: Civilians Inside the Siege of Boston

❦ ALEXANDER R. CAIN ❦

Over the years, historians have written countless works on the military and political aspects of the Siege of Boston. Unfortunately, little attention has been given to the impact of the siege upon the residents of the city. As British military and political authorities attempted to recover from the disaster of April 19, 1775, the residents of Boston found themselves trapped inside a town that was on the verge of social and economic collapse.

On the evening of April 18, many of the residents knew a military operation was in motion and thus got little sleep. "I did not git to bed this night till after 12 o'clock, nor to sleep till long after that, & then my sleep was much broken, as it had been for many nights before."[1] Many Bostonians were oblivious of plans to seize and destroy supplies located in Concord, Massachusetts. Instead, most believed the British objective was the arrest of Samuel Adams and John Hancock. As Sarah Winslow Deming recalled "the main was to take possession of the bodies of Mesrs Adams & Handock, whom they & we knew where were lodg'd. We had no doubt of the truth of all this."[2]

Shortly after dawn, word of the fighting at Lexington reached Boston residents. Predictably, fear set into the populace. "Early on Wednesday the fatal 19th April, before I had quited my chamber, one after another came runing up to tell me that the kings troops had fired upon & killed 8 of our neighbors at Lexington in their way to Concord. All the intelligence of this day was dreadfull. Almost every countenance expressing anxiety & distress."[3] As the day progressed, Boston broke into a state of panic. Many residents wandered about aimlessly, unsure

1. Sarah Winslow Deming Journal, Page 3, Historic Winslow House Association, Marshfield, Massachusetts.
2. Ibid.
3. Ibid.

of what the future held. In a letter to his son, the Rev. Andrew Elliot stated "I know not what to do, not where to go . . . poor Boston, May God sanctify our distresses which are greater than you can conceive— Such a Sabbath of melancholy and darkness I never knew . . . every face gathering paleness—all hurry & confusion—one going this way & another that—others not knowing where to go—What to do with our poor maid I cannot tell—in short after the melancholy exercises of the day—I am unable to write anything with propriety or connection . . . Everything distressing."[4]

Over the next few days, as the American army surrounded the town and settled into a siege, scores of Bostonians discovered they were prohibited from fleeing the town. Gen. Thomas Gage was fearful that if the residents were permitted to leave, they would provide material assistance to the American army. As a result, he issued orders barring residents from leaving Boston. Boston resident Sarah Winslow Deming despaired "I was Genl Gage's prisoner—all egress, & regress being cut off between the town & country. Here again description fails. No words can paint my distress."[5]

According to merchant John Rowe, Boston's economy immediately collapsed. Businesses stopped operating and fresh provisions for market stopped coming into town. "Boston is in the most distressed condition."[6]

Residents gathered at a town meeting on April 22, 1775 to address their declining situation. A resolution was drafted to General Gage and highlighted the level of desperation they felt with the town being shut off to the outside world. "Inhabitants cannot be Supplied with provisions, fewell & other Necessarys of Life by which means the Sick & all Invalids must Suffer greatly, & Imediatly & the Inhabitants in general be distressed espesically Such which is by much the greatest party as have not had the means of laying in a Stock of provisions, but depend for daily Supplies from the Country for their daily Support & may be in danger of perishing unless the Communication be opened."[7]

Representatives from the town also voted to approach General Gage to secure his permission for Americans to evacuate Boston. After a tense meeting, the general ultimately agreed to let the residents vacate to the

---

4. Reverend Andrew Eliot to His Son, April 23, 1775, Miscellaneous Manuscripts, Massachusetts Historical Society, Boston, Massachusetts.
5. Deming Journal, Page 4.
6. Letters and Journal of John Rowe, Merchant, April 21, 1775, Boston Public Library, Boston, Massachusetts.
7. Minutes from the Town of Boston, April 22, 1775, Miscellaneous Manuscripts, Massachusetts Historical Society, Boston, Massachusetts.

countryside on the condition they surrender their weapons. Reluctantly the Bostonians agreed. A minister recalled the state of the civilian populace on the eve of the evacuation. "I not impelled by the unhappy Situation of this Town . . . all communication with the Country is cut off, & we wholly deprived of the necessaries of Life, & this principal mart of America is become a poor garrison Town . . . almost all are leaving their pleasant habitations & going they know not whither- The most are obliged to leave their furniture & effects of every kind . . . now I am by a cruel Necessity turned out of my House must leave my Books & all I possess, perhaps to be destroyed by a licentious Soldiery; my beloved Congregation dispersed, my dear Wife retreating to a distant part of the Country, my Children wandering not knowing whither to go, perhaps left to perish for Want, myself soon to leave this devoted Capital, happy if I can find some obscure Corner wch will afford me a bare Subsistence. I wish to God the authors of our Misery could be Witnesses of it. They must have Hearts harder than an adamant if they did not relent & pity us."[8]

Those who chose to flee made their way to Boston Neck, the sole land route out of the town. At least four checkpoints along the neck were set up by the British army. Residents were searched for weapons and carriages and chaises were prohibited from leaving the city. Some residents pleaded with family and friends not to leave the "safety" of Boston.[9] Most pleas were rebuffed as many believed once British reinforcements arrived, the town would become a killing field.[10] This belief was only strengthened as rumors of atrocities being committed by soldiers inside Boston quickly spread.[11] Once again panic set in and residents pressed harder to get "out of ye city of destruction."[12] At the height of confusion, British officials closed Boston Neck and the inhabitants were ordered back into the town.

On April 27, 1775, General Gage again reversed himself and gave permission for the remaining American residents to leave Boston.[13] Sur-

8. Andrew Eliot to Thomas B. Hollis, April 25, 1775, Miscellaneous Manuscripts, Massachusetts Historical Society, Boston, Massachusetts.
9. Deming Journal, Page 4.
10. Ibid. "I had been told that Boston would be an Aceldama as soon as the fresh troops arriv'd, which Mr. Barron had told me were expected every minute." Ibid.
11. Ibid. "I saw, & spoke with several fri[ends] near as unhappy as myself . . . while we were waiting . . . there was a constant coming & going; each hinder'd ye other; some new piece of soldiary barbarity, that had been perpetrated the day before, was in quick succession brought in." Ibid.
12. Ibid.
13. At the same time, Loyalist refugees trapped behind American lines were permitted to enter the town.

prisingly however, British authorities undermined Gage and made it difficult, if not impossible, for Bostonians to leave. Passes were now required to cross over Boston Neck and their number was limited. "Near half the inhabitants have left the town already, & another quarter, at least, have been waiting for a week past with earnest expectation of geting Passes, which have been dealt out very Sparingly of late, not above two or three procur'd of a day, & those with the greatest difficulty. its a fortnight yesterday Since the communication between the town & country was Stop'd, of concequence our eyes have not been bless'd with either vegetables or fresh provisions, how long we Shall continue in this wretched State."[14] On May 5, a large number of passes were issued and many residents quickly left via Boston Neck. "You'll see parents that are lucky enough to procure papers, with bundles in one hand and a string of children in the other wandering out of the town (with only a sufferance of one day's permission) not knowing whither they'll go."[15] The following day General Gage inexplicably revoked all outstanding passes again, declared no more were to be issued and those who wished to leave were prohibited from doing so.[16]

By the end of May, Boston more closely resembled a post-apocalyptic world than a bustling seaport community. While many had abandoned the town, others barricaded themselves inside their homes and had private guards watching over their property. The Reverend Eliot accurately described the state of Boston on the eve of the Battle of Bunker Hill: "I have remained in this Town much ag: my inclination . . . Most of the Ministers being gone I have been prevailed with to officiate to those who are still left to tarry . . . Much the greater parts of the inhabitants gone out of the town . . . Grass growing in the public walks & streets of this once populous & flourishing place—Shops & warehouses shut up—business at an end every one in anxiety & distress."[17] Fresh provisions were increasingly scarce and trapped occupants were often forced to survive on food of questionable quality. "Its hard to Stay

14. John Andrews to William Barrell, May 6, 1775, Papers of Andrew Eliot, 1718-1778, Harvard University Archives, Harvard University.
15. Ibid.
16. Ibid. "You must know that no person who leaves the town is allow'd to return again & this morng an order from the Govr has put a stop to any more passes at any rate not even to admit those to go, who have procurd 'em already." Ibid. In a letter to her husband, Abigail Adams chastised Gage and other British officials for the continuous issuing and revoking of passes and the resulting stress to the Americans trapped inside the town. Abigail Adams to John Adams, May 7, 1775, Adams Family Papers, Massachusetts Historical Society, Boston, Massachusetts.
17. Draft letter from A. Eliot to Unknown Recipient, May 31, 1775, Miscellaneous Manuscripts, Massachusetts Historical Society, Boston, Massachusetts.

coop'd up here & feed upon Salt provissions . . . We have now & then a carcase offerd for Sale in the market, which formerly we would no thave pickd up in the Street, but bad as it is, it readily Sells."[18]

The combination of British troops, Loyalist refugees and Boston residents all occupying a small amount of space only exacerbated a very dangerous situation. Press gangs roamed the town looking for civilian men to force into manual labor.[19] Inhabitants were arrested for merely being suspected of espionage or providing aid to the enemy.[20] Many of the soldiers and camp followers abused the inhabitants, stole from them and plundered their property, particularly that of residents who had left the city. John Andrews complained that the "Soldiery think they have a license to plunder evry ones house & Store who leaves the town, of which they have given convincing proofs already."[21] According to John Leach, Boston had devolved into a complicated "scene of oaths, curses, debauchery, and the most horrid plasphemy committed by the provost martial, his deputy and Soldiers who were our guard, Soldier prisoners, and Sundry Soldier women."[22]

Nor were Loyalist refugees immune from the hardships of the siege. Dorothea Gamsby was ten years old when the war broke out. In a letter written years later to her granddaughter, Gamsby accurately described how tenuous the situation inside Boston had become by the eve of the Battle of Bunker Hill. Residents continued to hide in fear and were under constant stress. Most believed that the town would be invaded by the rebels and its inhabitants slaughtered at any moment. As Gamsby recalled the Battle of Bunker Hill, "then came a night when there was bastle, anxiety, and watching. Aunt and her maid, walked from room to room sometimes weeping. I crept after them trying to

---

18. Andrews to Barrell. "Was it not for a triffle of Salt provissions that we have, twould be impossible for us to live, Pork & beans one day, & beans & pork another & fish when we can catch it, am necessitated to Submit to Such living or risque the little all I have in the world." Ibid.

19. "Press-Gangs parading the Streets in quest of Labourers . . . likewise several Persons taken up and imprisoned upon Suspicion. The usual Consequences of martial Law" William Cheever Diary, June 19, 1775, Miscellaneous Manuscripts, Massachusetts Historical Society, Boston, Massachusetts.

20. "Yesterday Mr. James Lovell and John Leach with others were imprisoned by martial Authority." Ibid, July 1, 1775. "Martial Law has had a full Swing for this month past. The Provost with his Band entering houses at his pleasure, stoping Gentlemen from enter:g their Warehouses and puting some under Guard: as also pulling down Fences, etc., particularly Mr. Carnes's Rope Walk and our Pasture." Ibid, July 21, 1775.

21. Ibid.

22. "Diary of John Leach, From July 1st to July 17th, 1775," *The New England Historical and Genealogical Register,* Vol. XIX (1865), 255-263.

understand the cause of their uneasiness, full of curiosity, and unable to sleep when everybody seemed wide awake, and the streets full of people. It was scarcely daylight when the booming of the cannon on board the ships in the harbour shook every house in the city . . . My aunt fainted. Poor Abby looked on like one distracted. I screamed with all my might."[23]

As the siege progressed, conditions inside the town continued to decline. Some houses of worship were demolished for fuel or converted into riding stables. Disease and sickness began to spread inside Boston.[24] As Timothy Newell noted, there were "several thousand inhabitants in town who are suffering the want of Bread and every necessary of life."[25] The end result was a general sense of despair throughout the surviving civilian population. Some of the common emotional descriptions by residents during the siege include such negative words as "anxiety," "distress," "forsaken" and "darkness." Some accounts even expressed what only could only be interpreted as hopelessness or borderline suicidal thoughts. "It is impossible to describe the Distress of this Unfortunate Town . . . I try to do what Business I can but am Disappointed & nothing but Cruelty and Ingratitude falls to my lot."[26]

A final humiliating blow to the occupants came on the eve of the British evacuation of Boston. British troops and Loyalist refugees roamed the streets plundering homes, warehouses and businesses of the local populace. According to merchant John Rowe, "They stole many things and plundered my store . . . I remained all day in the store but could not hinder their Destruction . . . they are making the utmost speed to get away & carrying . . . everything they can away, taking all things they meet with, never asking who is Owner or whose property—making havoc in every house & destruction of of all kinds."[27] By March 17, 1776, British soldiers were suspected of committing acts of arson in the northern part of town. Troops repeatedly threatened, robbed and intimidated the inhabitants. To the horror of many Bostonians, even officers participated in the illegal activities.[28] The army did not turn a

23. Dorothea Gamsby Manuscript, Chapter 5, private collection.

24. "Social life is almost at the last gasp. We have passed favorably through the smallpox." "Letter of Isaac Winslow," January 15, 1776, *The New England Genealogical Register*, Vol. LVI (1902), 48-54.

25. "Journal of Timothy Newell," October 10, 1775, *Collections of the Massachusetts Historical Society*, Series 4, Vol. I (1852), 261-276.

26. Letters and Journal of John Rowe, March 7 and 8, 1776.

27. Ibid, March 11, 1776. Rowe later noted "There was never such Destruction and Outrage committed any day before this . . . the inhabitants are greatly terrified & alarmed for Fear of Greater Evils." Ibid, March 11 and 12, 1776.

28. Ibid, March 13—17, 1776.

totally blind eye to these crimes; during the siege and in the two months following the evacuation, at least twenty-seven military personnel, including two officers and three followers, were tried by general courts martial for crimes against inhabitants, primarily robbery and plunder.[29] Others may have been tried by lesser courts, but in spite of efforts, crimes by the soldiery were widespread.

Following the British and Loyalist evacuation of Boston, American troops entered the town and were joyfully greeted as liberators. "Thus was this unhappy distressed town . . . relieved from a set of men, whose unparalleled wickedness, profanity, debauchery and cruelty is inexpressible."[30] For the next several years, Loyalist and "Patriot" inhabitants of Boston petitioned the Continental Congress and the Massachusetts government for compensation for property lost or damaged as result of the siege.[31] Some claims were paid, others were ignored or denied. In the weeks after the conclusion of the siege, American troops moved south to New York City. Never again in Boston's history were residents subjected to the horrors of a military siege or occupation.

29. Proceedings of these trials are in the Judge Advocate Papers, WO 71, British National Archives.
30. Journal of Timothy Newell, March 17, 1776.
31. For an example of a Loyalist petition for compensation, see William Jackson to the Continental Congress, July 6, 1776, Miscellaneous Manuscripts, Massachusetts Historical Society, Boston, Massachusetts.

Preventing Slave Insurrection in South Carolina and Georgia, 1775–1776

❦ JIM PIECUCH ❦

As the colonies of South Carolina and Georgia moved closer to open rebellion against Great Britain in the summer of 1775, leaders of the revolutionary movement found themselves facing a host of potential threats. In addition to the numerous loyalists in both colonies, the tribes of pro-British Indians on their frontiers, and the possibility of an attack from British forces, the risk of a slave uprising loomed large in the minds of the rebels. Even in times of stability, slave revolts were a constant danger; in the crisis resulting from an impending war between Britain and the colonies, a slave insurrection might doom the southernmost colonies' attempt to resist the British.

In 1775 slaves outnumbered whites by 104,000 to 70,000 in South Carolina, and the disparity was greater in the low country, where the province's rice plantations were located. Georgia's white and slave populations were approximately equal, each group numbering about 25,000.[1] Revolutionary leaders in these colonies recognized that their large slave populations made them uniquely vulnerable to a British attack. While attending the Second Continental Congress in Philadelphia, Georgia delegates Archibald Bulloch and John Houstoun told John Adams that if the British sent just one thousand troops to Georgia, "and their commander be provided with Arms and Cloaths enough, and proclaim freedom to all the Negroes who would join his Camp, 20,000 Negroes would join it from the two Provinces in a fortnight." Their only security against the British taking such a step, they told Adams, was that "all the Kings Friends and Tools of Government have large Plan-

---

1. Rachel Klein, *Unification of a Slave State: The Rise of the Planter Class in the South Carolina Backcountry, 1760-1808* (Chapel Hill: University of North Carolina Press, 1990), 9; John Richard Alden, *The South in the Revolution, 1763-1789* (Baton Rouge: Louisiana State University Press, 1957), 9.

tations and Property in Negroes. So that the Slaves of the Tories would be lost as well as those of the Whiggs."[2]

Bulloch and Houstoun were unaware that many British leaders were actively pressing the government to adopt the kind of measures the Georgians feared. Generals Thomas Gage and John Burgoyne both urged the government to arm slaves, while another officer offered a more specific plan to enlist a corps of slaves in the Chesapeake Bay area to operate against the rebels there. William Lyttelton, a former royal governor of South Carolina, proposed in the House of Commons on October 26, 1775, that a few British regiments be sent to the southern colonies expressly to encourage and support a slave uprising, but the House rejected the measure.[3] Arthur Lee, a revolutionary who was still residing in London, sent news of these proposals to America where they circulated widely and created panic in South Carolina. The newly arrived royal governor of the province, Lord William Campbell, wrote that Lee had convinced the inhabitants that the king's ministers planned "to instigate and encourage an insurrection among the slaves," and that people in Charleston believed that the vessel that had brought Campbell to the city carried "14,000 Stand of Arms" to be issued to slaves.[4] South Carolina rebel Thomas Lynch denounced the British for offering "every incitement to our Slaves to rebel—and murder their masters."[5]

Lynch did not yet know it, but five days earlier, on November 14, the royal governor of Virginia had already taken steps to arm slaves without waiting for approval from London. John Murray, the Earl of Dunmore, believed that it was more important to use all available means to suppress the rebellion, and then worry about reconciliation. Accordingly, he issued a proclamation granting freedom to all rebel-owned indentured servants and slaves who would fight for King George

2. John Adams, *Diary and Autobiography of John Adams*, L. H. Butterfield, ed. (Cambridge, MA: Belknap Press, 1961), Vol. 2, *Diary*, 1771-1781, Sept. 24, 1775, 182-183.
3. Sylvia R. Frey, *Water from the Rock: Black Resistance in a Revolutionary Age* (Princeton, NJ: Princeton University Press, 1991), 60, 67; John Brooke, *King George III* (New York: McGraw-Hill, 1972), 178; "Project for Strengthening General Howe's Operations in the North by a Diversion in the South," [1775], Lord George Germain Papers, Vol. 4, William L. Clements Library; William Lyttelton's Speech, Oct. 26, 1775, in R. C. Simmons and P. D. G. Thomas, eds., *Proceedings and Debates of the British Parliaments Respecting North America, 1754-1783*, Vol. 6 (White Plains, NY: Kraus International Publications, 1987), 96.
4. Quoted in William R. Ryan, *The World of Thomas Jeremiah: Charles Town on the Eve of the American Revolution* (New York: Oxford University Press, 2010), 47.
5. Thomas Lynch to Ralph Izard, Nov. 19, 1775, in Anne Izard Deas, ed., *Correspondence of Mr. Ralph Izard of South Carolina, from the Year 1774 to 1804; with a Short Memoir*, Vol. 1 (New York: Charles S. Francis and Co., 1844), 154.

III. Dunmore's proclamation caused an uproar throughout the southern provinces; South Carolinian Edward Rutledge denounced it as the worst measure the British could have ever taken against the colonies.[6] George Washington declared that "if that man [Dunmore] is not crushed before spring he will become the most formidable enemy America has; his strength will increase as a snowball by rolling, and faster, if some expedient cannot be hit upon to convince the slaves and servants of the impotency of his designs."[7]

Like Washington, South Carolina's rebel leaders may have been shocked by Dunmore's actions, but they were not caught unprepared. By the summer of 1775 they had tightened enforcement of the slave codes, so that "regulations which had gone unenforced for years were given new life."[8] Militia patrols were strengthened, with their primary responsibility being, said Whig Josiah Smith, "to guard against any hostile attempts that might be made by our domesticks."[9] Some planters labored to persuade their slaves not to be seduced by offers of freedom, which, they warned, would surely prove false. A committee charged with planning South Carolina's defense proposed, in the event of a British invasion, to relocate the slaves in the vicinity of Charleston to the interior of the colony. Afterwards, constant militia patrols would prevent any communication between the slaves and the British.[10] No effort was ever made to carry out this scheme, which would have been nearly impossible to implement and may actually have created opportunities for slaves to escape.

Officials took more concrete measures against slaves suspected of rebellious intentions. In June, several low country slaves were tried on charges of plotting an insurrection. The evidence proved inconclusive,

6. Benjamin Quarles, *The Negro in the American Revolution* (Chapel Hill: University of North Carolina Press, 1996), 19; Edward Rutledge to Ralph Izard, Dec. 8, 1775, *Correspondence of Izard*, 165-166.
7. Quoted in Ryan, *World of Thomas Jeremiah*, 18.
8. Ira Berlin, *Many Thousands Gone: The First Two Centuries of Slavery in North America* (Cambridge, MA: Belknap Press, 1998), 292.
9. Robert Olwell, *Masters, Slaves, and Subjects: The Culture of Power in the South Carolina Lowcountry, 1740-1790* (Ithaca, NY: Cornell University Press, 1998), 238.
10. Henry Laurens to James Laurens, June 7, 1775, in Henry Laurens, *The Papers of Henry Laurens*, Vol. 10, David R. Chesnutt, ed. (Columbia: University of South Carolina Press, 1985), 162-163; "Report of the Committee for Forming a Plan of Defence for the Colony," 1775, in Robert W. Gibbes, ed., *Documentary History of the American Revolution, Consisting of Letters and Papers relating to the Contest for Liberty Chiefly in South Carolina, From Originals in the Possession of Gen. Francis Marion, by Gen. Peter Horry, of Marion's Brigade: Together with Others from the Collection of the Editor*, Vol. 1 (New York: D. Appleton & Co., 1853), 205.

but one or two slaves were whipped as an example to those who might be considering rebellion. The following month, reports reached the Council of Safety that slaves in St. Bartholomew's Parish were plotting an insurrection, abetted by a white preacher named John Burnet. Several slaves were arrested and tried; one was hanged and others whipped. Burnet was acquitted.[11]

Rebel leaders also worried about a free black, Thomas Jeremiah of Charleston, who had amassed considerable wealth from his skills as a harbor pilot and was himself a slave owner. One of the suspected slaves arrested in June had, during his interrogation, claimed that Jeremiah had asked him to carry guns to another slave, "to be placed in Negro's Hands to fight against the Inhabitants of this Province, and that He Jeremiah was to have the chief Command of the said Negroes." A second slave stated that he had sought Jeremiah's advice on what to do if war came, and that Jeremiah had told him to "join the [British] Soldiers; that the War was come to help the poor Negroes." The Whigs tried Jeremiah on August 11, sentenced him "to be hanged and afterwards burned," and carried out the sentence a week later despite the protests of the royal governor, Lord William Campbell.[12] Campbell sought the assistance of the provincial attorney general, James Simpson, and several judges to demonstrate that Jeremiah had not been tried according to proper legal practice and that the evidence of his guilt was insufficient, but neither this effort nor the support for Jeremiah offered by the prominent Anglican ministers Robert Cooper and Robert Smith were sufficient to alter the decision of the rebel leaders.[13]

Most historians, like the judges whose opinions were sought by Campbell, have since called into question the legality of Jeremiah's trial as well as his guilt. In all likelihood, the rebels targeted Jeremiah because of the danger he represented as a prosperous free black man in a society based on slavery. Rebel leader Henry Laurens, normally considered a moderate revolutionary, maligned Jeremiah as "a forward fellow, puffed up by prosperity, ruined by Luxury & debauchery & grown to an amazing pitch of vanity & ambition."[14] J. William Harris, author of a study of

11. Henry Laurens to John Laurens, June 18, 1775, and June 23, 1775; Thomas Hutchinson to Council of Safety, July 5, 1775; Council of Safety to St. Bartholomew Committee, July 18, 1775, in Laurens, *Papers*, 10:184-185, 191-192, 206-208, 231.

12. Lord William Campbell to the Earl of Dartmouth, Aug. 31, 1775, in K. G. Davies, ed., *Documents of the American Revolution, 1770-1783 (Colonial Office Series)*, Vol. 11 (Dublin: Irish University Press, 1977), 95-96.

13. J. William Harris, *The Hanging of Thomas Jeremiah: A Free Black Man's Encounter with Liberty* (New Haven, CT: Yale University Press, 2009), 140-146.

14. Henry Laurens to John Laurens, Aug. 20, 1775, in Laurens, *Papers*, 10:320-322.

the Jeremiah incident, pointed out with more than a hint of sarcasm that "if this sort of character was a sign of guilt, half of South Carolina's political leaders would have deserved hanging."[15] Nevertheless, Jeremiah's execution served both to remove the potential threat posed by a wealthy free black man with great influence among Charleston's African American community, and, in the words of one witness to Jeremiah's hanging, to "deter others from offending in the like manner."[16]

Jeremiah's execution brought an end to white South Carolinians' fears of slave insurrection, although its deterrent effect was limited as many slaves continued to make their way to the coast and seek refuge aboard British warships, while others fled overland to British East Florida. Some of the former joined British sailors in nighttime raids along the South Carolina coast. By December, a further five hundred fugitive slaves were camped on Sullivan's Island at the entrance to Charleston harbor, awaiting an opportunity to board Royal Navy vessels.[17]

Amid the tensions produced by Dunmore's proclamation, Whig leaders could not tolerate this outright defiance of white authority. On December 9, Gen. William Moultrie ordered Maj. Charles Cotesworth Pinckney to take 150 troops and capture the slaves in a surprise night attack. Pinckney, however, was unable to find a ford. A second attempt on December 18 succeeded. The troops, reinforced by fifty-four Catawba Indians, struck before dawn and killed an estimated fifty blacks. Several more were captured, along with a few British sailors. Fewer than twenty slaves escaped and were picked up by boats from British warships.[18] The Council of Safety expressed satisfaction with the operation, declaring that it would "serve to humble our Negroes in general."[19]

The Royal Navy's policy of granting refuge to fugitive slaves caused the Whigs to repudiate an agreement whereby they sold provisions to the naval vessels at Charleston in exchange for the officers' pledge not

---

15. Harris, *Hanging of Thomas Jeremiah*, 148.
16. Ibid., 1.
17. Peter H. Wood, "'The Facts Speak Loudly Enough': Exploring Early Southern Black History," in Catherine Clinton and Michele Gillespie, eds., *The Devil's Lane: Sex and Race in the Early South* (New York: Oxford University Press, 1997), 7.
18. William Moultrie, *Memoirs of the American Revolution, So Far as It Related to the States of North and South-Carolina, and Georgia*, Vol. 1 (New York: David Longworth, 1802), 113-114; Terry W. Lipscomb, *The Carolina Lowcountry, April 1775-June 1776, and the Battle of Fort Moultrie* (Columbia: South Carolina Department of Archives and History, 1994), 20.
19. Council of Safety to Richard Richardson, Dec. 19, 1775, in Laurens, *Papers*, 10:576.

to take supplies by force. On December 10, a Whig accused Capt. John Tollemache of HMS *Scorpion* of harboring fugitive slaves. Tollemache replied that the blacks "came as free men, and demanded protection," and he refused to return them.[20] When the *Scorpion* left Charleston shortly afterward, the Whigs believed that between thirty and forty slaves were on board.[21] Henry Laurens denounced the British "robberies" of slaves as "sufficient to alarm every man" in the colony.[22]

Slaves continually tried to escape to British warships through the spring and summer of 1776. Two who stole a schooner and attempted to reach a naval vessel were caught, and hanged on April 27. Five slaves employed as bargemen used the craft to reach a British ship in May. Some of the slaves took an active role in raiding parties that the British dispatched to seize supplies.[23] In August, a party of forty sailors and twenty armed blacks from a British frigate landed on Bull's Island, taking cattle and six slaves. Henry Laurens observed that "many hundreds" of slaves had by then "been stolen & decoyed by the Servants of King George the third."[24]

In Georgia, royal governor Sir James Wright clung to a vestige of his authority until the beginning of 1776, so that rebel leaders in that colony could not undertake any measures of their own to forestall a slave rebellion. However, when a Royal Navy squadron arrived in Savannah in January, the Whigs placed Wright under arrest. Then, in concert with South Carolina, the rebel militia searched slave quarters on both sides of the Savannah River, confiscating all arms and ammunition they found. The militia also searched the homes of overseers, leaving each of them with only one musket and thirteen rounds of ammunition. That measure was ordered by the Georgia Council of Safety to give overseers the means to defend against a slave revolt, but to deny slaves access to larger quantities of arms and ammunition should an insurrection succeed.[25]

As in South Carolina, slaves in Georgia did not rebel; instead, those most determined to bid for freedom tried to reach British ships. Many succeeded, while other fugitives gathered on Tybee Island to await their

20. Moultrie, Memoirs, 1:112.

21. Henry Laurens to James Laurens, Jan. 6, 1776, in Laurens, *Papers*, Vol.11 (1988),7.

22. Henry Laurens to Stephen Bull, Jan. 20, 1776, in Laurens, *Papers*, 11:50.

23. Quarles, 128; Richard Hutson to Isaac Hayne, May 27, 1776, "Letters of the Hon. Richard Hutson," *Year Book, City of Charleston, South Carolina*, 1895, 315.

24. Henry Laurens to John Laurens, Aug. 14, 1776, in Laurens, *Papers*, 11:223-224.

25. Harvey H. Jackson, "The Battle of the Riceboats: Georgia Joins the Revolution," *Georgia Historical Quarterly*, Vol. 58, No. 1, Summer 1974, 30; South Carolina Council of Safety to Georgia Council of Safety, Jan. 19, 1776, in Laurens, *Papers*, 11:44.

opportunity. By mid-March, about two hundred slaves were there. Col. Stephen Bull of the South Carolina militia, who had taken a detachment southward to assist the Georgians, urged his colony's Council of Safety to authorize harsh measures against the runaways. If the slaves managed to board British vessels, Bull asserted, it would "enable an enemy to fight us with our own . . . property."[26] Bull wanted to mount an attack on Tybee using Creek warriors who were then at Savannah. He suggested that the attackers execute all of the slaves who could not be recaptured, with their owners compensated at public expense. In addition to eliminating the fugitive slave refuge and setting an example for other slaves who might try to escape to the British, Bull hoped that employing the Creeks against the blacks would "establish a hatred or aversion between the Indians and negroes."[27]

South Carolina officials approved Bull's plan, although they stipulated that the attack should be carried out by the Georgians, who should also decide whether or not the Creeks should participate. The governments of South Carolina and Georgia would share the cost of reimbursing owners of any slaves who were killed in the operation. Finally, the Council told Bull to blame the violence on the British: "to those Royal Miscreants who are carrying on an inglorious picaroon Warr let every inglorious unavoidable act of necessity which we may be driven to commit for our self preservation, be imputed."[28] The Georgia militia, dressed and painted like Indians and assisted by about thirty Creeks, attacked the fugitive slaves on Tybee Island on the night of March 25. A dozen slaves were captured, and the rest were killed.[29] The exact number of dead was never reported, but if Bull's estimate was correct, perhaps as many as 200 slaves died in the one-sided battle. The British later denounced the "savage barbarity" of the attackers, and claimed that the white militiamen had acted more brutally than the Creeks.[30]

Georgia slaves nonetheless continued to flee to the British when opportunities offered. The Georgia Council of Safety noted in July that "negroes are daily inveigled and carried away" by British warships.[31]

26. Stephen Bull to Henry Laurens, March 12, 1776, March 13, 1776, and March 14, 1776, in Gibbes, *Documentary History*, 266, 268.
27. Bull to Henry Laurens, in Gibbes, *Documentary History*, 268-269.
28. South Carolina Council of Safety to Bull, March 16, 1776, in Laurens, *Papers*, 11:172.
29. Martha Condray Searcy, "The Introduction of African Slavery into the Creek Indian Nation," *Georgia Historical Quarterly*, Vol. 66, No. 1, Spring 1982, 27.
30. Laurens, *Papers*, 11:173n.
31. "Proceedings of the Georgia Council of Safety, July 5, 1776, in *Collections of the Georgia Historical Society*, Vol. 5 (Savannah: Braid & Hutton, 1901), 71.

Others took advantage of the colony's proximity to East Florida to escape overland to that staunchly loyalist province.[32]

The slave rebellion feared by South Carolinians and Georgians alike never came. The vigilance of Whig leaders, the harsh punishments meted out as examples to blacks like Thomas Jeremiah, and the brutal assaults on fugitive encampments on Sullivan's and Tybee Islands convinced most slaves that rebellion could not succeed, at least in the circumstances of 1775 and 1776. Yet it was also clear that many slaves ardently desired a chance at freedom, saw the British as the agents of that freedom, and endured the risks and hardships involved in attempting to reach British vessels or on the trek to East Florida. The Whigs would maintain control over the vast majority of their slaves during the next two years, until British troops landed in Georgia at the end of 1778. From that time onward, as the British occupied Georgia and South Carolina by mid-1780, thousands of slaves would leave their plantations and attach themselves to the Royal Army. They would provide valuable support in various military departments as pioneers, laborers, teamsters, and artisans. Some would take a more active role as spies and even soldiers. Many would lose their lives, be retaken by their masters, or reenslaved by the British, but a considerable number would find the freedom they sought. The extensive and often brutal efforts employed by the South Carolinians and Georgians at the start of the Revolution to maintain control over their slaves delayed, but did not prevent, the flight of thousands of African Americans from bondage.

32. Lachlan McIntosh to Lachlan McIntosh, Jr., Aug. 14, 1776, in "Papers of Lachlan McIntosh," *Georgia Historical Quarterly*, Vol. 39, No. 1, March 1955, 56.

A Republic of Wool: Founding Era Americans' Grand Plans for Sheep

BRETT BANNOR

Only 1,457 pounds of wool? George Washington was astonished. He had 568 sheep, so that meant the recent shearing at Mount Vernon and his other farms yielded an average of just over two and a half pounds of wool per animal. Washington was not home to supervise the process; it was June of 1793 and he was in Philadelphia beginning his second term as President of the United States. He learned the details of the shearing through a letter from his farm manager, Anthony Whitting. The President's response detailed exactly why he was so distressed by the news:

> From the beginning of the year 1784 when I returned from the Army, until Shearing time of 1788, I improved the breed of my Sheep so much by buying, & selecting the best formed, & most promising Rams & putting them to my best Ewes—by keeping them always well culled & clean—and by other attentions—that they averaged me ... rather over than under five pounds of washed wool each.[1]

What could be causing the dramatic reduction in the productivity of Washington's sheep? The President implied that insufficient attention had been paid to selectively breeding the animals. Showing a disdainful aspect of Virginia plantation life, Washington also reminded Whitting to be mindful of "the roguery of my Negros."[2] It was the enslaved doing the actual shearing; Washington snarled that in the past they had skimmed wool for themselves between the shearing and delivery of the fleeces.

---

1. Christine Sternberg Patrick, *The Papers of George Washington, Presidential Series* vol. 13 (Charlottesville: University of Virginia Press, 2007), 9.
2. Ibid.

In no way was Washington unusual in his attention to sheep and their husbandry. All through the Revolutionary and Founding eras, men of considerable distinction extensively discussed and wrote about sheep. For them this was not simply a matter of running an efficient farm. Sheep in the new nation were closely tied to economic policy and the promotion of republican virtue. The founding generation even saw a productive flock of American sheep as a matter of national security.

A WORLD DEPENDENT ON WOOL

In Washington's lifetime, wool was the dominant fiber for fabrics, particularly for durable and cold-weather wear. Furs also provide warmth, but wool is inherently more sustainable, since sheep do not have to be killed to yield fibers and flocks could be selectively bred to produce desired characteristics. Furthermore, by the end of the seventeenth century, the fur trade in Britain's Atlantic colonies was already in serious decline due to over-harvesting.[3]

Considering wool's importance, it is understandable that when the British first colonized North America they imported sheep, which had originally been domesticated in the Old World. But sheep did not prosper on American shores as readily as did the similarly imported cattle and hogs. In the uncultivated lands of the New World, sheep tended to forage in thickets where the wool was torn off their backs by briars and thorns. Worse, the sheep fell easy prey to wolves. It is not surprising then that sheep did best on islands such as Nantucket and Martha's Vineyard, where the wolves could most readily be extirpated.[4]

These occasionally prosperous insular flocks notwithstanding, when the Americans began to quarrel with the mother country in the 1760s there was a shortage of sheep in North America. Thus, the colonists were dependent on Great Britain for their wool clothing and blankets. They knew this. And so did the British.

"WE WILL USE OUR UTMOST ENDEAVORS TO IMPROVE THE BREED OF SHEEP"

It is likely the mood in Parliament was tense on February 13, 1766, when Benjamin Franklin was called on to answer questions about the Amer-

---

3. Eric Jay Dolin, *Fur, Fortune, and Empire: The Epic History of the Fur Trade in America* (New York: W.W. Norton & Company, 2010), 103.

4. Virginia DeJohn Anderson, *Creatures of Empire: How Domestic Animals Transformed Early America.* (New York: Oxford University Press, 2004), 110, 147-48. In contrast to the colonial situation, wolves had been eradicated from England by the fifteenth century; see Keith Thomas, *Man and the Natural World: Changing Attitudes in England 1500-1800* (New York: Oxford University Press, 1983), 273. Of the elimination of English wolves Thomas writes: "It made English sheep-farming less labor-intensive, for shepherds no longer had to guard their flocks by night . . . or lock them up in stone sheepcotes."

ican colonists' opposition to the Stamp Act. In Franklin's papers, the
session is referred to as his "examination" before the House of Commons, but really it was more of an interrogation. Franklin was peppered
with inquiries, some particularly hostile. "Do you think it right that
America should be protected by this country, and pay no part of the
expense?" a questioner demanded.[5] "Are not the lower rank of people
more at their ease in America than in England?" another asked of
Franklin, pointedly and probably rhetorically.[6]

Showing the importance of sheep in the trans-Atlantic politics of the
time, Franklin also was called on to answer several specifics about the
state of these livestock in America. Isn't the wool in the northern
colonies of bad quality because of the severe winters?[7] And don't the
harsh winters require the people there to provide fodder for their sheep
for many months?[8] Isn't the wool in the southern colonies also poor,
being coarse and really only a kind of hair?[9]

Franklin answered the sheep questions as best as he could, although
he clearly was out of his realm, as some of his replies were
noncommittal. But when asked the very general question "Can [the
people] possibly find enough wool in North America?" Franklin
confidently asserted that they could:

> They have taken steps to increase the wool. They entered into
> general combinations to eat no more lamb, and very few lambs were
> killed last year. This course persisted in, will soon make a prodigious
> difference in the quantity of wool. And the establishing of great man-
> ufactories, like those in the clothing towns here, is not necessary, as
> it is where the business is to be carried on for the purposes of trade.
> The people will all spin, and work for themselves, in their own
> houses.[10]

Franklin's appearance in Parliament did not alleviate the worsening
relationship between Britain and the colonies, and in September 1774
the First Continental Congress assembled to determine a unified

---

5. Leonard W. Labaree, ed. *The Papers of Benjamin Franklin*, vol. 13, *January 1 through
December 31, 1766* (New Haven, CT: Yale University Press, 1969),133.
6. Ibid,137.
7. Ibid,140.
8. Ibid,141.
9. Ibid,140.
10. Ibid,140. As T.H. Breen has shown, the popular notion of American self-sufficiency
in their consumption of goods during the colonial, revolutionary, and early republic
years is largely incorrect; see generally *The Marketplace of Revolution: How Consumer Politics Shaped American Independence* (New York: Oxford University Press, 2004).

American action. The assembly quickly decided that the most effective means of expressing their resolve was to no longer import goods from Britain or its possessions, nor export goods to them. This policy was formally declared in the Articles of Association, the primary document produced by the First Continental Congress.[11]

If the colonies planned to give up all British goods, that meant no more British woolen cloth or clothing. What would the Americans do to alleviate that foreign dependency? The seventh article of the Association addressed this important matter:

> We will use our utmost endeavors to improve the breed of sheep, and increase their number to the greatest extent; and to that end, we will kill them as seldom as may be, especially those of the most profitable kind; nor will we export any to the West Indies or elsewhere; and those of us, who are or may become overstocked with, or can conveniently spare any sheep, will dispose of them to our neighbors, especially to the poorer sort, on moderate terms.[12]

Article seven is a particularly vivid expression of virtue, a quality the founding generation often stressed as vital for the success of a republican government. Historian Gordon Wood has defined virtue as "the willingness of the individual to sacrifice his private interests for the good of the community."[13] The delegates to the First Continental Congress, many of whom were men of some means, were asserting that it would be improper to take advantage of a wool shortage to charge top dollar for surplus sheep; in tough times, virtue commanded that extra animals be dispersed "on moderate terms."

Not all the colonists supported the Articles of Association. Prominent among American Loyalists who advocated reconciliation with the crown was Samuel Seabury, the first American Episcopal Bishop. In a ninety-page pamphlet written in December of 1774 under the pseudonym "A.W. Farmer," Seabury mustered every argument he could think of against the actions of the recalcitrant Americans; not surprisingly, he brought up the matter of sheep. "Continue the non-importation" Seabury warned:

> and the first winter after our English goods are consumed, we shall be starving with cold. Kill your sheep ever so sparingly, keep every

11. Richard R. Beeman, *Our Lives, Our Fortunes & Our Sacred Honor: The Forging of American Independence 1774-1776* (New York: Basic Books, 2013), 155-162.
12. *Journals of the Continental Congress 1774-1789*, vol. 1 (Washington: Government Printing Office, 1904), 78.
13. Gordon S. Wood, *The Creation of the American Republic: 1776-1787* (Chapel Hill: The University of North Carolina Press, 1998), 68.

weather as well as ewe, to increase the number and improve the breed of sheep; make every other mode of farming subservient to the raising of sheep, and the requisite quantity of wool to clothe the inhabitants of this continent, will not be obtained in twenty years: if they increase only as they have done, not in fifty.[14]

A "weather"—now spelled "wether"—is a male sheep that has been castrated.

Given the timing of Reverend Seabury's tract, written just two months after the Articles of Association were signed, it is natural to assume that his warning of colonials "starving with cold" was a response to article seven. Actually there was another catalyst: Seabury was in the middle of a pamphlet war with a brash nineteen year old who yearned for American independence: Alexander Hamilton.[15] In defending the non-importation policy of the Continental Congress, Hamilton asserted in an earlier pamphlet that British wool was not needed in America. Writing under the pseudonym "A Friend to America" he boasted "We have sheep, which, with due care in improving and increasing them, would soon yield a sufficiency of wool."[16]

In this battle of booklets, the squabble about sheep was just one of the many points debated by Seabury and Hamilton. As events would show, however, Reverend Seabury had a far better understanding of America's wool vulnerability.

THE SHEEP OF WAR

For American colonists, having sheep on coastal islands protected them from wolves but left them vulnerable to another predator: the British Navy. As the war progressed, the British targeted insular sheep. For example, at Martha's Vineyard a September 1778 raid plundered nine thousand of the valuable animals.[17] Given the American need for wool, these were military actions analogous to bombing oil fields or refineries in modern wars.

---

14. Samuel Seabury, *A View of the Controversy between Great Britain and Her Colonies* (New York: James Rivington Press, 1774), 57-58; emphasis in the original.

15. Wayne Lynch, "Reverend Seabury's Pamphlet War," *Journal of the American Revolution* (July 9, 2013).

16. Alexander Hamilton, "A Full Vindication of the Measures of the Congress, &c.," in Harold C. Syrett, ed. *The Papers of Alexander Hamilton*, vol. 1, *1768–1778* (New York: Columbia University Press, 1961), 55 (hereafter *Hamilton Papers.*)

17. L. H. Butterfield and Marc Friedlaender, eds., *The Adams Papers, Adams Family Correspondence*, vol. 3, *April 1778–September 1780* (Cambridge, MA: Harvard University Press, 1973), 97.

The British sheep incursions had the desired effect; wool shortages were felt even before the disastrous September 1778 raid. Nine months prior to that, from his Valley Forge headquarters General Washington dashed off a grim letter to the American Board of War detailing how meager the supplies had become for his troops that cold, disheartening winter. One shortage particularly concerned the General:

> As to Blankets, I really do not know what will be done. Our situation in this instance is peculiarly distressing. I suppose that not less than from 3 to 4000 are now wanted in Camp—Our Sick want—Our Unfortunate men in captivity want.[18]

The men on the Board of War obviously knew that the lack of blankets was a direct effect of the shortage of wool and the lack of imported woolen goods. Washington was expounding on the natural outcome of America's sheep deficit.

When we picture the soldiers at Valley Forge shivering in the frigid winter air due to threadbare clothing and lack of blankets, we should recall what Reverend Seabury had warned about "starving with cold." The failure to adequately equip the American troops is often seen as a problem with the supply system—a shortage of funds to purchase provisions plus a dearth of wagons and suitable roads.[19] But when it came to wool goods there was a more basic problem—America just did not have enough sheep. Nor did it have sufficient manufacturing facilities to turn whatever domestic product existed into enough clothing and blankets for all the troops. On top of all their other wartime difficulties, the colonials faced a wool crisis.

POSTWAR WOOL—AS HAMILTON WOULD HAVE IT

In spite of its sheep shortage, America prevailed in the war. Peace may have come, but winters were still cold, and citizens of the new nation continued to need wool. There was wide agreement that the United States should continue its efforts "to improve the breed of sheep" as the Articles of Association had put it. But there was disagreement in two key areas. Should government policy promote sheep farming, or did this need to be left to the private virtue of gentlemen? And should Americans strive to produce only enough wool for essential domestic use, or consider full scale manufacturing to provide fancier clothing and even a commodity for export?

18. Edward G. Lengel, *The Papers of George Washington, Revolutionary War Series,* vol. 13 (Charlottesville: University of Virginia Press, 2003), 111.
19. e.g., John Ferling, *A Leap in the Dark: The Struggle to Create the American Republic* (New York: Oxford University Press, 2003), 217.

During a debate on revenue at the Constitutional Convention of 1787, Pennsylvania delegate Thomas Fitzsimons declared that he was against taxing American exports at that time, but that he thought the federal government should have the power to tax exports in the future, when America became a manufacturing country. According to James Madison's notes on the convention, Fitzsimons then "illustrated his argument by the duties in G. Britain on wool &c."[20] The delegates speaking immediately after Fitzsimons did not challenge his assertion that America would become a manufacturing nation, nor did a thorough discussion of wool policy follow. (It would not have been surprising if this had occurred.) But loud voices would soon be raised concerning what role, if any, the American government should play in the world of domestic and imported wool.

The Constitution crafted by Madison and the other delegates instructed the President of the United States to recommend to Congress "such Measures as he shall judge necessary and expedient."[21] When President Washington did that for the first time in January of 1790, the former general used his State of the Union Address to suggest that the legislature turn its attention to America's need for self-sufficiency as a matter of national defense:

> To be prepared for war is one of the most effectual means of preserving peace …. (The) safety and interest (of a free people) require that they should promote such manufactories, as tend to render them independent on others, for essential, particularly for military supplies.[22]

A week later, the House of Representatives passed a resolution instructing the Secretary of the Treasury to prepare a report consistent with Washington's recommendation. The House, like the President, framed the matter in terms of national security, stressing that the goal was "the encouragement and promotion of such manufactories as will tend to render the United States independent of other nations for essential, particularly military supplies."[23]

Neither Washington's speech nor the House resolution said anything specific about wool. But given the highlighting of military supplies by both the Executive and the Legislative branches, it is not surprising that when Treasury Secretary Alexander Hamilton presented his *Report on*

20. Max Farrand, ed. *The Records of the Federal Convention of 1787* vol. 2 (New Haven, CT: Yale University Press, 1911), 362.
21. United States Constitution, Article II, section 3.
22. *Annals of Congress,* Senate, 1st Congress, 2nd Session (1790), 969.
23. *Annals of Congress,* House of Representatives, 1st Congress, 2nd Session (1790), 1095.

the Subject of Manufactures to Congress, a discussion of wool was included. Hamilton had, after all, served as Washington's Aide-de-camp during the Revolutionary War.[24] He wrote: "The extreme embarrassments of the United States during the late War, from an incapacity of supplying themselves, are still matter of keen recollection."[25] Hamilton remembered that shortage of blankets.

Historians have discussed the influence of Adam Smith's *An Inquiry into the Nature and Causes of the Wealth of Nations* on the *Report on Manufactures*.[26] References to sheep and their wool figure prominently in Smith's treatise—it could scarcely be otherwise in an eighteenth century volume on economic policy written by a Briton. From his study of Smith's book, Hamilton would have learned some striking minutiae of the wool trade. He read about an archaic unit of measure for wool called a "tod;" which was equal to twenty-eight pounds of English wool and which, back in 1339, sold for around ten shillings.[27]

More significantly, reading *Wealth of Nations* would expose Hamilton to Smith's criticism of the protectionist wool laws of his homeland. Smith lamented that Great Britain's wool manufacturers had for many years convinced Parliament that the prosperity of the nation depended on a thriving wool industry. As a result of this successful lobbying, Parliament had passed some very harsh legislation to prevent exportations of either live sheep or their wool. A law enacted in Queen Elizabeth's time punished a first sheep exporting offense by making the offender forfeit all his goods forever, imprisoning him for a year, and cutting off his left hand. A second offense led to the death penalty. Later, during the reign of Charles II, the law was expanded to ban the exportation not just of live sheep, but also of sheared wool. The severe penalties were also applied to the new act. "For the honor of the national humanity," Smith solemnly wrote, "it is to be hoped that

24. John Ferling, *Jefferson and Hamilton: The Rivalry that Forged a Nation* (New York: Bloomsbury Press, 2013), 67-68.
25. *Hamilton Papers* vol. 10 (1966), 291. Hamilton also stressed that foreign commerce was at risk due to America's lack of a navy.
26. See editorial notes, *Hamilton Papers* vol. 10 (1966), 230-340. Other Founders were similarly influenced by *The Wealth of Nations*; see Forrest McDonald, *Novus Ordo Seclorum: The Intellectual Origins of the Constitution* (Lawrence: University Press of Kansas, 1985), 128: "Most public men in America acquired at least a passing acquaintance with the work, almost all praised it, and many gave it thorough study."
27. Edwin Cannan, ed., *The Wealth of Nations* by Adam Smith (New York: Bantam Classic, 2003), 312, (hereafter *The Wealth of Nations*).

neither of the statutes were ever executed."[28] Even if there had been no capital punishment, however, the economic sanctions alone were effective deterrents.

Parliament also prohibited the exportation of wool from Ireland to any country other than England, and permitted duty-free importation of wool from Spain.[29] The effects of these actions, Smith reported, had caused an artificial depression in the price of wool in Great Britain, such that its value at the time he wrote *Wealth of Nations* was less than it had been in the fourteenth century.[30] The capitalist Smith concluded that an absolute prohibition on the exportation of wool was not justified, but that a significant tax on exports would be sound fiscal policy.[31]

Hamilton hoped to put some of Smith's ideas into practice in America. Envisioning the United States becoming a factor in the international market, Hamilton recommended in *Report on Manufactures* that Congress offer financial incentives to assist the development of a wool manufacturing commerce to rival Britain's.[32]

While Hamilton did not have the hands-on experience with sheep common among the founders, his report briefly addressed the state of the live animals required to power his proposed wool manufactures. He praised the condition of Virginia wool, asserting that it was the nation's best because "Virginia embraces the same latitudes with the finest Wool Countries of Europe," by which he meant Spain in particular.[33] Hamilton also backtracked a bit from his argument with

28. *The Wealth of Nations*, 822-823. On capital punishment in Britain for sheep crimes, a remark in John Adams' diary for September 28, 1787 bears mention: "In the afternoon, a man was convicted of stealing a couple of sheep; for which he was fined 30 shillings. Parsons, said in England he would have been hung, but I a little doubt." By "Parsons" Adams meant John Murray, minister of the First Presbyterian Church in Newburyport, MA. *The Adams Papers, Diary of John Quincy Adams*, vol. 2 (1981), 296.

29. *The Wealth of Nations*, 313. Smith's mention of Spanish wool is a reminder that during this time Britain itself was largely dependent on wool imports. In 1791 the Scottish agricultural writer John Sinclair warned his fellow Britons: "We are obliged to import considerable quantities of clothing wool from another kingdom (Spain)... (And) the quantity... is daily diminishing." Sounding much like an American of the same era, Sinclair then pleaded for his countrymen to put their best efforts towards sheep improvement. Sir John Sinclair, *Address to the Society for the Improvement of British Wool* (Edinburgh: The Society for the Improvement of British Wool, 1791), 6.

30. *The Wealth of Nations*, 827.

31. Ibid, 830.

32. *Hamilton Papers* vol. 10 (1966), 332.

33. Ibid, 295. In stating that Virginia's wool was as good as Spain's simply because the two places sit on similar latitudes, Hamilton was expressing an imperfect view of climate that was common until a few decades later when Alexander von Humboldt synthesized meteorological data. See Andrea Wulf, *The Invention of Nature: Alexander von Humboldt's New World* (New York: Alfred A. Knopf, 2015), 177-179.

Reverend Seabury seventeen years earlier. While he still lauded the concept of American farmers working hard towards "raising and improving the breed of sheep" Hamilton conceded that U.S. wool might never be improved enough "to render it fit for the finest fabrics" for which the nation would still depend upon foreign imports.[34] In the short term Hamilton got this backwards; almost two decades later it would be common fabrics—not the finest ones—that were particularly vulnerable to dependency on Britain.

In any case, the effort was for naught. Unconvinced by Hamilton's arguments on wool or any other commodity, Congress shelved his report.[35]

Where in the Constitution that Hamilton helped formulate did he find justification for the United States government offering premiums and bounties to support the wool trade? He argued that this was authorized by congressional power "To lay and collect Taxes . . . for the common Defense and General Welfare of the United States."[36] That is a rather broad reading of the General Welfare clause, and Hamilton's expansive interpretation would be challenged by his frequent rival, Thomas Jefferson. It is striking that the political and constitutional disagreements between Hamilton and Jefferson extended even to policies regarding sheep.

POSTWAR WOOL—AS JEFFERSON WOULD HAVE IT

Thomas Jefferson's friendship with James Madison led him to often candidly share his feelings with the younger Virginian.[37] In a letter written in 1810, when Madison was the sitting President and Jefferson the recently retired one, Jefferson confessed his irritation with the profits made by the sellers of Merinos, a breed of sheep particularly prized for the quality of their wool:

> I have been so disgusted with the scandalous extortions lately prac-
> ticed in the sale of these animals, and with the description of patri-
> otism and praise to the sellers, as if the thousands of dollars apiece
> they have not been ashamed to receive were not reward enough...
> No sentiment is more acknowledged in the family of Agriculturists
> than that the few who can afford it should incur the risk and expense

34. *Hamilton Papers* vol. 10 (1966), 332.
35. Ron Chernow, *Alexander Hamilton* (New York: Penguin Books, 2004), 378.
36. United States Constitution Article 1, section 8; *Hamilton Papers* vol. 10 (1966), 302-303.
37. See generally Andrew Burstein and Nancy Isenberg, *Madison and Jefferson* (New York: Random House, 2010).

of all new improvements, and give the benefit freely to the many of more restricted circumstances.[38]

In reading this, we are reminded of the First Continental Congress, three and a half decades earlier, promising that those who could provide sheep to their poorer neighbors would do so on moderate terms. Jefferson's use of similar language demonstrates that the concept of public virtue still held a warm place in the heart of this revolutionary.

Jefferson's letter suggested a solution to the "scandalous extortions." He proposed an elaborate scheme for selective breeding of Merinos so that he and Madison, as virtuous Virginia gentlemen, could see that their state was well stocked with these valuable sheep, provided free or at a reasonable cost.[39]

What Jefferson did not write in the letter gives as much insight into his political philosophy as the words he actually composed. He does not propose legislation—either federal or state—to regulate the sale of Merinos, nor any plan for taxation that might curtail the selling practices Jefferson so despised. No, to Jefferson the way to end inflated Merino sales was not through government action, but through the private actions of noble, civic-minded men.

Another letter from Jefferson concerning sheep is even more pointed in this regard. Early in his second term as President, Jefferson wrote to J. Phillipe Reibelt, a French immigrant he sometimes purchased books from. Jefferson wished very much for more Merinos to be imported from Europe, but, he declared, "Congress could not, by our constitution give one dollar for all in Spain, because that kind of power has not been given them."[40] Even though the Constitution gave Congress authority "To regulate Commerce with foreign Nations, and among the several States," and even though wool and woolen goods were clearly items of commerce sorely needed in the United States, for Jefferson this was not a sufficient nexus to permit Congress to purchase sheep from overseas.[41] Given this strict construction of the Constitution, it is unsurprising that Jefferson also said nothing about wool as a military necessity, which might arguably authorize purchase of Spanish Merinos under his own executive power as Commander in Chief.

38. J Jefferson Looney, ed., *The Papers of Thomas Jefferson, Retirement Series,* vol. 2, 16 November 1809 to 11 August 1810 (Princeton: Princeton University Press, 2005), 388-390.
39. Ibid.
40. Thomas Jefferson to J. Phillipe Reibelt, December 21, 1805, *Founders Online,* National Archives, http://founders.archives.gov/documents/Jefferson/99-01-02-2859.
41. United States Constitution, Article I, section 8.

Legal historians commonly contrast Jefferson's argument for a strict construction of the Constitution that would disallow a national bank with Hamilton's advocacy of a looser construction that would authorize it.[42] Their differing views on wool demonstrate that the two men were no less at odds in their constitutional interpretation when it came to America's sheep. Hamilton declared that the General Welfare clause enabled Congress to financially aid the development of wool manufactures; Jefferson believed that no provision even gave Congress authority to acquire additional sheep necessary to produce the wool in the first place.

Jefferson did not, however, mean to imply that since Congress could not act that there was no way to bring Merinos across the Atlantic. As in his later letter to Madison, Jefferson emphasized to Reibelt the significance of the personal virtue of gentlemen. "It is probable that private exertions will transplant & spread [Merinos]," he wrote, following that prediction with the proud remark: "I have possessed the breed several years, and have been constantly distributing them in my neighborhood."[43]

But even if Jefferson had conceded a constitutional power to purchase sheep or to regulate wool, he would still have disagreed with Hamilton over the scope of the new nation's wool business. While Hamilton saw the development of woolen manufacturing in the United States to rival that in Britain as a positive good, Jefferson deplored such a possibility. Often he expressed his hope that America would remain an agricultural land rather than an industrial one. "While we have land to labor … Let our work-shops remain in Europe," he pleaded in his book *Notes on the State of Virginia*.[44]

To that end, Jefferson stressed his agrarian view that sheep should primarily provide homespun garments, not factory made ones. In a letter to John Adams, he painted a blissful picture of his native Virginia:

> Every family in the country is a manufactory within itself, and is very generally able to make within itself all the stouter and middling stuffs for its own clothing & household use. We consider a sheep for every person in the family as sufficient to clothe it.[45]

42. e.g., Kermit L. Hall, William M. Wiecek and Paul Finkelman, *American Legal History: Cases and Materials,* 2nd ed. (New York: Oxford University Press, 1996), 105-107.
43. Jefferson to Reibelt, December 21, 1805.
44. Thomas Jefferson, *Notes on the State of Virginia*, William Peden, ed. (Chapel Hill: The University of North Carolina Press, 1954), 165.
45. Jefferson to John Adams, January 21, 1812," *Founders Online,* National Archives, http://founders.archives.gov/documents/Adams/99-02-02-5743.

Jefferson did, however, follow that remark with a reservation. He admitted that while homespun woolens would do for everyday wear, they were not suitable for Sunday best. "For fine stuff," he told Adams "we shall depend on your Northern manufactures."[46]

Since Jefferson thought that one sheep was needed to clothe one person in the family, it is tempting to expand this and assume the same ratio would hold for the nation at large.[47] An earlier Founding era estimate, however, viewed one sheep per person as insufficient. In 1791, Connecticut legislator William Hillhouse opined that it would take one million sheep just to provide clothing for Connecticut's nearly 240 thousand people, a ratio of more than four sheep to every person.[48] Of course, it is simplistic to dwell merely on the raw number of stock when the amount of wool produced per "improved" sheep is so consequential. As George Washington bellowed in the letter to his farm manager, there was a world of difference between a flock averaging five pounds of wool per animal and a flock averaging two and a half pounds—and this is without even considering the difference in quality of fiber depending on the breed or condition of the livestock.[49] What is clear is that when Jefferson wrote Adams in 1810, America lacked sufficient flocks to meet anyone's notion of the necessary sheep-to-human ratio. The census conducted that year counted over 7.2 million people. But the young nation likely had fewer than 5 million sheep.[50]

It is significant that in his correspondence with John Adams on the need for one sheep per family member, Jefferson referred to "northern manufactures" rather than British ones. This letter was written in

46. Ibid.

47. A discussion of how the amount of wool needed to clothe Americans was related to its enslaved population is beyond the scope of this article, but Jefferson kept careful account of blankets and clothing distributed to his enslaved; see generally Robert C. Baron, ed. *The Garden and Farm Books of Thomas Jefferson* (Golden, CO: Fulcrum, 1987).

48. *Hamilton Papers* vol. 9, 332-334. The figure for the population of Connecticut is from the 1790 U.S. Census.

49. John L. Hayes, "Origin and Growth of Sheep-Husbandry in the United States," *Journal of the Executive Proceedings of the Senate of the United States of America*, 45th Congress, 3rd Session (Ex. Doc. No. 25), 30-31. Hayes notes that when the number of sheep reported are compared to the pounds of wool reported in the mid nineteenth century censuses there are major discrepancies. This makes it impossible to say for certain to what degree sheep were producing more wool due to "improvement."

50. The figure of fewer than five million sheep is my own. I have been unable to ascertain how many sheep the U.S. had at any point in the Revolutionary and Founding eras. An 1888 report by the United States Treasury Department estimates that in 1810 there were about ten million sheep in the country (Anon., *Wool and Manufactures of Wool* (Washington, D.C.: Government Printing Office, 1888) XLII.) The report admits that this estimate is "of doubtful accuracy" and the source is of this figure is unclear. The

January 1812, a few months before quarrels with Britain would once more erupt in war. In the years that led up to the conflict, again the matter of American wool shortage would come to the forefront.

BANNING BRITISH WOOL—OR AT LEAST SOME OF IT

Joseph Nicholson's survey of potential non-British sources for wool did not look promising, as the Maryland Congressman conceded when he shared his findings on the House floor in February of 1806. Nicholson told his colleagues that neither Germany, Holland, nor any other place on the European continent could provide goods in the amounts Americans consumed. "With coarse woolens," he unhappily concluded, "we are supplied altogether from Great Britain, and we cannot procure them elsewhere."[51]

As Nicholson spoke, Britain was at war with Napoleon's France. As a consequence of the hostilities, British ships seized goods on American ships to keep them out of French hands. The British also boarded United States ships to impress seamen believed to be Royal Navy deserters. Angered by these actions, considered an affront to America's official position of neutrality, Congress debated banning British imports in retaliation.[52]

In light of America's dependence on British wool, Congressman Nicholson argued that it would be nonsensical to enact a complete embargo. Prohibit all imports, he warned, and "we shall be laughed at by Great Britain and all other European powers for adopting a system altogether impracticable, because we cannot adhere to it."[53]

Nicholson then floated an idea. While he had declared in his speech that the "coarse woolens"—those worn by Americans of ordinary means—could only be acquired from Britain, he hastened to add that there were other options for "those who moved in the higher walks of

1810 census attempted to count sheep, but only five states and one territory submitted returns. These totaled 1,584,652 head of sheep, ranging from a reported 1,000 in the Michigan Territory to 618,223 in Pennsylvania. For America in 1810 to have 10 million sheep, the number of animals not reported in the other twelve states and several territories in existence at the time, plus possible undercounts from the states reporting, would have to total nearly 8.5 million. The possibility of this is remote. I have accordingly—and conservatively—cut the 1888 Treasury Department estimate in half. Note that by writing that there were probably no more than 5 million sheep I am by no means asserting confidence in this figure—it is possibly still too high.

51. *Annals of Congress*, House of Representatives, 9th Congress, 1st Session (1806), 450.

52. Gordon S. Wood, *Empire of Liberty: A History of the Early Republic, 1789-1815* (New York: Oxford University Press, 2009), 639-646.

53. *Annals of Congress*, House of Representatives, 9th Congress, 1st Session (1806), 450-451.

life." This being so, he suggested the ban not of all British woolens, but only the import of expensive ones.[54]

And that is precisely what happened. In April of 1806 Congress passed an embargo prohibiting the import of a number of British goods. The list included a total ban on several items used for clothing—articles of leather, silk, and hemp—but the legislation only banned "woolen cloths whose invoice prices shall exceed five shillings sterling per square yard" and "woolen hosiery of all kinds." The act also prohibited the import of all "clothing ready-made." [55] Americans could still get from England cheap wool, not already assembled into garments. Only the well-off who favored British-made clothing would have to change their consumption habits. The United States had by this time developed a small domestic manufacturing industry to provide some high end wool to those who could afford it—especially if out of patriotism they insisted on American-made.[56]

The half-hearted regulation of wool in the 1806 Embargo Act stood as stark acknowledgment that three decades into its founding, America still lacked enough sheep to be self-sufficient. This was forty years after Benjamin Franklin had stood before Parliament and assured them their North American colonies were taking strong steps to increase the wool. It was thirty-two years after the Articles of Association pledged to do the utmost to improve the breed of sheep—after banning import of *all* British wool, not just the expensive ones—and the same number of years since Alexander Hamilton in his pamphlet bragged that America would soon have a sufficiency of wool. The 1806 Act was twenty-eight years after George Washington wrote in despair of the lack of blankets at Valley Forge. It had been fifteen years since Hamilton presented his *Report on Manufactures*, encouraging Congress to financially support the development of factories turning out wool clothing.

Yet, in spite of the intentions, hopes, and efforts of some of the most influential men in American history, the dawn of a second war with Great Britain—the world's wool merchant—still found the USA with too meager a sheep flock to put garments on the backs of all its citizens.

---

54. Ibid.
55. "An Act to prohibit the importation of certain goods, wares, and merchandise," *United States Statutes at Large*, 9th Congress, 1st session (1806), 379.
56. Margaret Byrd Adams Rasmussen, "Waging War with Wool: Thomas Jefferson's Campaign for American Commercial Independence from England. *Material Culture* 41 (2009), 17-37, esp. 29-31. Note, however, that as a result of my research I disagree with Rasmussen's assertion that "At the outbreak of the Revolution in 1776, the United States was already self-sufficient with the coarse, homespun variety of woolen cloth that was produced in cottage industry," 19.

This was soberly put by Robert R. Livingston of New York, a member of the Second Continental Congress who served with Jefferson, Adams, and Franklin on the committee that drafted the Declaration of Independence. In 1809 he published a small, widely read book entitled *Essay on Sheep*. There, Livingston noted that the human population of the United States was rapidly increasing—but the nation "does not grow one-fifth of the wool necessary for its own consumption."[57]

FLOCKS IN THE FOUNDERS' FUTURE

It would be a mistake, however, to think that the dream of founding Americans for an expanded sheep population never came true. After the passing of the Revolutionary generation the flocks steadily grew, spurred in large part by the country's western expansion. By 1879, the United States produced four-fifths of the wool that its industry required.[58] Thanks to its empire Britain's wool economy also expanded; within a century of claiming Australia in 1770 that colony was the world's largest wool producer.[59] By the late nineteenth century, the rising numbers of sheep in both America and Australia insured that virtually the entire English speaking world had become what the Founders envisioned—a vast Republic of Wool.

57. Robert R. Livingston, *Essay on Sheep* (New York: T. and J. Swords, 1809), 136.
58. John L. Hayes, "Sheep-Husbandry in the United States," 4.
59. *Wool and Manufactures of Wool*, XLV.

Francis Dana and America's Failed Embassy to Russia

❧ BOB RUPPERT ❧

The war between Britain and her North American colonies shut off the availability of raw materials, specifically timber, tar, and pitch, for the British Royal Navy and her commercial fleet. This placed greater concern on protecting their second biggest supplier, the Baltic States. Part of that protection included confiscating all contraband and naval stores aboard any Baltic ships headed for France or Spain. On February 28, 1780, the Empress Catherine II of Russia, believing the action was in violation of maritime law, announced the Declaration of the Principles of Neutrality and invited all of the other Baltic states to join her. She believed that she and her country had with "scrupulous Exactness"

> observed the Rules of Neutrality, during the course of this War . . . [but] the Subjects of her Majesty [were] often times troubled in their Navigation, or interrupted and retarded in their Commerce, by the Subjects of the Belligerent Powers. These interruptions, having come upon Business in general, and that of Russia in particular, are of a Nature to awaken the Attention of all the neutral Nations, and oblige her . . . to seek to deliver herself from them.[1]

The declaration sought to secure for neutrals the freedom to navigate from one port to another as well as along the coasts of the belligerents, asserted the principle "free ships make free goods," restricted contraband to munitions and the essential instruments of war, and set forth the conditions which constitute a blockade.

It was Article 2 and Article 3 of the declaration that Britain took most issue with. Article 2 read, "That the Effects belonging to the Sub-

1. J. B. Scott, *Armed Neutralities 1780 and 1800* (New York: Oxford University Press, 1918), 295-6.

jects of the belligerent Powers, shall be free, in neutral Ships, except always, contraband Goods."[2] For five hundred years, the status of neutral property was based on the notion of *consolato del mare*—neutral property, except contraband, was safe from capture at sea on enemy ships, but enemy property was subject to capture on neutral ships. This favored countries with large navies because countries with small navies could not protect their commercial shipping. They were forced to negotiate treaties with the countries with large navies that would allow them to carry enemy property freely; as a concession they had to agree that neutral property on enemy ships could be confiscated. This was not much of a concession seeing as the smaller countries shipped their goods on their own ships. From this understanding came the maxim, *free ships, free goods*. Even though the maxim had no standing in the law of nations, it was at the time a more common practice than *consolato del mare*. Between 1650 and 1780, thirty-six treaties were signed establishing *free ships, free goods* and only fifteen adhered to *consolato del mare*.[3] Britain, however, believed that the law of the sea was founded on *consolato del mare* and that *free ships, free goods* was nothing more than a treaty privilege.

Article 3 read:

> That her Imperial Majesty, in Consequence of the Limits above fixed, will adhere strictly, to that which is stipulated by the tenth and eleventh Articles of her Treaty of Commerce with Great Britain concerning the manner, in which She ought to conduct towards all the Belligerent.

The articles referenced were part of the Anglo-Russian Treaty of 1766. They specifically defined what was considered contraband. Only contraband could now be considered; this meant raw materials and naval stores could not be confiscated as contraband.

Empress Catherine also expressed her determination to use her maritime forces to maintain and to protect "the Commerce of her States and also . . . the navigation of her Subjects against all those to whom it may concern."[4] The situation escalated for Britain when Sweden on July 21 and the United Provinces (Holland) on November 20 joined with Russia in an Armed League of Neutrality.

---

2. "Declaration of her Majesty the Empress of Russia, made to the Courts of Versailles, Madrid, and London, mentioned in the foregoing Memorial," in *The Adams Papers*, Papers of John Adams, Vol. 9, *March 1780-July 1780*, ed. Gregg L. Lint and Richard Alan Ryerson (Cambridge, MA: Harvard University Press, 1996), 121-26.

3. Matzen, in J. B. Scott, *Armed Neutralities*, 167.

4. "Declaration of her Majesty the Empress of Russia." in *The Adams Papers*, 9:121-26.

Seizing the opportunity to expand their trade relations and develop "a good understanding and friendly intercourse between the subjects of her Imperial majesty the Empress of all the Russias and these United States," the Continental Congress on December 15, resolved

That an envoy a minister charged with the affairs of the United States to reside at the Court of the Empress of Russia be appointed . . . that Monday next be assigned for electing such envoy minister . . . and that a committee of three be appointed to prepare a commission and draught of instructions for the said envoy minister.[5]

On December 19, the Continental Congress elected Francis Dana, minister plenipotentiary to the Court of the Empress of Russia.[6] Dana, who had been serving as John Adams' secretary in Paris, was not informed of his appointment until the middle of March 1781.[7] Little did he know that between his election and learning of his appointment, Denmark had joined the League on January 5. The goals of his embassy to St. Petersburg were

to engage her Imperial Majesty to favor and support the sovereignty and independence of the United States . . . [that it was] "a leading and capital point that these United States shall be formally admitted as a party to the conventions of the neutral maritime powers.... [and to propose a treaty of amity and commerce with Russia which was to be] "founded upon principles of equality and reciprocity and for the mutual advantages of both nations and agreeable to the spirit of the treaties existing between the United States and France.[8]

He was directed by the President of the Continental Congress upon his arrival in France to "communicate your powers and instructions to our ministers plenipotentiary at the court of Versailles . . . and avail yourself of their advice and information." He was also to "communicate the general object of your mission to the minister of his most Christian majesty at the court of Petersburgh, and endeavor through his mediation to sound the disposition of her Imperial majesty or her ministers towards these United States." [9]

5. *Journals of the Continental Congress*, 18:1155.
6. Ibid, 18:1167.
7. Francis Wharton, *The Revolutionary Diplomatic Correspondence of the United States* (Washington DC: Library of Congress, American Memory, 1888), *Diplomatic Correspondence*, 4, 325-27.
8. "Secret Journals of Congress," *Foreign Affairs*, Vol. 2, 362-65.
9. "Instructions to Francis Dana, as Minister Plenipotentiary to the Court of St. Petersburgh, 19 December 1780," in Wharton, *Diplomatic Correspondence*, 4:202.

On March 24, Dana informed the President of the Continental Congress that he had safely arrived in France and had already communicated his instructions and commission to Dr. Franklin who recommended that he speak with the Count de Vergennes, the French Foreign Minister, about "whether it would not be proper to make [his] communication also to the court of St. Petersburgh and obtain their approbation of the measure before [he] should set off for that country."[10] One week later, he informed Vergennes of his commission and then stated,

> It is not my intention to assume any public character on my arrival there, but to appear only as a private citizen of the United States, until the result of my inquiries shall point out a ready and honorable reception. I shall most cheerfully obey my instructions to communicate the general object of my mission to his majesty's minister at St. Petersburgh, whose able advice and assistance I hope your excellency will be pleased to assure me.[11]

On April 4, in an interview with Dana, Vergennes did not oppose his mission, but reinforced that he

> should appear as a mere private gentleman travelling with a view of obtaining some knowledge of that country; . . . [and] advised me to mention my design of going to the [Russian] minister at The Hague.[12]

On April 18, he sought the advice of one more person, John Adams. Adams said,

> I should think it altogether improper to communicate your design to the ambassador of traveling to St. Petersburgh as a private gentleman, secreting from him at the same time your public character . . . and [if he] advised against the journey, or to postpone it for instructions from his court, it would be less respectful to go than to go now when the circumstances of the times are very favorable . . . America, my dear sir, has been too long silent in Europe. Her cause is that of all nations and all men.[13]

This was the advice he chose to follow. Unfortunately, in doing so, it set off a series of actions that would eventually make Dana's embassy an unmitigated disaster. John Adams did not hide the fact that he had

10. "Dana to the President of Congress, 24 March 1781," in ibid., 4:326.
11. "Dana to the Count de Vergennes, 31 March 1781," in ibid., 4:343.
12. "Dana to the President of Congress, 4 April 1781," in ibid., 4:350-51.
13. "J. Adams to Dana, 18 April 1781," in ibid., 4:368.

little regard for Vergennes. So when Vergennes secured a promise from Dana not to proceed in presenting his Letters of Credence, that is, making the Russian Court aware of his mission, Adams felt an American diplomat was being held accountable to a foreign ministry. Because Dana had been Adams' secretary before receiving his commission, he had a strong affinity for Adams. It was not surprising that such admiration would lead to the appropriation of many of his opinions.

While he was en route to St. Petersburg, a fourth country, Prussia, joined the League on May 19; it was the second country since Dana's appointment.

On November 29, 1775, the Continental Congress established a committee to oversee their agents in Britain and their "friends in . . . other parts of the World." Because of the nature of its role, soon the word "secret" was added to the committee's title. On April 17, 1777, owing to the growing demand of their duties, Congress renamed the committee; it was now the Committee of Foreign Affairs. On August 10, 1781, Robert R. Livingston was elected the first Secretary of Foreign Affairs.[14] Dana was to report directly to him.

Dana reached St. Petersburg on August 27, 1781. On the 31st, he wrote to the Marquis de Verac, the French Minister to Russia, announcing his arrival. That same day, Verac wrote back stating that Vergennes had prepared him for his arrival. On September 1, Dana again wrote to Verac, this time informing him of his commission. The next day, Verac wrote back warning Dana to "reflect much before you display the character with which you are clothed, or make advances which will be more injurious than beneficial to the success of your views"[15] and that without the intervention of any other belligerent parties, not even that of the two imperial courts, [before] their mediation shall be formally asked and granted for this object."[16] This was a major point of misunderstanding for the Continental Congress and Dana. The Empress had directed the Declaration to the three European belligerents only, Britain, France and Spain; it was not directed to the United States because if it had been, Empress Catherine would have been recognizing the United States as a sovereign state when in fact they were colonies of one of the belligerents. Belligerents could accede to the principles of the League, but this did not mean that they would be allowed to be part of the League.

14. *Journals of the Continental Congress,* 21:851-52.
15. "Verac to Dana, 2 September 1781," in Wharton, *Diplomatic Correspondence,* 4:684.
16. "Verac to Dana, 12 September 1781," in ibid., 4:705.

Francis Dana, left, American minister plenipotentiary to the Court of the Empress of Russia; Empress Catherine II of Russia, right, by an unknown artist, c. 1780. (*Kunsthistorisches Museum*)

Frustrated, Dana wrote back,

the United States of America have been, ever since the 4th of July 1776, a free, sovereign, and independent body-politic. Your illustrious sovereign made this declaration in the face of the world more than three years since; and I flatter myself the time has now come when other sovereigns are prepared to make the same, if properly invited to do it . . . [and ignoring his promise to Vergennes wrote] I see no difficulty in adopting the measure I shall presently mention . . . it appears to me to be betraying the honor and dignity of the United States to seclude myself in a hotel, without making one effort to step forth into political life [therefore] . . . the measure I propose to take is make a confidential communication of my public character to the proper minister of her majesty and of the general object of my mission.[17]

Dana could not accept that diplomatic recognition could not be rendered after he made his mission known. What made the communication between Dana and Verac even more difficult was that Dana did not speak Russian or French, the language of the royal court, and Verac did not speak English. All communication between them had to be through translators.

17. "Dana to Verac, 4 September 1781," in ibid., 4:698.

Over the next six months, Dana waited patiently for his audience with the Empress Catherine. He strongly believed that "the critical moment for the Maritime Provinces of Europe {had] arrived. They may never, or at least for a long time to come, again see so fair an occasion to promote their essential Interests."[18] During this time he received a surprising letter from Livingston and had to combat a rumor that could jeopardize his embassy.

In the letter the Secretary of Foreign Affairs was adamant about how Dana was to carryout his mission. He wrote that Dana's

> eager desire to render essential service to your country had in some measure biased your judgment . . . [but] that you entertain serious thoughts of making and immediate display of your powers to the Russian ministry, notwithstanding the cautions given you [by those] whom you were expressly directed to consult . . . if you have not yet made a communication of your powers, to delay doing it till the Marquis de Verac shall agree in sentiment with you that it will be expedient . . . [because] The conclusions of the Marquis de Verac on the plan of the proposed mediation are sound and just.

Before sending the letter off, Livingston requested the approval of its contents from Congress. Two weeks later, Congress directed him to add the following:

> That Mr. Dana be instructed not to present his Letters of Credence to the Court of Petersburg until he shall have obtained satisfactory assurances that he will be duly recd. and recognized in his public Character.[19]

With this weighing on his mind, Dana was confronted with a piece of information that had been spread at the Court in Madrid by Russian Ambassador Brandenburg:

> If North America confirms its independence and the number of inhabitants increases, they will then begin to raise there flax and hemp; and they already have timber, tar, pitch, wax, and other products which come from the North (the Baltic), and are in a position to satisfy with these all the southern areas at a better price and more conveniently than the North is able to do.[20]

18. "To John Adams from Francis Dana, 23 April 1782," in *The Adams Papers,* Papers of John Adams, *October 1781-April 1782,* ed. Gregg L. Lint, Richard Alan Ryerson, Anne Decker Cecere, et al... (Cambridge, MA: Harvard University Press, 2004), 12:455-57.
19. "Livingston to Dana, 10 May 1782," in Wharton, *Diplomatic Correspondence,* 5:412; *Journals of the Continental Congress,* 22:301.
20. A.V. Efimov, *Iz istorii velikikh russkikh gepgraficheskikh otkrytii v severnom ledovitom i tikhom okeanakh XVII i pervaia polovina XVIII v* (Moscow, 1950), 222.

In other words, if the United States gained its independence, her "free commerce . . . would be highly prejudicial to their [Russian] commerce." Dana, believing that commerce was the main obstacle which prevented Russia's recognition of the United States, wrote a polemic entitled, *Reflections to refute the Assertion of the British that the Independence of the United States will be injurious to the commercial Interests of the Northern Nations, and of Russia in Particular.*[21] In it he made three points: first, that there was no difference if Russia sold her commodities in total to one country or in total to two or more countries; second, that there was a market in the United States for iron bar, sailcloth, cordage, and hemp and in Russia there was a market for rice and a higher quality of tobacco; and third, an independent United States could trade with Russia without undergoing the middleman expense currently imposed by Britain. The arguments changed few minds because in Russia commerce was thought of as a fixed market for exports only and not as the balance between imports and exports—she could not comprehend that two countries could export the same commodity, and the commerce of both could increase rather than decrease due to the nature of each country's imports.

As the months continued to pass, Dana became convinced that Verac had no intention of allowing him to present his Letters of Credence to the Court under any circumstances. Verac opposed the presentation in September of 1781 when Dana had just arrived in St. Petersburg, in December when he learned of Cornwallis's defeat at Yorktown, in March of 1783 when Parliament enacted a series of new policies just prior to the fall of Lord North's Ministry, in October when Richard Oswald was empowered to negotiate a peace treaty with the American Commissioners, in November when Charles James Fox, the new Secretary of State for the Northern Department under the Rockingham ministry, announced that there would be no pre-conditions to the peace negotiations, and in February of 1783 when the preliminary treaty was signed.[22]

On February 22, Dana received a letter from Adams. In it he stated,

You can no Longer hesitate to make known your Errand. Whether the advice of the Marquis de Verac is for it or against it, I should

---

21. "Dana to Livingston, 28 June 1782," in Wharton, *Diplomatic Correspondence*, 5:529-32 and 780.
22. "Verac to Dana, [translation] 2 September 1781," in ibid., 4:685; "To John Adams from Henry Grand, 21 November 1781," in *The Adams Papers*, 12:77; "To the American Peace Commissioners from Francis Dana, 14 January 1783," in Ibid., 14:194-5; "Dana to Livingston, 18 November 1782," in Wharton, *Diplomatic Correspondence*, 6:54; "Dana to Livingston, 25 February, 1783," in ibid., 6: 263.

think you would now go to the Minister.—Your Instructions are
Chains Strong Chains.—Whether you shall break them or no as We
have been obliged to do, you are the only judge.—There is a Vulcan
at Versailles [Vergennes] whose constant Employment it has been
to forge Chains for American Ministers.—But his Metal has not been
fine and strong enough . . . My advice to you is immediately to communicate your mission.[23]

On March 5, a member of Catherine's cabinet visited Dana and informed him that he could communicate his mission to the Vice-Chan-
cellor, Count Ostermann, as soon as he pleased. Ostermann was
serving, *de facto*, as Russia's Foreign Minister with Catherine's secretary,
I. A. Bezborodko, as his advisor, after the dismissal of Count Nikita
Ivanovich Panin in May of 1781. On March 7, without consulting Verac,
Dana communicated his mission to Ostermann and requested an audience so that he might present his Letters of Credence.[24] Five days later,
he received a message from Osterman confirming that he had received
the letter and would present it to her majesty. There was no further
communication between the two men until they met on April 23. In
the meeting, much to Dana's surprise, the Count stated that Russia, in
order to maintain her neutrality, could not recognize the United States
as an independent and sovereign state, that Dana needed new Letters
of Credence dated "prior to the acknowledgment of the independence
of the United States by the King of Great Britain," and that a minister
from the United States could not be received by Russia before one had
been received by Great Britain. Dana, after being assured by a member
of the Empress's cabinet that there would be no obstacles to his reception, was stunned, confused, and angry. He told Ostermann that he
needed to some time to consider his response. On May 8, he sent a memorial to Ostermann explaining why he would not apply to Congress
for the revocation of his Letters of Credence:

1. Because it would be to desire the United States of America to
strike seven years of their existence as free, sovereign, and independent
State

2. Because their compliance with it would, in effect, annul their resolution contained in the declaration of their independence. . . .

3. Because it would imply on their part that they owed their existence as a free nation to the acknowledgment of their independence by
the King of Great Britain

23. "To John Adams from Francis Dana, 22 February 1783," in *The Adams Papers*, 14:285-
7.
24. "Dana's Communication of his Mission to Count Ostermann, 7 March 1783," in
Wharton, *Diplomatic Correspondence*, 6: 275.

4. Because . . . it would go to annul all their acts of sovereignty prior to that period, and among others, the most important ones of their treaties with France and Holland, as well as their commissions granted to their ministers at the court of Madrid and other courts. . . .

5. Because the requisition of new letters of credence bearing date since the period above-mentioned involves in itself a decision on the part of her Imperial majesty, that the United States of America ought [not] of right to be considered as a free, sovereign, and independent power, but in virtue of the acknowledgment of them as such by the King of Great Britain

6. Because the granting of new letters of credence would amount to a confession on the part of the United States of the justice of such a decision and

7. Because a compliance with such a requisition would . . . in every point of view, be highly derogatory to the dignity of the United States, and is a sacrifice which circumstances by no means require to be made.[25]

The next day Dana sent a copy of the memorial to Livingston and added,

> What the effect of this memorial will be, is impossible to say. I have no sanguine hopes from it . . . but if [Congress] should be inclined, would it not be more eligible for me to return, when they would have an opportunity to get rid of the matter without any revocation . . . by nominating another minister after I had quitted the empire.[26]

One week later, Dana wrote to John Adams, "If they [Congress] have not lost all sense of their own Dignity, and I believe they have not, they wou'd sooner resolve never to send a Minister to this Court, during the life of the present Sovereign."[27]

Unbeknown to Dana, on May 21, the Continental Congress resolved to permit him to bring his embassy to an end

> That Mr. Dana be informed, that the treaties lately entered into for restoring peace have caused such an alteration in the affairs of these states, as to have removed the primary object of his mission to the Court of Russia. . . .That with respect to a commercial treaty with Russia, they consider the benefits of it to this country . . . as rather remote, and have therefore little present inducement to enter into it. . . . That . . . , unless Mr. Dana shall have already formed engagements

25. "Dana to Ostermann, 8 May 1783," in ibid., 6:411-15.
26. "Dana to Livingston, 9 May 1783," in ibid., 6:418.
27. "To John Adams from Francis Dana, 15 May 1783," in *The Adams Papers*, 14:480-1.

or made proposals, from which he cannot easily recede . . . he be permitted to return [to the United States].[28]

Livingston had expressed a similar opinion to the President of the Continental Congress on February 26[29] and again in his report to the Continental Congress on June 3. Dana would not receive a copy of the resolution until July 27.

On June 14, Dana met with Ostermann for the second time. He informed Dana that the Empress

> will receive him with pleasure in that quality as soon as the definitive treaties which are now on the eve of being concluded between the powers who have been at war shall be consummated.[30]

He told him that in a few days the Empress Catherine would be travelling to Finland and probably would not return until the end of September at which time she would receive him. On July 27, Dana received the Continental Congress's resolution attached to a letter from Livingston. The good news was that he would be allowed to return home; the bad news was that Congress refused to pay the customary fee for a settling a commercial treaty and that his power only permitted him "to communicate with her Imperial Majesty's ministers on the subject of a treaty, etc. . . , but not to assign it. He was taken aback with this assertion,

> But it is useless to spend a moment's consideration upon the extent of my powers, when you say you are persuaded that it is the wish of Congress rather to postpone any treaty with Russia rather than buy one at this day, as I am persuaded no treaty is to be obtained, or could be honorably postponed, without conforming, as other nations have done, to the usage of this court in that respect.[31]

Dana vented his frustration and anger in a letter to Adams two days later. He was commissioned a minister plenipotentiary

> with full power on behalf of the United States, to propose a treaty of amity and commerce between these United States and her said Imperial Majesty, and to confer and treat thereon with her ministers, vested with equal powers . . . ; transmitting such treaty for our final ratification.

28. *Journals of the Continental Congress,* May 21, 1783, Vol. 24, 350-1.
29. "Livingston to the President of Congress, 26 February, 1783," in Wharton, *Diplomatic Correspondence,* 6:264.
30. "Dana to Livingston, 14 June 1783," in ibid., 6:494.
31. "Dana to Livingston, 27 July 1783," in ibid., 6:597-8.

Then he referenced point number six in his instructions:

> . . . and you are authorized to communicate with her Imperial Majesty's ministers on the form and terms of such treaty, and transmit the same to Congress for their ratification.[32]

Dana was confounded by Livingston's position since there would be no point for Dana or any Russian ministers to enter into any negotiations if he, Dana, could not sign what they concluded. This would also make what they concluded nothing more than a draft, leaving nothing for Congress to ratify. On August 8, Dana informed Ostermann that there was no need to schedule an audience with the Empress because he was departing for America in a couple of weeks.[33] Concerned that Ostermann might misinterpret his motives for departing, he explained that his health was poor and he had some private affairs that needed his attention. On August 16, Dana paid Ostermann one final visit to extend personal wishes.

On September 29, 1783, Dana boarded the *Duchess of Kingston* and set sail for the United States. He arrived in Boston on December 13. Four days later, he wrote to the President of the Continental Congress:

> Sir: I do myself the honor to acquaint your excellency of my arrival at Boston . . . on Friday last . . . I wish that your excellency would be pleased to write to me . . . whether it is the expectation of the Congress that I should come to the place of their session, and without loss of time, to render a more particular account of my late mission. There is nothing I should more earnestly wish than to meet a strict inquiry into my conduct during the time I have had he honor of being a servant of the public.[34]

The failure of Francis Dana's embassy has numerous reasons. Putting aside any alleged subversion by Minister Verac or British Minister Harris, the following appear to be more than enough:

• the effort of the Continental Congress to send ministers to European courts where there appeared no remote prospect of obtaining aid to or recognition of the United States was over-zealous;

• the United States had nothing to offer Russia by way of a military alliance—all they had to offer was a trading partner;

---

32. *Journals of the Continental Congress,* 18:1166-73.
33. "Dana to Livingston, 8 August, 1783," in Wharton, *Diplomatic Correspondence,* 6:264.
34. "Dana to the President of Congress, 17 December 1783," in ibid., 6:739.

• the United States had a lack of understanding of the military al-liances on the continent and their influence on political policies;
• communication between the Continental Congress and Dana roundtrip took between five and six months;
• Empress Catherine was concerned first and foremost with what transpired on the continent. She was nearing a war with the Turks which meant at some time she needed the support of Britain;
• Empress Catherine needed to maintain her commercial rela-tionship with Britain and;
• Empress Catherine needed to maintain Russia's neutrality in order to protect her commerce and be viewed as a fair and just mediator.

The 3rd New Jersey Regiment's Plundering of Johnson Hall

PHILIP D. WEAVER

The newly formed 3rd New Jersey Regiment, commanded by Col. Elias Dayton, was mustered into the Continental Army on May 2, 1776. It was reviewed in New York City by Generals Washington, Putnam, Sullivan, and Greene. The regiment's Capt. Joseph Bloomfield noted in his personal journal that the generals claimed they were the "compleatest and best regiment in the Continental service"[1] Bloomfield's 2nd lieutenant, Ebenezer Elmer noted that "Gen Washington made bold to say we were the flower of all the North American Forces"[2]

Wasting no time, the regiment embarked in sloops for Albany the very next day. They were bound for Canada, with several other regiments belonging to Brig. Gen. John Sullivan's relief force.[3] Apparently Colonel Dayton was not with them. He received the following order by Adjutant General Horatio Gates from Headquarters in New York, dated May 9, 1776:

> It is his Excellency General Washington's orders, you proceed to Albany, where you will receive and obey the orders of Major-General Schuyler, with respect to joining your Regiment upon their march to Canada, and to the assistance he thinks proper to order you to give in transporting ammunition, artillery, stores, and provisions, to

1. Description of activity from late April until early May, Mark E. Lender & James K. Martin, editors, *Citizen Soldier: The Revolutionary War Journal of Joseph Bloomfleld* (Newark, NJ: New Jersey Historical Society, 1982), 39.
2. Entry for May 2, 1776, Ebenezer Elmer, "Journal Kept during an Expedition to Canada in 1776," *Proceedings of the New Jersey Historical Society*, 2 (1846):102.
3. Lender & Martin, *Citizen Soldier*, 40, May 3, 1776. Elmer, *Journal*, 2 (1846):102, May 3, 1776. Elmer only named the 1st New Jersey regiment, where Bloomfield explained that all six regiments in the division, including the 1st New Jersey, departed for Canada.

Quebeck. As the service requires despatch, his Excellency depends upon your utmost diligence in forwarding every part of it that you are, or may be hereafter commanded to execute.[4]

Not long after arriving in Albany, New York, Maj. Gen. Philip Schuyler changed those plans to move north when he wrote Colonel Dayton, on May 14, and informed him that Brig. Gen. John Sullivan would order him to proceed out the Mohawk Valley to Johnstown, with a detachment of his regiment. After performing some other business, he was to:

> . . . let Sir John Johnson know that you have a letter from me, which you are ordered to deliver in person, and beg his attendance to receive it. If he comes as soon as you have delivered the letter, and he has read it, you are immediately to make him close prisoner, and carefully guard him, that he may not have the least opportunity of escape. When you have done this you are to repair to his house, taking him with you; and after having placed proper sentinels to prevent any person belonging to the family from carrying out papers, you are to examine his papers in his own presence . . .
>
> Although Sir John Johnson is to be closely guarded, he is by no means to experience the least ill-treatment in his own person, or those of his family; and you are to be particularly careful that none of the men under your command, or any person whatever, destroy or take away the most trifling part of his property, except arms and ammunition, which you are to secure, and bring down with you, and deliver to Mr. Philip Van Rensselaer, Storekeeper, with a charge to keep them safe until further orders from me.
>
> In securing Sir John Johnson, and in searching his house, I wish the least tumult possible; and, to that end, you are not to suffer a private soldier to enter it, unless by your immediate order.[5]

On the evening of May 16, all able-bodied, effective, and fully accoutered men in the 3rd New Jersey were assembled in Albany, New York. By directions from Major General Schuyler, Brigadier General Sullivan had the men drawn up and strictly examined. He then ordered that forty of the best and most able men, plus two officers, be selected from each company and be mustered at six o'clock the next morning, with all things in order and six days provisions in their knapsacks. In-

---

4. Adj. Gen. Horatio Gates to Col. Elias Dayton, May 9, 1776, Peter Force, ed., *American Archives* (Washington, D.C., 1837-53), 4th Series, 6:397.
5. Maj. Gen. Philip Schuyler to Col. Elias Dayton, May 14, 1776, Force, *American Archives*, 4th Series, 6:447-448.

tended for a secret expedition, they were provided with flints, powder, ball, and required provisions. However, they were lacking enough cartridges, so they did not step off until one o'clock in the afternoon.[6] The rest of the officers and men, except the sick and unfit for duty, followed at five o'clock in the evening of May 20.[7]

The select men of the 3rd New Jersey began arriving in Johnstown, New York, late in the afternoon on May 19 and immediately started working on various issues in the area regarding the Indians and tracking down Loyalists.[8] Within the week, Colonel Dayton sent a letter to General Schuyler summarizing how the regiment's mission was proceeding and his intentions for Johnson Hall:

> Sir: In my letter sent yesterday, by the Rev. Mr. Caldwell, I informed you of my intentions of possessing Johnson-Hall. A guard and sentries are so placed as to intercept effectually any communication with any part of the country. Previous to this, I sent an officer with a letter to Lady Johnson, informing her of my design, and requesting all the keys, in order to examine Sir John's papers. Colonel White, Major Barber, and myself, waited upon her shortly after. She immediately produced all the keys, with a considerable number of papers. The letters were carefully perused in presence of herself, and a few selected, copies of which I transmit you by this express, retaining the originals in my own hands until I shall have the pleasure of seeing or conveying them more safely to you. The house, also, was examined in every part. Since Mr. Caldwell left this place, I am more assured that Sir John, with his party, marched from these settlements on Monday last, for Niagara or Canada. Lady Johnson assures me he is on his road to Niagara, and that we soon shall hear where he is. As the guards and sentries around the Hall must increase the pain of her situation, I have requested her to remove to Albany, where, as I understand, she has several friends. To this she seems averse, but for what reasons I know not; and I would therefore be glad to receive your directions on this head also . . . .[9]

6. Lender & Martin, *Citizen Soldier,* 46, May 17, 1776. Elmer, *Journal,* 2 (1846): 108, entries for May 16 and 17, 1776.
7. Elmer, *Journal,* 2 (1846):108-109, entries for May 20, 1776. Soldiers, during this period, did not usually march between locations in the middle of the day. Period writings seem to indicate they normally started in the wee hours of the morning and stopped by midday. In this case the officers appear to have flipped the process and opted to march in the evening and probably stopped for the day sometime after midnight.
8. Lender & Martin, *Citizen Soldier,* 47-55, entries for May 19-24, 1776.
9. Col. Elias Dayton to Maj. Gen. Philip Schuyler, May 24, 1776, Force, *American Archives,* 4th Series, 6:581.

The officer Colonel Dayton sent to deliver the letter was Captain Bloomfield, who wrote in his journal on May 22:

I was early this Morning directed by Col. Dayton to take a file of Men & go to Johnson Hall with my side arms only & wait on Lady Johnson with a Letter, The substance of which was to demand the key of the Hall & drawers in the Rooms with directions for her immediately to Pack up her own apparel only and go to Albany, that an Officer & a Guard should wait on her Ladyship to Albany if she choses. Accordingly I went to the Hall & after directing the Sarjant of My Guard to place Centuries round the Hall & Fort I asked for her Ladyship who was then a Bed and after waiting an hour she came into the Parlour. I gave her the Letter with assuring her Ladyship it gave me Pain that I was under the disagreable necessity of delivering her a Letter that must give her Ladyship a great deal of uneasiness and which my duty oblidged me to do in obedience to the orders of my superier Officer. She hastily broke open the Letter & immediately burst into a flood of Tears, wh[ich] affected me, so that I thought proper to leave her alone. After some time she sent for me, composed herself, ordered the Keys of the Hall to be brought in & given to me & which I desired might lay on the Table till the Coll. came. After which I breakfasted with her Ladyship & Miss Jenny Chew whose Father is in England Acting the part of a Violent Tory. After Breakfast Col. Dayton & Major Barber came & we in the presence of her Ladyship or Miss Chew Examined every Room & Every Drawer In Johnson-Hall & Sr. John's office, but found no Letters of a publick Nature inimical to the cause worth mentioning.[10]

Things began to settle down in the region as the regiment went about its business for the next couple of weeks. Then, on Wednesday, June 5, a serious breach in security was discovered. 2nd Lt. Ebenezer Elmer, of Bloomfield's company, noted in his journal that:

There began to be great suspicion among the people that the officers had been plundering at the Hall, which coming to the Colonel's ears, and he making strict enquiry and search, it appeared to be true, and that to a considerable value. And as a great part was taken last night when Capt. ******** was Captain of the guard there which was entirely contrary to orders, his place being at town, yet pushing himself

10. Lender & Martin, *Citizen Soldier*, 52-53, May 22, 1776. When soldiers are formed up into two or three ranks, the men, one behind the other, are known as a file. So, depending on how many ranks the 3rd New Jersey formed up in, "a file of men" would be two or three men.

The front of Johnson Hall, in Johnstown, New York, as it stands today as a New York State Historic Site. A small courtyard is located in he rear, between the two blockhouses.

there made it appear very evident that he and Col. ***** (many declared he took things) were confederates and had with Capts **** and ****** most of the booty, which is supposed to be near £500. However, after evening roll call, the Colonel desired us all to attend in his room; when we got there, he informed us that many things were taken from the Hall contrary to orders; that altho' he did not deem that as the property of Sir John, yet we had by no means a right to take one farthing's worth from there until it is properly confiscated by Congress and delivered out in such a manner, or to such use as they saw fit—that he did not know who were guilty of it, neither did he want to know, as his duty would then oblige him to cashier those who were foremost in it; but as he imagined it was done inadvertently, he would therefore request every one to return whatever he had got that evening in the entry, for which purpose he would order the door left open And no one would know who brought then. This being a method which screened the guilty from any punishment, shewed the desire the Colonel had of not bringing it to light, which was exceedingly favoring; but as he was no doubt fully convinced in his own mind who were the principal ones, and his thus endeavoring to hide their faults, so that all would suffer equally alike, shewed, in my opinion, a small degree of partiality; and whether he, if it should have fallen upon others, would have acted in the same manner, time must discover. Capt. Bloomfield come up.[11]

Upon arrival, Capt. Joseph Bloomfield noted in his personal diary, using similar but far less verbose language than Elmer, that:

> Col. Dayton also informed me that some of our officers had imprudently (not to term it worse) last Night got the keys of & Plundered Johnson-Hall, of sundry goods & furniture to the amount of a considerable Value, that if those goods were not returned to the Hall this Night he would punish or rather prosecute those concerned with the utmost severity & of which He informed the officers of in general.[12]

By the next morning, things had not gone as Dayton hoped. Lieutenant Elmer noted in his journal that "it appears that not the quarter part was brought back."[13] Captain Bloomfield, who began as a neutral observer, quickly found himself in the middle of the mess:

> By order of the Col. Capt. Dickinson [Dickerson] & myself went this Morning to the Hall & took an Acct. of the goods returned, taken the Night before last from the Hall. After our Report the Coll. Judge Duer Mr. Adams & two Daughters (who have the care of the Hall) Capt. Dickeson & myself went to the Hall, saw that the goods & furniture were carefully packed & securely Stored in the Rooms, after which the Hall was Locked with strict directions for no Persons to enter without leave, which was particularly injoined on me to attend to as I mounted guard tonight. Mounted Guard all night, stayed myself In Johnson-Hall. Lieut. Lloydd Lt. McDonald & Ensign Reading mounted guard at the Camp.[14]

In an aside at the bottom of a letter to General Schuyler, sent from Fort Schuyler in August, Dayton wished "Captains Bloomfield & Dickenson's Companies were ordered here, they have Officers I can depend

---

11. Elmer, *Journal,* 2 (1846):120-121, June 5, 1776. The transcript of the original journal shows dots as a way to mask the names in this entry. Figuring each dot represents a letter, the colonel would be Lt. Col. Anthony W. White (lieutenant colonels are addressed as "colonel"). Capt. Thomas Patterson would be the captain of the guard and one of the confederates was probably Capt. John Ross. The other confederate is a bit harder to identify, so will leave that anonymous for now.
12. Lender & Martin, *Citizen Soldier,* 59-60, July 5, 1776.
13. Elmer, *Journal,* 2 (1846): 122, June 6, 1776.
14. Lender & Martin, *Citizen Soldier,* 60, July 5, 1776. The junior officers mounting the guard at the camp were not from either Bloomfield's or Dickerson's companies.

upon."[15] This provides insight into why these two captains were picked to handle this difficult matter. However, the above entry from Bloomfield's journal, listing the junior officers guarding the camp, illustrates that neither of these officers knew, at the time, who was involved.

As a final capper, on June 17, regimental orders included the written statement that "Col. Dayton positively orders that everything taken from Johnson Hall, either by officer or soldier, be returned this day to the Adjutant or Quarter Master."[16] Up until now the incident was an internal regimental matter that could be somewhat controlled, but with this, the plundering of the Hall was official and something formal had to be done about it.

It did not take long to find the first suspect, but General Schuyler, who was at German Flatts, got wind of it. A letter from him, dated July 22, sent to Colonel Dayton apparently brought about swift action:

From the advice contained in an intercepted letter which was yesterday delivered me, there is reason to suspect that Lieutenant McDonald, of your regiment, is concerned in the embezzlement of the effects at Johnstown. You will therefore be pleased to send him immediately, under arrest, to this place, together with such other officers, if any there are, who may lay under similar suspicions, and all such officers and soldiers who may, by their testimony, elucidate a matter which reflects so much disgrace on the regiment.

The Representatives of the United American States have lately transmitted me a resolution deprecating, in the most pointed terms, the abuses of like kind committed to the northward, and have ordered every military offender to be brought to justice. You will, I doubt not, exert your best endeavours to convict the delinquents, and to wipe away that stain which now sullies the whole corps. I beg you will attend here yourself, and bring with you the orders I sent you previous to your leaving Albany. I have a sufficiency of officers here to hold a general court-martial.[17]

The trial was quickly arranged to take place in about a week's time. In the interim, they needed another witness. Following the Sunday evening tattoo, on July 28, Lieutenant Elmer was ordered by Colonel Dayton to pursue Pvt. Jonathan Moore "with all speed." He had been sent off to Fort Schuyler by Lieutenant McDonald, supposedly with in-

---

15. Col. Elias Dayton to Maj. Gen. Philip Schuyler, August 15, 1776, Force, *American Archives*, 5th Series, 1:1033-1034.

16. Elmer, *Journal*, 2 (1846):127, regimental orders June 17, 1776.

17. Maj. Gen. Philip Schuyler to Col. Elias Dayton, July 22, 1776, Force, *American Archives*, 5th Series, 1:511.

structions from McDonald to Captains Thomas Patterson and John Ross. Catching up to Moore, Elmer found no papers, but brought him back the next day. Stopping by General Schuyler's location on the way, Elmer informed the general what had occurred. Schuyler questioned Moore on it and other matters. At the conclusion, he ordered Moore arrested and confined to quarters pending trial.[18]

Per the orders of Major General Schuyler, a court martial board sat on Tuesday, July 30. It consisted of thirteen officers, from within and without the regiment, including Lieutenant Elmer and Captain Bloomfield, and was presided over by a fourteenth, Col. Cornelius Van Dyck of the New York militia. This board issued the following charges, but pushed any other action to the next morning:

> Lieut. McDonald, of Col. Dayton's battallion, arrested for behaving unbecoming the character of a gentleman and officer, in taking, or assisting in taking, things from Johnson Hall, the property of Sir John Johnson or other persons unknown, for aiding and abetting others so to do, for concealing things so taken, and for disobedience of orders, is to be tried.[19]

When reconvened, a series of witnesses presented a very strong case that brought about Lieutenant McDonald's conviction. He had smuggled out of the Hall both a dressed beaver skin and an otter skin, a barrel full of unnamed items, a bow with two arrows, one or more canes, and some alcohol. He had apparently hidden the items in various places in the Johnstown area and had willing and unwilling accomplices assist in the cover-up. He did return most of the items, but he seemed attached to a particular cane. Several witnesses described that McDonald explained to them that the cane was lost, sent to his father, or sent to a friend in Albany.

The second charge of disobedience of orders, though true, was a bit excessive. Everyone involved with the theft was guilty of violating General Schuyler's expressed orders "to be careful not to molest or injure the property of the inhabitants" and to "hold the property of individuals inviolable." However, McDonald's downfall was not returning all the items he had taken when the participants were given a second chance and even a third chance to do so.[20]

---

18. Elmer, *Journal,* 2 (1847):165, July 28, 1776.
19. Elmer, *Journal,* 2 (1847):166-167, July 30, 1776.
20. Elmer, *Journal,* 2 (1847):167-170, copy of the General Court Martial of 2nd Lt. William McDonald. President Van Dyck was a former company commander in the 2nd New York in 1775. He was to be appointed second in command of the new establishment of the 1st New York in November 1776, a position he would hold for the duration of the war.

The Court, after reciting the charge and evidences, made the following report to General Schuyler:

> Whereupon the Court after the most serious & mature deliberation, were unanimously of Opinion that Mr. William McDonald is guilty of the whole Charge exhibited against him & consequently guilty of a breach of the 27th. article for the Government of the Continental Troops as also of the second & last Article of the Amendment (that part of the Charge of the 2d. article expressed by the Term *Fraud* being only excepted); & therefore this Court do Sentence the said Wm. McDonald to suffer the Penalties thereunto annexed.[21]

General Schuyler's general orders were read in the presence of Lieutenant McDonald at roll-call approving of the sentence of the court-martial. After reciting the above articles the following conclusion was added:

> The General therefore by Virtue of the said sentence & the said Articles of War hereby discharges the said Wm. McDonald from the Continental Service, as a person unfit for further service as an officer & Orders that any Pay due to him be detained.
>
> The General with great satisfaction observes from the Proceedings of the Court-Martial that the Gentlemen haveing conducted themselves with a regularity that reflects Credit on them, & haveing no further Business for them dissolves the Court & they are dissolved accordingly.[22]

Since nearly all the stolen items had been recovered, it looked like the regiment could put the break-in quickly behind it. Even the most neutral of observers would conclude that the trial was a classic attempt to whitewash the entire matter and make Lieutenant McDonald the scapegoat. One would hope this was not the case, but it was exactly what they were doing. A letter from Major General Schuyler to Com-

21. Ibid. Lender & Martin, *Citizen Soldier*, 93-94, August 1, 1776. Both Elmer and Bloomfield were members of the court martial board. Elmer's journal included a copy of the entire proceedings. It stated that McDonald breached the 47th article, where Bloomfield's journal, quoted here, only included the final charges, and cites the 27th article. It is likely that there is a transcription error in Bloomfield's journal. Articles of War, June 30, 1775, Worthington C. Ford, ed., *Journals of the Continental Congress, 1774-1789* (Washington: Government Printing Office, 1905), 2:116,118-119. Article 47 fits McDonald's court-martial perfectly and reads as follows: "Whatsoever commissioned officer shall be convicted before a general court-martial, of behaving in a scandalous, infamous manner, such as is unbecoming the character of an officer and a gentleman, shall be discharged from the service."
22. Ibid.

mander-in-Chief George Washington, dated August 18, sought his advice on whether to "bury the affair" or not:

> Soon after Colonel Dayton's regiment marched to Johnson-Hall, some of the officers broke open the doors and carried away a very considerable quantity of effects, contrary to mine and Colonel Dayton's orders. Soon after my arrival at the German-Flats, I was informed of this by some of the officers, who wished an inquiry, that the innocent might not share the scandal with the guilty. I ordered a Court-Martial on Lieutenant McDonald, witnesses with respect to his conduct being on the spot. He was tried and broke. In the course of his trial it appeared that a number of others were concerned; and I ordered Lieutenant-Colonel White and Captains Ross and Patterson down from Fort Stanwix. The two Captains delivered me the paper No.1, in answer to which I advised them candidly to narrate the whole transaction. No.2 is their narrative; and No.3 contains an account of what they took; No.4, with the paper enclosed in it, is what Colonel White delivered me. As I was apprehensive that a publick conviction of so many officers would reflect too much disgrace on our troops, I chose to defer any further proceedings until I should advise with your Excellency. Permit me, therefore, to entreat your opinion, whether it will be prudent for me to accept of the concessions they offer to make at the head of the regiment, and thus to bury the affair, or whether I ought to have them tried. Please to return the papers above alluded to, as I have not time to make copies of them.[23]

The four documents referenced by Schuyler were not included with the letter, so it seems safe to conclude they were returned to him by Washington, as requested. The following reply does not include them either, so the documents may be with either Schuyler's or Washington's original papers. If they were ever found, they would add much to this narrative.

Meanwhile, General Washington's reply is most interesting as he dances around the question a bit and wisely throws it back to General Schuyler to let a court-martial decide:

> I wish you had proceeded as your own judgment and inclination led in the case referred to me for my advice, respecting Colonel Dayton's officers. I am sorry that persons of their rank and of their connexions should have given in to such dishonourable and disgraceful practices;

23. Maj. Gen. Philip Schuyler to Gen. George Washington, August 18, 1776, Force, *American Archives*, 5th Series, 1:1031-1033.

and I feel myself much concerned for themselves and friends. But as the matter is with me to determine; as their making concessions at the head of the regiment would not answer any purpose but that of rendering them objects of ridicule and contempt; as they could never after claim and support that authority over their inferiors that is necessary to good government and discipline; as publick justice and a regard to our military character require that matters of such a nature should meet every possible discouragement; as my conduct might otherwise be deemed reprehensible; and to deter others from the like conduct, which is but too prevalent, I cannot but advise that the several persons concerned be subjected to the trial of a Court-Martial. If the Court should be of opinion that they ought to be broke and dismissed the service, Colonel Dayton, his Major, and other officers, will recommend such as will be proper persons to fill the vacancies occasioned by their removal.[24]

Since Washington was in favor of the court-martial process, the search for any other suspects and additional witnesses continued.

One such instance occurred on August 19, when a letter arrived, from General Schuyler, ordering Captain Bloomfield to apprehend and secure the 3rd New Jersey's former sutler "for takeing things from Johnson Hall." This was done, so the next day, Bloomfield questioned him and sent him under guard to General Schuyler.[25]

By mid-September 1776, a court of inquiry was held in camp at German Flatts along the Mohawk River. Captain Bloomfield sat as a member of that board:

Engaged on the Court of Inquiry Ordered by Col. Dayton . . . To Inquire by hearing Evidences of the Conduct of Lt. Col. White, Capts. Patterson & Ross touching their plundering Johnson-Hall, which Evidence being taken before the Court was Certifyed & transmitted to Albany to be laid before the Genl. Court Martial ordered for those Gentlemen being tryed.[26]

From this point on, the investigation and trial of Lieutenant Colonel White and Captains Patterson and Ross regarding the plundering was moved to Albany, New York. A series of potential witness were sent

24. George Washington to Philip Schuyler, August 24, 1776, Force, *American Archives,* 5th Series, 1:1142.
25. Lender & Martin, *Citizen Soldier,* 101, August 19 and 20, 1776. During the period, a sutler was, usually, a third party attached to the army, who dispensed alcoholic beverages to the soldiers. Other merchants might sell dry goods, trinkets, etc. to the soldiers.
26. Ibid., 106, September 16–18, 1776.

there. 1st Lt. William Gifford, Ens. Edmund Thomas, and two soldiers were sent on September 24, 1776 "to be examined respecting the embezzlement at Johnson Hall."[27] Maj. Francis Barber and four or five of the regiment's junior officers were sent from Fort Schuyler to Albany on October 5.[28]

This process went on for so long that both Captain Bloomfield and Lieutenant Elmer bluntly expressed frustration in their respective journals. Bloomfield noted that, "It seems if this imprudent plundering of Johnson-Hall will never be settled but that our Regimt. is to be convulsed during their being by this rash Action & not to call it worse." Elmer feared the matter "would not be settled until our regiment is broke up."[29] Neither should have worried, for on November 12, there was a final official resolution.

> Lt. Col. White, Capt. Patterson and Lt Gordon, of Col. Dayton's Regiment, tried by a general Court Martial held at Albany, whereof Col Van Schaick was President, for being concerned in the embezzlement of certain effects belonging to Sir John Johnson, the Court, after due examination, are unanimously of opinion that the charge against the prisoners was malicious and groundless, and therefore acquit them with honor. His Excellency Gen. Washington has approved of the proceedings of this Court Martial, and orders this testimony of his approbation to be inserted in the general orders of the northern army.[30]

Any resolution regarding Captain Ross or how 2nd Lt. William Gordon was brought into the mix is not explained. Allowing for the obvious gaps in documentation and the like, further investigation will be required.

Beyond that, there are two open-ended questions that were never answered by any of the above presented correspondence, orders, or trial transcript. First, all of the Hall's keys had been given by Lady Johnson to Captain Bloomfield, and left on the table for the regiment's field officers, Colonel Dayton, Lt. Colonel White, and Major Barber. Presuming Dayton did not take them, as he was traveling around the area

27. Dayton to Schuyler, September 22, 1776, Force, *American Archives*, 5th Series, 2:859. Last paragraph of this letter begins "24th."
28. Elmer, *Journal*, 3 (1848):32, October 5, 1776. *Lender & Martin, Citizen Soldier*, 109, October 5, 1776.
29. Ibid. The regiment was to serve a year and would break up come the spring of 1777.
30. Elmer, *Journal*, 3 (1848):41, November 12, 1776. Col. Goose Van Schaick commanded his own (un-numbered) Continental battalion at this time, but was soon to be named the commander of the new establishment of the 1st New York Regiment.

a lot, the question remains open on whom of the other two had them at the time the Hall was plundered. Since the thieves used the keys to gain access to the Hall, the holder of those keys had to have been involved or was responsible for someone else gaining access to them.

Secondly, a wrinkle appears on Monday, July 17, when after morning exercise, Lieutenant Elmer explains in his journal that he "was put upon guard and sent over to the Hall, where I staid taking particular care that nothing went amiss . . . ."[31] While there he could see that "something was taken from the Hall, especially the cellar door broken open, and wine taken; and notwithstanding the positive orders of the Colonel, very little was returned. Sad affair!"[32]

No known official report mentions the cellar doors ever being broken open. Therefore, unless Elmer phrased it incorrectly in his journal, the cellar was raided after the night of June 4. Considering the plunderers already had the keys at the time, there appears to be no reason to break those doors open. However, once the Hall was re-secured on June 5, more aggressive action would be required to get to the wine.

In summary, the actions of the 3rd New Jersey officer corps involved in the plundering of Johnson Hall were shameful and a violation of their orders. When given a chance to return the stolen items, few complied without additional prodding. The powers-that-be then found a scapegoat in Lieutenant McDonald, who was too foolhardy to get himself out of the mess by simply returning the items he stole. Luckily for him, despite all the trials and kerfuffle that took place, he got away with the relatively minor punishment of being cashiered from the service, instead of a far more serious one.

Ironically, had the officers waited until the property was "properly confiscated by Congress," they probably could have gutted the entire building and no one would have raised an eyebrow.

31. Elmer, *Journal,* 2 (1847): 127-128, July 17, 1776.
32. Ibid.

The Setauket Raid, December 1777

❀❄ PHILLIP R. GIFFIN ❀❄

On the 1st of December 1777 Colonel Samuel B. Webb noted in his journal, ". . . At Horseneck [Greenwich, Connecticut]. This day my Regiment marched in to this place. An expedition is intended on Long Island . . . . We expect to cross tomorrow evening." [1]

Sgt. Simon Giffin of Webb's Regiment was a busy man that day. At North Castle (today's Armonk, New York) he wrote in his diary, "turned out by gun fire this morning . Got the cartridges I went after and then set out for Rye." Sergeant Giffin had been sent to gather cartridges for his company, Capt. Caleb Bull's Company of Webb's 9th Connecticut Regiment. Fortunately, he had been provided with a horse for the fifteen-mile ride through Westchester County to rejoin his regiment at Rye. There were Tory partisans operating in the area and he was carrying a heavy load, "enough cartridges to complete 50 rounds per man for 53 men," a burden probably weighing some 125 pounds (less if some men already had some cartridges). Did he have a packhorse to carry his load? He doesn't mention one.

Giffin's diary, an unpublished manuscript in possession of the family, provides long-forgotten details about a time, place, and a host of fascinating characters, all neighbors, friends, patriots, soldiers, and writers.[2] He wrote in a personal form of shorthand that is challenging to read; the extracts that appear below are as much translation as transcription. During his seven years in the Continental Army he participated in some

1. Samuel B. Webb, *Correspondence and Journals of Samuel Blachley Webb*, Worthington Chauncey Ford, ed. (New York: Wickersham, 1893), 1:239.
2. Simon Giffin, *The Diary of Quartermaster Sergeant Simon Giffin of Col. Samuel B. Webb's Regiment 1777-1779*. See Also: *Record Book of Quartermaster Sergeant Simon Giffin 1779-1783*. Photocopies and microfilm of the originals are available at the Connecticut State Library and Archives in Hartford (CSLA). Originals are with the family. Special thanks to Robert E. Moser JR. for providing the author with an original photocopy for transcription.

well-known campaigns, but his most revealing insights concern the many smaller actions that only marginally affected the course of the war, but that were every bit as dangerous and demanding as the major events. The Setauket raid is one of those stories.

By 3 pm on December 1 Sergeant Giffin was back in Rye only to discover that his regiment had marched off to Horseneck on the shores of Long Island Sound. He rode off again for the final six miles of his journey, rejoining the regiment at sunset, but his day was not over yet. As the evening shadows lengthened, he made a quick visit to the commissary, gathered three days provisions, and distributed them to the men with instructions to cook everything immediately, as the regiment would be on the road again in the morning. After his long day, Giffin found lodgings on the nearby farm of a Mr. "P. Somers." Was he sleeping in the house or the barn, or a tent in the yard? He doesn't say.

Sergeant Giffin spent the following day, December 2, in camp at Horseneck where he recorded that Privates Josiah Burris and Amos Porter were brought before a regimental formation for punishment. They had been convicted of desertion, a serious offense which usually resulted in a sentence of one hundred lashes or a hanging, but in this case Burris was set free and Porter was "picketed for 19 minutes," a punishment that involved painfully balancing on one bare foot on a blunt peg, or picket.

The next morning, December 3, the regiment departed Horseneck, and marched east along the Connecticut shore through Stamford and on towards Norwalk. General Putnam had planned a three-pronged attack across Long Island Sound against three "lightly defended" British posts.[3] One wing of the attack under General Meigs would attack a Loyalist regiment at Jamaica. A second wing under General Parsons would assault British transports loading wood at "Hockaback" (modern Aquebogue) on Peconic Bay at the eastern end of Long Island. Colonel Webb's raiders were ordered to attack a garrison of Loyalist troops at the village of Setauket on Long Island, near Stony Brook.

Several such raids on Long Island had occurred already that year, each resulting in skirmishing but none in decisive victory for either side. Now, in December 1777, General Washington's spies in Setauket had informed him that the enemy garrison had been reduced in numbers and the depot at Setauket was bulging with supplies. Unfortunately, those same spies failed to notice that the British garrison had recently

---

3. Charles S. Hall, *Life and letters of Samuel Holden Parsons* (Binghamton, NY: Otseningo, 1905), 133-136. See also Richard B. Buell, *Dear liberty: Connecticut's mobilization for the Revolutionary War* (Middletown, CT: Wesleyan, 1980), 132-34.

been reinforced with four swivel guns (light cannons). For this assault on Setauket, General Parsons dispatched a force of some 400 Continentals. Among them would be men from the 9th Connecticut Regiment; both Colonel Webb and Sergeant Giffin recorded details about the events.

According to Giffin, on December 4 Colonel Webb sent a scouting party of thirty or so men across Long Island Sound from Connecticut in whale boats to explore enemy positions around the Setauket Church. The next day he divided his main force into groups, assigning them to two sloops, the *Mifflin* and *Spy,* and the schooner *Schuyler.* Sergeant Giffin was assigned a squad of twelve men plus a corporal and ordered to board the privateer *Spy* tied up in the harbor at Norwalk, Connecticut. The raid across the Sound was to proceed as soon as possible, weather permitting, but the weather didn't cooperate. Giffin described his week:

December 4, 1777 Clear and cold. We lay at Norwalk all day. There was a small ship that went over to Long Island with about 30 or 35 men as a scout in order to make discoveries. Nothing happened remarkable.

December 5: this morning orders came for all the Sergeants to parade before the Colonel; and I was ordered to take command of a guard of 12 men and a Corporal to go on board the Privateer that lay in the harbor at Norwalk.

We marched down as far as I could and haled the *Spy,* for the privateer was called by that name, but they could not hear us. I had to march back to my old quarter again. About sundown the boats came for us then I and the men with me went on board and we was divided into four watches with the men that belonged to the schooner. I was in the third watch. Nothing happened.

December 6: Severe cold weather. Lay in the harbor this day. The ice came down [the Norwalk River] by us rushing fast.

Cold weather, snow, and ice complicated the attack. On the evening of December 7 Captain Riglin of the *Spy* ordered his crew to "make sail" for Long Island. Giffin reported that the pilot, a local expert on sailing conditions in the area, "disappointed us." Was he disappointed because the mission was scrubbed? Or, was it because the pilot gave up too easily? Whatever the explanation, the *Spy* returned to Norwalk harbor that night. The next day was cloudy and the *Spy* remained in the harbor all day and all night. In the morning Giffin walked into town to gather supplies for his men. He rested for the remainder of the day and then "stood his watch" on the ship beginning at midnight. In his notes he reported that the wind was blowing hard all night.

The next day, December 9, the three ships remained in Norwalk harbor during the day, and then about 9 pm they sailed together out into Long Island Sound. The wind was blowing fresh from the northwest and the three ships soon parted ways. At 4 am Captain Riglin of the *Spy* ordered his crew to "take in a double reef" (reduce sail to a minimum) and return to Connecticut. They made harbor and spent the night at Black Rock Point, near Bridgeport. Giffin reported that the three ships had been separated in the storm and it would be several days before he learned of the fate of the other raiding parties.

Foul weather on December 9 wreaked havoc on all three wings of General Parsons' ambitious plan of attack. General Meigs' raiding party departed Sawpits (Port Chester) in whale boats for the twelve-mile trip across the sound to Hempstead Harbor. The whaleboats, each propelled by a single sail and sixteen oarsmen, floundered in the rough seas and gale force winds. They were forced back to Sawpits and the attack on Jamaica was cancelled. General Parsons' fleet of small vessels bound for the eastern end of Long Island was slowed by the storm; by the time they reached Aquebogue all but one of the enemy transports had sailed. Parsons' men captured a coastal merchant ship and a dozen Tory volunteers gathering firewood for the British garrison in New York.

Giffin's party of raiders on the *Spy* spent the 10th of December on shore at Bridgeport, where Private Burris deserted again "and went home to his family." Later that day the *Mifflin* sailed into Bridgeport, reporting that on the night of December 9–10 she had successfully fought through the storm and landed her party of raiders near Setauket before returning. The next day the other two vessels were ordered to sail up the coast of Connecticut to "Seamus Head" (not on modern maps), pick up more raiders, and then make a second attempt at landing men on Long Island.

Meanwhile at Smithtown Bay on the morning of December 10, General Parsons' party of raiders from the *Mifflin* marched off towards the Setauket Meeting House, about four miles away. Their landing did not go unnoticed. Loyalist observers rushed off to Setauket to warn the British garrison of the impending attack. The Loyalist troops were manning the barricades as the Americans approached. For the next several hours the raiders blazed away at the enemy breastworks, the old Church, its stained glass windows, and steeple all lined with enemy marksmen. By noon they were beginning to run out of ammunition and General Parsons was forced to order a retreat. They would spend the rest of the week, December 11 thru 17, avoiding enemy patrols and waiting to be rescued.

According to Sergeant Giffin's notes, General Parsons' headquarters in Connecticut made several attempts to reestablish contact and to ferry reinforcements and supplies to Parsons' men on Long Island. On Friday December 12, 1777, the *Mifflin* and the *Spy* again sailed out into the Sound, carrying reinforcements. At 3 AM Saturday morning the two vessels landed an additional 200 raiders at Smithtown Bay. This second wave moved inland towards Setauket but without Sergeant Giffin and his squad. They had been ordered to stay onboard the *Spy* as a security detail.

That afternoon, December 13, the two vessels returned to the coast of Connecticut, sailing past Old Saybrook and up the Connecticut River to East Haddam where they picked up more reinforcements from the local Colchester and East Haddam Regiment of Col. Henry Champion (the 3rd Connecticut Regiment). That evening the two ships returned to New London where they finally learned of the fate of Colonel Webb and the raiders on the schooner *Schuyler.*

On that stormy night of December 9-10, the *Schuyler* sailed alone, successfully fighting its way through the wind and waves. Then, at dawn as they approached Smithtown Bay, the *Schuyler* was confronted by a British warship, HMS *Falcon*. Colonel Webb later provided a report of his disastrous night to General Washington:[4]

> On Tuesday evening December 9, I embarked on board the armed sloop Schuyler with 3 other vessels and about 400 men for Long Island. The night being dark and blustery we (our ships) parted company. . . . At dawn on Wednesday morning we [on the Schuyler] were off Setauket when we discovered a ship crowding all sail for us, being to leeward we had only one chance to escape . . . grounding our ship on a beach about 200 yards from shore . . . The surf ran so amazingly high that She filled and sank . . . The enemy ship came within a half mile and was pouring in broadsides . . . in this cruel situation we were forced to strike. The British sloop of war Falcon brought us to Newport, Rhode Island . . . .

Giffin's notes reveal that his ship, the *Spy,* made several more attempts that week to return to Long Island to pick up survivors. It would be the 17th of December, however, before they made contact with Parsons and were able to evacuate the scattered remnants of his raiders.

Sabbath December 14, 1777 [we] sailed from New London in order to go to Long Island but the wind blew hard and a heavy sea going and we were obliged to put back again to New London . . . [Later] we were called up to sail for Long Island about 3 o'clock at night.

4. Webb, *Correspondence,* 1:410-412.

Monday December 15, 1777 we sailed for Long Island the wind blowing fresh. We came to anchor at Oyster Pond [near Montauk Point?] where we sent an express to General Parsons to see whether we were to wait for the troops or not as they were not here.

Tuesday December 16, 1777 we lay in Oyster Pond harbor waiting for the troops but they did not come as we expected to have them. Nothing more remarkable happened.

Wednesday December 17, 1777 this morning some of the troops came down and embarked on board the vessels that lay waiting. And, got the General on board and set sail for the lee breezes were brisk about 12 o'clock in the fore [noon]. [We] landed all the men and lay at Saybrook all the remainder of the day until night. It rained all night.

Webb's raid on Setauket was a disaster for the army and for the Connecticut River communities around Wethersfield, home to the men of Colonel Webb's Regiment. Among those captured were Colonel Webb, army Capt. Edward Bulkley, sea captain John Riley of the *Schuyler*, and some sixty-five enlisted men. Their families must have been devastated by the loss at one time of so many local men.

Following the calamity on Long Island, the balance of Webb's Regiment gathered at New London, Connecticut. On December 22 they received orders to return home for winter leave. It would be their first visit with their families in seven months. They were among the fortunate ones who would be spending a month at home rather than with the Grand Army at Valley Forge.

Lafayette—An Acerbic Tongue or an Incisive Judge of Character?

❦ GENE PROCKNOW ❦

A truly French and American hero, Marquis de Lafayette, a nineteen-year-old nobleman without significant military or political experience, joined the fledgling American Revolution at a low point. Among the plethora of French officers seeking a Continental Army commission, the young Marquis distinguished himself by volunteering to serve without commission and compensation. Worldly beyond his years, Lafayette rapidly sized up the Patriot situation and successfully navigated the complex politics of the Continental Congress and the Patriot officer corps. He quickly earned the respect of Washington and other senior Continental Army generals as a trustworthy subordinate and a loyal team player. Further, Lafayette facilitated vital French economic and military support for the Revolution.

In a cheeky assessment of Lafayette's maturation, character and judgment, Sarah Vowell observed in her recent book: "It's worth noting right from the start, America brought out the best in Lafayette, as if he had vomited up his adolescent petulance somewhere in the middle of the Atlantic and had come ashore a new and wiser self."[1]

The decision to come to America and the trans-Atlantic voyage might well have been transformative for Lafayette; however, it did not a completely mature his character and judgment. Although he incisively judged most people, from time to time he offered poorly nuanced, ill-informed perspectives, which were inconsistent with his overall character. As with any developing leader, life's lessons provided valuable leadership education and matured his wisdom.

Starting at the top and with his positive character assessments, Lafayette formed a close, effective and almost fatherly relationship with

1. Sarah Vowell, *Lafayette in the Somewhat United States* (New York: Riverhead Books, 2015), 85.

Washington, who he portrayed as: "my friend, my intimate friend, and since I like to choose my friends, I dare say that to give him that title is to praise him."[2]

In addition to Washington, Lafayette forged strong bonds with many fellow officers in the Continental Army. He especially held positive opinions of generals highly regarded by Washington, those who Lafayette served under and those who were intensely loyal to Washington with no designs on replacing him. Maj. Gen. Nathanael Greene is an example of a general highly valued by Washington. Lafayette offered this complimentary assessment of Greene: "it will be General Greene, our most senior officer after Gates and Heath, who really has talent and exceptional judgment."[3] An example of Lafayette's judgment of a general, under which he served, is Maj. Gen. John Sullivan. On being assigned to Sullivan's command, Lafayette expressed, "I both love and esteem you, therefore the moment we'll fight together will be extremely pleasant and agreeable to me."[4] An example of a general who was intensely loyal and no threat to Washington is Maj. Gen. William Heath. Lafayette concluded in a letter to Heath, ". . . one that looks upon you as an intimate friend. . . ."[5] Loyalty to Washington greatly influenced Lafayette's character judgment in all three cases.

As might be expected from someone his age, Lafayette did not always form opinions of people with sufficient understanding of the situation. A recent biographer noted that he was overly impulsive.[6] This impulsiveness led to Lafayette not being afraid to bluntly speak his mind about his fellow officers, offering biting criticism of their actual and perceived command failures. Some of these strong opinions suffered from not knowing all the facts and were politically naïve. From time to time, he offered uncharitable judgments not becoming a mature leader.

Perhaps the best example of Lafayette forming and expressing strong opinions too quickly and without the nuance of perspective is his assessment of Samuel and John Adams. Stridently in his memoirs of 1779, Lafayette questioned their competence by observing that the Adams' "were rigid republicans but more capable of destroying than preserving

2. Marie Joseph Paul Yves Roch Gilbert Du Motier Lafayette, Stanley J. Idzerda, and Marie Joseph Paul Yves Roch Gilbert Du Motier Lafayette, *Lafayette in the Age of the American Revolution: Selected Letters and Papers, 1776-1790* (Ithaca, N.Y: Cornell University Press, 1977), 1:130.
3. Ibid., 2:202.
4. Ibid., 2:111.
5. Ibid., 3:53.
6. J.T. Headley, *Washington and His Generals* (New York: A. L. Burt Company, n.d.), 449.

the republic."[7] While many people have characterized John Adams as rigid and Samuel a firebrand, this hyperbolic overstatement may have resulted from Lafayette's unquestioned, protective support of Washington during political disagreements with the Adams'. Late in the war, Lafayette changes his opinion of John Adams. In a fawning congratulatory letter to Adams for inking the 1782 Dutch Treaty of Amity and Commerce, Lafayette concluded, "Your long Professed friend and Admirer."[8] The change of heart is consistent with an emerging leader who, when learning more about someone, will alter his opinion as a result. Also, Lafayette changed his view after Adams was no longer a threat to Washington's leadership.

An illustrative example of Lafayette forming opinions without understanding all the facts is his assessment of the military command capabilities of Maj. Gen. Israel Putnam. Lafayette concludes that in the October 1777 Hudson Highlands battles, the British ". . . were hardly bothered by old Putnam, the man who, when the troubles first began, had left his plow and given the army more zeal than talent."[9] In a second letter, Lafayette stated: "I am told general putnam is recalled, and goodell (good deal) is expected on that part—but your excellency knows better than I do what could be convenient; therfore I do'nt want to mind those things myself."[10]

Clearly, Lafayette had little confidence in Putnam and advocated relieving him of command. A more dispassionate and informed view concludes that Putnam was held in high regard by his officers and soldiers, was especially important for new recruits and political support from Connecticut, and acquitted himself courageously on the battlefield. In all three battles in which he commanded, Putnam faced vastly superior British forces supported by uncontested naval superiority. In the Hudson Highlands campaigns referenced by Lafayette, Putnam had only a small force to cover multiple strategic points and the British firmly controlled the Hudson River. Being massively outnumbered by superior

7. Lafayette et al., *Lafayette in the Age of the American Revolution*, 1:171.
8. The Marquis de Lafayette to John Adams, May 7, 1782, *Founders Online*, National Archives, founders.archives.gov/documents/Adams/06-13-02-0009 (Original source: *The Adams Papers*, Papers of John Adams, vol. 13, *May–October 1782*, ed. Gregg L. Lint, C. James Taylor, Margaret A. Hogan, Jessie May Rodrique, Mary T. Claffey, and Hobson Woodward. Cambridge, MA: Harvard University Press, 2006, 12–14).
9. Lafayette et al., *Lafayette in the Age of the American Revolution*, 1:99.
10. Lafayette to George Washington, February 23, 1778," *Founders Online*, National Archives, founders.archives.gov/documents/Washington/03-13-02-0552 (Original source: *The Papers of George Washington*, Revolutionary War Series, vol. 13, *26 December 1777–28 February 1778*, ed. Edward G. Lengel. Charlottesville: University of Virginia Press, 2003, 648–650).

mobile forces that could move more rapidly using the river, Putnam preserved his command to fight another day. Never having superior military forces, Putnam "rose to the occasion" to competently serve his country and was not as incompetent as Lafayette portrayed.[11]

Lafayette's assessment of the French volunteer Philippe Charles Tronson Du Coudray, an expertly trained artillery and engineering officer, is a good example of Lafayette's ability to discern character while adding an impolitic and unseemly barb. Of Du Coudray's character Lafayette opined, "A cleaver but imprudent man, a good officer, but vain to the point of folly."[12] Most senior Continental Army contemporaries would concur with the description of Du Coudray's vanity, but with an absence of taste Lafayette added a less than charitable comment not found in the writings of more mature leaders: ". . . M. Du Coudray was drowned in the Schuylkill, and the loss of that troublemaker was perhaps a fortunate accident."[13] Du Coudray gave his life for the Patriot cause and in respect, Congressional leaders offered one of only four Catholic masses in which the Continental Congress participated for his funeral.

Less acerbic, but still biting, was Lafayette's assessment of Maj. Gen. Lord Stirling's (William Alexander) judgment. Lafayette praised "brave Stirling" for his performance during the battle of Monmouth.[14] However two years earlier, Lafayette called into question Lord Stirling's battlefield judgment by remarking that Lord Stirling ". . . was more courageous than judicious."[15] This is another example of Lafayette changing his mind about a Patriot's capabilities.

Lafayette offered even more pointed comments about Maj. Gen. Charles Lee, a highly experienced though quirky former British Army officer with numerous pre-Revolution combat commands. Lafayette wrote in his memoirs on Lee:

His features were coarse, his personality was caustic, his heart ambitious and avaricious, his character inconsistent and his whole appearance was entirely peculiar.[16]

Many fellow officers also did not hold Lee in high personal regard, but they followed his orders and respected his military experience.

11. Eugene Procknow, "General Israel Putnam: Reputation Revisited," *Journal of the American Revolution*, August 11, 2016, https://allthingsliberty.com/2016/08/general-israel-putnam-reputation-revisited/.
12. Lafayette et al., *Lafayette in the Age of the American Revolution*, 1:11.
13. Ibid., 1:12.
14. Ibid., 2:11.
15. Ibid., 1:91.
16. Ibid., 2:9.

Lafayette did recognize Lee for making at least one good military decision but denigrated him in the same sentence.

He hated the general [Washington] and loved no one but himself, but in 1776 his advice had saved the general [Washington] and the remnants of the army.[17]

The 1778 Battle of Monmouth provided a major turning point for Lafayette's opinion of Lee. Hours before the battle, Washington replaced Lafayette with Lee as the commander of the Rebel advance guard. In the initial engagement with the British at Monmouth Courthouse, Lee's forces inexplicably retreated from the attacking British. Famously, Washington, accompanied by Lafayette, came upon the retreating Lee, relieved him on the spot, and rallied the Patriot forces. As a result of the battle, Lee lost the confidence of his fellow officers and his loyalty first came into question due to the seemingly unexplained retreat. Lafayette echoed the sentiments of many other Continental Army officers by stating that Lee's "first action would have been to sell out his friends and the whole American cause."[18] Again to protect Washington, Lafayette harshly criticized Lee.

However, Lafayette went much further than most contemporaries and uncharitably concluded on Lee, "He was later suspended by a court martial, he left the service, and he was not missed."[19] While not providing a complete vindication of Charles Lee's traitorous actions, but at odds with Lafayette's views, two recent biographers offer a more balanced assessment of Lee's contributions. They concluded that Lee's Monmouth battlefield performance was appropriate and that only with the additional Continental forces from Washington's main army did the Patriots have sufficient forces to occupy defensible terrain and engage the British. Lee's biographers posit that Washington may have overreacted due to Lee's previous insubordinate actions. Unwaveringly and vociferously, Lafayette supported Washington's decision.[20]

Further, Lafayette overstated his negative appraisals of officers who had pre-Revolution political disagreements with Washington. For example, he characterized Maj. Gen. Adam Stephen "as always drunk."[21] Certainly, Stephens was cashiered from the Continental Army after the Battle of Germantown for a critical and deadly friendly fire incident

---

17. Ibid. 2.
18. Ibid., 1:172.
19. Ibid., 2:11.
20. Phillip Papas, *Renegade Revolutionary: The Life of General Charles Lee* (New York: New York University Press, 2014); Dominick A Mazzagetti, *Charles Lee: Self before Country*, 2013, public.eblib.com/choice/publicfullrecord.aspx?p=1562499.
21. Lafayette et al., *Lafayette in the Age of the American Revolution*, 1:91.

under his command and for being intoxicated on too many occasions. However, it is not likely that Stephen was always drunk, and other factors besides the extent of Stephen's drinking impacted Lafayette's judgment. What is less known, is the pre-Revolutionary relationship between Washington and Stephen who were initially friends serving together in the French and Indian War. During the inter-war period, Stephen ran against Washington for a seat in the House of Burgesses that caused a subsequent, permanent personal rift between them. Improbable for someone "always drunk," Stephen after the Revolution engaged in a long, productive business career including the founding of Martinsburg, West Virginia. In 1788, Stephen attended the Virginia Continental Convention and persuasively argued for the adoption of the United States Constitution. A more mature leader might have criticized Stephen for the friendly fire incident and not focused on the intoxication with was endemic throughout the officer corps. This is especially true as Lafayette directly assumed responsibility for Stephen's division. Denigrating a previous leader appears unprofessional, especially one who ably commanded in previous battles and who became an accomplished civic and business leader despite being Washington's political antagonist.

Lafayette reserved his severest criticisms for those who conspired or were thought to have conspired to replace Washington as supreme commander. In a letter to Washington, Lafayette labeled the alleged eponymous leader of the famous cabal, and his fellow French Army officer, Maj. Gen. Thomas Conway "an ambitious and dangerous man."[22] Lafayette made his personal dislike of Conway widely known. Henry Laurens, the President of Congress, related to a fellow South Carolinian that Lafayette viewed Conway with the "utmost abhorrence."[23] Other officers including Knox, Greene and Lord Stirling also took a dim view of Conway, concurring with Lafayette that Conway was dangerous to Washington. But in a letter to the Continental Congress, Lafayette went much further by derisively referring to Conway's military abilities, stating: "I don't include St. Augustine because Gen. Conway will take it with fifteen hundred men coming from Mr. De Borre's country."[24]

Lafayette was referring to Conway's proposal to Congress to invade East Florida and capture the highly defended citadel at St. Augustine with an obviously undermanned force recruited from Europe. Sarcasti-

22. Ibid., 1:205.
23. Henry Laurens to Isaac Motte, January 26, 1780, Henry Laurens et al., *The Papers of Henry Laurens. Vol. 12: Nov. 1, 1777 - March 15, 1778*, 1. ed (Columbia, S.C: Univ. of South Carolina Press, 1990).
24. Lafayette et al., *Lafayette in the Age of the American Revolution*, 1:259.

cally, Lafayette cast doubt on Conway's judgment and military leadership by coy inferences of Conway overstating his military abilities.

Further, a suspicious Lafayette wrote to Washington that he was concerned that Conway would be named over Lafayette to take command of the proposed 1778 invasion of Canada. With a hint of ethnic elitism, Lafayette wrote to Washington about the potential for Conway to lead the attack:

> . . . there are some projects to send Connway to Canada—they will laugh in france when they'l hear that he is choosen upon such a commission out of the same army where I am, principally as he is an irishman, and when the project schould be to show to the frenchmen of that country a man of theyr nation who by his rank in france could inspire them with some confidence.[25]

Continuing with boyish sarcasm, Lafayette further denigrated Conway's military capabilities and character in another letter to Washington: "I fancy Mister düer will be with Mister Cannway [Conway] sooner than he had told me—they'l perhaps conquer canada before my arrival, and I expect to meet them at the governor's house in quebec."[26]

Eventually Lafayette was named to lead the planned Canadian invasion, but the invasion was abandoned due to the lack of personnel, supplies and funding. In France after the war, Lafayette's criticisms of Conway caused a scandal as Conway whispered to well-placed sources in French society that Lafayette in America ruined him with innuendo and slander.[27]

Lafayette also expressed an abrasive opinion of another officer rumored to be part of the Conway Cabal. While only rumored to be the cabal's choice for supreme leadership, Maj. Gen. Horatio Gates certainly had long standing personal designs on replacing Washington as Commander in Chief. On Gates, Lafayette opined;

25. Lafayette to Washington, January 20, 1778," *Founders Online,* National Archives, founders.archives.gov/documents/Washington/03-13-02-0251 (Original source: *The Papers of George Washington,* 13:291–292).
26. Lafayette to Washington, February 8, 1778, *Founders Online,* National Archives, founders.archives.gov/documents/Washington/03-13-02-0407 (Original source: *The Papers of George Washington,* 13:488–489).
27. Lafayette to Washington, March 9, 1784," *Founders Online,* National Archives, founders.archives.gov/documents/Washington/04-01-02-0143 (Original source: *The Papers of George Washington,* Confederation Series, vol. 1, *1 January 1784–17 July 1784,* ed. W. W. Abbot. Charlottesville: University Press of Virginia, 1992, 184–189).

He was a good officer, but he had neither the talent, the intelligence, nor the willpower necessary for supreme command. He would have been crushed by the burden.[28]

Clearly ambitious, but a major contributor, Washington assigned Gates to important command positions throughout the war. His victory at Saratoga paved the way for the vital French alliance and he was the only Patriot general to command five military departments.[29] Although his rout at the Battle of Camden and his likely participation in the Newburgh conspiracies were stains on his record, a more mature leader like Washington realized that he could employ Gates to aid in the successful outcome of the rebellion.

On most every account, Lafayette was a brilliant and gifted leader who succeeded despite his young age and lack of prior military experience. Lafayette accomplished so much. But like any young leader, from time to time he lacked tact, formed opinions too quickly without sufficient information, and overstated his characterizations. In several instances, he issued some excessively strident and biting character assessments. Clearly Lafayette saved his greatest vitriol for those generals who were threats to Washington's leadership. These flaws don't make Lafayette a lesser hero; examining them merely serves to better understand his nature and his maturation into a legendary leader on two continents.

In the end, those who succeed write history. To Lafayette's credit, Continental Army officers in their memoirs concurred with many aspects of his perspectives and character assessments. However, Lafayette would want to be remembered for his ability to accurately assess a person's character, not for his acerbic, sarcastic comments reveling in a comrade's death nor for dismissing a staunch Patriot as a teetering old man.

28. Lafayette et al., *Lafayette in the Age of the American Revolution*, 1:171.
29. Canada, Eastern, Northern, Hudson Highlands and Southern Departments.

William Bingham—Forgotten Supplier of the American Revolution

RICHARD WERTHER

William Bingham. Does the name sound familiar to you? Some readers will recognize it. For many others, it may be a name they have either never encountered or may vaguely recall from a footnote someplace. In this era of "Founders Chic"[1] where it seems everything remotely connected to the founding has been covered ad infinitum, Bingham remains remarkably obscure. The last biography of him (and the only one I could find) was published in 1969.[2]

Yet Bingham played a pivotal role in the success of the Revolution at a young age and more than merely rubbed elbows with the key figures of the Revolution and later the founding era. He had a record of achievement that is worth recalling.

William Bingham was born April 8, 1752, in Philadelphia. He was enrolled in the College of Philadelphia (now the University of Pennsylvania) at age 6(!),[3] started there in 1765, and graduated cum laude in 1768. Following the death of his father in 1769, he resumed his education there and earned a Master of Arts degree in 1771. He initially developed his business acumen managing his father's business interests in the Caribbean, and in 1770 at the age of 18 (living in America but still a British colonial subject), he was named British consul to Martinique. In early 1773, he travelled to Europe, furthering his business connections and experience.[4] He returned to Philadelphia to find a city and country

1. Michael D. Hattem, "The Historiography of the American Revolution", *Journal of the American Revolution*, August 27, 2013, accessed April 20, 2017, allthingsliberty.com/2013/08/historiography-of-american-revolution/.
2. Robert C. Alberts, *The Golden Voyage: The Life and Times of William Bingham* (Boston, Houghton Mifflin Company: 1969).
3. Ibid., 12.
4. Pennsylvania State Senate webpage biography, accessed April 24, 2017, www.legis.state.pa.us/cfdocs/legis/BiosHistory/MemBio.cfm?ID=5072&body=S.

embroiled in conflict with the British. The fever was stoked as the blows came one after the other—the Stamp Act, the Boston Massacre, the Boston Tea Party, the resulting Boston Port Bill, and eventually Lexington and Concord.

These events led to the convening of the First Continental Congress in Philadelphia in September 1774 and, shortly after the Lexington and Concord news rocked the city, the Second Continental Congress in 1775. In November of that year, the Congress formed the committee from which Bingham was to take his direction, the Committee of Secret Correspondence (later to become the Committee for Foreign Affairs). The Committee was chaired by Benjamin Franklin, with other members being John Jay, John Dickinson, Thomas Johnson, Benjamin Harrison, and soon thereafter banker Robert Morris.[5]

The Committee had authority to retain agents to engage in its mission, which was to supply the military and recruit foreign allies, particularly the French. It appointed Silas Deane as its agent in France (posing as a merchant) in March 1776. Soon thereafter, Bingham was assigned a similar role, his based on the French island of Martinique (often referred to in correspondence as "Martinico"). Bingham's previous experience in Europe and as British consul to Martinique, a position he resigned when the Revolution broke out, made him an ideal choice for the assignment. He set sail to the Caribbean aboard the sloop *Reprisal* (the vessel originally assigned, the *Hornet*, proving unseaworthy) on July 3, 1776, the day before independence was declared.

As with Deane, Bingham would have a dual role, acting as an agent for the Committee to promote American interests but doing it under the cover of a merchant transacting personal business. This mixing of personal and public business was not without controversy, and in fact Bingham, besides performing key duties for his country, did return to Philadelphia a rich man. On the other hand, there were many times Bingham would have to spend personal funds or borrow against not yet existing loans that Franklin and others were desperately trying to obtain in Europe to assist the cash-depleted United States. In turn, the fledgling country and army would also receive huge benefits from his activities in the form of arms and supplies. The instructions given to the twenty-four-year-old Bingham by the Committee can be summarized as follows:

1. To secure military supplies: They began: "You are earnestly to en-

5. Secret Committee of Correspondence/Committee for Foreign Affairs, 1775–1777, U.S. Department of State, Office of the Historian website, accessed April 20, 2017, history.state.gov/milestones/1776-1783/secret-committee.

deavor to procure from him (the French governor there) Ten Thousand good Musquets," but this was only the start—much more was needed.

2. To encourage privateering against British targets, particularly to obtain the aforementioned military supplies, but also to stir up animosity between the French and British in the vicinity. He came armed with a fistful of blank privateering commissions.

3. To pass intelligence findings to and from both the Committee and Deane in France.

4. To cultivate a strong relationship with the French and get them to do as much as they could, within the bounds of their official stance of neutrality, to help the Americans:

> You are to continue at Martinico untill we recall you and are to cultivate an intimate and friendly Correspondence with the General and other Persons of Distinction there, that you may be enabled to procure all the usefull Intelligence you can . . . you will take proper opportunities of sounding the Genl., and learn from him whether he could admit Prizes made by our Cruizers to be sent in and protected there until proper Opportunities offered for bringing them to the Continent.[6]

Bingham's arrival in Martinique proved auspicious. The *Reprisal* reached the Port of St. Pierre late Saturday afternoon on July 27, only to find the British sloop *Shark* stationed in the harbor. It was there to register a complaint with the French command. *Reprisal* captain Lambert Wickes decided to engage, even though shorthanded due to crew sent away with three prizes captured en route. Before going into battle, Wickes ensured his prized cargo, Bingham, was rowed safely to shore. The ensuing battle was eventually ended by the firing of French shore batteries on the *Shark*, causing it to flee to open waters. As Bingham reported:

> I was a Spectator of the whole of it from on shore. And to the honor of America, the Reprisal damaged the Shark so much, that She was forced to sheer off in order to refit, when the Fort fired upon her & put an End to the Engagement. Never did I feel the Sensation of Joy in a more lively Degree, than upon viewing the different Treatment which the two Commanders met with from the Inhabitants of St Pierre; Capt [Lambert] Wickes was complimented & caressed be-

6. The Committee of Secret Correspondence: Instructions to William Bingham, June 3, 1776, U. S. National Archives, The Founders Online, accessed April 20, 2017, founders.archives.gov/?q=william%20bingham%20Recipient%3A%22Bingham%2C%2 0William%22%20Author%3A%22Committee%20of%20Secret%20Correspondence%22 &s=1111311112&r=1.

yond measure, whereas Capt [John] Chapman was under the necessity of procuring a Guard of Six Men to protect him from the Insults
of the Mob.[7]

This early support from the French boded well for the future. Now
that Bingham was safely ensconced in Martinique came the hard part—
delivering on his assigned tasks.

In letters to the Committee, Bingham laid out what he thought was
the best method of conducting goods from Europe to America, which
was transshipment through the West Indies with the last leg being carried to the mainland by French vessels. In a letter from Willing, Morris
& Co., they agreed with Bingham's approach; however, they expressed
concern as to the funding difficulties that would plague not only Bingham's mission but the entire war effort:

> The observations you make on the different modes of Conducting a
> Commerce between Europe & this Continent through the Islands
> of Martinico & St Lucia are very proper, they are what have fre-
> quently occurred to us, but do not remove the only difficulty we have
> to encounter, which is the establishing proper Funds in Europe as a
> foundation to Trade on.[8]

He would end up using credit that was predicated on loans from
France, Spain and other European countries, which were only hoped
for at the time, coming through. He made frequent draws against
Franklin, who was in Paris.

The French were more than predisposed to participate in activities
against their ancient enemy, making Bingham's job of establishing a
strong relationship with the governor there, comte Robert D'Argout,
much easier. Indications from the Shark encounter were positive, with
D'Argout stating, "If the American cruisers should bring prizes into our
ports, we will not prevent their selling or disposing of them as they
should think proper." The commander of the *Shark* was ordered to
never again "engage battle in our roads or under our forts . . . an act of
hostility which I will never tolerate . . . I again assure you, Sir, of my
entire neutrality in this affair."[9]

7. William Bingham to Silas Deane, August 5, 1776, in William Bell Clark, et al., eds,
Naval Documents of the American Revolution, 12 Volumes (Washington, DC: The Naval
History and Heritage Command, 1964-2013), 6:77, accessed April 20, 2017, www.his-
tory.navy.mil/content/dam/nhhc/research/publications/naval-documents-of-the-
american-revolution/NDARVolume6.pdf.
8. Willing, Morris & Co. to Bingham, Martinique, September 14, 1776, in *Naval Documents*, 6:824, accessed April 20, 2017.
9. Alberts, *The Golden Voyage*, 29-30.

Bingham's fleet of privateers undertook further activities against the British, with French support in sheltering prizes in their harbors and helping escort supply ships and captured vessels to American ports. Per one British intelligence report:

> Property belonging to Philadelphia upon going out of the Bay saluted a Sloop of War then lying there who instantly returned the Salute. This happened about the 1st of May. Mr Bingham a Native of Philadelphia has for some time been there, the professed and pub-lick Agent of the Congress and resides publickly at No 252 Rue du Petit Versailles, from whence he deals out Commissions against the English to all such as apply for them. He had access whenever he pleased to Comte D'Argout & was upon the best terms with him.[10]

Also funneled through Martinique (some went directly to American ports) were the supplies received from a certain Roderique Hortalez & Co. in France. This was the cover name for the operation run by the French playwright and polymath Pierre Augustin Caron de Beaumar-chais, author of *The Barber of Seville*. Bingham worked with Franklin and Deane in France to help arrange routing these supplies.

The Bingham-sponsored privateering activities brought many British protests, indicating how successful he was at egging on these two long-time foes. A letter from Thomas Shirley, British Colonial Governor in the Bahamas, provides one example from what became a steady stream of complaints. Addressing D'Argout, it stated:

> It is with concern Sir that I am obliged to take this oppertunity to acquaint your Excellency that I am informed . . . that Vessells are fit-ted out Armed and Commissioned from the Port of St Pierre's in Order to make Piratical Depradations upon the Coasts of this Island; This I am told is done by one of His Britannick Majesty's Rebellious Subjects now residing at St Pierre's in the Character of an Agent (here he refers to Bingham) . . . from a Number of my Masters Re-bellious Subjects in America who Stile themselves the Congress; This proceeding . . . is matter of great concern and Alarm to His Majesty's Loyal Subjects here, looking upon this Piratical kind of War never made use of even at times when there was an open Rupture between the Two Nations, which is by no means the Case at present.[11]

10. Intelligence Regarding Martinique Received From Arthur Piggott, in *Naval Docu-ments*, 9:460, accessed April 20, 2017.
11. Governor Thomas Shirley to Count D'Argout, January 8, 1777, in William Bell Clark, et al., eds, *Naval Documents*, 7:902, accessed April 18, 2017.

Maybe Bingham was a little too successful in stirring things up, because eventually even the French admitted D'Argout had overstepped his bounds. The Marquis de Bouille arrived in early May 1777 to take his place. He tightened the rules, at least for a time. As Beaumarchais noted in a letter to French Foreign Minister comte de Vergennes:

> I Am very sorry to receive confirmation of the troublesome announcement that the Marquis de Bouille made at Martinique on arriving there. It seems certain that France has conceded to England, the right of stopping and seizing any French vessel, coming from the Islands, which Will be loaded with produce for the mainland - what distress can have induced us to make such an agreement?[12]

With time, Bingham was able to cultivate a close relationship with de Bouille and win back a good measure of the operating freedom he had with D'Argout.[13]

The goal was to edge the French toward outright support of the American cause. This depended heavily on demonstrating success in the war, thus bad news from the States was often soft-pedaled to Bingham and then in turn by him to the French. For example, witness this highly optimistic portrayal of the outcome of the battle of New York:

> They have been ten or twelve weeks with a powerfull Fleet and a [i.e., are] well provided and appointed with every thing necessary and what have they done? They have got possession of three small Islands on the Coast of America, these were hardly disputed with them and yet if every Acre of American teritory is to cost them in the same proportion the Conquest woud ruin all Europe. Our Army are now collected to a point and are strongly entrenched on New York Island and at Kingsbridge, so that in fact Mr. Howe is hemmed in as he was at Boston, except that he has more Elbow Room and a powerfull Fleet commanding an extensive Inland Navigation.[14]

After the war yielded nearly constant setbacks, the American victory at Saratoga tipped the balance, and the French shortly thereafter abandoned all pretense of neutrality. Thanks to the hard work of Franklin and others in Paris, they signed a treaty of alliance with the Americans. Bingham was not informed of the treaty and its contents and, somewhat

---

12. Beaumarchais to Vergennes, July 1, 1777, in *Naval Documents*, 9:451, accessed April 19, 2017.
13. Alberts, *The Golden Voyage*, 70.
14. Committee of Secret Correspondence of The Continental Congress to William Bingham, Martinique, September 21, 1776, January 8, 1777, in *Naval Documents*, 6:938, accessed April 20, 2017.

embarrassingly, had to learn them from de Bouille. After the French officially joined the war, Bingham's role diminished. He was relegated to more administrative tasks, and he asked to return home. He received no response for nineteen months, part of a general blackout on information that was likely due to miscarried correspondence. Still, without an official recall, he nonetheless boarded the *Confederacy* on March 12, 1779, to sail for Philadelphia, armed with a lengthy account of his time in Martinique ("A Clear and Succinct Account of My Agency")[15] and a letter of commendation from de Bouille. The coda to his time in Martinique was in Latin at the end of his account: "*Quod, potui, feci;—facient meliora potentes*": "I've done my best—let abler men do more."[16]

Bingham's postwar life continued his chain of success, though it was to be somewhat abbreviated. In 1779, he returned to Philadelphia a rich man from his private dealings during his stay in Martinique, as well as from inheritance.[17] On the other side of the ledger, he was saddled with debts to settle for credit he used to perform some of his official duties. These included a lawsuit that had placed a lien against the property at home, originating from a dispute over ownership of a privateering prize.[18] This case would plague him the rest of his life and was not settled until after he died. With help, he was eventually able to resolve the other debt issues, and he was generally regarded as one of the richest men in America until his departure to England in the early 1800s.[19]

As to military activities, in August 1780 he is recorded as a private in the Second Company of the Fourth Battalion of Philadelphia Association.[20] Later, in 1788, he would organize his own military unit, the Second Troop of the Philadelphia Light Horse, of which he was the

15. Alberts, *The Golden Voyage*, 454-463 has the complete text of this document, which provides a fascinating account of Bingham's time in Martinique.

16. Ibid., 80-82.

17. Margaret L. Brown, "William Bingham, Eighteenth Century Magnate," *The Pennsylvania Magazine of History and Biography*, volume LXI, Issue 4, October 1937, published by The Historical Society of Pennsylvania. Google Books edition. Page 387, accessed April 20, 2017, journals.psu.edu/pmhb/article/download/29420/29175.

18. Alberts, *The Golden Voyage*, 78-79.

19. University of Virginia: Social Networks and Archival Content (SNAC) Online, accessed April 19, 2017, socialarchive.iath.virginia.edu/ark:/99166/w6w37zvc.

20. W. A. Newman Dorland, "The Second Troop Philadelphia City Cavalry," Chapter V, *The Pennsylvania Magazine of History and Biography*, volume XLVI, Issue 4, October 1922, free e-Book, page 57, accessed April 18, 2017, books.google.com/books?id=sNY-LAAAAYAAJ&printsec=frontcover&dq=Pennsylvania+magazine+of+history+and+biography&hl=en&sa=X&ved=0ahUKEwi5trrbyLPTAhXJv1QKHViRCLQQ6AEIJTAA#v=onepage&q=Pennsylvania%20magazine%20of%20history%20and%20biography&f=false.

William Bingham, in an undated engraving.

captain. The company was largely ceremonial; its primary claim to fame was its role in escorting George Washington through the area on his way to New York to assume the presidency.[21]

The early 1780s brought much personal happiness as he courted and married Anne Willing on October 26, 1780, at Christ Church in Philadelphia.[22] Anne, only age 16 at the time, though with beauty and grace beyond her years, was the eldest child of Thomas Willing, in his own right a powerful merchant and banker of the Revolution and the early Federal period. William and Anne would become in modern day terms a "power couple" in Philadelphia.

A few days after the wedding a Philadelphia girl wrote to her mother about Anne (note the jab at her husband!):

> Speaking of handsome women brings Nancy Willing to my mind. She might set for the Queen of Beauty, and is lately married to Bingham, who returned from the West Indies with an immense fortune. They have set out in highest style; nobody here will be able to make the figure they do; equipage, house, cloathes, are all the newest

21. Alberts, *The Golden Voyage*, 195.
22. Anne Bingham, American National Biography Online, accessed April 20, 2017, www.anb.org/articles/20/20-00070.html.

taste,—and yet some people wonder at the match. She but sixteen and such a perfect form. His appearance is less amiable.[23]

As to politics, views differed as to Bingham's ambitions, and these are perhaps driven by his strong Federalist affiliation. Writing later, in 1787, Federalist opponent Thomas Jefferson took a decidedly dim view:

> He will make you believe he was on the most intimate footing with the first characters in Europe & versed in the secrets of every cabinet. Not a word of this is true. He had a rage for being presented to great men & had no modesty in the methods by which he could effect it. If he obtained access afterwards, it was with such as who were susceptible of impression from the beauty of his wife.[24]

Jefferson might have added that he was one of those people charmed with Mrs. Bingham, though he was far from alone on that score!

Others were more favorable in their views of Bingham's value in the political arena. Upon his failed bid for election to Congress in 1782, fellow Federalist James Wilson provided some consolation:

> I was much disappointed and indeed mortified to find that you are not in the Delegation to Congress: I lose a particular Pleasure, which I should have enjoyed in serving with you. However, you must still direct your Attention to public Life: Your Country will soon call for you; and you must, as others have done, obey the Call, notwithstanding previous unhandsome Treatment.[25]

According to Bingham's thinking, politics were only a part of the picture. Commerce came first, but "the Interests of Commerce, as connected with Politics, are So Striking, that it is difficult to Separate one from the other."[26]

William and Anne departed the U.S. in 1783 for a three-year stint in Great Britain:

23. Margaret L. Brown, "Mr. and Mrs. William Bingham of Philadelphia: Rulers of the Republican Court," *The Pennsylvania Magazine of History and Biography*, volume LXI, Issue 3, July 1937, page 286, accessed April 20, 2017, journals.psu.edu/pmhb/article/download/29408/29163.

24. Jefferson to James Madison, January 30, 1787. U. S. National Archives, The Founders Online, accessed April 19, 2017, founders.archives.gov/documents/Madison/01-09-02-0126.

25. Margaret L. Brown, "William Bingham, Eighteenth Century Magnate," *The Pennsylvania Magazine of History and Biography*, volume LXI, Issue 4, October 1937, Google Books edition, page 388, accessed April 20, 2017, journals.psu.edu/pmhb/article/download/29420/29175.

26. Ibid.

where they established friendships with French and English nobility, especially Lord Lansdowne, as well as with visiting Americans such as Thomas Jefferson. Anne quickly adopted French manners and fashions and dazzled the French and English courts. She became a public figure in England and an engraving of her was sold in London shops. Abigail Adams arranged that Anne be presented at court and recorded that Anne was very much admired.[27]

They returned in 1786, and this time Bingham was elected to the Continental Congress, representing Pennsylvania. He was also elected to the prestigious American Philosophical Society in 1787.[28] This was of course around the time of the Constitutional Convention. Some disagreement exists as to whether Bingham wanted to preserve the union, having observed first hand its initial dysfunction during his time in the Continental Congress. In his notes on the debate about holding the convention, James Madison reported that the feeling was unanimous that the existing government could not long continue, but that "Mr. Bingham alone wishes that the Confederacy might be divided into several distinct confederacies, its great extent and various interests being incompatible with a single government."[29]

Perhaps Madison identified the wrong person or was taking a partisan shot at the Federalist, as Bingham's thinking did not appear to support this interpretation. Less than two weeks after Madison made his note, Bingham, in a letter to former British Prime Minister Lord Shelburne about conditions in America, indicated:

> There must be Power lodged Somewhere, to form Commercial Regulations, whose Effects must be general & pervade every Part of the Union. . . . [America] wants nothing now but a strong efficient Government, which will command Respect & Confidence abroad, & act with Vigor & Energy at home . . . I was very active in promoting this Measure [the Federal Convention], as I am convinced that all our political Misfortunes flow from the Weakness of our foederal Government.[30]

Bingham exerted his efforts at both getting Pennsylvania (and other states) to approve the proposed constitution and to have the seat of

27. Anne Bingham, American National Biography Online, accessed April 20, 2017, www.anb.org/articles/20/20-00070.html.
28. Member History, American Philosophical Society, accessed April 10, 2017, www.amphilsoc.org/memhist/search?creator=William+Bingham&title=&subject=&subdiv=&mem=&year=&year-max=&dead=&keyword=&smode=advanced.
29. Brown, "William Bingham, Eighteenth Century Magnate, 389.
30. Ibid.

government established in Philadelphia. The former effort was successful, the latter not (other than as the temporary capital while the capital
city was being constructed).

He would eventually assume a role in the new government, but this
was preceded by work at the state level with a term in the Pennsylvania
State House of Representatives, 1790–1791, serving as speaker in 1791.[31]
This was followed by a term in the Pennsylvania state senate (1794–
1795). His principal work here was the formation of a company to build
the Lancaster Pike, an important internal improvement that facilitated
commerce with the interior of the state.[32]

The theme of commerce and his role as one of the country's leading
businessmen and bankers would come into play in his next assignment.
Secretary of the Treasury Alexander Hamilton, in the process of building the new nation's financial system, asked Bingham as a leading
banker in the states for his input. Bingham had been a founder and large
contributor to the Bank of Pennsylvania, established to fund the supplying of the army.[33] In 1781, this became the Bank of North America,
the first bank in the country where he was one of 12 directors and also
a large stock subscriber.[34] He and Hamilton, probably the two greatest
financial minds in the country, generally saw eye-to-eye on banking
and financial systems.

He responded to Hamilton's request with a 5,000-word document
(not known to historians until 141 years later, when it was found amidst
the papers of Hamilton's successor as Treasury Secretary, Oliver Wol-
cott, Jr.).[35] These were passed to Hamilton in a letter in late 1789,[36] and
to a large extent they were of the same mind on the plan, though some
changes recommended by Bingham were made.[37] Following a stormy
debate, Congress in February 1791 passed the banking bill establishing
the Bank of the United States, the first national bank. Bingham was
elected one of its 25 directors.[38]

31. University of Pennsylvania Biographies, University of Pennsylvania website, accessed
April 17, 2017, www.archives.upenn.edu/people/1700s/bingham_wm.html.
32. Brown, "William Bingham, Eighteenth Century Magnate", 410.
33. Bingham, W, MSS, Lilly Library Manuscript Collections website, University of Indiana, accessed April 25, 2017, www.indiana.edu/~liblilly/lilly/mss/index.php?p=bing-
hamw.
34. Brown, "William Bingham, Eighteenth Century Magnate", 403.
35. Alberts, *The Golden Voyage*, 202.
36. Bingham to Alexander Hamilton, November 25, 1789. U. S. National Archives, The
Founders Online, accessed April 25, 2017, founders.archives.gov/documents/Hamil-
ton/01-05-02-0344-0001.
37. Alberts, *The Golden Voyage*, 202.
38. Bingham, W, MSS, Lilly Library Manuscript Collections website, University of Indiana, accessed April 25, 2017, www.indiana.edu/~liblilly/lilly/mss/index.php?p=bing-
hamw.

The outbreak of hostilities between France and Great Britain would help provide the opportunity Bingham needed to assume a formal political role in the new government. In 1793, a meeting was held in Philadelphia, headed by Federalists Bingham and Thomas Fitzsimons, for the purpose of protesting against any action being taken by Congress against England. This was successful, and put both in the mix for future Senate consideration.[39] Bingham was selected to run, and won a seat in the Fourth Congress in 1795, eventually rising to President pro tempore.[40]

The tumultuous 1790s represented the apex of his role in national politics. According to accounts of the time when Philadelphia was temporarily the nation's capital, Bingham played host to the so-called Federalist court. He used his large, extremely elegant Philadelphia mansion to entertain the political and social elites of the new country.[41]

Bingham was also a statesman with considerable political power. Washington, Franklin, Hamilton, and Lord Lansdowne, England's prime minister were counted among his friends both politically and socially. They, along with business acquaintances, foreign visitors, relatives and friends, were frequent guests at the Bingham mansion in Philadelphia, where he and his wife, the former Anne Willing, were the social leaders of the nation's first capital.[42]

And speaking of Washington and Lansdowne, it was the Binghams who commissioned Gilbert Stuart to paint the iconic Lansdowne portrait of the General. The portrait was a gift from the Binghams to Lansdowne. A copy of this painting was rescued from the White House as it burned in the War of 1812.

Then things slowly started to turn for Bingham. His finances began to suffer due to the financial panic of 1796–1797. Investments in land speculations in Maine, Pennsylvania and New York caused Bingham to be land rich but cash poor. Unlike many others (the eminent Robert Morris, for one, ended up in debtor's prison), he was able to survive.

As the century turned, the decline in Bingham's fortunes, political and personal, accelerated. On the political front, the election of Jefferson ended the Federalist reign. The expiration of Bingham's Senate term

39. Brown, "William Bingham, Eighteenth Century Magnate", 392.
40. William Bingham, University of Pennsylvania Biographies, University of Pennsylvania website, accessed April 17, 2017, www.archives.upenn.edu/people/1700s/bingham_wm.html.
41. Brown, "William Bingham, Eighteenth Century Magnate", 392.
42. University of Virginia: Social Networks and Archival Content (SNAC) Online, accessed April 19, 2017, socialarchive.iath.virginia.edu/ark:/99166/w6w37zvc.

(he did not seek re-election) coincided with Jefferson's inauguration. More tragically, Anne developed tuberculosis. The Binghams made a desperate trip to Bermuda in an attempt to get a better climate for her recovery, but she succumbed there to the disease on May 11, 1801.[43] Among others, Jefferson, a widower himself, reached across the political divide to offer his condolences:

> I had before felt a sincere concern for the circumstance which has made you wish for a change of scene, having myself entertained a very high esteem for the character which has left us and learnt from experience the indelible effects of such a loss. time is the only medicine & but an imperfect one.[44]

From here, Bingham moved to England, where his two daughters resided. He reportedly never regained his equilibrium after Anne's death. The ensuing health problems eventually led to his death there at age 51 on February 7, 1804, possibly of a stroke.[45] He is interred in the abbey in Bath, England. In more than one way, he lived on: his estate, placed into a complex trust, was not settled until 1964 ($838,000 divided among 315 heirs, some British).[46] Oh, and Binghamton, New York? Yes, that's named for him, on one of his many landholdings, though he never set foot there.[47]

So, with this sparkling array of accomplishments and posts held, where in the pantheon does William Bingham rate? He probably does not merit founder status, which I would reserve for a limited list of the most influential players in the drama that created America. He was nonetheless a prodigy and a man of diverse talents. During his life, he served his country in multiple ways, many of which were crucial to the establishment and eventual viability of the nation. Regardless of where one ranks him among the figures of the period, he clearly deserves to be remembered more than he has been.

43. Anne Bingham, American National Biography Online, accessed April 20, 2017, www.anb.org/articles/20/20-00070.html.
44. Jefferson to Bingham, July 29, 1801, U. S. National Archives, The Founders Online, accessed April 20, 2017, founders.archives.gov/documents/Jefferson/01-34-02-0508.
45. University of Pennsylvania Biographies, University of Pennsylvania website, accessed April 17, 2017, www.archives.upenn.edu/people/1700s/bingham_wm.html.
46. *New York Times* website archives; article appeared on November 15, 1964, accessed April 20, 2017, www.nytimes.com/1964/11/15/heirs-of-1804-trust-to-divide-838000.html.
47. Binghamton New York—A Brief History, City of Binghamton website, accessed April 20, 2017, www.binghamton-ny.gov/history.

General George Washington: Diplomat

❧ BENJAMIN L. HUGGINS ❧

An important facet of Washington's generalship has gone largely un-explored by historians: his role as a diplomat. For a top-level military leader in a coalition, maintaining good relations with allies is of the first importance. With the signing of the military alliance with France in 1778, Washington had to add this role to his generalship. As soon as French vice admiral d'Estaing arrived with his naval squadron on the American coast to cooperate with Washington's army, the American commander in chief had to become a diplomat. The American general had to cultivate harmonious relations with his French counterpart as well as with the French ministers plenipotentiary, who often visited his headquarters to discuss strategy.

During the Rhode Island campaign of 1778, Washington's diplomacy saved the fledgling Franco-American alliance. Shortly after d'Estaing's arrival in early July, the two commanders decided to make the capture of Newport, Rhode Island the allies' first objective. Early on, Washington recognized the importance of accord between the allied forces. "Harmony & the best understanding between us, should be a Capital & first Object," he reminded Maj. Gen. John Sullivan, the commander of the American troops in the state of Rhode Island.[1] Sullivan and d'Estaing planned to land their respective forces on Aquidneck Island and in a joint offensive drive the British from Newport. But after a promising start to the campaign, d'Estaing, with several ships damaged in a storm and facing the threat of a superior British fleet, chose to sail his squadron to Boston where he could safely repair and refit his ships. Reacting angrily to the Frenchman's strategic decision, Sullivan's general officers issued a "Protest" that declared "the Honor of the French Nation . . . injured by their Fleet abandoning their Allies." Sullivan followed

---

1. Washington to John Sullivan, July 27, 1778, in *Papers of George Washington, Revolutionary War series* (*PGWRW*), 16:187-88.

this protest by writing a letter to the general officers in which he accused d'Estaing of "having abandoned us." The next day he issued a general order in which he accused the French of failing the "great dependance" the Americans had placed on their assistance. As might be expected, the allied commanders-in-chief did not react well to these rash pronouncements. Washington thought Sullivan's order had been "very impolitic." The French admiral was "much displeas'd" and "much wounded" by the protest.[2]

In this potentially damaging situation, Washington's overarching concern became protection of the French alliance. He could not allow public censure of the French that would hazard the partnership, and he so instructed Sullivan and Maj. Gen. William Heath at Boston. According to Washington, "at so critical a moment" the situation had to be "prudently managed" to avoid "injurious consequences" to the alliance.[3] The American commander then took a personal hand in resolving the crisis. He called on his generals to protect the military partnership with France. Washington urged Heath to use his "utmost influence to palliate and soften matters." To Sullivan, Washington revealed his deep concern for the preservation of the coalition. The disagreement had given him a "very singular uneasiness." "The Continent at large is concerned in our cordiality," he wrote, "and it should be kept up by all possible means that are consistent with our honor and policy. . . . Permit me to recommend in the most particular manner, the cultivation of harmony and good agreement."

Letting his generals conduct the local diplomacy, Washington took a statesmanlike approach to d'Estaing's withdrawal. He ignored the controversy and focused on his chief concern: keeping the French fleet in American waters. He wrote the French admiral: "The importance of the fleet under your command to the common cause and the interest I take in your personal concerns would not permit me, but to be deeply affected with the information of the disappointment and injuries you sustained in the late unfortunate storm. I flatter myself, and I most ardently hope, my countrymen will exert themselves to give you every aid in their power, that you may as soon as possible recover from the damage you have suffered and be in a condition to renew your efforts

2. Sullivan to Washington, August 23, 1778, n.1, *PGWRW,* 16: 360-61; Lafayette to Washington, August 25-26, 1778, n.4, *PGWRW,* 16:374; Washington to Nathanael Greene, September 1, 1778, *PGWRW,* 16:458-59; Washington to Lafayette, September 1, 1778 (second letter), *PGWRW,* 16:461-64; and John Laurens to Washington, September 2, 1778, *PGWRW* 16:479-80.
3. Washington to William Heath, August 28, 1778, and Washington to Sullivan, August 28, 1778, *PGWRW,* 16:401-2, 406-7.

against the common enemy." D'Estaing's final words on the incident reveal the effectiveness of the general's diplomatic policy. The French commander told Washington that he remained "devoted to the common cause, and the union of the two nations," and he graciously credited the general's letters with smoothing over the crisis, assuring the American commander that Sullivan's words were "intirely forgotten."[4]

In addition to averting a dangerous breach with d'Estaing, Washington extended his diplomacy to relations with the Marquis de Lafayette. Although historians have generally recognized the father-son aspect of the general's relationship with Lafayette, they have failed to recognize the alliance diplomacy involved in their association. Washington held Lafayette in highest esteem of all the foreign officers in the army.[5] Not only was the young and sensitive marquis a major general in the Continental army, he was its highest-ranking French officer and a nobleman who could be influential at the French Court. Realizing Lafayette's importance to the alliance, the American commander had to treat him with careful consideration.

During the Newport crisis, Washington believed pacifying Lafayette most crucial as the other French officers looked up to him as their head. He also realized Lafayette's influence with d'Estaing and the French commanders.[6] In two letters to the young French general Washington praised him and appealed to him for help in holding the coalition together. After assuring Lafayette that he felt for him and "for our good & great Allys the French," the American commander characterized the protests of Sullivan and his generals as "illiberal" and "unthinking." Washington applauded Lafayette as the patron of the army's French officers, reminded him of the importance of his leadership to the alliance, and appealed to him to offer a "healing hand" to a wound "unintentionally" made. He had no doubt that the Frenchman would use his "utmost endeavours to restore harmony" so that the alliance would be "promoted and cemented in the firmest manner."[7] In a second letter, Washington expressed his friendship and praised Lafayette's assistance

4. Washington to d'Estaing, September 2, 1778, *PGWRW*, 16: 468-70; d'Estaing to Washington, September 5, 1778, *PGWRW*, 16:522-25; d'Estaing to Washington, September 17, 1778, *PGWRW*, 17:33-37.
5. Washington to Gouverneur Morris, July 24, 1778, *PGWRW*, 16:153-55.
6. Washington to Nathanael Greene, September 1, 1778, *PGWRW*, 16:458-59. For Lafayette's influence with d'Estaing, see Lafayette to Washington, August 6, 1778, *PGWRW*, 16: 261-62, Lafayette to Washington, September 21, 1778, *PGWRW*, 17:69-72. For his influence with the French court, see Greene to Washington, September 16, 1778, *PGWRW*, 17:22-25.
7. Washington to Lafayette, September 1, 1778 (first letter), *PGWRW*, 16:460-61.

to the Revolution, speaking of his "love of liberty" and his "noble, & disinterested exertions in the cause of [liberty]." He extolled Lafayette's "ardent Zeal" in the campaign and offered his "warmest thanks" for the Frenchman's "endeavours to cherish harmony."[8] When Lafayette decided to return to France in late 1778, Washington wrote an effusive letter of recommendation for him to present to Benjamin Franklin, the American minister in Paris, in which he praised the French general's "Zeal, Military ardour & talents." He hoped the letter would give Franklin "an idea of the value this country sets upon you."[9] Washington's diplomacy bore valuable fruit. Lafayette praised Washington and his army at the French court, and his efforts were instrumental in France's sending Lieutenant General Rochambeau's expeditionary army to America in 1780.[10]

Though the Continental Congress was primarily responsible for diplomatic relations with the French, Washington played an important part in maintaining good relations with their ambassadors. The general proved just as skilled at dealing with these officials as he had with d'Estaing and Lafayette. When the King of France sent a new minister plenipotentiary, the Chevalier de La Luzerne, to America to replace Conrad Alexandre Gérard, Washington had to once again become a diplomat.

During La Luzerne's three-day visit to West Point in September 1779, the general deployed all his diplomatic skill. La Luzerne's secretary, the Marquis de Barbé-Marbois, described their meeting with the American commander and their boat trip downriver to the fortress: "In spite of all the objections of M. de la Luzerne, General Washington came to meet him at Fishkill. He received us with a noble, modest, and gentle urbanity and with that graciousness which seems to be the basis of his character. . . .. We embarked with the General on ... the Hudson, and sailed down it with the tide to West Point where the headquarters are, surrounded by the chief posts of the American army. The general held the tiller, and during a little squall which required skill and practice, proved to us that this work was no less known to him than are other bits of useful knowledge." The dinner that Washington served the Frenchmen became part of his diplomacy. "All the generals and the

8. Washington to Lafayette, September 25, 1778, *PGWRW,* 17:128-32.
9. Washington to Benjamin Franklin, December 28, 1778, and Washington to Lafayette, December 29, 1778, *PGWRW,* 18:521-22, 526-27.
10. See James Lovell to Washington, August 25, 1779, *PGWRW,* 22:254-56; and Arnold Whitridge, *Rochambeau* (New York, 1965), 72-73. Lafayette had decided to return to France to take part in any French offensive against Great Britain. After a French cross-channel invasion proved abortive, he returned to America in May 1780.

higher officers were there," Barbé-Marbois wrote. "It was interesting to see this meeting of these warriors, each of them a patriot renowned for some exploit, and this military meal, served in a tent in the midst of the apparatus of arms, in the heart of the former possessions of our enemies, to a French minister and officers, was to all of us a remarkable novelty. [The general] spoke of the fine behavior of my compatriots and of the glory which they had won in America. ... A few steps away from us musicians played military and tuneful French airs. The banks and the forests of the mountain answered long to the cannon shots fired to the health of the King and Queen."

The next day Washington, who, Barbé-Marbois noted, "wanted to conduct us himself," led La Luzerne on an inspection tour of West Point's newly expanded and strengthened fortifications, and the party observed the maneuvers of the army's brigades with Barbé-Marbois commenting on the Continentals: "They had hardly any clothes, but were very well armed, and the men were strong and robust." That afternoon at four o'clock the party dined at the quarters of Brigadier General Duportail, Frenchman and chief of the American army's Corps of Engineers. Following the dinner, Washington held a strategic planning conference with La Luzerne. At the conclusion of La Luzerne's visit Washington and "the chief officers of his army" escorted him away from West Point and the American commander in chief had two of his generals continue the escort across New York and New Jersey. Showing the effectiveness of Washington's diplomacy, Barbé-Marbois, who himself later became French minister to the United States, commented, "I shall always recall with pleasure the time which I spent with that man who is so much to be respected."[11]

Washington excelled at this aspect of coalition leadership. No American general would have to act as a diplomat in such circumstances as this until Dwight D. Eisenhower in World War II. By the end of the war, Washington would be expert in diplomacy, but even in the first two years of the alliance he demonstrated a talent for this new and difficult task.

11. Substance of a Conference with La Luzerne, September 16, 1779, source note, *PGWRW,* 22: 442-44.

Elite Regiment, Delinquent Behavior

JOSHUA SHEPHERD

Its list of battle honors nearly constitutes a history of the Revolution itself. During seven years of service, the Delaware Regiment earned a staggering combat record at the most legendary engagements of the war, including Long Island, White Plains, Trenton, Brandywine, Germantown, Monmouth, Camden, Cowpens, Guilford Courthouse, Hobkirk's Hill, Ninety-Six, and Eutaw Springs.[1] They were eventually regarded as crack troops, and regularly given tough assignments. "The State of Delaware furnished one regiment only," Henry Lee famously observed, "and certainly no regiment in the army surpassed it in soldiership."[2]

But the Delaware Regiment, like all military units, spent far more time subjected to the monotony of camp life than the crucible of combat. Even the best of troops could grow a little testy, creating a seething atmosphere of raw nerves that could snap with little warning. Despite its elite status, the Delaware Regiment was composed of mere mortals who were prone to ill manners, short tempers, and bad behavior.

By the end of the war, the regiment had been reduced to a mere two companies under the overall command of Capt. Robert Kirkwood, who had the reputation of one of the hardest fighting company commanders in the Continental Army; thankfully, he was also a dutiful record keeper. Among the materials he recorded is information about disciplinary proceedings in the regiment. Unfortunately, most surviving court-martial summaries are often just brief snippets that offer limited details of events. Kirkwood did a little better than the average officer and - when active campaigning didn't intervene—was better at preserving the particulars of regimental courts-martial. Kirkwood's order book offers a

1. The standard history of the regiment remains Christopher L. Ward, *The Delaware Continentals, 1776-1783* (Wilmington: The Historical Society of Delaware, 1941).
2. Henry Lee, *Memoirs of the War in the Southern Department of the United States* (New York: University Publishing Company, 1869), 185.

priceless glimpse into the inner workings of one of the Continental Army's most legendary units, and contains fascinating tidbits of authentically fallible human interaction that would otherwise have been lost to history.[3]

ENCORE, ENCORE

Diverting the attention of a robbery victim is an age-old ploy for criminals, and nearly worked for Private William Dowers. Dowers was in company with Sgt. Marmaduke McCain late in October, 1777, when McCain, who apparently possessed a fine singing voice, burst into sweet refrain. It must have been a stunning performance; to McCain's delight, Dowers asked him to sing it again. Like any good vocal artist, McCain was happy to oblige, but must have been a little distracted by the sound of his own voice. When the encore performance was over, McCain suddenly noticed that his pocketbook, which had been lying close by and contained a $5 bill, was missing. He immediately accused Dowers of stealing it, but was met with sharp denials. Dowers was searched after the incident, but had no money on him.

The affair might have ended there if Dowers had exercised a little more caution. The day after he had been searched, Dowers was heading off to sentry duty with Private Henry Gardner when he asked Gardner to stop off to see a sutler. While there, Dowers made a disastrous mistake: he changed a $5 bill, and did so in front of several witnesses.

He would pay dearly for it. At his court-martial on October 25, Dowers could present little in the way of a defense, and came up with the rather lame excuse that he had "found" the $5 bill by a campfire. Nobody bought it. He was found guilty of stealing the money and sentenced to receive 500 lashes "well laid on." The court mercifully reduced the sentence to 200 lashes, but had another minor instructive lesson for Dowers. He was ordered to pay McCain $5.[4]

MARCHING LEFT OF CENTER

The trouble started on the evening of November 26, 1777, when Private William Howell, parading with his company but "disguised in liquor", was seen having a little trouble walking in a straight line. Sgt. Thomas Thompson observed his wobbly meanderings and ordered him to incline to the left and rejoin his own company. Howell snapped back "that he would not," at which Thompson gave him a helpful shove in the

3. All of the following stories are from Joseph Brown Turner, ed., *The Journal and Order Book of Captain Robert Kirkwood of the Delaware Regiment of the Continental Line* (Wilmington: The Historical Society of Delaware, 1910).
4. Ibid., 216-217.

right direction. A good bit irritated at the affront, Howell glared back at the sergeant and offered that, in his opinion, Thompson was a "Chuckleheaded Son of a bitch."

It was an ugly thing to say, and sure to result in a regimental court-martial. Judgement was swift when the court convened the following day. Charged with "abusing" the sergeant, a contrite Howell pleaded guilty and confessed that "he was heady, & was rather rash in contradicting Serjt Thompson." His forthrightness elicited little mercy. Although two other soldiers had their sentences reduced by the same court, Howell was sentenced to receive his full share of punishment: twenty lashes for mouthing off to a sergeant, and ten lashes for being intoxicated.[5]

OH, YOU MEAN THAT HANDKERCHIEF

Sometimes the cover-up is worse than the crime, particularly if one is really bad at cover-ups. While the Delaware Regiment was camped at Hanover, New Jersey during August of 1777, one of the locals, John Tappan, walked into a tavern to witness one of the most brazen—if clumsy—heists of the century. There were several people present, including the landlady, a girl, an unidentified soldier, and Private Dennis Maanna. In the privacy of an anteroom, the girl let it be known that she had "lost" her handkerchief, but apparently insinuated that it had been stolen. The unidentified soldier then entered another room with Maanna and asked him if he knew anything about it. Maanna played dumb and claimed "he had not got it." The soldier then pointed to the tail of the handkerchief, which was clearly visible and hanging out of Maanna's pocket, and said "there it is." The game was up. Maanna sheepishly surrendered the handkerchief, and the girl announced that she knew about it all along but had been afraid to say anything.

At the court-martial on August 14, Maanna might have been better off to keep his mouth shut. He had consumed a gill of gin that day, he explained. Then he noticed the handkerchief on a chair, picked it up, put it in his pocket "by accident", and forgot about it. The presiding officers of the court not only found Maanna guilty of stealing the hanky, but unanimously rejected his unlikely story. Maanna was sentenced to receive 75 lashes for stealing and an additional 25 lashes for lying to the court, to be administered "on his bare back well Laid on with the Cat o nine tails."[6]

5. Ibid., 255-256.
6. Ibid., 142-143.

NICE WATCH

Being confined under suspicion of "stealing a watch" was no laughing matter, and could result in an entirely unwanted encounter with the cat o' nine tails. John Chambers explained that during the regiment's stay in Philadelphia in the summer of 1777, John Pemberton had the habit of stopping by his room in the barracks to visit friends. During one such visit, Pemberton happened to notice a watch hanging on the wall, asked who owned it, and was told it was the property of Drummer Joseph Purdie. Pemberton clearly liked the looks of the timepiece. When he asked if Purdie might be willing to sell, Chambers thought he might. At that, Purdie took the watch down, "opened her" to have a better look, and then put the watch back.

At some point after that, the watch disappeared. Pemberton, the only suspect, was arrested on suspicion of the crime, and his case came before a court-martial on July 19, 1777. At least two men witnessed Pemberton admire the watch, but no one saw an actual theft. In his defense, Pemberton confessed that he had been "in Liquor" during the incident, and "seeing the Watch took her down & looked at her, and then put her up again." There was simply no evidence that he had done more than that, and the court ordered that Pemberton "be immediately Releas'd from his Confinement."[7]

BE CAREFUL WHAT YOU WISH FOR

There's nothing quite so mind-numbing as redundant paperwork. That was obviously the sentiment of Sgt. James Stenson in June of 1777, when a quartermaster ordered him to fill out a return for provisions. Stenson demurred, observing that "he thought there was no Necessity of making one as he has already given in one." According to the quartermaster, Stenson "absolutely refused" to turn in the requested paperwork.

Maj. Joseph Vaughan happened to overhear the conversation, and intervened on the quartermaster's behalf, ordering Stenson to go and draw up the return "immediately." As a thoroughly sour Stenson walked off, he did so mumbling that "it was better not to be a Serjt in this Rejt then be one." Vaughan, assuming the mantle of a stern father figure, asked Stenson to repeat himself. It was better not to be a sergeant, Stenson barked as he spun around, "thats what I say."

The presiding officers of his court-martial on June 29 were glad to oblige. "After Due Consideration", Stenson was sentenced "to be reduced to the Rank And Serve as A Private Centinel."[8]

7. Ibid., 119-120.
8. Ibid., 91-92.

AN UNFORTUNATE MISUNDERSTANDING

Picket duty might be less appealing than staying warm by a cozy fire, but far better than the alternative of a court-martial. During the last week of November 1777, Sgt. Adam Johnston was busy with his morning rounds, turning out men for routine picket duty at the Continental camp at White Marsh, Pennsylvania. Johnston noticed Private Martenius Sipple sitting by a campfire in front of his tent, but Sipple, seemingly lost in a world of his own, wasn't stirring. The sergeant asked if he hadn't heard the call to picket duty, but Sipple didn't answer. As Johnston continued walking by, he prodded Sipple once again, and then heard the unthinkable: Sipple distinctly snapped "Go along you yellow Son of a Bitch."

It seemed to be an open and shut case of insubordination, but at Sipple's court-martial on November 30, the case took an unexpected turn. The surprise witness was Benjamin Moody, who explained that during the apparent confrontation with Sergeant Johnston, Sipple was already engaged in a heated argument with another soldier, William Ploughman, when he uttered the fatal words. That fact cast doubt on the entire prosecution. Moody testified that he couldn't say if the expletive had been hurled at Johnston or Ploughman. Johnston also confessed that he wasn't sure if the abuse was meant for him, but that he "understood it so at that time."

With that in mind, the officers of the court decided that the nasty words had been intended for a lowly private—Ploughman—and not Sergeant Johnston. Sipple, relieved, no doubt, at the outcome of his court-martial, was spared the lash. Although a good mouth washing with a bar of soap might have sufficed, Sipple was forced to ask Ploughman's forgiveness in front of their commanding officer.[9]

9. Ibid., 260-261.

Benjamin Franklin: "Our Salvation Depends on You"

❀❧ BOB RUPPERT ❧❀

Benjamin Franklin was appointed an American Commissioner to France on September 26, 1776.[1] One month later he set sail for France where he arrived safely on December 3. His mission was to gain French support for American Independence. Little did he know that shortly after he arrived he would be confronted with an issue that he had not considered and that was not a declared part of his commission. On March 7, 1777, he received a letter from Patience Wright, an American living in England. She begged for his assistance in securing the freedom of Ebenezer Platt, a merchant from Georgia, whose vessel and person were seized in Jamaica, and who was currently detained in a British prison. Platt's situation concerned Franklin, but something Mrs. Wright wrote at the end of the letter also caught his attention:

> There is 23 more unhappy Prisoner at Portsmout and gosport and the Same perdiecterment of Mr. Platt they wish to Know what to hope from You. For gods Sake have Compasion on those Strangers whos Property is all taken from them and they in Iorns No one to Comfort them, and it is not in the powe of the People to help them without You. You must be our Delivier our Salvation depends on you and you Sir have it in your Powr to Set us all in order.[2]

On February 23 and April 2, Franklin wrote to Lord Stormont proposing an exchange of prisoners; only after the second letter did he receive a brief and abrupt response: "the king's ambassador receives no applications from rebels, unless they come to implore his Majesty's

---

1. *Journals of the Continental Congress,* Worthington Chauncey Ford, ed. (Washington DC: Library of Congress, 1906), 5:827.
2. "From Patience Wright, after March 7, 1777," *The Papers of Benjamin Franklin* (Yale University Press, 1954-), hereafter "PBF," 23:447.

mercy."[3] To show their further resolve, on March 3, Parliament adopted the Treason Act; it suspended habeas corpus for persons "charged with or suspected of a crime of High Treason committed in any of His Majesty's colonies or Plantations in America, or on the High Seas, or the crime of Piracy."[4] Americans could now be detained at the King's pleasure for piracy provided that adequate evidence could be shown. Over the next two months, because a substantial number of American sailors were detained, the British government was forced to consider how and where they should be held. On May 8, the Admiralty ordered that two locations be established as "places of confinement for such Rebel Prisoners." One of the prisons, Mill Gaol, was located near Plymouth and the other, Forton Gaol, was located near Portsmouth.[5] Charles Herbert, a prisoner at Mill, described the conditions:

> Many are strongly tempted to pick up the grass in the yard and eat it and some pick up old bones in the yard that have been laying in the dirt a week or ten days and pound them to pieces and suck them. Some will pick up snails out of the holes in the wall and from among the grasses and weeds in the yard, boil them and eat them and drink the broth. . . . Our meat is very poor in general; we scarcely see a good piece once in a month, Many are driven to such necessity by want of provisions that they sold most of the clothes off their backs for the sake of getting a little money to buy them some bread.[6]

It would not be until November that the Commission of Sick and Hurt Seamen, a commission under the Lords Commissioners of the Admiralty, made it known that there was "a great want of clothing and of Shoes and Stockings amongst many of the prisoners."[7]

On June 4, Franklin received a letter from Dr. Josiah Smith. He had been captured aboard a ship en route to France. He told Franklin,

> When I left Plymouth there were about 200 of my country men, prisoners there; and as many more at Portsmouth; the former of which I frequently visited; and informing them that I should go directly to

3. "The American Commissioners to Lord Stormont, April 3, 1777," PBF, 23:548; Reported by Lord Stormont to Lord Weymouth, April 3, 1777, S.P. 78/302.
4. 17 Geo.3 c.9.
5. Francis Abell, *Prisoners of War in Britain, 1756-1815* (London: Oxford University Press, 1914), 214-234.
6. Gardner Weld Allen, *A Naval History of the American Revolution* (Boston and New York: Houghton Mifflin Company, 1913), 2:642-43.
7. "Commissioners for Sick and Hurt Seamen to Admiralty, November 25, 1777," Adm/M/404, National Maritime Museum, Greenwich, England.

France, they beged of me to represent their situation to your Honour.[8]

With the future of exchanges in doubt, Franklin at least wanted to relieve some of the prisoners' distresses. On October 14, he wrote to his friend and Member of Parliament, David Hartley.

> With Regard to the Prisoners now in your Gaols—They complain of severe Treatment. They are far from their Friends and Families, and a Winter is coming on, in which they must suffer extremely . . . I shall content myself with proposing that your Government would allow us to send or employ a Commissary to take some Care of those unfortunate People . . . If you could have Leisure to visit the Gaols in which they are confined . . . I wish you would take the Trouble of distributing among the most necessitous according to their Wants five or six hundred Pounds, for which your Drafts on me here should be punctually honour'd . . . If you cannot obtain for us Permission to send a Commissary, possibly you may find a trusty humane discrete Person at Plymouth, and another at Portsmouth, who would undertake to distribute what Relief we may be able to afford, those unhappy brave Men.[9]

Franklin was going to create a relief program. On December 4, he again wrote to Hartley.

> We have requested the Bearer Mr. Thornton, to visit your Goals and bring us a true Account of the Situation of the American Prisoners, believing it too much to request of you during the Session of Parliament: When you see his Account you will judge in what manner the Relief I requested you to distribute can best be given, and whether you can make any Use of that Account in Parliament favourable to those unhappy People.[10]

John Thornton was given the following instructions: to deliver "a Letter to Lord North and another to Sir Grey Cooper Secretary of the Treasury;" "to obtain Permission to visit and examine into the Situation of our People in their Gaols;" "administer the relief" (the money); and "wait on Mr. Hartley and desire his Advice or Orders."[11] Unbeknownst to Franklin, there already were men offering such assistance. They were

8. "From Josiah Smith, June 4, 1777," PBF, 24:117.
9. "To David Hartley, October 14, 1777," PBF, 25:64-67.
10. Ibid.
11. "The American Commissioners: Instructions to John Thornton, December 11, 1777," PBF, 25:269.

Deacon Robert Heath, a Calvinist Methodist, at Mill Gaol and Rev. Thomas Wren, a Presbyterian, at Forton Gaol. Both men were supported by Thomas Digges, a London merchant, who visited both prisons.[12]

The plight of the American prisoners was also known in London. On December 1, Lord Abingdon called for an investigation into prison conditions and ten days later, pleaded the American prisoners' case in Parliament before announcing that he intended to encourage the creation of a subscription on their behalf. On December 24, a meeting was held at the King's Arms Tavern in the Cornhill section of London for "relieving the Distresses of the American Prisoners." Nearly 100 were in attendance. A decision was made to create a subscription on the prisoners' behalf. By the end of the meeting about £1500 was pledged; by January 8, 1778, the amount had risen to £3815; and by January 15, to £4657.[13]

For the next eighteen months, individual allotments were distributed each week—2s per sailor and 5s per officer. [14] The funds were used by the prisoners to purchase additional food at the merchants' market set up each day in the gaol's courtyard. Other items distributed to the prisoners were warm clothing, tobacco, medicine, books, writing necessities, and tea.

John Thornton visited Forton Gaol between December 28 and 30. In his memorandum to the American Commissioners he stated that on the first day he had "to bribe the Invalid centries to permit [me] to speak to the prisoners" . . . and on the second day, he was allowed to speak with the prisoners but he had to be accompanied by the Agent's Clerk of the gaol.

> There is not the least distinction made between the Officers and common Sailors, and the Prison having no glazed windows, they can not have any light without having the Northern and Westerly Winds, their provisions are but scanty at best . . . There are now in the Infirmary 20, and few days ago 27 in the black hole . . . the 27 were con-

12. William Bell Clark, "In Defense of Thomas Digges," *Pennsylvania Magazine of History and Biography* (1953), 77:389-90.
13. *The Annual Register, or a View of the History Politics and Literature for the Year 1778*, 3rd edition (London,1778), 79; *Gentleman's Magazine*, (1777), 47:607; (1778), 48:43; *The Public Advertiser* (London), January 2, 1778; *The London Evening Post*, December 23-25, 1777, January 8-10, 1778; *The Public Advertiser*, January 10,1778; *The London Evening Post*, January 13-15, 1778.
14. "From Thomas Wren, March 25, 1778," PBF, 26:165.

fined on 2d December and till lately were not let out at all . . . these men have only the half allowance of provisions.[15]

There were 119 prisoners at Forton Gaol at the time; he implied that similar conditions existed for the 289 American prisoners at the Mill Gaol. He also reported that Rev. Wren provided "the greatest service and behaved with great Humanity to the American prisoners."[16]

Franklin's relief plan received unexpected assistance between October 1777 and May 1778; first came news of the surrender of Burgoyne and his army at Saratoga on October 17, 1777; then came news of the Treaty of Amity and Commerce and the Treaty of Alliance between France and the American Colonies on February 6, 1778; and finally the success that Capt. John Paul Jones had in taking British ships in European waters and turning over the crews as prisoners of war. With British manpower being threatened, it did not surprise Franklin when the Lords Commissioners of the Admiralty expressed interest in an exchange.

The letter that Franklin had given to Thornton on December 11 for Lord North was a request for a prisoner exchange. North agreed to the request as well as to Hartley serving as the intermediary between the Commissioners of Sick and Hurt Seamen and the American Commissioner. Six months later, on May 25, Franklin wrote to Hartley, "I wish to know whether your Ministers have yet come to a Resolution to exchange the Prisoners they hold in England."[17] Hartley wrote back "you should send me the number and rank of the prisoners which you have on your side to deliver upon the receipt of which an equal number shall be prepared on this side for the Exchange."[18] The exchange would take place at Calais, France.

The American Commissioners were given more reason to be optimistic when they received news that Captain Jones had captured the *Drake,* a twenty-gun British Sloop-of-War, in Belfast harbor. He was bringing the prize and 200 prisoners to Brest.

Some of the prisoners were not about to sit around and wait for an exchange. They devised a number of ways to escape; they dug tunnels, assumed disguises, bribed guards, stole keys, and some even feigned ill-

15. [John Thornton]: Memorandum for the American Commissioners, Between January 5 and 8, 1778," PBF, 25:414.
16. Ibid.
17. "The American Commissioners: Instructions to John Thornton, December 11, 1777," Answer appended to PBF, 25:269.
18. "From David Hartley, June 16, 1778," PBF, 26:628.

ness in order to be sent to the infirmary where there was little security. Once beyond the gaol's walls, however, they were far from safe. Men called "five pounders" were waiting in the countryside and nearby towns. Their name referred to the amount of money they were paid for each escapee caught and returned to gaol. Thomas Digges set up a series of safe houses that provided escapees with clothing, food, and money. If they were lucky, they were able to make their way to London and then to France. In London many found refuge in the homes of Thomas Digges, Dr. George Williams, and John Blyth.[19] Caleb Foote, a prisoner at Forton, described the emotional journey: "We fled from the Valley of Destruction to the City of Refuge, where we spent but little time, and then we crossed the Gulf of Despair and arrived safely at the Promised Land."[20] Once in France some made their way to Franklin's home in Passy where they hoped to secure further assistance. If they received money, they were required to sign a promissory note handwritten by Franklin stating taht they would repay the amount to the Superintendent of Finance for the United States shortly after arriving home.

On July 13, Franklin sent Hartley the list that he had requested on June 16. Hartley promptly responded,

> The prisoners to be exchanged from hence will be taken from Forton and Plymouth [Mill] in proportion to their numbers in each place, and to consist of those who have been the longest in confinement . . . As to the passport . . . I am authorized to say that it will be granted by our Admiralty, if you will give me assurance that our ship going to Calais shall have free entrance without molestation, and free egress with the prisoners in Exchange.[21]

Franklin knew that for the exchange to occur in France, he would need a passport from Minister Sartine, the Secretary of State for the French Marine. On August 18 he submitted the request. On September 14, Franklin informed Hartley that the passport had been secured but "The Port of Calais was not approv'd of, and I think the Ports mention'd (Nantes and L'Orient) are better for you as well as for us . . . as being nearer to Plymouth."[22] The American Commissioners, confident that

19. "From [Thomas Digges], November 10, 1779," PBF, 31:79; "From Dr. George Williams, October 2, 1778," PBF, 27:491.
20. Caleb Foote, compl., *Reminiscences of the Revolution. Prison Letters and Sea Journal of Caleb Foote,* "October 14th, 1780," *The Essex Institute Historical Collections,* XXVI (1889), 22.
21. "From David Hartley, July 14, 1778," PBF, 27:94.
22. "To David Hartley, September 14, 1778," PBF, 27:399.

an exchange would occur in the near future, wrote to the Prisoners at Forton and at Mill.

> We have not been unmindful of your interests, your comfort, or your liberty. We have been engaged a long time in negotiating a cartel of exchange. This work we found attended with many difficulties, but at last have obtained assurances from England that an exchange shall take place . . . we can not certainly say, however, that all will be immediately exchanged, because we fear we have not an equal number to be sent to England. Those that remain, if any, will be those who have been the latest in captivity, and consequently have suffered the least.[23]

Four weeks later, Franklin received, by way of Hartley, a letter from the Admiralty Office requesting the exact number of prisoners to be exchanged. He wrote back,

> I cannot at present give it to you, they being dispers'd in different Ports . . . the Number continually changing by new prisoners brought in, and some escaping . . . we make this Proposition, that if their Lordships will send us over 250 of our People, we will deliver all we have in France. If the Number we have falls short of the 250, the Cartel Ship may take back as many of those she brings as the Deficiency amounts to, delivering no more than she receives.[24]

Hartley told Franklin that as soon as he was informed of the place and the name of the exchange agent, he would send it on to the Commissioners of Sick and Hurt Seamen.[25] On January 1, 1779, Franklin informed Hartley that the exchange would take place at Nantes and the American Agent would be a Mr. Schweighauser.[26]

On the 22nd, Franklin responded to a letter from Minister Sartine. Sartine wrote,

> You are undoubtedly aware that American seamen escaping from English prisons often arrive in French ports without the basic necessities. I can instruct the commissioners in ports where you have no agents to treat these men as they would French escapees.[27]

---

23. Francis Wharton, *The Revolutionary Diplomatic Correspondence of the United States*, Serial Set 2585 (Washington, DC: Library of Congress, 1889), 2:729.
24. "To David Hartley, October 20, 1778," PBF, 27:574.
25. "From David Hartley, December 10, 1778," PBF, 28:218.
26. "From David Hartley, January 1, 1779," PBF, 28:321.
27. "Sartine to the American Commissioners, December 22, 1778," PBF, 28:262.

Franklin wrote back

We . . . are much obliged to you for the interest you take in what concerns the unhappy prisoners who may escape from England. We had not been inattentive to that subject. There are persons who supply them at Bordeaux, Brest, L'Orient, Nantes, and Dunkirk [and] a gentleman at Calais has voluntarily done this service.[28]

Franklin's agents in place were merchants already engaged in commercial business on behalf of the United States, John Bondfield at Bordeaux, Berube de Constentin at Brest, James Moylan at L'Orient, J. D. Schweighauser at Nantes, Francis Coffyn at Dunkirk, and Jacques Leveux at Calais. They served in similar roles as Wren, Heath, and Digges, but on French soil. When the Americans arrived in France, without proof that they were Americans, they were arrested by French officials because they were thought to be English spies. They were detained in places such as St. Malo Prison, Dinan Castle, Dunkirk Prison, and Calais Prison. It was the responsibility of Franklin's agents to assist them until they were aboard a ship bound for the United States, but when some were detained, Franklin had to bring their situation before Sartine and request their release himself.

The first formal exchange of prisoners occurred on April 2. According to David Hartley, the first ship departing Spithead for Plymouth was "beat back twice [by the wind] . . . between the Downs and Plymouth."[29] Schweighauser reported that 97 prisoners eventually arrived in port and were exchanged. Franklin informed the Committee of Foreign Affairs in Philadelphia that "this is to continue till all are exchanged."[30]

On June 24, Hartley informed Franklin that a second shipload of prisoners for exchange would be coming from Forton gaol.[31] Three weeks later, Digges informed Franklin that 92 prisoners were exchanged at Nantes. Hartley proposed that the next exchange take place at Morlaix since it was much closer than Nantes. This meant that Franklin needed a new passport from Sartine. At first Sartine was reluctant because Morlaix was only fifty miles from the port of Brest, a French naval base, but eventually he agreed to issue it. On October 8, Digges reported to Franklin that on September 23, Capt. John Paul Jones fought and defeated two British men of war, the *Serapis* and *Countess of Scarborough*,

28. Wharton, *The Revolutionary Diplomatic Correspondence*, 3:7.
29. "From David Hartley, March 30, 1779," PBF, 29:233.
30. "To the Committee of Foreign Affairs, May 26, 1779," PBF, 29:57.
31. "From David Hartley, June 24, 1779," PBF, 29:732.

and that "Mr Paul Jones has . . . got 350 Seamen besides the Crews of thirty odd vessels which he took & destroyd on his late cruise."[32] Jones wanted to take his prizes and prisoners to Dunkirk, but his French captains insisted on Texel, Holland. Franklin now believed he had more than enough British prisoners to exchange and Morlaix was the closest French port to Holland for the exchange. On October 19, Franklin wrote to Hartley,

> Having just received the Passport desired for the Cartel to make use of the Port of Morlaix, I take this first Opportunity of sending it to you, in hopes of releasing by more expeditious Voyages of the poor Prisoners on both Sides before the Severity of Winter comes on.[33]

It is unclear if Franklin was planning to move the prisoners from Holland to Morlaix or to conduct the exchange in Holland. He would receive three letters over the next nine days, two from Hartley and one from Hodgson. Each requested the number of British prisoners in France as well as the name of the American exchange agent in Morlaix. It was the letter from Hodgson, however, that changed whatever Franklin was planning. William Hodgson, in David Hartley's absence, had just returned from a meeting with the Commissioners of Sick and Hurt Seamen.

> They do not mean to send any Vessell to Morlaix untill your Answer returns . . . I mentioned to them the Crews of the Serapis & C of Scarbro captured by P. Jones. I found that the objection against sending to the Texel was that those Vessells & their Crewes might possibly be retaken on their Return to Dunkirk or elsewhere.[34]

Jones, not long after arriving, was urged by the Dutch government to leave the Texel as soon as possible because Holland was a neutral country and feared retaliation from the British for harboring a rebel and a pirate. Because the British were not going to accept an exchange of prisoners in Holland and with "eight of the enemy's ships laying in wait for him at the south entrance and four more at the north entrance to the port," if he was going to escape, Jones needed to leave his prizes and prisoners behind. He entrusted them to the French Ambassador to the Hague, the Duc de la Vauguyon, who wrote to Franklin,

---

32. "From T[homas] D[igges], October 8, 1779," PBF, 5:94.
33. "From David Hartley, October 19, 1779," PBF, 30:559.
34. "From David Hartley, November 15, 1779," PBF, 31:349; ibid, "November 17, 1779," 31:118; "From William Hodgson, 23 November 1779," 31:142.

All his representations were reduced to soliciting that his crew was not deprived of the rights he had over the prizes, and that his prisoners were exchanged for Americans; I have promised to join him and you to M. de Sartines in order to obtain all the satisfaction he desires in this respect.[35]

On December 6, Captain Jones's prizes and prisoners were placed under the French flag.[36]

At the beginning of 1780, Thomas Digges reported to Franklin that there were 183 prisoners at Mill gaol and 227 at Forton gaol. [37] Franklin, knowing that Hartley was out of town and learning that the prisoners would be arriving on two separate ships, secured a second Morlaix passport and sent it to Hodgson. Franklin assured him that he would request Minister Sartine to send the 48 British prisoners at L'Orient and the 36 at Brest to Morlaix. One week later he informed Hodgson that the Duc de la Vauguyon had exchanged all of Jones' prisoners for French prisoners. Sartine planned for the prisoners to man the two French-captured ships, the *Serapis and Countess of Scarborough* as well as the French frigate *Pallas,* and French brig *Vengeance* that were trapped in the port.

On February 2, Franklin told Hartley, who had returned, that he would have enough prisoners with a French complement to exchange at Morlaix:

The Number of Prisoners we now have in France is not easily ascertained. I suppose it exceeds 100; but you may be assured that the Number which may be brought over by the Two Cartels, Shall be fully exchanged by adding to those taken by us as many as will make up the Compliment out of those taken by the French.[38]

The following day Franklin received a letter from the prisoners at Forton prison. It may have been the most painful letter he received during the war. The prisoners wrote,

The Season being Cold and blusterring our donation has been of great Service to us but it is now almost Exhausted being For this Some months past only a three pence per week. We are Very discontented amongst us being Informed by Mr. Newsham [the British Agent at the prison] that it is intirely owing to your Neglect that we have not gone for Long ago.[39]

35. "From Duc de la Vauguyon, November 25, 1779," PBF, 31:150.
36. "To John Paul Jones, December 6, 1779," PBF, 31:203.
37. "From Thomas Digges, January 10, 1780," PBF, 31:364.
38. "To David Hartley, February 2, 1780," PBF, 31:436.
39. "Two Hundred Eighty American Prisoners to Franklin, February 3, 1780," PBF, 31:442.

Because he had expected the exchange to take place before winter set in, Franklin had not replenished the relief fund. If anything, this letter was an impetus for Franklin to work even harder on behalf of the prisoners. On February 12, he wrote to Minister Sartine as promised, requesting the above transfers, and to Hodgson informing him that the American agent at Morlaix was a Mr. Pitot.

In anticipation of the large prisoner exchange, Franklin decided to change the form of his financial assistance from the handwritten notes he had used up to this time to printed ones. He needed to "standardize and [better] account for the money he anticipated distributing." The forms he designed were a *blank order* and a *promissory note*. The *blank order* read,

> Pay to _____ or order, the Sum of _____ Livres Tournois, to assist _____ in returning to the United States of America; being lately from Prison in England. —Charge the same to the PUBLICK ACCOUNT of .

The order was to be taken to Mr. Grand, Franklin's banker for cashing. This order was used only for money paid to an American who had escaped from a prison or who had been exchanged. The *promissory note* read

> I Promise to Pay to the Honourable the Superintendent of Finances, for the Time being, _____ of the United States of America, Livres Tournois, which I have received here from Benjamin Franklin, esquire, Minister Plenipotentiary of the said States; and for which I have signed three Notes, all of this Tenor and Date: one of which being paid, the others are to be void.

This note was used for an American who had been on board a ship captured by the British. If a loan of a large sum of money not limited to any specific purpose was necessary, a different promissory note had to be signed. It was similar to the first promissory note except it stated payment was to be made to "the President, for the time being" and the amount of money lent was in *Louis d'ors* and not *Livres Tournois*.[40]

One copy of every order and note was kept by Jean l'air de Lamonte, an aide to Franklin, in a list. They were entered by bearer, date, and sum. The first series of promissory notes was used until June, 1781; the second series in a different typeface was used until March, 1782; and

---

40. earlyamericanists.com/2014/06/16/benjamin-franklin-and-our-seamen-who-were-prisoners-in-england/.
41. "Thomas Digges to Franklin, March 10, 1780," PBF, 32:80.

the third series set in italics was used until the end of his embassy in France.

On March 10 Franklin received a letter Thomas Digges:

> A vessel saild from Plyo. with 100 [actually 119] on the 5th Int. There remains but 86 and what is rather singular there is pardons lodgd for 68 of that number agt. The return of the vessel . . . the next Cargoe by the rotine must go from Portso . . . The Revd Mr heath— has been a second Wren to those people.[41]

Franklin thought the exchange had taken place as planned until he received a letter from Hodgson on March 28,

> I am much concerned to find that the Cartel vessel is returned from Morlaix without a single prisoner in Exchange—I heard from Plymo & have since been desired to go to the Sick and Hurt office who confirmed the Acc't. They appear to be much disgusted at the proceeding & say it is a breach of Faith . . . I hope Sir you will furnish me with such an explanation of this Affair as shall be satisfactory and expedite future exchanges at present untill the Affair is cleared up all further progress in this business must be put a Stop to.[42]

Franklin was astonished. He believed that Sartine, as part of the agreement between the two of them, was going to deliver a complement of British prisoners held by France to Morlaix for exchange.

> I applyed for 100 English to be rendered at Morlaix for the Exchange and was told that orders should be that Day given; . . . I have now desired of M. De Sartine that two hundred may be immediately sent over. One to pay for the 100 Americans received and the other to Exchange a fresh Parcel. His verbal Answer is, that the request is just, and shall be complyed with, and he will write a Letter to me to morrow, which I may send over to be shewn to The Board of Sick & Hurt, that will explain the matter, and clear me from any Charge of bad Faith.[43]

Sartine never offered a satisfactory explanation to Franklin as to why the prisoners were not delivered, but the reason may be found in a letter from Sartine to Franklin near the end of April: "These prisoners [the British captured by John Paul Jones] having been regarded as taken in the sea by a French Wing, and their Exchange having been arrested by the two Ministers under this denomination."

42. "From Hodgson, March 28, 1780," PBF, 32:167.
43. "To Hodgson, April 11, 1780," PBF, 32:236.

Sartine was claiming that because the *Bon Homme Richard* had been fitted out and belonged to the King of France that any prisoners taken at sea by its captain and crew belonged to France. This allowed the French Ambassador to the Hague to exchange them for French prisoners. With regard to the 48 British prisoners at L'Orient, they had been captured by the *Black Prince*, another privateer with a captain and crew that were American and Irish but which was fitted out and belonged to the King of France. It seems that Sartine was going to exchange every British prisoner detained in a French prison, if he could present an argument that their capture was due to a ship or ships that belonged to the King of France. This would explain why no British prisoners were transferred to Morlaix. To make the entire situation even more questionable Sartine told Franklin that if he wished to appeal his decision regarding who had the right to exchange which prisoners, he could appeal to the king. On May 16, Franklin wrote to Charles Gravier de Vergennes, the Foreign Minister of King Louis XVI. He laid out the entire timeline and communications between Sartine and himself.[44] This author has not found any response from Vergennes.

On the same day, Franklin received a letter from Hodgson:

> The Board [of Sick & Hurt Seamen] were of Opinion it wou'd be better to wait those further explanations (which you promised to send to Mr. Hartley . . . after receiving them from Monsieur de Sartine) & lay the whole before the Admiralty at one View.[45]

By mid-1780 William Hodgson began to take on the role formerly performed by David Hartley. The need for this was first brought to Franklin's attention by Thomas Digges on October 8:

> There seems a strange detention of the [cartel] ship in every voyage and Mr H[artley] being in the Country & not sticking close to the Agents here, I fear helps in this detention.[46]

Hartley's private affairs were causing him to be away from London. Because Hodgson had worked at Hartley's side, he was the obvious choice to serve as Franklin's new intermediary in London. Hodgson was a well-respected merchant which gave him status with the Board and Digges knew that as an American he could not appear before the Board. On February 10, Digges again wrote to Franklin,

---

44. John Bigelow, ed., *The Works of Benjamin Franklin,* Vol. VIII Letters and Miscellaneous Writings 1779-1781 (New York and London: G. P. Putnam's Sons, 1904), 227-27.
45. "From William Hodgson, May 12, 1780," PBF, 32: 377.
46. "From T[homas] D[igges], October 8, 1779," *The Benjamin Franklin Papers,* (The Historical Society of Pennsylvania), 5:94.

I think more might be done thro Him [Hodgson] than by D[avid] H[artley], (at least at the Office on Tower Hill, for, with the best intentions & wishes to do good, that Gentn is so much out of Town & employed in other Par[liamentar]y matters, that the necessary business for the Prisoners cannot be duly attended to by Him.[47]

Digges' recommendation proved to be fortuitous because in the fall elections David Hartley was not returned to Parliament. In August, Hodgson reported,

I had a Message from the Board of Sick & Hurt desiring to see me, I waited upon them accordingly & they shewed me a Letter from the Lords of the Admiralty ... It consisted of the recital of my propositions & concluded by the Declaration that having taken into Consideration they could not depart from their former Resolution, viz to exchange Man for Man of the American Prisoners against Man for Man of his Majestys Subjects taken by American Vessels in Europe.[48]

It was the last six words of the letter that changed everything for Franklin. Little did he know that the exchange that had been scheduled for Morlaix would be the last exchange until the fall of Lord North's ministry. For the remainder of the year, Franklin encouraged John Paul Jones and all of the privateers to secure as many British prisoners of war as they possibly could. On December 4, he received a letter from Hodgson stating, "there remains due from you 41 Prisoners to make up the Number of the last Cartel, & untill that Debt is paid it is in Vain to expect any more exchanges."[49]

The year 1780 had been a difficult one for Franklin: in January, he had learned that Captain Jones' prisoners had been exchanged for French prisoners; in February, he received the letter from the prisoners at Forton prison; in March, there was the Morlaix exchange fiasco and he regretted not maintaining the relief fund; in August, he learned of the new restrictions on any future exchanges; and in September, David Hartley lost his seat in Parliament. The final disappointment occurred in the spring of 1781, when he learned that Thomas Digges had not been delivering the prisoners' allowances that had been sent to him,

47. Ibid., "February 10, 1780," 5:118.
48. "From William Hodgson, August 11, 1780," PBF, 33:180.
49. "From William Hodgson, December 4, 1780," PBF, 34:115.

but rather had absconded with an estimated £300.[50] Franklin fumed over Digges' misappropriations:

> He that robs the Rich even of a single Guinea, is a Villian, but what is he who can break his sacred Trust by robbing a poor Man and a Prisoner of Eighteen Pence given charitably for his Relief, and repeat that Crime as often as there are Weeks in a Winter . . . we have no Name in our Language for such atrocious Wickedness. If such a Fellow is not damn'd, 'tis not worth while to keep a Devil.[51]

Fortunately, he had the financial resources to continue the prisoners' allowances, or so he thought. In December, he sent £150 to Hodgson only to hear back,

> I observe that you wish the allowance for provisions & Cloathes during the Months of Jany. Feby & March shou'd be equal to 16p. per week per each Man, have you Sr considered how soon so large a distribution will swallow up the present remittance, there are not many Prisoners [short of] 500, so that in that proportion they will Require a supply of near £150 per month.

In April, Franklin had to send an additional £250; in June, another £100; in July, £110; in September, £200 and in October, £400.[52] The money was enough to maintain the allowances for the 500 prisoners until he learned in April that the number had risen to near 600, then on September 18 that "the Prisons here are now much crowded—there being upwards of 700 in Confinement & the Commissioners told me they expected very soon near as many more—it gives me much concern" and then on December 21, "there now being nearly if not quite 800 Prisoners."[53] The reason for the increase was that the Lords Commissioners had permitted the transfer of American prisoners from North America to England in addition to their refusal to exchange any Americans for Englishmen not taken by American vessels.

---

50. "Franklin to Robert R. Livingston, June 25, 1782," in Wharton, *The Revolutionary Diplomatic Correspondence*, 5:512; "To Thomas Digges, December 5, 1780," PBF, 34:118; "To William Hodgson, January 30, 1781," 34:326; "To Ferdinand Grand, February 23, 1781," 34:399; "From William Hodgson, March 20, 1781," 34:475; "To William Hodgson, April 1, 1781," 34:507; "From William Hodgson, April 12, 1781," 34:537; "To William Hodgson, April 25, 1781," 34:572; "From William Hodgson, May 8, 1781," 35:44.
51. "To William Hodgson, April 1, 1781," PBF, 34:507.
52. "From William Hodgson, January 9, 1781," PBF, 34:256. Ibid., "April 1,1781," 34:507; Ibid., "June 29, 1781," 35:198; Ibid., "July 8, 1781," 35:233; Ibid., "September 4, 1781," 35:439; Ibid., "October 31, 1781," 35:673.
53. "To William Hodgson, April 1, 1781," PBF, 34:507; Ibid., "From William Hodgson, September 18, 1781," 35:508; Ibid., "From William Hodgson, December 21, 1781."

Franklin, concerned about the growing number of prisoners and aware of Lord Cornwallis's surrender at Yorktown, hoped the Admiralty would give new consideration to an exchange. On November 19, he wrote to Hodgson,

> I would make a Proposal thro' you to the Commissioners, which is, that if they will send me over hither all the American Prisoners, they possess, I will give an Acknowledgement of receiving them, and en-' gage that an equal Number of English shall be deliver'd for them in America, Soldiers or Sailors or both.[54]

Four weeks later, he heard back from Hodgson,

> On receipt of your Letter I immediately drew up a Memorial to the Sick & Hurt Board, proposing an Exchange of Prisoners under the Terms & Provisos . . . I called upon them a few days ago to know the result, I rec'd for answer that my paper had been sent to the Admiralty Board.[55]

Hoping that the response would be positive, Franklin needed an up-to-date assessment of the gaol conditions similar to the one that John Thornton had supplied in December of 1777. This time he sent Matthew Ridley to conduct the visits, with the following instructions:

> To wait on Edmd. Burke . . . and request to know whether he has done anything . . . on the Subject of [an exchange]; [to] "wait on Mr. William Hodgson . . . [and learn] what Answer [to the Proposal] , if any, has been received; and "to procure the best Acct of the present Situation of our People in the English Prisons . . . and if . . . they suffer for want of Necessaries . . . to obtain Leave for the residence of a Commissary near each of those Prisons, for the purpose of taking proper Care of them.[56]

On January 15, 1782, Hodgson, probably after working with Ridley, wrote to Franklin,

> I shall enclose you a state of the Acc't with the Prisoners, they now are near 900 & however strange it may appear to you, I have not yet been able to procure a reply to the memorial I presented on the 4th of Decr . . . I am sorry to have to Call upon you for more Cash, from Plymo they have only a supply for this week.[57]

54. "To William Hodgson, November 19, [-20] 1781," PBF, 36:61.
55. "From William Hodgson, December 21, 1781," PBF, 36:276.
56. "To Matthew Ridley, before December 26, 1781," PBF, 36:301.
57. "From William Hodgson, January 15, 1782," PBF, 36:439.

Near the end of February, Hodgson wrote, "the Prisoners are now so numerous that they take from £50 to £60 per week at 1*s*. each & little extraordinaries."[58] The next day Franklin received a letter from Richard Hare, an Irish merchant, delivered by Job Whipple and Elijah Lewis, two gaol escapees. He learned that there was a British gaol in Kinsale, near Cork, Ireland. Originally a French gaol, it was located in Desmond Castle. The gaol at one point held 336 prisoners.[59] This was the second letter from a prisoner who had been detained at Kinsale in the last four months; the first was from Jonathan Avery, a surgeon aboard the brig Wexford commanded by Captain John Rathburn.

The Sufferings of a number of our unfortunate Brethren, whom the Fortune of Warr have thrown into the Hands of People, void of Humanity, can be releated by either of the above Gentlemen, . . . near two hundred are at present confined in a wretched prison . . . Your Excellency will be pleased to take their pityable case into your serious Consideration & endeavour to have an Exchange effected, which, if speedily done , may be the means of saveing the Lives of a number of brave, tho' unfortunate Men.[60]

While Franklin was preparing a letter to Hodgson on how to relieve the prisoners' distresses at Kinsale, he received a letter from him which stated,

the Number of Prisoners which I have before [me is] about 1000 . . . the Administration of this Country . . . the whole of the Old Ministry, so hostile & so inimical to America are to Retire . . . [and] Burke has introduced into Parliament a Bill for the exchange of American Prisoners.[61]

Within days he finished his letter to Hodgson regarding the American prisoners at Kinsale.

I just hear from Ireland, that there are 200 of our People, prisoners there, who are destitute of every Necessary, and die daily in numbers. You are about to have a new Ministry. If a sincere reconciliation is desired, Kindness to the Captives on both sides may promote it greatly. I have no Correspondent in Ireland. Can you put me in a way of sending those poor Men some Relief?[62]

58. "From William Hodgson, February 22, 1782," PBF, 36:605.
59. *John How was Agent for Prisoners of War at Kinsale* by James Coleman in "Antiquarian Remains and Historic Places in Kinsale District," *Journal of the Cork Historical & Archeological Society*, 2nd Series, XVIII (Cork, 1912), 136.
60. "From Richard Hare, Jr., February 23, 1782," PBF, 36:607.
61. "From Hodgson, March 22, 1782," PBF, 37:31.
62. "To William Hodgson, March 31, 1782," PBF, 37:79.

Franklin did not realize that, like Reverend Wren at Forton and Deacon Heath at Mill gaols, the prisoners at Kinsale were cared for by Rev. William Hazlitt, a Unitarian minister; and similar to Thomas Digges, he was assisted by Reuben Harvey, a Quaker merchant. From this day forward, Franklin made sure the Americans at Kinsale were included in every exchange.

Because of the change in the Ministry, Franklin and Hodgson's appeal for an exchange had to be presented to the new ministers. Franklin delegated the writing of a memorial to Hodgson. On April 6, the memorial was presented to the Lords Commissioners of the Admiralty:

> In December last . . . I presented, to the late Lords of the Admiralty
> . . . Propositions of an Exchange, to which Memorial their Lordships
> did not make a reply. Since . . . the Legislature have passed an Act
> for the removal of certain Difficulties, which obstructed the exchange—
>
> I take the Liberty therefore of renewing to your Lordships, those
> Propositions. The first proposition is, that . . . all American prisoners
> in Great Britain and Ireland to be sent over to France, Dr. Franklin
> will give an acknowledgement of receiving them and will engage
> that an equal Number of English Prisoners shall be delivered for
> them in America Soldiers or Sailors or both. Or 2dly that the Prisoners
> now here shou'd be sent to America in English Ships, and be
> exchanged there, under the directions of his Majestys Admirals or
> Generals, commanding on that Station.
>
> My Lords . . . my Propositions are founded upon the Principles of
> Humanity, they go to the relief of Englishmen. Languishing in Confinement,
> and equally to the relief of Americans, who have suffered
> a much longer Duration of it.[63]

"The removal of certain Difficulties, which obstructed the exchange" referred to a bill proposed in the House of Commons by Edmund Burke on February 26, "An Act for the Better Detaining, and More Easy Exchange, of American prisoners brought into Great Britain." The House of Commons passed the bill on March 19 and the House of Lords and the King approved the bill on March 25.[64] The American prisoners would no longer be viewed as rebels, but rather as prisoners of war. Eight days later, Hodgson sent Franklin an exchange agreement worked out between himself and Mr. Nepean, an under-secretary. He stated

---

63. "William Hodgson to the British Board of Admiralty, April 6, 1782," PBF, 37:124.
64. 22 Geo III, ch. 10; *Journals of the House of Commons* (London), 38:859, 866, 900, 904, 907.

"that the Transports, to take the Prisoners on board, will be ready, in a short Time; therefore no Time shou'd be lost, in finishing the business." Near the bottom of the letter he added "alltho the Propositions agreed upon, do not mention Ireland, yet, I have been assured, that a Vessell shall call at Kinsale, to take on board, the Prisoners, that remain there." The principle parts of the agreement read as follows:

> The American prisoners now in Forton & Mill Prisons, are to be sent forthwith to America in Transports . . . & to be supplyed with provisions for their Subsistence during the passage at the expense of the [British] Government: The Prisoners who belong to Massachusetts Bay & the Colonies adjacent, to be conveyed to Boston & those belonging to the southern Colonies to be conveyed to the Chesapeak or Philadelphia . . . The Master of the Transport is to be furnished with a Certificate of the Number he receives from such agent as may be appointed to superintend their Embarkation & upon such Certificate being produced by the Commander in chief of his Majestys Forces in North America the like Number of British Seamen, soldiers or Marines, as are specified in the said certificate, who have been made Prisoners by the Americans, shall be immediately released . . . It is expected that the Transports which are to receive them on board are to be furnished with a proper Proportion of Provisions for the Subsistence of the British Troops so exchanged.[65]

On April 26, Franklin wrote that he had sent

> the Passports and Powers [to sign the agreement] . . . which I hope will be sufficient . . . I confide the whole Transaction to your Judgement and Equity, and shall be satisfied with any Agreement you make . . . Whatever Allowance [Lord Sherburne] makes for the Prisoners in England, I suppose he will extend also to those in Ireland.— If not, I request you will desire your Friends at Kinsale to furnish it, and I will pay the Account upon Sight.[66]

Hodgson reported to Franklin on May 10 that the Lords Commissioners at his request gave orders to the British agent at each port of embarkation "to supply such Prisoners as may stand in need with Slops to an Amount not exceeding 20s. each Man, so that they will gt away decently & comfortably provided with necessary's for the Voyage."[67]

65. "From William Hodgson, April 14, 1782," PBF, 37:152; "To William Hodgson, April 26, 1782," ibid, 37:228-229.
66. "To William Hodgson, April 26, 1782," PBF, 37:228-229.
67. "From William Hodgson, May 10, 1782," PBF, 37:356.

Four weeks later, Hodgson reported,

The Prisoners from Portsm to the amount of 330 are gone . . . The wind having been contrary the Transports for the Plymo prisoners were not arrived, but I imagine they are by this Time . . . there will be upwards of 700 Prisoners from Plymo—the greatest part of those from Kinsale being arrived at Plymo—some few sick will remain so that another Vessell will be required as a Cartel in a short Time.[68]

Robert R. Livingston, the Secretary of State of Foreign Affairs, learned of the agreement between Franklin and the Lords Commissioners for the first time on June 25.

I had obtained from the British Ministers a Resolution to exchange all our Prisoners . . . it was made by an Act of Parliament declaring us Rebels, and our People being committed as for high treason. I impower'd Mr Hodgson . . . to treat and conclude on the Terms of the Discharge, and have approved of the Draft he sent to me of the Agreement. I hope Congress will see fit to order a punctual Execution of it.[69]

Because he did not get Livingston's input regarding or approval for the agreement beforehand, Franklin was not sure how the agreement was going to be received. So until he heard back, he was going to continue with the exchange.

On July 13, Hodgson proudly informed Franklin, "The Prisoners are all gone except about 120—who remain for some [are] sick in the Hospitals & they I expect will go in a very few days." One month later, he wrote, "I have made application for another Cartel Vessell to carry what America Prisoners have been collected since the last sailed—with those who were left behind sick the No. is about 130 and I am promised they will be sent away [as soon] as a Vessell can be procured for the purpose."[70]

There would be minor issues to resolve before all of the prisoners on both sides were exchanged. Congress threatened not to release their British prisoners because the exchange of a soldier for a sailor was an unequal proposition; the British claimed they did not have any American soldiers to exchange and that this was once again a breach of faith on the part of the Americans. Congress knew they possessed two groups of prisoners that Britain wanted returned forthwith, Burgoyne's Convention Army and Cornwallis's Yorktown Army (less those who

68. "From William Hodgson, June 7, 1782," PBF, 37:446.
69. "To Robert R. Livingston, June 25, 1782," PBF, 37:535-539.
70. "From William Hodgson, July 13, 1782," PBF, 37:625; "From William Hodgson, August 26, 1782," PBF, 38:420.

had escaped), and appeared ready to hold out. Finally, on January 9, 1783, the Lords Commissioners of the Admiralty "ordered Vessells to depart immediately with all the American prisoners." Congress however still refused to release any British Prisoners until the Provisional Articles of Peace became the Definitive Articles of Peace. This occurred on April 15, when Congress "resolved, unanimously, that the said articles be ratified, and that a ratification in due form be sent to our Ministers Plenipotentiary at the Court of Versailles, to be exchanged if an exchange shall be necessary."[71] Three weeks later, Livingston wrote to Franklin "A great part of the [British] Prisoners are on their way to New York, and the whole will be sent in a few days—they will amount to about six thousand Men."[72]

Franklin's relief program had accomplished what it set out to do: bring home as many imprisoned Americans as it could. The efforts ended as quietly as they began and since have been relegated to a mere footnote in history. There is no definitive number of prisoners directly or indirectly Franklin saved. The records are far from complete. Most biographies of Benjamin Franklin give little attention to this chapter in his life. He risked a great deal and asked for nothing in return. This is just one more reason why he truly deserves to known as one of the greatest founding fathers.

71. *Journals of the Continental Congress,* Gaillard Hunt, ed. (Washington DC: Library of Congress, 1922), 24:242.
72. "From Robert R. Livingston, May 9, 1783," PBF, 39:578.

The "P" is for Profit: Revolutionary War Privateers and the Slave Trade

❧ MIKE THOMIN ❧

The American Revolutionary War was fought largely by armies on the North American continent, however, like waves in a pond the conflict inevitably rippled out across the Atlantic world. The flow of people, supplies, and information was crucial to waging war across the Atlantic, and they were linked by who could control the sea. While studies of the use of naval power during the American Revolution abound, an in depth consideration and focus on the use of privateers during this time finally is receiving fresh scholarly attention in the twenty-first century.[1] Yet, for all the studies examining privateering during the American Revolution thus far, one aspect remains to be explored more fully: their role in the slave trade.

Privateers were privately armed ships legally sanctioned by a government to attack the merchant vessels of a nation with which the sponsoring country was at war. Privateering commissions, the documents issued by governments that granted privately owned ships the

---

1. Kylie Alder Hurlbert, "Vigorous and Bold Operations: The Times and Lives of Privateers in the Atlantic World During the American Revolution," Ph.D. dissertation, University of Georgia, 2015. E.J. Martin, "The Prize Game in the Borderlands: Privateering in New England and the Maritime Provinces, 1775-1815," Ph.D. dissertation, University of Maine, 2014. James Richard Wils, "In behalf of the continent": Privateering and Irregular Naval Warfare in Early Revolutionary America, 1775-1777," Ph.D. dissertation, East Carolina University, 2012. Michael J. Crawford, "The Privateering Debate in Revolutionary America," *The Northern Mariner*, XXI No. 3 July 2011, 219-234. Sarah Vlasity, "Privateers as Diplomatic Agents of the American Revolution 1776-1778", PhD dissertation, Department of History, University of Colorado at Boulder, 2011. Robert H. Patton, *Patriot Pirates: The Privateer War for Freedom and Fortune in the American Revolution* (New York: Pantheon Books, 2008). Richard Pougher, "Averse ... to remaining idle spectators': The Emergence of Loyalist Privateering During the American Revolution, 1775—1778," Ph.D. dissertation, The University of Maine, 2002.

right to be armed and outfitted for these types of cruises, often stipulated the vessel size, crew number, and basic rules they had to follow in order to have a legitimate claim on captured vessels. Captured vessels, or prizes, were to be determined legitimate or not by prize courts or vice admiralty courts. Similarly, letters of marque were also issued by governments to authorize merchant ships to seize enemy prizes they came across during a voyage. Unlike commissions, letters of marque primarily still functioned as merchant vessels hauling cargo while privateers were specifically outfitted as warships for capturing prizes. Either way, the value of the captured ship and cargo was shared by the privateer owners and crew.[2] The practice of commerce raiding was a maritime activity throughout the eighteenth century. The outbreak of the American Revolutionary War was an opportunity for privately armed ships to obtain permission from states, the Continental Congress, and Great Britain to wage war on their enemy's trade. Later as Spain, France, and the Netherlands entered the war, so too did they bring more privateer vessels into the "prize game."[3]

Maritime historian David Starkey noted that during the American Revolution British privateering, in particular, reached "its *apogee*, by most measures, for the 'long' eighteenth century as a whole."[4] While earlier histories of the American War of Independence treated privateering as a quasi-legal activity that was peripheral to the main theater, maritime historians have shown it was in fact widespread and a major

2. Donald A Petrie, *The Prize Game: Lawful Looting on the High Seas in the Days of Fighting Sail* (Annapolis, MD: Naval Institute Press, 1999). Matthew Taylor Raffety, *The Republic Afloat: Law, Honor, and Citizenship in Maritime America* (London: The University of Chicago Press, 2013), 31. For a thorough discussion on the anachronistic meaning between piracy and privateering, the difference between commission and letters of marque, and the limits of government authority on the practice see Guy Chet, *The Ocean is a Wilderness: Atlantic Piracy and the Limits of State Authority, 1688-1856* (Boston: University of Massachusetts Press, 2014). For an overview of the historic context and use of privateering in Europe and the Americas see Janice E. Thomson, *Mercenaries, Pirates, and Sovereigns: State-Building and Extraterritorial Violence in Early Modern Europe* (Princeton University Press, 1994), 21-68. Also see Alejandro Colas and Bryan Mabee, ed., *Mercenaries, Pirates, Bandits and Empires: Private Violence in Historical Context* (New York: Columbia University Press, 2010).
3. Carl Swanson, *Predators and Prizes: American Privateering and Imperial War, 1739-1748* (Columbia: University of South Carolina Press, 1991). Patrick Crowhurst, *The French War on Trade: Privateering 1793-1815* (Leicester: Scolar Press, 1989). David J. Starkey, *British Privateering Enterprise in the Eighteenth Century* (Exeter: University of Exeter Press, 1990).
4. Starkey, *British Privateering Enterprise*, 194.

wartime pursuit.[5] All the belligerent nations that participated in the American Revolution issued commissions to privateers to attack merchant vessels in order to harm or improve economic power, hamper or bolster political will, and increase or diminish access to resources.

For the Americans, privateers were particularly important since they captured desperately needed supplies, such as firearms, gun powder, ammunition, and goods. They also seized ships, gathered intelligence, and at least for a time effectively became the de facto American naval force since the Continental Navy remained relatively weak throughout the war. Even early in the war, during the siege of Boston in 1775 when Gen. George Washington was desperate for supplies, it was ultimately an American privateer ship that captured a British military supply vessel and delivered thousands of arms for use by the American army.[6] Additionally, the British were forced to redirect ships from convoy or blockade duties to police the privateers who operated in the Caribbean and brought ruin to West Indian traders.[7] Some estimates put American privateers as being responsible for taking 16,000 British seamen as prisoners and capturing 3,386 British ships, with an estimated value of $66 million.[8]

For the British, privateering vessels were an important aspect of naval operations as well. The British faced a major land war in North America that required the logistics of their navy to convey and transport supplies and men over 3,000 miles of water. With the entrance of the Dutch, French, and Spanish, Britain was forced to stretch its navy to protect its colonial interests throughout North America, the Caribbean, Mediterranean, and the Far East. With its resources spread out across the Atlantic world and its navy on the defensive, privateer vessels allowed the British to be on the offensive. Privateers also opened up op-

5. Edgar Stanton Maclay, *A History of American Privateers* (New York: D. Appleton and Co., 1899). Wils, "In Behalf of the Continent," 75-93. Michael Scott Casey, "Rebel Privateers—the Winners of American Independence," MA thesis, U.S. Army Command and General Staff College, 1990.

6. David McCullough, *1776* (New York: Simon & Schuster, 2005), 64.

7. Selwyn H. H. Carrington, "The American Revolution and the sugar colonies, 1775-1783," in Jack Greene and J. R. Pole, *A Companion to the American Revolution* (Oxford: Blackwell Publishing, 2004), 515-517. Also see Andrew Jackson O'Shaughnessy, *An Empire Divided: The American Revolution and the British Caribbean* (Philadelphia: University of Pennsylvania Press, 2000), 154-157. Nathan Miller, *Sea of Glory: A Naval History of the American Revolution* (Annapolis, MD: Naval Institute Press, 1992), 261.

8. Miller, *Sea of Glory*, 260-261. While Miller devotes several pages to privateering, he only mentions the slave trade a single time in the book. Starkey, *British Privateering Enterprise*, 200, 221, 279.

"The Southwell Frigate On the Coast of Africa Tradeing," by Nicholas Pocock, about 1760. (*Bristol Culture*)

portunities for British merchants who suffered from the declining economic situation due to the loss in trade.[9]

Historians in recent years have appreciated how privateers shaped the American, British, and Spanish war efforts throughout the Age of Revolutions.[10] While from a legal standpoint privateers were widely deployed and perhaps necessary for smaller naval powers, they were not always seen in a positive light or on equal terms with other revolutionary actors. One of the reasons for privateers being seen as less patriotic compared to other actors in the Revolution is because they were often perceived as fighting for their own self-interests of making a profit. In-

9. Starkey, *British Privateering Enterprise*, 193-195. See also John O. Sands, "Gunboats and Warships of the American Revolution," in George Bass, ed., *Ships and Shipwrecks of the Americas: A History Based on Underwater Archaeology* (London: Thames and Hudson, 1996), 149-168.

10. David Head, *Privateers of the Americas: Spanish American Privateering from the United States in the Early Republic* (Athens: University of Georgia Press, 2015). Matthew McCarthy, *Privateering, Piracy and British Policy in Spanish America, 1810-1830* (Suffolk: Boydel Press, 2013). Edgardo Perez Morales, "Itineraries of Freedom: Revolutionary Travels and Slave Emancipation in Colombia and the Greater Caribbean. 1789-1830," Ph. D dissertation, University of Michigan, 2013. Edgardo Perez Morales, *El gran diablo hecho barco. Corsarios, esclavos y revolución en Cartagena y el Gran Caribe. 1791-1817* (Bucaramanga: Universidad Industrial de Santander, 2012). Vanessa Mongey, "Cosmopolitan Republics and Itinerant Patriots: The Gulf of Mexico in the Age of Revolutions (1780s—1830s)," Ph. D dissertation, University of Pennsylvania, 2010.

dividual privateersmen could potentially make small fortunes from a single cruise, but that depended on their success at capturing prizes and their rank on the ship.[11] Some contemporary Americans viewed privateers as taking desperately needed manpower away from the army and navy and occasionally acting like nothing more than pirates.[12] Lucy Knox, the wife of American Gen. Henry Knox, wrote to her husband that she did "not like privateering," and that often property is taken from "innocent persons, who have nothing to do with the quarrel—[it] appears to me to be very unjust."[13] Although clearly at odds with his wife's conscience, Henry Knox invested their money in a privateer cruise a month after she wrote him this letter. Several other prominent American military officers, politicians, and shipping merchants invested their own money in privateer cruises during the war, and some made fortunes from these investments.[14]

Of course not all privateers were simply war profiteers. In some instances a lack of other sailing opportunities because of wartime disruption limited available options.[15] Mary Port Macklin describes how her life was turned upside down while living in Charleston when the war

11. See Christopher Prince, *The Autobiography of a Yankee Mariner: Christopher Prince and the American Revolution,* ed. Michael Crawford (Washington D.C.: Potomac Books, 2002), 144-145, 162. See John Palmer Papers, "Sloop REVENGE (Privateer) abstract log, Jul.-Sep. 1777, and journal Feb.-Jun. 1778, Joseph Conkling, master; contains Articles of Agreement for privateering voyage," *G. W. Blunt White Library*, Mystic Seaport Collection, Coll. 53—Box 1, Folder 12 , 39, accessed library.mysticseaport.org/manuscripts/coll/coll053.cfm. John Palmer was a Revolutionary War soldier and mariner from Stonington, Connecticut. He served on the *Revenge* on two cruises lasting four months each under Captain John Conkling spanning 1777-1778. In his diary he noted that "things taken the second cruise with Captain Conkling on and brought home into the family": 13 pounds of coffee, 9 pounds chocolate, 9 pounds of sugar, 2 ¼ gallons molasses, and 1 gallon rum valued at 21 pounds 12 shillings. See "John Palmer Diary," John Palmer Papers, *G. W. Blunt White Library*, Mystic Seaport Collection 53, Box 1, Folder 10, 22, accessed library.mysticseaport.org/manuscripts/coll/coll053.cfm.
12. See Hurlbert, "Vigorous and Bold Operations," 13, 164-220.
13. Lucy Knox to Henry Knox, March 18, 1777, Gilder Lehrman Collection GLC02437.00553, www.gilderlehrman.org.
14. George Washington, Benjamin Franklin, John Hancock, Henry Knox, Jonathan Jackson, Tristan Dalton, and William Pickman are just a few of these American leaders who made investments in privateering enterprises during the American Revolution. See *Gilder Lehrman Institute of American History* Collection GLC01411 for letters, court cases, and receipts demonstrating these specific individuals' business ventures with privateering. www.gilderlehrman.org/collections, accessed September 9, 2016. Also see Kevin Philips, *Wealth and Democracy: A Political History of the American Rich* (New York: Broadway Books, 2003), 13-14.
15. Daniel Vickers and Vince Walsh, *Young Men and the Sea: Yankee Seafarers in the Age of Sail* (New Haven: Yale University Press, 2007), 164-165.

broke out. In her diary Mary wrote that she emigrated from England to Charleston in 1775 with her husband Jack Macklin where they operated an eatery for three years. After refusing to take an oath of fidelity to the revolutionary cause when the British Fleet arrived in Charleston harbor in 1778, her husband was thrown into jail and all their property was seized and sold. Eight months later they were sent as Loyalists to St. Augustine. When they arrived they had no money or work, so her husband "took the command of the Privateer named the Polley."[16] Undoubtedly not all privateers had just their own self-interest at heart. Wills written by privateers before they left on cruises demonstrate that they had families back at home whom they were concerned about. David Harrison, a British mariner from Liverpool belonging to the privateer *Sart*, set up his last will and testament before his cruise in 1782. In his will he left his "dear wife Ellen Harrison . . . all wages at prize money bounty money and all other sums of money and all goods chattels cloaks and etc."[17]

Nonetheless, making a profit remained an important motivation even among the patriotic.[18] The American privateer Christopher Prince wrote that during the Revolution he had "two motives in mind, one was for the freedom of my country, and the other was the luxuries of life."[19] As Paul Gilje has clearly demonstrated, in many cases joining a privateer ship was not for patriotic reasons at all, but rather for the better pay.[20] In fact, some of the proceeds from prizes they made during the American Revolution included engaging in the slave trade.

16. Mary Port Macklin, Mary Port Macklin Journal, 1823, P.K. Yonge Library of Florida History, Special Collections, Diary Box 16, 22-23, accessed September 12, 2016, ufdc.ufl.edu/AA00017213/00001.
17. "Will of David Harrison otherwise George Greaves, Mariner now belonging to the Sart Privateer of Liverpool , Lancashire," July 31, 1782, The National Archives, Kew, Wills and probate, PROB 11/1093/396.
18. Hurlbert, "Vigorous and Bold Operations," 164-165.
19. Prince, *The Autobiography of a Yankee Mariner*, 210. Also see Crawford, "The Privateering Debate in Revolutionary America," 225-226.
20. For more discussion on sailors who sought out privateer service, especially to earn a living or make a "small fortune" during the American Revolution, see Paul Gilje, *Liberty on the Waterfront: American Maritime Culture in the Age of Revolution* (Philadelphia: University of Pennsylvania Press, 2007), 106-116. Sometimes the line between public or private ventures on ships outfitted for cruises against the enemy were confused and ill-defined in wartime. See Louis Arthur Norton, "America's Unwitting Pirate: The Adventures and Misfortunes of a Continental Navy Captain," CORIOLIS, Volume 6, Number 1, 2016.

Historians documented that from the sixteenth through the nineteenth centuries privateers in general were active agents in the entan-
gled world system of the Atlantic slave trade. Linda Heywood and John
Thornton found that the first Englishmen to bring Africans to the
Americas as slaves were in fact privateers.[21] David Head demonstrated
that privateers remained involved in this activity well after the foreign
slave trade was banned in 1808.[22] Nevertheless, to date there appears
to be no comprehensive examination of the role privateers during the
American Revolution played in the Atlantic slave trade.[23] Historians
have documented the practice of arming slaves to fight on both sides,
and about a thousand known black slaves served on American naval
and privateer ships during the war.[24] Going to sea in general offered enslaved black sailors some forms of freedom, and they served on many
types of vessels throughout the eighteenth century Atlantic world including whalers, fishing ships, merchant vessels, naval warships, and
even slavers.[25] In fact, at least half of the men sailing in Bermudian vessels on the eve of the American Revolution were enslaved people of
African descent. According to historian Michael Jarvis these enslaved
sailors "propped up the operations of Bermuda's merchant fleet."[26]

21. Linda M. Heywood and John K. Thornton, *Central Africans, Atlantic Creoles, and the
Foundation of the Americas, 1585-1660* (New York: Cambridge University Press, 2007).
22. David Head, "Slave Smuggling by Foreign Privateers: Geopolitical Influences on
the Illegal Slave Trade," *Journal of the Early Republic*, 33, 2013.
23. There are a few studies that mention privateers capturing slaves, but do not attempt
to more fully explore the subject. See Joseph Inikori, *Africans and the Industrial Revolution
in England: A Study in International Trade and Economic Development* (Cambridge: Cambridge University Press, 2002), 253-265. See Hurlburt, "Vigorous and Bold Operations".
See E. Arnot Robertson, *The Spanish Town Papers: Some Sidelights on the American War
of Independence* (New York: Macmillan Company, 1959), 128-143. See Benjamin Quarles,
The Negro in the American Revolution (Williamsburg: The University of North Carolina
Press, 1996).
24. Philip D. Morgan and Andrew Jackson O'Shaughnessy, "Arming Slaves in the American Revolution," in Christopher Leslie Brown and Philip D. Morgan, ed. *Arming Slaves:
From Classical Times to the Modern Age* (New Haven: Yale University Press, 2006), 198.
Black slaves also served aboard British privateer vessels during the American Revolu-
tion. See Michael Jarvis, "Maritime Masters and Seafaring Slaves in Bermuda, 1680-
1783," *The William and Mary Quarterly* 59, no. 3 (2002): 585-622. See Cassandra Pybus,
*Epic Journeys of Freedom: Runaway Slaves of the American Revolution and Their Global
Quest for Liberty* (Boston: Beacon Press, 2006), 29, 237. Also see Quarles, *The Negro in
the American Revolution*, 91-93.
25. W. Jeffrey Bolster, *Black Jacks: African American Seamen in the Age of Sail* (Cambridge:
Harvard University Press, 1997). Emma Christopher, *Slave Ship Sailors and Their Captive
Cargoes, 1730-1807* (New York: Cambridge University Press, 2006), 51-90, 60-61.
26. Michael J. Jarvis, *In the Eye of All Trade: Bermuda, Bermudians, and the Maritime Atlantic World, 1680-1783* (Williamsburg: University of North Carolina Press, 2012), 149.

However, the outbreak of the war and issuing of privateering commissions could work for or against both free and enslaved people of African descent. James Forten, a free African-American who joined a privateer crew in 1781 when he was fourteen, feared that if he was captured he would be sold as a slave in the West Indies since "rarely . . . were prisoners of his complexion exchanged."[27] His worries were not without grounds. In one particular case a group of enslaved black Bermudian sailors who made up the crew of a British privateer ship were sold when they were captured. In 1780 an American sailor named Joseph Bartlett serving on board a British privateer ship out of Bermuda was captured by an American letter of marque from Philadelphia. Afterwards, Bartlett joined the American crew and bragged that his fifty former slave shipmates were sold for a "hefty price" in the Havana slave market.[28] In her journal Mary Macklin wrote that part of her husband's first prize share included "3 negro lads," and the second "prise he sherd for his part" an enslaved couple named Robert and Nancy.[29] These were not isolated incidents; privateers took an active role in the slave trade.

Since slaves were considered property, terrestrial-based revolutionary actors engaged in this practice as well. After all, slaves were considered spoils of war.[30] While some accounts of slaves becoming crew on board privateers suggests agency, like their counterparts on land privateers did capture and sell slaves for a profit to a notable degree. This included capturing slave ships at sea like the cases mentioned above, as well as amphibious raids on plantations. Don Francisco Saavedra de Sangronis was a Spanish soldier and government official sent on a mission by General Bernardo de Galvez during the American Revolution to help plan to retake Pensacola, Florida, and eventually to capture Jamaica. He spent over a year in Jamaica after his ship was captured by the British and kept a diary of his experiences during the war. Of particular interest is a story he related of a British officer complaining to him of how Spanish *corsarios*, or privateers, frequently sailed from the port of Trinidad in canoes "authorized with the royal letter of marque" and raided plantations in British Jamaica for slaves. They then smuggled

27. Julie Winch, *A Gentlemen of Color: The Life of James Forten* (Oxford: Oxford University Press, 2005), 43.

28. Gilje, *Liberty on the Waterfront*, 116. For another case of black sailors on a British privateer being sold as slaves in Maryland see Quarles, *The Negro in the American Revolution*, 107.

29. Macklin wrote that Robert and Nancy became their house slaves, while the three "negro lads" went with her husband. Mary Port Macklin Journal, 24.

30. Quarles, *The Negro in the American Revolution*, 107, 156.

these slaves to Cuba and sold them.[31] In 1777 two plantations on the island of Tobago owned by Charles Gustavas Meyers and Henry Kelly
were raided by an American privateer named Paschall Bonavita. When
Bonavita and his crew raided the Meyers and Kelly plantations they
stole a small schooner at anchor as well as thrity-seven black slaves and
"2 Carib Indians born in the Island of St. Vincents." They sold the slaves
to their Spanish contacts in Trinidad.[32] Spanish and American privateers
reportedly raided plantations at New Smyrna in East Florida for slaves
as well.[33] In 1781 a British privateer captured thirty slaves from an American plantation in Westmoreland, and there were several other incidents
of both American and British privateers raiding plantations for "slave
loot" as well.[34]

The Atlantic slave trade declined during the American Revolutionary
War and in some years decreased by half. Nevertheless, slavers continued to transport "captive cargoes" throughout the conflict.[35] A British
slave ship captain noted that in the year 1777 "The trade [to the Gold
Coast of Africa] in general has suffered greatly since I have known it,
both as to the difficulty in obtaining slaves, and the price at which they

31. Saavedra De Sangronis Francisco, and Francisco Morales Padrón, *Journal of Don
Francisco Saavedra De Sangronis during the Commission Which He Had in His Charge from
25 June 1780 until the 20th of the Same Month of 1783* (Gainesville: University of Florida
Press, 1989), 45-47.
32. See Michael J. Crawford, *Naval Documents of the American Revolution Volume 10*
(Washington D.C., U.S Government Printing Office, 1994), 277-279.
33. Jennifer Snyder, "Revolutionary Repercussions: Loyalist Slaves in St. Augustine and
Beyond," in In Jerry Bannister and Liam Riordan, *Loyal Atlantic: Remaking the British
Atlantic in the Revolutionary Era* (Toronto: University of Toronto Press, 2012), 174-176.
34. Quarles, *The Negro in the American Revolution*, 118, 131-132.
35. According to *The Trans-Atlantic Slave Trade Database*, before the war began in the
year 1775 over 92,000 slaves embarked on voyages. As the Revolutionary War continued
this number declined dramatically, reaching its lowest level during the war in 1779 with
37,758 slaves embarking on voyages for the year. The number of slaves embarking on
voyages did not recover to prewar levels until after the war ended. In 1784 the number
of slaves embarking on voyages rapidly increased to its highest number for a year in
over three decades to 104,364. slavevoyages.org/assessment/estimates. The slave trade
declined by a quarter in the early years of the war and twelve out of thirty Liverpool
slave companies went out of business before 1778. See O'Shaughnessy, *An Empire Divided*, 166. Some vessels involved in the slave trade before the American Revolution
began did in fact fit out to become privateers during the war. See David Eltis and David
Richardson, *Atlas of the Transatlantic Slave Trade* (New Haven: Yale University Press,
2010).

are purchased."[36] Contemporaries observed that in some areas of the Atlantic world the prices for slaves declined while in others they increased dramatically. In 1788 Thomas Clarkson wrote that during the American war "while the price of a slave was as low as seven pounds on the coast, and as high, on an average, as forty-five in the colonies, the adventurer, who escaped the ships of the enemy, made his fortune."[37] The *Annals of Commerce, Manufactures, Fisheries and Navigations* listed the average price for slaves from the years 1764 to 1788 in Africa as eight to twenty-two pounds Sterling compared to twenty eight to thirty five pounds Sterling in the West Indies.[38] In general slave prices increased throughout the war and created abnormally large profits in the trade.[39] Even though a quarter or more of slave vessels were captured during wartime, the demand for slaves in the Americas made it a risky but worthwhile business venture.[40]

In her study of British Admiralty records, E. Arnot Robertson wrote that it made no difference for slaves who were rerouted from capture,

36. "Minutes of Enquiry into Administration of the West African Trade: Volume 84," in *Journals of the Board of Trade and Plantations: Volume 14*, January 1776—May 1782, ed. K. H. Ledward (London: His Majesty's Stationery Office, 1938), 126-146. British History Online, www.british-history.ac.uk/jrnl-trade-plantations/vol14/pp126-146, accessed September 10, 2016.

37. Thomas Clarkson, *An Essay on the Impolicy of the African Trade* (London: J. Phillips, 1788), 25.

38. David Machperson, *Annals of Commerce, Manufactures, Fisheries, and Navigation Vol. IV* (London: Nicols and Son, 1805), 153.

39. David Eltis, Lewis, and Richardson, "Slave Prices, the African Slave Trade, and Productivity in the Caribbean, 1674-1807," *The Economic History Review*, New Series, 58, no. 4 (2005): 679-686. Elizabeth Donnan wrote that "The information about the price of slaves during the early years of the Revolution is curiously conflicting." See Elizabeth Donnan, *Documents Illustrative of the History of the Slave Trade to America: Volume II: The Eighteenth Century* (New York: William S. Hein & Col., 2002), 554. The price of goods in general fluctuated geographically during the American Revolution. See O'Shaughnessy, *An Empire Divided*, 160-167. Also see Mary M. Schweitzer, "The Economic and Demographic Consequences of the American Revolution," in Greene, *A Companion to the American Revolution, 559-577*. Joseph Inikori, "Measuring the unmeasured hazards of the Atlantic slave trade: documents relating to the British trade," *Revue Francais D'Histoire D'Outre Er* 83 (September 1996), 88.

40. See David Eltis, Lewis, and Richardson. "Slave Prices." According to one study, two thirds of the British slave ships lost were captured by an enemy nation during wartime. See Christopher, *Slave Ship Sailors and Their Captive Cargoes*, 75.

41. Robertson, *The Spanish Town Papers*, 135.

"except that they worked till they died in Jamaica, and not in Barbados or the Southern States of America."[41] Yet, one might argue that the trauma of capture alone certainly mattered to "the experience of the historical subjects" involved in such instances.[42] Robertson wrote this book in 1959, and since that time historians have demonstrated to some extent it mattered where the enslaved ended up geographically at least in terms of individual experience, and thus for the lives of their descendants.[43] We must remember, as Vincent Brown stresses, that numbers alone "cannot represent the wrenching personal trials endured by the enslaved."[44]

Nonetheless, according to *The Trans-Atlantic Slave Trade Database* (TASTD), 480,929 slaves embarked on 1,551 voyages across the Atlantic world during the years of the American Revolutionary War from 1775–1783.[45] Of these, 31,768 slaves were captured on 107 different voyages by naval and privateer vessels during the course of the conflict. These slaves were rerouted from their intended point of disembarkation to ports allied to the flag the privateer vessel flew under, or where supporters or agents could secure their anchorage. Utilizing the TASTD variable query of slave ships captured specifically by a "pirate/privateer," shows that 1,690 slaves were captured by six different privateer vessels from 1775–1783. By using various primary and secondary source materials and cross referencing them with the voyage outcomes recorded as captured in the TASTD, it is clear that the number of slaves captured by privateers during the years of the American Revolution actually exceeds what the TASTD currently shows. In fact, at least 8,519 slaves

42. See Vincent Brown, *Reaper's Garden: Death and Power in the World of Atlantic Slavery* (Cambridge: Harvard University Press, 2008), 29.

43. Ibid, 48-57. See Ira Berlin, *Generations of Captivity: A History of African-American Slaves* (Cambridge: Harvard University Press, 2003), 55.

44. Brown, *Reaper's Garden*, 29.

45. This is according to the summary statistics for the years 1775-1783 on the *The Trans-Atlantic Slave Trade Database*. In 1775 the war at sea was not yet significant at that time, and the several months of that year when the war was not impacting numbers of the slave trade do somewhat skew the results. This database is the most comprehensive source on slave voyages ever compiled by researchers. The web resource allows researchers to query specific variables and dates to analyze over 34,000 slave voyages that transported over 10 million Africans to the Americas. David Eltis, et al. *The Trans-Atlantic Slave Trade Database.*, www.slavevoyages.org.

were captured on 43 privateer cruises during the American Revolution.[46] This is nearly twenty-seven percent of the slaves listed as captured by vessels in the TASTD throughout the war.

Part of this discrepancy is because some of the slave vessels captured by privateers recorded in the TASTD are listed under the variable queries of "unknown" or "captor unspecified." The privateers recorded were predominantly American or British, but also include French and Spanish (26 American ships, 9 British, 1 French, 2 Spanish, 4 unspecified). America and Britain should be expected to have the highest numbers of privateers since they were the two main belligerents during the conflict and were likely responsible for issuing most of the commissions. Also, the sources utilized here are primarily Anglo-American. If Dutch, French, and Spanish sources are included the overall number of privateer ships involved in transporting and selling captive cargoes during the war will undoubtedly increase.[47]

Nearly half the American privateer ships recorded in this study took their captured prizes with cargoes, including slaves, to the French island of Martinique. Others sailed to various ports in North America (New Orleans, Philadelphia, Connecticut, South Carolina, Georgia) or other French and Spanish Caribbean islands (Haiti and Trinidad). In contrast, the British privateer vessels recorded in this study took almost all their captured prizes with cargoes including slaves to Jamaica or the West Indies (a few were adjudicated in British East Florida in St. Augustine). The highest number of slaves captured by a privateer on one voyage

46. Three primary sources were utilized for this purpose. These include the *Naval Documents of the American Revolution, Lloyd's List*, and incidents reported in British and American colonial newspapers and court records. Clark, William Bell, Ernest McNeill Eller, et al. *Naval Documents of the American Revolution. Volumes 1-12* (Washington: U.S. Govt. Print. Off., 1964-2013). *Lloyd's List* 1774-1775, 1775-1776, 1776-1777, 1777-1778, 1778-1779, 1779-1780, 1780-1781, 1781-1782, 1782-1783, 1783-1784 (Westmead, Great Britain. Gregg International, 1969), catalog.hathitrust.org/Record/000549597. Newspaper Archives 1690-2010, NewsBank and/or the American Antiquarian Society, 2004, geneaologybank.com. A database of privateers mentioned in these sources as capturing slaves was compiled with relevant information recorded by the author in a Microsoft Excel spreadsheet. Other primary sources utilized include court records, ship logs, and diaries.

47. Moreover, the number of slaves captured by privateers might easily double from what this study documented. According to a report filed in 1777 by the Board of Trade, which investigated the African Company of Merchants after a request from the House of Commons, "During the last two years, the colonies did not receive 16,000 annually from all parts of Africa, even when any of those purchased there escaped, being taken by American privateers on their passage to the West Indies." See Donnan, *Documents Illustrative of the History of the Slave Trade*, 553.

was 697, and the lowest number of slaves recorded captured by a privateer on a single voyage was one.[48]

When compared to overall operations, privateer ships that sailed on cruises during the American Revolution did not regularly capture slave ships or raid plantations. At least qualitatively, the bulk of the prize ships privateers captured carried goods, raw materials, or war contraband.[49] Yet, for the thousands of enslaved individuals who found themselves onboard privateer ships against their will, the actions of privateers certainly mattered because being captured added to the trauma of their voyage and ultimately determined their final place of disembarkation. Although the number of slaves imported as "prize cargo" was small compared to the overall number of enslaved people shipped during the conflict, new questions should be asked pertaining to the role privateers played in the slave trade during the war.[50]

48. No. 1036, February 26, 1779, *Lloyd's List 1779 & 1780* (Westmead: Gregg International Publishers, 1969). Henry Yonge, Court of the Vice Admiralty, "Claim Made on the Sloop Lucky Strike," 1779, *The Gilder Lehman Institute of American History*, GLC01411.10: Legal Documents relating to captured American Privateers, 1776-1779.
49. When the American sailor Jacob Nagle served aboard two different privateer vessels from April 1780 to November 1781, he claims they took dozens of prizes. Although Nagle identifies some of types of the cargo and items they captured from ships, he does not mention slaves being onboard any of these prizes. This was probably the typical case for most privateer cruises during the American Revolution. Jacob Nagle served as a sailor for both the British and American navies throughout his decade's long career. Chapter two in this published diary cover his service on board an American privateer ship from April 1780 to November 1781, providing a unique first-hand account on life on privateer cruises during the American Revolutionary War. See Jacob Nagle, *The Nagle Journal: A Diary of the Life of Jacob Nagle, Sailor, From the Year 1775 to 1841*, John C Dann, ed. (New York: Weidenfeld & Nicolson, 1988), 15. Christopher Prince does not mention capturing slaves on board prizes in his account of the privateer cruises he served on from 1777-1781 either. Neither do Christopher Hawkins (American privateer ship Eagle) or Andrew Sherburne (American privateer ships Ranger and Greyhound). See Christopher Hawkins and Charles I. Bushnell, ed. *The Adventures of Christopher Hawkins* (New York: 1864) and Andrew Sherburne, *Memoirs of Andrew Sherburne: A Pensioner of the Navy of the Revolution*, 2nd edition (Providence: H.H. Brown, 1831).
50. One important question to research further is what was the economic impact of these slave cargoes on the privateering enterprise (e.g. recruiting), privateering ports, and the American war effort? This was raised by Dr. Guy Chet in a comment on an earlier draft of this paper. Lydia Towns noted in an unpublished paper that "Historians of the transatlantic slave trade have been lax in evaluating the impact of piracy on the transatlantic slave trade during the sixteenth and seventeenth centuries, relegating phenomena of piracy to a side note in many of their texts." Lydia Towns, "English Privateers and the Transatlantic Slave Trade," www.academia.edu/14696017/English_Privateers_and_the_Transatlantic_Slave_Trade.

The American War of Independence is often remembered by the public as a revolution led by colonial patriots who fought for liberty against oppressive British masters.[51] Yet, some of these revolutionary actors who participated in the conflict, such as privateers, were at least partially motivated to fight for the large profits they could receive from prizes, and not just for the ideals of "liberty and equality." Moreover, some of these same revolutionary privateers helped deny individual freedom to others through their role in the slave trade by stealing and selling "captive cargoes." While some politicians, generals, merchants, and even common Jack Tars certainly lost all they had during the war, others profited handsomely from the human beings and property they captured and sold throughout the conflict.

---

51. Gary Nash, *The Unknown American Revolution: The Unruly Birth of Democracy and the Struggles to Create America* (New York: Penguin Group, 2006), xiv-xv.

Joseph Addison's *Cato*: Liberty on the Stage

❈ ERIC STERNER ❈

The study of ancient Greece and Rome was a significant part of upper class education in Colonial and Revolutionary America. The founders were familiar with spread of Greek democracy, the fall of the Roman Republic, concepts of citizenship, and the rise of tyrants and dictators. They drew cautionary lessons, particularly about the vulnerabilities of democracies and republics to demagogues, dictators, and mob rule. Those lessons did not merely come from reading ancient histories, but were also frequent subjects of discussion, in which events in the classical word were mutually understood touchpoints for events in the early eighteenth century. Contemporary letters and essays make frequent references to events in Pericles' Athens, Cicero's commentaries, the fall of the Roman Republic and the rise of Julius Caesar. Indeed, questions of governance, citizenship, duty, and liberty entered popular culture. One vehicle was Joseph Addison's drama *Cato: A Tragedy*.

First performed on the London stage in 1713, Addison's play made its way to the colonies in 1732.[1] Addison, a Whiggish essayist and co-founder of the *Spectator*, was already widely read in the colonies. His play was performed, among other places, in Charleston in 1736, New York in 1750, Philadelphia in 1759, Providence in 1762, and Boston and Portsmouth in 1778. (Earlier attempts to perform the play in Boston had been quashed; Joseph Warren and his fellow students put on a private production at Harvard in 1758.[2]) Some consider it to have been

1. Thomas Fleming, "George Washington's Favorite Play," *Journal of the American Revolution*, December 11, 2013, allthingsliberty.com/2013/12/george-washingtons-favorite-play/.
2. Robert M. Keller, compiler, Performance Notices in The Colonial Music Institute database, www.cdss.org/elibrary/PacanNew/index.htm, accessed September 20, 2016;

Washington's favorite play.[3] (In his biography of Washington, Ron Chernow notes Cato's importance, but believes a comedy, *The School for Scandal*, was Washington's favorite play.[4])

Two famous, or possibly infamous, quotes from American history allegedly trace their roots to *Cato*. Nathan Hale's ubiquitous quote during his execution, "I only regret that I have but one life to lose for my country," may have been inspired by Act IV, when Cato glorifies his son's death, "-How beautiful is death when earned by virtue? / Who would not be that youth? What pity is it / That we can die but once to serve our country!"[5] Similarly, Patrick Henry's "Give me liberty or give me death!" cry during the Second Virginia Convention may owe its heritage to a scene in Act II, in which Cato declares, "It is not now a time to talk of aught / But chains or conquest, liberty or death."[6] In truth, Henry often spoke extemporaneously from notes and no complete text of the speech has survived. Instead, it was re-constructed decades later by a Henry biographer, who Ray Raphael concludes likely wrote the speech.[7] Similarly, few were present at Hale's execution and his quote comes through the memoir of a classmate, who claimed to be repeating the story told him by John Montressor, the British chief engineer sta-

Robert Brand Hanson, ed., *The Diary of Dr. Nathaniel Ames of Dedham, Massachusetts, 1758-1822* (Camden, ME: Picton Press, 1998), www.drjosephwarren.com/2016/03/cato-more-perfect-than-before/, accessed September 20, 2016; Jason Shaffer, *Performing Patriotism: National Identity in the Colonial and Revolutionary American Tradition* (Philadelphia: University of Pennsylvania Press, 2007), 45.

3. Harlow Giles Unger, *The Unexpected George Washington: His Private Life* (New York: John Wiley & Sone, 2006), 52; David McCullough, *1776* (New York: Simon and Schuster Paperbacks, 2005), 47. According to Austin Washington, his great uncle George kept a copy of *Cato* by his bed. Austin Washington, *The Education of George Washington* (Washington, DC: Regnery History, 2014), 279.

4. Ron Chernow, *Washington: A Life* (New York: The Penguin Press, 2010), 126. *The School for Scandal* was first performed in 1777 and lacked the political themes that made Addison's *Cato* relevant to the politics of the day.

5. *Cato*, act IV, scene 4, 84.

6. Christine Dunn Henderson and Mark E. Yellin, eds., Joseph Addison, *Cato: A Tragedy, and Selected Essays* (Indianapolis: Liberty Fund, 2004), 44. The play went through several iterations and the text contained here is from the 8th edition, which does not differ from the 7th edition that Addison considered definitive. Performances included additional material that Addison preferred not to see in printed editions. References to the play's text are hereafter cited as *Cato*, with reference to the act, scene, and page number.

7. Ray Raphael, "Patrick Henry's 'Liberty or Death'-Granddaddy of Revolution Mythologies," *Journal of the American Revolution*, July 13, 2015, allthingsliberty.com/2015/07/patrick-henrys-liberty-or-death-granddaddy-of-revolution-mythologies/.

tioned nearby.[8] In either case, a certain class of Americans were already familiar with the ideas and sentiments attributed to Henry (liberty or death) and Hale (martyrdom for cause and country), thanks in no small part, to the play. It was only natural for those recreating Henry's and Hale's words to borrow from a well-understood source, just as today's writers often refer to contemporary memes as a way of connecting with their readers.

Cato (the play) may have resonated in early eighteenth century America because of the themes it touches upon and the dilemmas which confront its individuals living in an increasingly dictatorial system, as the colonists believed themselves to be facing. Cato the Younger (95 BC–46 BC), was a Roman aristocrat and statesman best known as a leader of the opposition to the centralization of power in the Roman Republic. A confirmed republican, Cato commanded a legion, embraced a stoic philosophy and lifestyle, was elected to a government position where he rooted corruption out of public institutions, and eventually became the tribune elected by the plebian (lower) classes. Fearing the rise of Caesar and Pompey after their military successes, he opposed their political maneuvering to reward their soldiers at the expense of the public good. When the political alliance among Caesar, Pompey, and Crassus broke down, Cato led efforts to strip Caesar of some his power, prompting the latter to move against the Senate and begin his pursuit of sole power. As the civil war grew, Cato allied with Pompey. After Pompey lost the battle of Pharsalus, Cato and some of his allies escaped with part of their army to Utica on the African coast, in present-day Tunisia. When it became apparent that the military situation was irretrievable after the anti-Caesar forces lost the battle of Thapsus, Cato killed himself.

Cato became an example of a life lived in service of higher principle and, by the eighteenth century, he had evolved into a symbol of committed republicanism in the face of the threat posed by tyranny, represented in the person of Caesar.[9] While the basic facts of his life came down through the centuries from Plutarch and other writers, Addison's play popularized the Roman and turned him into a martyr for liberty. It was no accident that Washington allowed, if not encouraged, the play's performance at Valley Forge in the midst of a Congressional ban on drama as an indulgent extravagance.[10]

8. Barnet Schecter, *The Battle for New York* (New York: Penguin Books, 2002), 213-24.
9. Carl J. Richard, *Greeks & Romans Bearing Gifts: How the Ancients Inspired the Founding Fathers* (Laurel, MD: Rowman & Littlefield Publishers, Inc., 2008), Chapter 7.
10. David Malinsky, "Congress Bans Theatre!" *Journal of the American Revolution*, December 12, 2013, allthingsliberty.com/2013/12/congress-bans-theatre/.

Addison's play opens after the battle of Thapsus, the latest defeat for republican forces, surely something the army under Washington's command understood well after a series of high profile defeats at British hands outside Philadelphia. Their situation at Valley Forge may have reminded them of Cato's army holed up in Utica. The first act introduces one of the play's major's themes: the struggle between virtue and passion. Virtue in the eighteenth century was not mere chastity, but a commitment to self-improvement and self-control through the embrace of reason to overcome the passions that led individuals and societies astray in the pursuit of self-aggrandizement and indulgence. Thus, virtue had both a public and private nature.

In *Cato*, Addison presents the public aspects in the conflict between Caesar, who represents the pursuit of personal glory, and the benefits of civilization, represented by Cato and the Roman Republic. More narrowly, he brings that conflict home to Utica in a conspiracy between two people holed up in Utica with pro-republican forces, Sempronius and Syphax. Working together for slightly different motivations, they scheme to betray Cato. Sempronius anticipates a reward from Caesar, preferably the hand of Cato's daughter Marcia. Syphax is a Numidian general who, recognizing the hopelessness of their situation, wants to prevent his prince, Juba, from joining the fate of Cato when Caesar finally wins the conflict. For his part, Juba admires Cato's philosophy and seeks to emulate it; he also loves Marcia.

Addison captures the private aspects in two love triangles. The first concerns the aforementioned Marcia; Juba the virtuous and Sempronius the opportunistic traitor both love her. Juba hopes to win her by emulating her father.[11] Sempronius hopes to receive her as a prize from Caesar. The second concerns Cato's sons, Marcus and Portius, and Lucia, one of Marcia's friends. Both sons love her, but also strive to emulate their father's pursuit of higher purpose at the expense of their personal desires and passions. Marcus, in particular, struggles with the battle between his emotional desire for Lucia and his commitment to the noble purposes of his father. Unfortunately for him, his difficulty in controlling his emotions leads Lucia to prefer Portius.

When Sempronius first makes his appearance in act I, he confides to the audience that he is up to something and must dissemble when he encounters Portius. After discussing the situation, the latter takes his leave, telling Sempronius:

11. In a 1758 letter to Sally Fairfax, Washington flirtatiously suggested they might enjoy playing the parts of Marcia and Juba. See Rob Hardy, "Cato," The *Digital Encyclopedia of George Washington*, September 11, 2016, www.mountvernon.org/digital-encyclopedia/article/cato/.

> *I'll animate the soldiers' drooping courage,*
> *With love of freedom, and contempt of life,*
> *I'll thunder in their ears their country's cause,*
> *And try to rouse up all that's Roman in 'em.*
> *'Tis not in mortals to command success,*
> *But we'll do more, Sempronius, we'll deserve it.*[12]

Both John Adams and George Washington were familiar with the line. Adams paraphrased it in a letter to his wife and Washington in letters to Nicholas Cooke and Benedict Arnold.[13] To Arnold, then engaged in the disappointing Canadian campaign and facing circumstances only slightly less bleak than Cato, Washington wrote, "It is not in the power of any man to command success, but you have done more—you have deserved it."[14] It was a none-too-subtle way of placing Arnold on a pedestal with a first century Roman many admired.

Ironically, for a play named after him, Cato does not appear in the first act. Instead, he hovers in the background, the standard of virtue to which his sons and Juba aspire despite their private passions, and the pillar of Roman civilization that stands against Caesar's tyranny and Sempronius' conniving manipulations. Fortunately for the audience, Cato is in the first scene of act II.

Having established his broader theme, Addison sharpens the conflict between mankind's higher and baser self in presenting his characters with temptations and choices. For Cato, the choice is between liberty and slavery, freedom and servitude. He clearly prefers liberty and freedom, telling a fellow senator, "A day, an hour, of virtuous liberty / Is worth a whole eternity in bondage."[15] In act II a messenger from Caesar arrives, offering peace and elevation to Cato if he submits to Caesar's rule. Cato, of course, dismisses the offer out of hand and instead demands that Caesar surrender and face the judgment of Rome. (He also declines to inform his allies in Utica of it, forcing them to share his fate). Juba, meanwhile, confesses his desire for Cato's daughter, Marcia. Cato promptly rebuffs him as well, chastising the young man for pursuing his personal desires when such momentous events are in play. (Indeed, the liberty or death phrase arrives with Cato's rejection of Juba's petition.) Syphax attempts to take advantage of Juba's heartbreak and sway

---

12. *Cato*, act I, scene 3, 14.
13. *Cato*, act I, scene 3, n 19, 14.
14. "George Washington to Benedict Arnold, 5 December 1775," in George Washington, *Selected Writings* (New York: Library of American Paperback Classics Edition, 2011), 81.
15. *Cato*, act II, scene 1, 33.

him from Cato's noble cause, offering to carry Marcia off for his prince, but fails. Juba reacts angrily and Syphax finally joins Sempronius in Caesar's cause, secretly forsaking his prince. He and Sempronius have laid the groundwork for a mutiny by the army.

Whereas Juba succeeds in his test of virtue, remaining true to Cato in the face of Syphax's temptation, Marcus and Portius fail. The former surrenders to his passion and enlists his brother to convince Lucia to pledge herself to him. Portius, who undertakes the mission somewhat reluctantly, cannot hide his own passion for Lucia. He confesses his love to her even as he begs her not to hurt Marcus by rejecting him. Ironically, whereas Cato's sons fail this personal test, Lucia rejects Portius because he asks the impossible of her and instead foreswears him. Thus, Addison posits that failure to place a higher priority on one's public duty leads to personal failure. Indeed, no one in the play who indulges his personal interests and desires truly succeeds.

While Cato's sons spend their time and energy on an impossible love triangle, Sempronius begins to spring his trap. Even as mutinous soldiers confront Cato, Sempronius pledges his fealty to the exiled leader. It serves him well, as Cato talks the soldiers out of abandoning their cause immediately by shaming them. However, urged on by Sempronius, Cato condemns the leaders to death. Sempronius is quick to have the sentence carried out, lest his own part be revealed and, no doubt, with the expectation that the executions will spread yet more discord in the army. Addison returns to his "liberty or death" motif in words that any American revolutionary would appreciate:

> *Meanwhile we'll sacrifice to liberty.*
> *Remember, O my friends, the laws, the rights,*
> *The generous plan of power delivered down,*
> *From age to age, by your renowned forefathers,*
> *(So dearly bought, the price of so much blood,)*
> *Oh let it never perish in your hands!*
> *But piously transmit it to your children.*
> *Do thou, great liberty, inspire our souls,*
> *And make our lives in thy possession happy,*
> *Or our deaths glorious in thy just defence.*[16]

The call to a higher, more noble, sacred purpose—liberty—is clear.

Although Cato turns back Sempronius' initial mutiny attempt, the latter attempts to kidnap Marcia. Juba kills him in the process, leading

---

16. *Cato*, act III, scene 5, 68.

Marcia to confess her love for Juba. At the same time, Syphax leads Juba's army out of camp, fleeing to Caesar. In the process, the Numidians kill Marcus, but not until the latter kills Syphax. Upon reuniting with his son's corpse, Cato bewails the want of more than one life to lay before his country. Heartbroken at his son's death and disheartened by the Roman republic's collapsing situation, he tells Portius and his allies to flee and live a life of quiet contemplation someplace safe. Determined not to become Caesar's prisoner or to bow down to his tyranny, Cato kills himself. Addison spares his audience the gruesome end. The real Cato's first attempt to disembowel himself was not fatal. So, amidst his family's efforts to restrain him and treat his wounds, he stabbed himself again. The Roman intends his final act to mock Caesar, who, having conquered the republic, will be denied its most prominent symbol, at least to Cato's mind.[17]

In *Cato: A Tragedy*, Addison offered the Revolutionary generation an example of an individual uncompromising in his defense of liberty, who closely identified it with republicanism and the fruits of civilization. Before the war, it was an inspiring message about the individual's duty to a larger cause and the ancient defense of liberty. During the war, Cato's persistent commitment to his principles in the face of overwhelming force, even to the point of death, made the play an appropriate drama to present to the troops at Valley Forge. Every other individual who chose his personal interest over the duty to defend liberty failed in his private pursuits. Only Juba, who remained true to Cato and his cause in the face of temptation, received his heart's desire in Marcia's love. While Steuben trained the army, Addison, and even Cato after a fashion, instructed its mind.

17. *Cato*, act V, scene 2, 90.

The Remarkable Spanish Pilgrimage of John Adams

❀ JOHN L. SMITH, JR. ❀

The ship carrying John Adams was sinking in the middle of the Atlantic Ocean!

The awful thought must have been crippling for Adams, chosen almost unanimously by Congress to travel to France for this second time. It was November 1779 and Adams was being sent as minister to negotiate treaties of commerce, and most importantly—peace with Great Britain, if it should come. Ocean voyages were always dangerous, but a winter crossing was especially so. As the threat of sinking shot through Adams' mind, he probably regretted bringing his two sons on board with him, twelve-year old John Quincy and nine-year old Charles, even though John Quincy had already accompanied his father on his first trip to Paris the year before. How was Abigail, back in Braintree, Massachusetts going to react when she found out her husband and two sons were drowned at sea?

When a sailing ship of those days ran into trouble on the vast Atlantic Ocean, the captain and crew were totally alone. No SOS distress signal could be sent to nearby vessels; no GPS coordinates could be flashed to friendly coast guard monitoring stations of all nations. The ship just silently sank with all crew and passengers on board. Usually no sign of the vessel or people was ever found.

Just a couple days after having set sail from Boston on November 15, 1779, the doomed French frigate—*le Sensible*—with the Adams entourage on board, sailed into a "very violent Gale of Wind"[1] and then —the worst nightmare that could be imagined during an eighteenth-

1. John Adams autobiography, part 3, "Peace," 1779-1780, sheet 5 of 18 [electronic edition]. Adams Family Papers: An Electronic Archive. Massachusetts Historical Society, www.masshist.org/digitaladams/, accessed September 4, 2016.

century ocean crossing—the vessel *sprang a large leak!* The captain immediately began to have the icy water pumped out, crew and passengers alike all working the pump frantically twenty-four hours a day. Even young John Quincy took his turn. But the leak got worse, so a second pump had to be installed and used. Even with the group's best pumping efforts, the leak was getting worse. The ship was sinking! The question was whether the boat would make it to *any* land before it totally sank into the freezing Atlantic waters. Captain Chevalier De Chavagne decided their only chance would be to try to make it to the first friendly port they could get to. In 1779, that meant Spain, an ally with France against their common enemy—Great Britain.

In the morning mist of December 7, 1779, the rocky piece of triangular land called Cape Finisterre was spotted. It was the westernmost tip of Spain and for many centuries considered to be the end of the earth. It meant they had survived the perilous ocean crossing. To make Abigail feel better (but it most likely just increased her anxiety), John Quincy cavalierly later wrote his mother: "One more storm would very probably [have] carried us to the bottom of the sea."[2] On December 8, the *Sensible*[3] limped into the Spanish port of El Ferrol which opened to the Atlantic Ocean at the tip of the Bay of Biscay. As soon as the ship docked and the pumping had stopped, the *Sensible* filled up with seven feet of sea water. John Adams was now stuck on the northwestern tip of Spain, almost 1,000 miles from Paris, not knowing if he should wait for ship repairs (which could take months, if possible at all) or just hoof it from Spain to France. "Whether to travail by Land to Paris, or wait for the Frigate,"[4] Adams mused in his diary. Just the year before, in March 1778 on his first diplomatic mission, Adams had traveled from Bordeaux, France, somewhat near the northeastern Spanish border, into Paris – in 1780 a trip of approximately five days. Adams didn't know it, but the Spanish countryside was vastly different than the flat, lush, cultivated countryside of France. But John Adams, a type-A personality of his time, couldn't just sit around. He had to get to work, even if it meant a difficult commute. He just didn't have any idea of difficult!

2. John Quincy Adams to Abigail Adams, Bilbao January 16, 1780, in *Adams Family Correspondence*, L. H. Butterfield and Marc Friedlaender, eds., Vol 3; (Cambridge, MA., Belknap Press, 1973), 260.
3. Adams didn't think much of their vessel. He wrote in his autobiography, "The Sensible was an old Frigate, and her Planks and timbers were so decayed, that one half the Violence of Winds and Waves which had so nearly wrecked the new and strong Ship the Boston the Year before, would have torn her to pieces."
4. John Adams diary, 1779 DECEMBER.[5.] SUNDAY, page 4; John Adams diary 30, November 13, 1779—6 January 1780, Adams Family Papers.

For the week following the port landing, Adams was wined and dined in El Ferrol by Spanish and French officers, chief magistrates and local dignitaries like the French Consul from Coruña. Adams was gracious, but impatient. "Yesterday, I walked about the Town but there is nothing to be seen"[5] . . . . "very few Horses and those very small and miserably poor; Mules and Asses were numerous but small. There was no Hay in the Country: The Horses, Mules &c. eat Wheat Straw."[6] One night he was taken, grudgingly, to an Italian opera, ". . . a dull Entertainment to me."[7] But Adams' sweet tooth perked things up a bit for him: "Breakfasted on Spanish Chocolate which answers the Fame it has acquired in the World."[8]

On the final evening in El Ferrol, Adams was the special dinner guest of the French Consul and his other invitees. In the true combative style of John Adams, the touchy subject of American independence came up. Yipes. Adams wrote that a certain "Mr. Linde an Irish Gentleman a Master of a Mathematical Academy here" was "of Opinion that the Revolution in America was of a bad Example to the Spanish Colonies and dangerous to the Interests of Spain."[9] Adams always relished a good debate, especially "when I know I am right."[10] He went on to explain to Mr. Linde how that "opinion" was in error and how Spain should get onboard the independence train to overthrow its own king before it was too late. Then Adams, *very wisely* apologized, saying he had early morning travel to attend to and must take his leave. Later in his autobiography, Adams reflected,

> If, in 1807, We look back for seven and twenty Years, and . . . had the United States remained subject to Great Britain, Mr. Linde and the Consul and the whole Spanish Nation might be convinced, that they owe much to the American Revolution.[11]

5. John Adams diary, 1779 DECEMBER.[13.] MONDAY, page 7.
6. John Adams diary, 1779 DECEMBER.[14.] TUESDAY, page 9.
7. John Adams diary, 1779 DECEMBER.[9.] THURSDAY, page 6.
8. John Adams diary, 1779 DECEMBER.[10.] FRYDAY, page 7.
9. John Adams diary, 1779 DECEMBER.[14.] TUESDAY, page 11.
10. John Adams to Edmund Jenings, September 27, 1782, Founders Online, National Archives, founders.archives.gov/documents/Adams/06-13-02-0217, accessed September 3, 2016 (original source: *The Adams Papers, Papers of John Adams*, vol. 13, May–October 1782, ed. Gregg L. Lint, C. James Taylor, Margaret A. Hogan, Jessie May Rodrique, Mary T. Claffey, and Hobson Woodward (Cambridge, MA: Harvard University Press, 2006), 494–495). The full quotation: "Thanks to God that he gave me stubbornness when I know I am right" begins the fourth chapter in the HBO/Playtone miniseries *John Adams*, and is producer/writer Kirk Ellis' favorite Adams quote.
11. John Adams autobiography, sheet 7 of 18, December 14, 1779, page 2.

The next morning, Tuesday, December 14, "We arose at five O Clock;"[12] Adams and entourage[13] were sailed around to the southern tip of the bay from El Ferrol to La Coruña. There Adams wrote, they "mounted our Mules. Thirteen of them in Number and two Mulateers . . . We rode over very bad roads, and very high Mountains" to reach the old, walled city of "Corunna."[14] But the train of men and mules had barely arrived when John Adams was immediately invited to dine that evening with the "General who is Governor of the Province"[15] in Coruña. The dinner conversation was going great because "The Governor of the Province, told me he had orders from Court to treat all Americans as their best friends."[16] It was going great . . . until . . . "He asked me when this War would finish?"[17] Oh oh. But Adams was diplomatic this time and only gave a very veiled slight to the governor and the Spanish king, replying,

> *Pas encore* [not yet]—But when the Kings of France and Spain would take the Resolution to send 20 or 30 more line of Battle Ships to reinforce the Comte d'Estain and enable him to take all the British Forces and Possessions in America.[18]

All along, Adams had been weighing the decision to either wait for ship repairs in Spain, assuming the *Sensible* wasn't to be condemned, or to hit the road by foot. The governor and advisors gave Adams probably the final advice. At least enough so that on December 16, Adams wrote his decision to Samuel Huntington, the president of Congress,

> I am advised by every body to go to France by Land.—The Season, the Roads, the Accommodations for travelling are so unfavourable, that it is not expected I can get to Paris in less than thirty days. But if I were to wait for the Frigate it would probably be much longer. I am determined therefore to make the best of my Way by Land.[19]

---

12. John Adams autobiography, ibid, December 15, 1779, page 3.
13. Besides Adams himself, there were John Quincy and Charles Adams, Francis Dana (Congressional secretary to Adams' commission), John Thaxter (Adams' Congressional private secretary), and two servants.
14. John Adams diary, 1779 DECEMBER.[15.] WEDNESDAY, page 13.
15. Ibid.
16. Ibid.
17. John Adams diary, 1779 DECEMBER.[15.] WEDNESDAY, page 14.
18. Ibid.
19. John Adams autobiography, part 3, "Peace," 1779-1780, sheet 8 of 18, December 16, 1779; page 1.

The next morning the governors of both the province and the town called upon Adams at his "Lodgings at the Hotel du grand Amiral"[20] and invited him to dinner again the following evening. Adams was then given a passport for credentialed free movement within the Spanish provinces, signed by the governor-general of the province of Gallicia, Don Pedro Martin Sermenio.[21]

Once the Adams group arrived in Coruña and the transportation method had been decided, things started to take shape for their overland trek; everything needed for the trip was being collected. Along with Adams' diplomatic papers were clothes and personal items,[22] food and drink,[23] mules (John Quincy wrote in his diary that one of the mules in their traveling party "had near a Hundred little bells tied round it's neck"[24]), Spanish guides, and calashes (small, crude two-wheeled carts). And while preparations were being made, the ever-curious John Adams found himself able to take in the local sites—an ancient lighthouse, "two noble Windmills,"[25] convents and churches, and watching a "Souvereign Court of Justice" in session—where Adams noted, "The Robes, Wigs and bands both of the judges and Lawyers are nearly like ours at Boston."[26]

But before the journey would begin, *another* official dinner banquet was to be thrown on Sunday, December 19, in which Adams was to be the honored guest. It would be attended by the Spanish attorney general, the chief justice, the "President of the Souvereign Court of the Kingdom of Gallicia"[27] and many other dignitaries. Adams wrote that

20. John Adams diary, 1779 DECEMBER.[16.] THURSDAY, page 14.

21. In 1779-1780, northern Spain was still divided into distinct provinces – Gallicia (northwest), Castille and Leon (northcentral) and Basque country (northeast). Adams would be traveling through all three "kingdoms," as he called them, and as a diplomatic foreigner would need valid credentials for traveling the provinces. It turned out that it was a good thing Adams had the signed official passport. The party was stopped by military guards at Puente de la Rada, on the road to Bilbao.

22. "Indeed, We were obliged to carry . . . our own Beds, Blanketts, Sheets, Pillows" John Adams autobiography, December 28, 1779, page 4.

23. "Bread and Cheese, Meat, Knives and Forks, Spoons, Apples and Nutts," ibid.

24. John Quincy Adams diary 1, 12 November 1779—31 December 1779, page 37; December 26, 1779, Massachusetts Historical Society, A Digital Collection www.masshist.org/jqadiaries/php/doc?id=jqad01_37.

25. John Adams autobiography, sheet 7 of 18, December 16, 1779, page 4. Fellow traveler John Thaxter had already written of the likeness of the Adams entourage to that of *Don Quixote*.

26. John Adams diary, 1779 DECEMBER.[17.] FRYDAY, page 16.

27. John Adams autobiography, part 3, "Peace," 1779-1780 sheet 9 of 18, December 19, 1779; page 1.

he was determined to answer any questions the group had "civilly and candidly"[28]... for a change. But it didn't take long before two Spanish officials started berating Adams about his last name. "I thought these questions very whimsical and ridiculous,"[29] wrote Adams. But the officials kept it up, claiming that Adams *must* have been born in Spain, as if "this was a peculiar Kind of Spanish Compliment."[30] Perhaps from the vast amount of wine being consumed that Adams described, it got weird from there. Adams wrote that it was told

> that in several Provinces there were very ancient, rich and noble Families of the Name of Adams and that they were all remarkable for their Attachment to the Letter S. at the End of Adam. They were so punctillious in this that they took it as an Affront to write their Name without this final Letter and would fight any Man that did it.[31]

John Adams made it out of that dinner conversation successfully, but just three days later decided to give a little of a come-back when, "I ventured to ask the Attorney General a few Questions concerning the Inquisition. His answers were guarded and cautious as I expected."[32]

Adams figured it was time to go. Besides, he was exhausted and wrote he hadn't slept one single night in the sixteen nights he'd been in Spain. "The Universal Sloth and Lazyness of the Inhabitants suffered not only all their Beds but all their Appartments to be infested with innumerable Swarms of Ennemies of all repose."[33] He was talking about sharing beds with the constant lice, fleas, and bedbugs. Some nights he thought he'd never live to see France.

Ten days after getting to Coruña, the supplies were gathered and the strange caravan was packed up for their eastward journey. Examining Spanish maps, Adams at first was inclined to want to take the most direct way to Bilbao, the last Spanish town at the French border. It would be a straight line right across the northern coast from Coruña to Bilbao. A guide and an interpreter explained that an almost-impassable mountain range ran across almost the entire length of the Spanish coastline

28. Ibid.
29. Ibid.
30. Ibid.
31. John Adams autobiography, part 3, "Peace," 1779-1780 sheet 9 of 18, December 19, 1779; pages 1-2.
32. John Adams autobiography, part 3, "Peace," 1779-1780 sheet 9 of 18, December 22, 1779; page 4.
33. John Adams autobiography, part 3, "Peace," 1779-1780 sheet 9-10 of 18, December 24, 1779; page 4. On January 4, 1780, Adams wrote, "Found clean Beds and no fleas for the first Time in Spain."

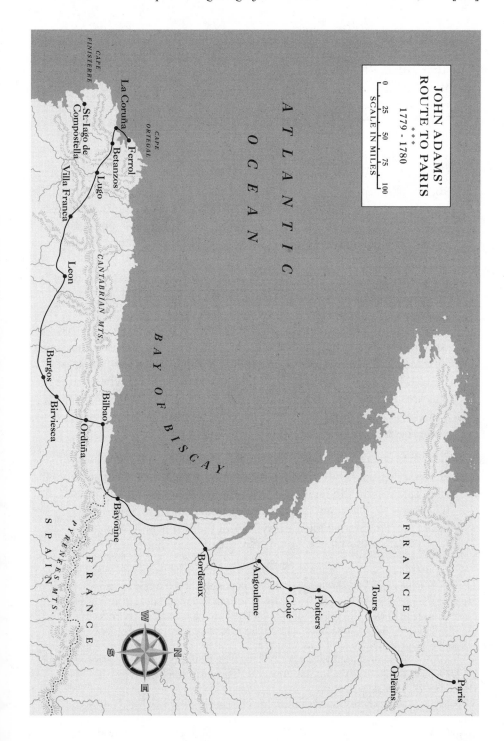

of the Bay of Biscay. What the travelers would have to do, it was explained, was to go southeast from Coruña, and then traverse the straight
path that Adams had wanted, through some plains and less-rocky
mountains before turning northeast to travel up to Bilbao. In fact, a little
history was also passed along to John Adams that day.

The trail recommended by the Spanish guides was, in fact, a famous
pilgrimage route that had been traveled for centuries since the middle
ages. The road was called El Camino de Santiago ("The Way of Saint
James"[34]) and the Adams entourage would be traveling the road, in reverse, of the pilgrims walking the route. Tradition has it that the remains
of the apostle St. James are buried in a cathedral shrine in Santiago de
Compostella, which ironically is just south of Coruña where John
Adams and group began their own pilgrimage eastward. Adams speaks
of this pilgrimage road and the story behind it in his autobiography.
One of his biggest disappointments, he writes, is that he didn't visit the
cathedral in "St. Iago de Compostella"[35] while he was near it. But now
they had to get on their way.

It was Sunday, December 26, 1779 and finally the strange Adams
caravan was on its journey to France. "At half after two We mounted
our Carriages and Mules and rode four Leagues[36] to Betanzos, the ancient Capital of the Kingdom of Gallicia, and the place where the
Archives are still kept."[37] In the coming days, the travelers would express
shock at the squalid conditions that average Spanish citizens lived in
and while the trekkers were staying in wayside inns.

> The House where We lodge is of Stone . . . No floor but the ground,
> and no Carpet but Straw, trodden into mire, by Men, Hogs, Horses,
> Mules, &c . . . . On the same floor with the Kitchen was the Stable .
> . . There was no Chimney. The Smoke ascended and found no other
> Passage . . . The Smoke filled every Part of the Kitchen, Stable, and
> other [Parts] of the House, as thick as possible so that it was very

---

34. This famous medieval pilgrimage route is still popular and traveled by many hundreds of thousands of walkers each year from Europe and the Middle East. It gained
more fame in 2010 with the independent film "The Way" in which Martin Sheen walks
the El Camino de Santiago with the ashes of his son, played by Emilio Estevez—who
is also the film's writer, director and producer.
35. John Adams autobiography, part 3, "Peace," 1779-1780 sheet 10 of 18, December
26, 1779; page 1. Adams describes the story of St. Iago in his autobiography – Tuesday,
December 28, 1779, page 4.
36. A league is somewhere around three miles. The equivalent length has changed over
time.
37. John Adams autobiography, part 3, "Peace," 1779-1780 sheet 10 of 18, December 26,
1779; page 1.

difficult to see or breath . . . The Mules, Hogs, fowls, and human Inhabitants live however all together . . . The floor had never been
washed nor swept for an hundred Years—Smoak, soot, Dirt, every
where.[38]

But in spite of it all, by reaching the town of Castillano, Adams
wrote, "Nevertheless, amidst all these horrors I slept better, than I had
done before since my Arrival in Spain."[39] He doesn't say why he slept
better. Maybe Adams was that tired. Or maybe it was because he knew
he finally was on the road to France. Speaking of roads, Adams was
equally horrified at those: "The Road was very bad, mountainous and
rocky to such a degree as to be very dangerous"[40] . . . . "The Roads, the
worst without Exception that ever were passed"[41] . . . . "Steep, sharp
Pitches, ragged Rocks."[42]

Sometimes Adams rode in one of calashes, but most of the time he
rode a mule or (when the terrain ran almost vertically), "sometimes all
walk."[43] The road was so rough, one of the calashes broke an axle, which
required that they stop and fix it. As they traveled "The Way" through
Spain, Adams formed certain overall lasting impressions:

> I see nothing but Signs of Poverty and Misery, among the People. A
> fertile Country, not half cultivated, People ragged and dirty, and the
> Houses universally nothing but Mire, Smoke, Fleas and Lice. Noth-
> ing appears rich but the Churches, nobody fat, but the Clergy[44] . . .
> . The Houses are uniformly the same through the whole Country
> hitherto—common habitations for Men and Beasts—the same
> smoaky, filthy holes.[45]

But in the easternmost part of Spain, John Adams also beheld a ma-
jestic spectacle he had never seen before: the Pyrenees Mountains in

---

38. John Adams autobiography, part 3, "Peace," 1779-1780 sheet 10 of 18, December
27, 1779; pages 2-3. John Quincy Adams characterized the common people as, "Lazy,
dirty, Nasty and in short I can compare them to nothing but a parcel of hogs." John
Quincy Adams diary, January 3, 1780.
39. John Adams autobiography, part 3, "Peace," 1779-1780 sheet 10 of 18, December
27, 1779; page 3.
40. John Adams diary, 1779 DECEMBER.[26.] SUNDAY, page 25.
41. John Adams autobiography, part 3, "Peace," 1779-1780 sheet 11 of 18, December
30, 1779; page 1.
42. John Adams diary, 1780 JANUARY.[1.] SATURDAY, page 34.
43. John Adams diary, 1779 DECEMBER.[28.] TUESDAY, page 29.
44. John Adams autobiography, part 3, "Peace," 1779-1780 sheet 11 of 18, December
30, 1779; page 1.
45. John Adams diary, 1780 JANUARY.[1.] SATURDAY, page 35.

winter, "an uninterrupted succession of Mountains of a vast hight,"[46] "white with Snow."[47] He also found in small villages near Leon towns- folk merrily dancing something called "Fandango" with "a Pair of Clack- ers in his and her Hand."[48] Adams and the caravan were drawing up on the noticeably larger city of Leon, situated maybe two-thirds of their way on the trail to Bilbao. "This was one great Plain, and the road through it was very fine,"[49] Adams noted.

The final leg of their journey might be less stressful than the first half, if only John Adams could keep his strong-minded opinions to him- self while traveling through a Catholic countryside. But it was not to be. One last affront had to be made. Not intentionally; it was just Adams being Adams.

John Adams had noted while traveling through towns, big and small, that the majority of the inhabitants were dirt poor, with their homes and buildings decaying to dust, except for the numerous beautiful and well-kept churches and cathedrals easily dominating each scene. It struck the Protestant-Congregationalist nerve in Adams that the well- fed followers of the various Catholic religious orders he had noted (mostly "Franciscans" and "Dominicans") didn't seem very virtuous. But he kept his feelings to himself . . . and his diary, of course[50].

But on Thursday, January 6, 1780, while stopped in Leon, Adams was invited by one of their guides to attend High Mass for "The Feast of the King"[51] at the Leon Catholic church. No less than the Bishop would be at the ceremony, so Adams eagerly accepted. "We saw the Procession of the Bishop and of all the Canons, in rich habits of Silk, Velvet, Silver and gold."[52] But then, to have Adams explain it, as the Bishop turned the corner inside the church and with his hands out-

---

46. John Adams diary, 1780 JANUARY.[1.] SATURDAY, page 3.

47. John Adams diary, 1779 DECEMBER.[31.] FRYDAY, page 33, Adams Family Pa- pers.

48. John Adams diary, 1780 JANUARY.[6.] THURSDAY, pages 40-41.

49. John Adams autobiography, part 3, "Peace," 1779-1780 sheet 11 of 18, January 5, 1780; page 4.

50. Young John Quincy Adams wasn't quite as reserved as his father. In his dairy, John Quincy gave his own unvarnished observation of the religious domination of the com- mon people, "Poor Creatures they are eat up by their preists. Near three quarters of what they earn goes to the Preists and with the other Quarter they must live as they can. Thus is the whole of this Kingdom deceived and deluded by their Religion. I thank Almighty God that I was born in a Country where any body may get a good living if they Please." John Quincy Adams diary, January 3, 1780.

51. John Adams autobiography, part 3, "Peace," 1779-1780 sheet 11 of 18, January 6, 1780; page 4.

52. Ibid.

stretched, all the people around him ". . . prostrated themselves on their Knees as he passed. Our Guide told Us We must do the same."[53] Ha. Protestant Adams was not about to lay prostrate for any religious clergy, so he wrote that he had been content just to bow. Of course, the Bishop spotted John Adams right off – partly by the way he was dressed, and partly because he was the only one standing in the whole church line. "The Eagle Eye of the Bishop did not fail to observe"[54] him, Adams wrote in his autobiography. As the Bishop walked along through the procession, his eyes were squinting solidly on John Adams, as if "I was some travelling Heretick."[55] But Adams kept his tongue and said nothing, thereby averting a final Spanish scene. Abigail would've been proud of him.

The Adams cavalcade arrived in Burgos on Tuesday, January 11, "sneezing and coughing,"[56] having slogged through "fog, rain, and Snow all the Way, very chilly and raw."[57] Almost all of them were sick with a "violent Cold . . . all of Us in danger of fevers."[58] Adams wrote to himself that in the last twenty years of his "great hardships, cold, rain, Snow, heat, fatigue, bad rest, indifferent nourishment, want of Sleep &c. &c. &c.", he "had never experienced any Thing like this journey."[59]

The grueling Spanish leg of their journey was almost over. From Burgos, the pilgrims headed almost due north to the coast of the Bay of Biscay, to the seaport town of Bilbao. This point, two months earlier, would've been their final destination after a quick shipboard jaunt from El Ferrol or Coruña. But live and learn. Finally, *finally*, the party reached "St. John De Luz, the first Village in France"[60] on Thursday, January 20, "And never was a Captive escaped from Prison more delighted than I was."[61] They reached Bayonne three days later. "Here We paid off our Spanish Guide with all his Train of Horses, Calashes, Waggon, Mules, and Servants."[62] From this point, Adams was back in familiar, friendly

53. Ibid.

54. Ibid.

55. Ibid.

56. Ibid.

57. John Adams autobiography, part 3, "Peace," 1779-1780 sheet 11 of 18, January 11, 1780; page 3.

58. John Adams autobiography, part 3, "Peace," 1779-1780 sheet 11 of 18, January 11, 1780; page 4.

59. Ibid.

60. John Adams autobiography, part 3, "Peace," 1779-1780 sheet 15 of 18, January 20, 1780; page 3.

61. Ibid.

62. John Adams autobiography, part 3, "Peace," 1779-1780 sheet 15 of 18, January 23, 1780; page 3.

country, and from the next French town of Bordeaux and all the way into Paris, Adams would be back on the same path that he'd traipsed just a year before. The Adams procession would all arrive in Paris on February 9, 1780. If the young Adams boys—John Quincy and Charles—thought their school vacation would continue once they all arrived in Paris, they were quickly disappointed. The very next morning of their arrival, their father immediately enrolled them in a Passy boarding school.

John Adams always held that he'd had just three regrets while on this strange pilgrimage through Spain. The first was electing to take the land route at all rather than waiting for a ship. (He would only admit that in a letter to Abigail and never to anyone else). He regretted not seeing the famous terminus point of "The Way," the cathedral of Santiago de Compostella.

And he regretted that at Bayonne, he had to say goodbye to his mule, "for which I was very sorry, as he was an excellent Animal and had served me very well."[63] Strangely similar travel companions they were, John Adams and his mule.

---

63. John Adams autobiography, part 3, "Peace," 1779-1780 sheet 15 of 18, January 23, 1780; page 3.

Under Appreciated Allies: Choctaws, Creeks, and the Defense of British West Florida, 1781

❄ JIM PIECUCH ❄

Two months after Spain entered the American Revolutionary War on June 21, 1779, the governor of Spanish Louisiana, Don Bernardo de Galvez, launched an invasion of the British province of West Florida on August 27. The defenders, consisting of two British infantry regiments, a detachment of the Royal Artillery, two understrength provincial battalions, a regiment of hired German troops from Waldeck, and local loyalists, were heavily outnumbered by Galvez's forces. The disparity in numbers increased as Galvez quickly overwhelmed several British posts along the Mississippi River and captured their garrisons.[1] In these circumstances, the British commander in West Florida, General John Campbell, was forced to rely upon the assistance of Britain's Indian allies, the Choctaws and Creeks in particular, to defend the province. Although Campbell badly bungled relations with both Indian nations, the Choctaws and Creeks contributed greatly to the defense of West Florida until the Spanish capture of Pensacola in May 1781. Unfortunately for the Indians, Campbell failed to acknowledge the full extent and effectiveness of their support. While neither a larger number of Indians nor a more capable deployment of them could likely have prevented the loss of West Florida to Spain, given Campbell's mediocre leadership and the lack of assistance to his garrison from British naval and land forces in the West Indies theater, the Choctaws and Creeks delayed the progress of the Spanish siege of Pensacola and inflicted considerable casualties on the attackers. The information provided in

---

1. George C. Osborn, "Major-General John Campbell in British West Florida," *Florida Historical Quarterly*, Vol. 27, No. 4 (April 1949), 319, 325, 326.

Spanish accounts and from British sources other than Campbell's biased reports testifies to the Indians' valuable support during operations in 1781.

Campbell had been assigned to command the British forces in West Florida in the fall of 1778. During his long service, he should have acquired an understanding of Indian culture and military practices that might have enabled him to interact more appropriately with the Native allies whose cooperation he needed to succeed in his new assignment. From 1764 to 1766 he had commanded Fort Detroit in the wake of Pontiac's Rebellion, and had received orders to negotiate a peace agreement with Pontiac. The extent and nature of his dealings with Pontiac and the Indians of the Great Lakes region remain unknown; however, based on the policies he adopted in dealing with the Natives during his time in West Florida, it would be reasonable to say that his interactions with the northern Indians were not positive. Campbell was the lieutenant colonel of the 57th Regiment of Foot, which joined General William Howe's army in New York after participating in the abortive southern expedition in early 1776. He was promoted to brigadier general in 1777 and took command of a brigade that was part of the British garrison of New York City.[2]

When Campbell arrived in Pensacola early in February 1779, he found affairs in the Indian Department in disarray. John Stuart, superintendent of Indian affairs for the region south of the Ohio River, was, Campbell reported, "in the last stage of consumption," and Stuart died the following month. Campbell worried that Stuart's death would cause "great confusion" in Indian affairs.[3] While waiting for the government in London to appoint a replacement for Stuart, Governor Peter Chester, in consultation with Campbell, decided to appoint a five-member commission to manage Indian relations. Lord George Germain, Secretary of State for the American Department, subsequently decided to divide responsibilities for the southern region between Alexander Cameron, Stuart's deputy at Pensacola, and provincial lieutenant colonel Thomas Brown, who commanded the garrison at Augusta, Georgia. Cameron was to manage the Choctaws and Chickasaws, and Brown the Creeks and Cherokees. Both men were made subordinate to the British military

2. Osborn, "Major-General John Campbell," 317; Virginia Parks, "Scotsman in Retreat: Major General John Campbell," in Virginia Parks, ed., *Siege! Spain and Britain: Battle of Pensacola, March 9-May 8, 1781* (Pensacola, FL: Pensacola Historical Society, 1981), 33-34.

3. John Campbell to Sir Henry Clinton, February 10, 1779, in K. G. Davies, ed., *Documents of the American Revolution, 1770-1783 (Colonial Office Series)*, Vol. 17 (Dublin: Irish University Press, 1977), 62.

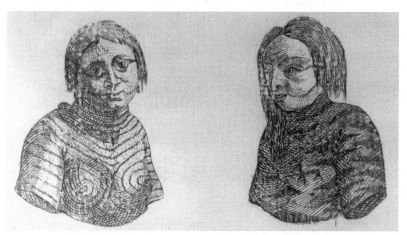

Choctaws sketched in 1775. Many southern Indians decorated their bodies with elaborate tattoos, to which the men added war paint before going into battle.

command.[4] This new arrangement created a cumbersome situation for West Florida, in that Cameron now lacked authority to deal directly with the Creeks, who were considered crucial to the province's defense.

Further complicating the employment of Indians to protect West Florida were Spanish efforts to win the support of the Choctaws. One faction among the Choctaws had long been partial toward Spain, and Galvez hoped to capitalize on this by sending agents among the Choctaws in November to distribute coats, medals, and other gifts. Cameron responded by lavishing gifts of his own upon the Choctaws, and by October 31, 1780, he was able to report to Germain that "the Choctaw partisans, whom Governor Galveze gained over to the Spanish interest by virtue of great bribes and fear together, have entirely deserted him, came down to Pensacola, and delivered up their Spanish medals, commissions, and colours to me." He added that he believed the Choctaws' pledges of loyalty to Britain "to be genuine."[5]

As proof of the Choctaws' allegiance, Cameron noted that "small parties" of their warriors had been hovering near Mobile, which the Spanish had captured in March, "and not a Spaniard can venture out of sight of the fort but they knock him up and carry off his scalp. . . .

4. Lord George Germain to Clinton, June 25, 1779, Lord George Germain Papers, Vol. 9, William L. Clements Library, Ann Arbor, MI; Osborn, "Major-General John Campbell," 322.
5. Thomas Brown to Germain, March 10, 1780, and Alexander Cameron to Germain, Oct. 31, 1780, in Davies, *Documents*, Vol. 18 (1978), 55, 219.

The Spaniards are in the greatest distress being cooped up by the Indians, and it's my own opinion as well as that of many others, that if the Indians were encouraged and proper white leaders who could speak their language kept in pay with them, that they would have routed the Spaniards from Mobile in a short space."[6]

The chief obstacle to employing the Indians effectively, Cameron complained, was Campbell. The general refused to provide either provisions or presents to the Indians who came to Pensacola, insisting instead that Cameron pay such expenses from Indian Department funds. Cameron declared that Campbell "does not understand anything of Indians or their affairs he thinks they are to be used like slaves or a people void of natural sense. He will not be prevailed upon that presents are necessary, or that Indians have a right to demand any unless he calls them upon actual service."[7] This lack of harmony between the Indian superintendent and the general commanding in the province did not bode well for future cooperation between the two men, or between the Indians and the military garrison at Pensacola.

Campbell had already made his own views clear on the only method he saw as suitable for converting the Indians into effective allies. After complaining to Germain about the "extravagance and unbounded waste" that in his opinion plagued the Indian Department, Campbell had offered his version of a plan that Americans had been attempting to impose on the Indians since shortly after the founding of New England in the seventeenth century. Campbell's plan had five points, the first of which reflected his opinion of the Crown's Native allies in its key phrase, "civilizing these barbarians." The general then went on to urge that the Indians be taught European concepts of property ownership, forced to settle along navigable waterways, and compelled to live in European-style towns. He also urged intermarriage between Indians and white settlers to speed up the civilization process.[8] Such plans had never received a warm reception among the Natives anywhere in North America, and had the Choctaws and Creeks learned of Campbell's real opinions, the British-Indian alliance might have been damaged beyond repair.

Not everyone in Pensacola shared Campbell's view. Philipp Waldeck, a chaplain in the Waldeck regiment assigned to the town's garrison, recorded his observations on the parties of Choctaws and Creeks that visited Pensacola. He described the Creeks as "most wonderfully de-

---

6. Cameron to Germain, October 31, 1780, in Davies, *Documents*, 18:219-220.
7. Cameron to Germain, October 31, 1780, in ibid., 220, 221-222.
8. Osborn, "Major-General John Campbell," 334.

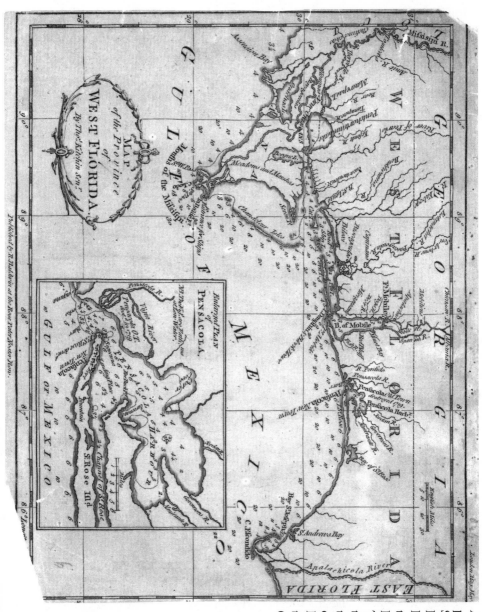

A map of West Florida published in 1781. After Spain ceded Florida to Britain in 1763, the British divided the territory into two colonies, East and West Florida. The latter extended from the Apalachicola River to the Mississippi, including the towns of Mobile and Pensacola, the capital, on the Gulf Coast.

veloped, large and strong," and the Choctaws as "braver in war" than the Creeks but physically less impressive. "What a wonderful regiment could be made of them," Waldeck marveled. "But would they accept discipline? Discipline is something about which they know nothing. Even the chief does not control them." He also recognized the need to be generous with the Indians, as in his opinion the failure to do so might cause them "to take up arms against us."[9]

Another individual who recognized the Indians' value to the defense of West Florida was Campbell's adversary, Bernardo de Galvez. On April 9, 1780, Galvez had tried to deprive the British of their Native allies with a proposal that neither side employ Indians in future campaigns. "The Indians who are in the English Interest believe that it is their Duty to Pillage and destroy all the Inhabitants which are of another Nation," the Spaniard wrote in a letter to Campbell. "Those who have taken part with Spain, think that by right of retaliation they may commit like hostilities against the English. . . . In order that a War . . . might not be rendered still more bloody I hope your excellency will join me in a reciprocal agreement which may shelter us from the horrid imputation of inhumanity," Galvez proposed. Despite his dislike of Indians, Campbell recognized that Galvez was trying to manipulate the situation to Spain's advantage. The British general replied with a denunciation of the proposal as "insulting and injurious to reason and common sense," and went so far as to admit, albeit in all likelihood grudgingly, that it was the Indians' presence that had thus far prevented Galvez from undertaking an attack on Pensacola.[10]

Nevertheless, Campbell's relations with the Choctaws remained strained. When a Choctaw party arrived in Pensacola on August 26 and reported that they had met with Galvez and "received presents . . . but were dissatisfied with them," Campbell concluded that the Choctaws intended to auction their support to the highest bidder. He therefore refused to give them presents, whereupon they apologized. To prove their allegiance to the British, the Choctaws then proceeded toward Mobile, and en route encountered a Spanish truce party and killed and scalped three soldiers. Returning to Pensacola with their trophies, they "received no reward, and for their cruelty . . . were treated with con-

9. Philipp Waldeck, *Eighteenth Century America: A Hessian Report on the People, the Land, the War as Noted in the Diary of Chaplain Philipp Waldeck (1776-1780)*, Bruce E. Burgoyne, trans. (Bowie, MD: Heritage Books, 1995), 129, 134, 154-156.
10. Bernardo de Galvez to John Campbell, April 9, 1780, and Campbell to Galvez, April 20, 1780, Sir Guy Carleton Papers, Vol. 22, Nos. 2681 and 2692, microfilm, David Library of the American Revolution, Washington Crossing, PA.

tempt."[11] When Campbell later received a letter from Galvez protesting the incident, Campbell reprimanded the Choctaw leader Mingo Pouscouche. Angered, the chief replied that in the future he and his followers would kill any Spaniard they encountered, and the Choctaws departed. In the autumn they attacked the Spanish near Mobile, and arrived in Pensacola with three scalps and a captured family. Apparently aware that he could not risk further alienating the Choctaws, Campbell did not reproach them and gave them presents to obtain the family's release.[12]

As it became increasingly apparent that Galvez was planning a major operation against Pensacola, Campbell became skittish and began demanding that the Creeks and Choctaws come to the aid of the Pensacola garrison. In mid-November 1780 Campbell urgently requested that Thomas Brown dispatch the Creeks and Cameron the Choctaws to defend the town against the expected attack. The Indians "have it still in their power, by frequent attacks & constant alarms, in short by continually harassing & hanging on the enemy's rear, in case of siege, greatly to impede the operations, if not totally defeat & disconcert the designs of any force they can send against us," Campbell told Brown. The imminent threat had clearly caused Campbell to reassess the Indians' value.[13] However, when a hurricane dispersed the Spanish invasion fleet, Campbell ordered the agents to send the Indians home. Rumors of another impending Spanish attack led Campbell to call for Creek aid a second time in January 1781, only to again order the one thousand warriors who had assembled to return home when he learned that British officials had promised to send reinforcements from Jamaica. The repeated calls for help and sudden dismissals angered the Creeks, whose hunting had been disrupted by Campbell's summons.[14]

Campbell decided to disrupt Galvez's plans by recapturing Mobile. In January 1781 he dispatched a force of 160 British and German regulars, 200 provincials, and over 400 Choctaws to attack the town. The attack was made on the morning of June 7, and broke the Spanish line, but the Waldeck officer commanding the force was killed and the

11. Waldeck, *Eighteenth Century America*, 168.

12. Waldeck, *Eighteenth Century America*, 169-171; Greg O'Brien, *Choctaws in a Revolutionary Age, 1750-1830* (Lincoln: University of Nebraska Press, 2002), 45-46.

13. Campbell to Brown, November 15, 1780, Carleton Papers, 26:3149.

14. J. Barton Starr, *Tories, Dons, and Rebels: The American Revolution in British West Florida* (Gainesville: University Presses of Florida, 1996), 178-179; James H. O'Donnell III, *Southern Indians in the American Revolution* (Knoxville: University of Tennessee Press, 1973), 105.

provincial officer who succeeded to command called off the assault. In the confusion, no one signaled the Indians to join the attack. However, two of Cameron's deputies who accompanied the Choctaws directed the Indians to open fire from their concealed positions, allowing the regulars and provincials to withdraw without molestation. The Indians' fire was so effective that some of the Spanish defenders fled and tried to escape by boat; the Choctaws pursued and cut them down, taking between forty and fifty scalps. Although Choctaw leaders urged the regulars and provincials to renew the attack, the officers refused and instead ordered a retreat to Pensacola. Cameron praised the "great resolution and coolness" that the Choctaws displayed, yet some British officers later blamed the Indians for the failure of the assault, despite the complete lack of evidence to support such an accusation.[15]

If Campbell shared this opinion of the Choctaws' culpability for the failure of his plan, he kept it to himself. He did appear to have altered his opinion of the Indians' importance from what he had previously expressed to Thomas Brown, if he had been truthful in that letter; Cameron wrote that "General Campbell will give himself no trouble in humouring or cultivating [the Indians'] friendship and I have it not in my power to use them as I am sensible they deserve." The Indian agent noted that some of the "principal gentlemen" of Pensacola had offered "to pay all the expense" of supporting the Indians properly, but added that he "could not with propriety accept of their offer while General Campbell was here and I was to be regulated alone by him."[16]

In early March the long-awaited Spanish attack on Pensacola began when Galvez appeared offshore with a powerful fleet and four thousand troops; he would later be reinforced by an additional three thousand Spanish and French soldiers. Against this army Campbell could muster some fifteen hundred British, German, and provincial troops along with some armed blacks, loyalist militia, and the crews of a few Royal Navy warships.[17] In addition, there were some four hundred Choctaws and about forty Creeks in Pensacola when Galvez arrived. A further eighty Creeks, led by Alexander McGillivray, joined the defenders during the

15. Albert W. Haarmann, "The Spanish Conquest of British West Florida, 1779-1781," *Florida Historical Quarterly*, Vol. 39, No. 2 (October 1960), 120-121; Starr, 183; O'Donnell, *Southern Indians*, 112; Cameron to Germain, February 10, 1781, in Davies, *Documents*, Vol. 20 (1979), 59.

16. Cameron to Germain, February 10, 1781, in Davies, *Documents*, 20:59.

17. O'Donnell, *Southern Indians*, 113; O'Brien, *Choctaws in a Revolutionary Age*, 10; Francisco de Miranda, "Miranda's Diary of the Siege of Pensacola," Donald E. Worcester, trans., *Florida Historical Quarterly*, Vol. 29, No. 3 (Jan. 1951), 176.

second week of April, and fifty-four Chickasaws reached the town on April 27.[18]

Campbell was prompt to criticize the Indians for perceived failures. He remarked in a report to Germain that Spanish troops from Mobile had joined Galvez outside Pensacola on March 22, stating that the Spaniards had "marched by land unopposed by the Indians (although they had been stationed at the Cliffs expressly for that purpose and re-inforced by near one hundred troops from Fort George to support and encourage them)." The British general failed to impart any blame to his own troops, even if they were equally culpable for allowing the Spanish force to pass unopposed. The next Indian activity reported by Campbell took place on the evening of March 28, when he described a skirmish between the Indians and Spanish that ended "without any advantage, only that of the savages showing themselves." On March 30, he wrote, the Indians fought "without the savages intending it, themselves led on by the countenance of some troops . . . without making any perceptible impression" on the enemy. Finally, he stated that a planned attack on the Spanish during the night of May 2 miscarried because "the regulars and Indians having separated and lost one another on their march," he was forced to cancel the assault. Again, the implication was that the In-dians required the presence and example of regular troops to fight, even though the regulars shared the responsibility for the two forces becom-ing separated.[19]

Other sources provide a very different account of the Indians' con-tributions to the British defense. Robert Farmar, a former British army officer turned planter who had been driven from Mobile when the Spanish captured that town, was in Pensacola during the siege and recorded important events in his journal. He wrote that on March 19, "a party of Indians . . . fell in with an enemy boat & crew consisting of eleven men ten of which were killed and one brought in prisoner."[20] Galvez recorded in his diary of the siege that on March 22, one column of his troops had repeatedly halted "with the object of waiting for a band of Indians that had harassed the rearguard with continual sniping.

18. Michael D. Green, "The Creek Confederacy in the American Revolution: Cautious Participants," in William S. Coker and Robert R. Rea, eds., *Anglo-Spanish Confrontation on the Gulf Coast during the American Revolution* (Pensacola, FL: Gulf Coast History and Humanities Conference, 1982), 71; Robert Farmar, "Bernardo de Galvez's Siege of Pen-sacola in 1781 (As Related in Robert Farmar's Journal)," James A. Padgett, ed., *Louisiana Historical Quarterly*, Vol. 26, No. 2 (April 1943).
19. Campbell to Germain, May 7, 1781, in Davies, *Documents*, 22:136-138.
20. Farmar, "Bernardo de Galvez's Siege of Pensacola," 316.

These followers, [though] pursued by our cazadores, remained very active." That evening, Galvez continued, "some Indians came to fire on the troops that were around the [camp] fires, killing three and wounding four of our soldiers, not leaving us at peace until morning."[21]

These attacks were only the beginning of the Indians' harassment of the besiegers. On March 25, the Indians brought into Pensacola twenty-three horses they had captured from the Spaniards and two Spanish scalps. Two days later, they repelled an attempted landing by five boats carrying Spanish troops, while on March 29 Indians battled with the Spanish near the shore of Sutton's Lagoon "and drove in the picket three times upon which their grenadiers turned out and fired twice at them and retired. 4 of the Indians were wounded. . . . The Indians report that they killed and wounded a number of the enemy."[22] The next day a larger battle occurred. In the morning a detachment of regular troops sallied over a mile from Pensacola's fortifications, and when joined in the afternoon by the Indians they attacked Galvez's soldiers. Despite being forced to retreat due to heavy Spanish fire, the Indians returned with four captured drums, the head of a Spaniard, and several scalps. One Indian was killed and two wounded. According to Galvez, the Indians initiated the action, were driven off by artillery fire, and then shifted position and resumed firing on the Spanish soldiers. Only then did the British troops join the fight. Galvez reported that the engagement lasted four hours and cost him three killed and twenty-eight wounded.[23]

Galvez further recounted that on April 3 his men began building entrenchments that were "necessary for all camps because of the Indians." He also noted that a skirmish between his advance guard and a party of Indians took place that morning. On April 5 the Spanish commander reported that during the night "the Indians have fired on the camp wounding two in their tents and disturbing the whole army."[24] Farmar confirmed the account, noting that "the Indians at night attacked both wings of the enemy's camp & kept them under arms the whole night." Farmar recorded another skirmish between the Indians and the besiegers on April 12, after which the Indians "brought in a couple of Spanish muskets."[25]

---

21. Bernardo de Galvez, "Bernardo de Galvez's Combat Diary for the Battle of Pensacola, 1781," Maury Baker and Margaret Bissler Haas, eds., *Florida Historical Quarterly*, Vol. 56, No. 2 (Oct. 1977), 181.
22. Farmar, "Bernardo de Galvez's Siege of Pensacola," 317-318.
23. Ibid., 318; Galvez, "Bernardo de Galvez's Combat Diary," 182-183.
24. Galvez, "Bernardo de Galvez's Combat Diary," 184-185.
25. Farmar, "Bernardo de Galvez's Siege of Pensacola," 319-320.

While Campbell generally kept his troops within the defensive works, the Indians continued to shoulder the burden of delaying the Spanish siege operations. Some Creeks captured a Spanish boat on April 17, killing three members of the crew and capturing a fourth. A more significant engagement was fought two days later; Farmar observed that "a party of Indians went and laid close to the enemys camp and this morning they had a skirmish with the Spaniards. The Indians brought in with them a scalp. One of the Indians got wounded."[26] The Indians inflicted additional casualties as well: Spanish officer Francisco de Miranda reported that Galvez had been "slightly wounded in one finger . . . and in the abdomen by a musket shot by savages." Another Indian marksman killed Col. Rey Rebollo.[27]

When the French and Spanish reinforcements disembarked on April 23, they immediately set to work, in accordance with Galvez's orders, to build fortifications around their camp. It was "indispensable" that the site be "immediately protected by bulwarks," Miranda explained, because the camp was situated "in the midst of woods and surrounded by savages who hid in the forest and insulted us at all hours."[28] Galvez noted the next day that the Indians continued to fire on his men, requiring him to send out "four detachments to drive them off." The troops "killed some Indians," but had one officer and nine enlisted men wounded. Miranda stated that some parties of regular troops had been operating with the Indians. On April 25 Galvez recorded yet another engagement with the Indians, during which six Spaniards were wounded. Miranda reported a further skirmish with the British and Indians on April 26 in which Spanish artillery drove off the attackers.[29]

On April 27 Farmar noted the arrival of the Chickasaw reinforcements in Pensacola, observing that they brought with them "a great number of scalps, firelocks, and bayonets" taken from the besieging Spaniards. He also noted that other Indians had fired on the rear of a Spanish field artillery battery.[30] Further fighting took place on April 30. "Some parties of savages came through the nearby woods toward our camp and . . . they fired on our advanced positions," wrote Miranda. The Spaniards "answered them immediately with field pieces and rifles,

---

26. Ibid, 320, 321.
27. Miranda, "Miranda's Diary," 174, 193-194. Galvez in his diary (187) wrote that he had been wounded on April 16, but neither Miranda nor Farmar reported any significant occurrences that day.
28. Ibid, 177.
29. Galvez, "Bernardo de Galvez's Combat Diary," 189, 190; Miranda, "Miranda's Diary," 177, 180.
30. Farmar, "Bernardo de Galvez's Siege of Pensacola," 323.

and they retreated after having mortally wounded a soldier in our camp." The Indians then moved to the shore of the bay and surprised a group of Spanish sailors, killing or capturing six.[31] Farmar reported that the Indians brought one prisoner into Pensacola who had been captured "close to the enemy work," making it likely that this was a different individual and that all the sailors had been killed.[32] The Indians made another sortie against Galvez's army on May 7, and returned with ten scalps in the attack that Campbell claimed to have canceled. Miranda confirmed the Indians' attack, asserting that Spanish casualties were one dead, one wounded, and another captured, while two Indians were killed and four wounded. Galvez likewise recorded that an engagement had taken place, and listed his casualties as two men of the New Orleans militia killed and scalped and three wounded, and an officer and four men wounded in a regular regiment. He stated that the total number of Spanish troops wounded in the skirmish with the Indians was sixteen.[33]

The next day, a Spanish shell struck the magazine of Fort George and destroyed that position, forcing Campbell to open surrender negotiations. The final terms of the capitulation were signed on May 10. Galvez reported taking 1700 prisoners from the British army and navy. The Indians, he wrote, looted the warehouses and other places where supplies were stored in Pensacola before leaving the town; they did not stay to be taken prisoner. Spanish casualties, according to Galvez, totaled 8 officers and 111 enlisted men killed, and 15 officers and 116 enlisted men wounded.[34] While many of these men were the victims of British artillery fire and a smaller number were lost in skirmishes with troops from the Pensacola garrison, a significant percentage, and doubtless a majority of those not killed in the artillery exchanges, were suffered at the hands of the Choctaws, Creeks, and Chickasaws. Indian losses, on the other hand, were comparatively light. Miranda remarked with frustration that "our people brought a dead savage whom they found on the battlefield with a shot in the head, and he has been the only one dead or alive that we have been able to take during the siege."[35]

Despite all of their efforts, the Indians received no credit from Campbell. In his official report to Germain on May 12, the British general

31. Miranda, "Miranda's Diary," 183-184.
32. Farmar, "Bernardo de Galvez's Siege of Pensacola," 323-324.
33. Ibid,. 326; Miranda, "Miranda's Diary," 190; Galvez, "Bernardo de Galvez's Combat Diary," 193, 196-197.
34. Galvez, "Bernardo de Galvez's Combat Diary," 194-195; Farmar, "Bernardo de Galvez's Siege of Pensacola," 326-327; Miranda, "Miranda's Diary," 194.
35. Miranda, "Miranda's Diary," 194.

praised the conduct of his officers and men but said not a word about the Indians.[36] Alexander Cameron naturally was of a different opinion; he informed Germain that the Indians had "behaved with great spirit and attachment; and had we but as many more of them, particularly on the 30th March, we would have driven the whole Spanish army into the sea. No men could behave better than they did that day." Cameron added that the Choctaws' leader, Franchimastabe, "seemed in a passion for not being supported with some of the [regular] troops." In a jibe at Campbell, who had alienated the Creeks by repeatedly summoning them to Pensacola and then ordering them to return home, Cameron declared that "had my advice been regarded by General Campbell . . . instead of having 500, I should have had 2000 Indians to oppose the Spanish at the siege of Pensacola."[37] It is possible that Cameron exaggerated both in terms of the number of Indians he could bring into action and in their capability to defeat the Spaniards, yet he did not understate the Indians' contribution to Pensacola's defense. While the garrison fought artillery duels with Galvez's gunners and made only a few sorties, the Indians harassed the Spanish throughout the siege, forced them to expend time and labor entrenching their camps, and inflicted a significant number of casualties. In repeatedly engaging a far superior and better armed enemy and doing so with great effectiveness, the Indians' role in the two-month campaign was important and deserving of recognition. If Campbell refused to commend the Indians' efforts, the accounts of their Spanish opponents provide ample testimony to the Natives' military skill.

36. See Campbell to Germain, May 12, 1781, in Davies, *Documents*, 22:138-142.
37. Cameron to Germain, May 27, 1781, in Davies, *Documents*, 22:150.

The Complex Character of John Paul Jones and His Polite Home Invasion

JOHN L. SMITH, JR.

To British aristocracy, John Paul Jones was a thieving rebel and a Scotch-borne traitor to the Empire. To seacoast citizens of the British Isles, Jones was portrayed as Blackbeard the pirate, a renegade rogue cutthroat. "Chap-books depicted Paul Jones as a buccaneer, armed to the teeth, in highly colored pictures, bloody and terrifying. Mothers frightened their children with the bare mention of his name."[1]

To American colonial ladies, however, he evoked images of a dashing, swashbuckling Patriot corsair. But Jones's actual character didn't always match up to his storybook images. When first meeting the famous "Chevalier Jones" in Paris, Abigail Adams wrote to her sister feelings of being charmed, yet "disappointed:"

> Chevalier Jones you have heard much of. He is a most uncommon Character. I dare Say you would be as much dissapointed in him as I was. From the intrepid Character he justly Supported in the American Navy, I expected to have seen a Rough Stout warlike Roman. Instead of that, I should sooner think of wraping him up in cotton wool and putting him into my pocket, than sending him to contend with Cannon Ball.
>
> He is small of stature, well proportioned, soft in his Speach easy in his address polite in his manners, vastly civil, understands all the Etiquette of a Ladys Toilite as perfectly as he does the Masts Sails and rigging of a Ship. Under all this appeerence of softness he is Bold enterprizing ambitious and active.

1. Anna De Koven (Mrs. Reginald de Koven), *The Life and Letters of John Paul Jones*, Vol. I (New York: Charles Scribners Sons, 1913), preface vii; Evan Thomas, *John Paul Jones – Sailor, Hero, Father of the American Navy* (New York, Simon & Shuster, 2003), 136.

He has been here often, and dined with us several times. He is said to be a Man of Gallantry and a favorite amongst the French Ladies: whom he is frequently commending for the neatness of their persons their easy manners and their taste in dress. He knows how often the Ladies use the Baths, what coulour best suits a Ladys complextion, what Cosmecticks are most favourable to the skin.[2]

THE COMPLEX CHARACTER OF JOHN PAUL JONES

The real John Paul Jones had a complex character and it would be a big mistake to think that he was a totally effeminate fop by what Abigail Adams wrote. Sure, he knew how to appeal to the ladies and he did it very well throughout his lifetime (and more than a few times this womanizing got him into some *really serious* trouble). However, he was also an incredibly brave and skillful seafaring battle captain and in every way, "an absolute nautical bad ass."[3] Totally fearless in battleship combat.

Another trait deemed as positive, aside from Jones's valiant charm, was that he wasn't very materialistic, which was exceptionally uncommon for the time. Jones wrote, "Personal gain was never the reason for my public actions; I had more noble motives. And far from making my fortune from the Revolution . . . I consecrated to this great cause the 10 best years of my life."[4] Jones was a self-made man with a high sense of honor and he truly felt that he was fighting for freedom from despotism, as he wrote many times.

Then again, those positive features were counterbalanced with qualities that kept Jones from advancing or receiving recognition as he should have, perhaps stemming from his poor childhood and feelings of inferiority that he possibly still harbored inside. Jones was argumentative and had a quick temper, which resulted in a couple of incidents in which Jones either threatened to or was actually charged with killing a mutinous member of his crew. That's why he fled to Virginia and added the fake name (even back then) of "Jones" to the end of his name. Many members of his various crews disliked, even *hated* him because he demanded strict adherence to his own shipboard standards and procedures—and because he *wasn't* materialistic. In fact, Jones put down

2. Abigail Adams to Elizabeth Cranch, December 3, 1784, Founders Online, National Archives, founders.archives.gov/documents/Adams/04-06-02-0002 (accessed March 3, 2017).

3. allthingsliberty.com/2015/01/the-real-immortal-words-of-john-paul-jones/ (accessed March 3, 2017).

4. "John Paul Jones's Memoir of the American Revolution – Presented to King Louis XVI of France," translated and edited by Gerard W. Gawalt (Washington, D.C., Library of Congress, 1979), 73.

more than a couple mutinies by his own crews on his own ships. That clash of values between Jones and his crew would come to a head with one particular upcoming assignment.

He also hated to be patronized by arrogant nobles, again possibly harkening back to his youth watching his father, a master gardener at Arbigland estate, being disrespected by the estate owner William Craik.[5] Another dominant character flaw was that Jones almost constantly complained about any perceived unfair treatment or biased P.R. that he thought he was receiving, and therefore Jones took an active interest in his own self-promotion and in guarding his own hard-earned reputation. His sensitivity to bad press and criticism guided his shore side activities, when he wasn't at sea fighting incredibly epic battles.

Nonetheless, the only personality trait that mattered to members of the Continental Congress was that John Paul Jones was a rough-and-tumble American master ship's captain. He broke enemy blockades, and ultimately captured "some sixty vessels from the foremost of naval powers . . . destroyed more than a million dollars' worth of property on the sea, and took hundreds of prisoners."[6] By 1778, the Congressional Marine Committee thought Jones also had the potential to wreak havoc and panic in the seacoast towns of the British Isles.

John Paul Jones was all of that and much more. He was a complicated hero of the Revolutionary War who deserves all of the fame and glory that he only started to earn during his brief lifetime. His life story up to the time he set to sea as a poor kid named John Paul Jr.[7] from Kirkbean, west Scotland, is aptly told in the *Journal of the American Revolution* article by Michael Shellhammer "The Real Immortal Words of John Paul Jones."[8] So I won't repeat what has already been so well described. Instead, we'll focus on a little-known incident that Jones and his (unruly, of course) crew encountered while out generally terrorizing the enemy—or trying to, with mixed results. The surprising, little-

5. If the name "Craik" sounds familiar, it's possibly because of William Craik's well-known womanizing. In a strange twist in fate, William Craik had an illegitimate son named James Craik, born in the same parish as John Paul Jones. James Craik went on to become George Washington's lifelong doctor and was at Washington's deathbed. Rumors in Kirkbean were that John Paul Jones himself was an illegitimate son of William Craik, as well.

6. *John Paul Jones – Commemmoration at Annapolis – April 14, 1906*, compiled by Charles W. Stewart, Superintendent Library and Naval War Records (Washington D.C., Government Printing Office, 1907), 29.

7. He added the dubious name of "Jones" to his name while in Virginia, running from law enforcement.

8. allthingsliberty.com/2015/01/the-real-immortal-words-of-john-paul-jones/ (accessed March 7, 2017).

known story and aftermath showcases many of Jones's character traits that have been described here.

JONES'S DARING TWO-PRONGED PLAN

By October 1776, John Paul Jones had already proven himself many times off the American coast as a fearless warrior, fighting battles with other British ships (and with his own surly American crews). He was promoted to the rank of captain in the Continental Navy, and in early 1778 sent to France commanding the eighteen-gun[9] sloop-of-war *Ranger.* Just recently built in Portsmouth, New Hampshire, the *Ranger* was set to receive still more upgrades in France to Jones's specifications, such as adding deck weapons of blunderbusses and swivel guns. Then, once fitted out, Jones would be setting sail into the Atlantic with "unlimited orders"[10] from the American commissioners[11] in Paris. The commissioners just assumed Jones would cruise around creating mayhem and destruction to British ships whenever he happened upon them.

But John Paul Jones had two specific goals that he wanted to accomplish. First, he wanted to execute hit-and-run raids on coastal enemy fleets. Aside from the obvious damage to local shipping, it would create a civilian panic along the coastlines of England, Scotland or Ireland, and therefore force British war officials to divert some of their maritime resources from American shores to protecting their own homeland.[12] Secondly, he wanted to kidnap an important official of the British Empire and hold him for ransom until imprisoned Americans were freed from British jails or impressment.

In a later account penned for King Louis XVI, Jones wrote,

> I had not communicated my plan to this end to the American ministers residing in Paris. I proposed to descend on some part of England and there destroy merchant shipping. My plan was also to take someone of particular distinction as a prisoner and to hold him as

9. The hull was pierced for twenty guns, but *Ranger* only had eighteen installed.
10. *John Paul Jones – Commemmoration at Annapolis,* 168.
11. Benjamin Franklin, Arthur Lee, and Silas Deane. At the time they issued Jones "unlimited orders," John Adams was enroute to Paris to relieve Silas Deane.
12. This idea had been first proposed to him by Robert Morris of the Congressional Marine Committee in a letter to Jones dated February 5, 1777. Library of Congress, *A Calendar of John Paul Jones Manuscripts in the Library of Congress,* February 5, 1777, books.google.com/books?id=q2JCOi7n9RQC&pg=PA235&lpg=PA235&dq=Robert+Morris+to+John+Paul+Jones+Feb.+5,+1777&source=bl&ots=OFYX2E0cQX&sig=GBo6qyovVmauiUTn5X3v8D2Z1Cw&hl=en&sa=X&ved=0ahUKEwinru7tvcrSAhUH-WCYKHYc2DbIQ6AEIHzAB#v=onepage&q=Robert%20Morris%20to%20John%20Paul%20Jones%20Feb.%205%2C%201777&f=false (accessed March 9, 2017).

hostage to guarantee the lives and exchange of Americans then imprisoned in England.[13]

THE BOTCHED RAID ON WHITEHAVEN

On April 10, 1778 Capt. John Paul Jones had just set sail out of Brest, France aboard *Ranger* when he, of course, was faced with a mutiny by his indignant, flea-infested crew. The "restless and sullen"[14] crew of *Ranger* hadn't signed on to get killed in battles for glory. They had fully been expecting loot or "prize money"[15] as it was called, when they captured merchant ships. Jones later wrote, "Their object, they said, was *gain not honor.*"[16] Of course, Jones hadn't been paid yet either from the sale of the loot collected so far, and the crews were paid from what Jones was paid. On the other hand, those were unimportant details now and the crew united for the mutiny.

Jones, however, ended the mutiny quickly when he placed his pistol against the head of David Cullam, the mutinous instigator. The steely iron nerve of their captain probably made the crew think that the rumors they'd heard about Jones having put down an earlier mutiny by running the mutineer through with a sword were true (they were!).

So with that understanding out of the way, *Ranger* and John Paul Jones began their usual assigned business of capturing and sinking British brigs, schooners and sloops in the Irish Sea, between Wales, England and Ireland. Jones saw the opportunity to attack the twenty-gun British frigate *Drake*. Unfortunately, at a strategic moment the key anchor detail mate-in-charge on *Ranger* failed because he "had drunk too much brandy."[17]

By Thursday, April 23 and with winds logged as "Fresh Gales and Squally,"[18] Jones put into action the first part of his own two-part plan—that of launching a slash-and-burn raiding party against British ships tied up in an English port town. He picked the English seaport of Whitehaven, located in John Paul Jones's old childhood neck-of-the-woods and where his seafaring career first began. However, before Jones could inflict devastation, a member of his crew jumped ship, deserted (surprise) and warned residents of the danger. At least Jones and select crewmen were able to spike the coastal defense guns and set one coal

---

13. "John Paul Jones's Memoir of the American Revolution," 16.
14. Thomas, *John Paul Jones,* 105.
15. Ibid.
16. "John Paul Jones's Memoir of the American Revolution," 17.
17. Ibid.
18. From the captain's log of *Ranger,* Thursday, April 23, 1778. *John Paul Jones and the Ranger, and the Log of the Ranger,* ed., Joseph G. Sawtelle (Portsmith, NH: The Portsmith Marine Society, publication 20, 1994), 142.

Left: "Helen, Countess of Selkirk" (*Lady Helen Hamilton Douglas–Lady Selkirk*); right, Captain John Paul Jones, 1780, after Moreau le Jeune. (*New York Public Library*)

ship on fire, hoping the blaze would spread quickly to the other wooden vessels. Nevertheless, the locals were able to put the fire out quickly.[19]

No problem, because now on to Part Two of John Paul Jones's Daring Plan.

THE HOME INVASION AND KIDNAPPING

When Jones had been growing up in Kirkbean, near the Craik estate in the County of Kirkcudbright, the most famous and powerful English noble he'd ever known of was the Earl of Selkirk. In young Jones's limited world, he probably thought the Earl and the King were on a first name basis, when in actuality nothing could be further than the truth. Lord Selkirk (Dunbar Hamilton Douglas) was the 4th Earl of Selkirk and had been rector of Glasgow University for a couple years. Otherwise, his job was just being a "representative peer" in the British House of Lords. His wife was Lady Selkirk (Helen Hamilton Douglas). Family records show that Lord Selkirk was a decent guy and didn't really put much value in his "peerage."

Jones didn't know any of that and either way, he was on course to execute his most daring undertaking to date. The exploit that would

19. Although the raid ultimately did little damage, it started a panic of sorts by civilians. Rumors of an expected French invasion were given traction aside from just the shock of an actual raid on English soil happening. A raid supposedly hadn't occurred since the seventeenth century when a town on the southeast corner of England had been burned by Dutch raiders.

make his name known throughout the Empire: the kidnapping of a British noble. And then, instead of accepting the expected ransom money like some loathsome pirate, Jones would nobly refuse it in lieu of freeing unjustly-imprisoned Americans. Although his crew would be enraged, Jones's chivalrous honor would make him a world-wide legend.

According to the log of *Ranger* for Thursday, April 24, at about 12:00 noon and with winds "Light Airs and hazey Weather,"[20] Jones guided the vessel the twenty miles across the Firth of Solway, water that he knew well from his youthful sailing days. The Earl's Georgian manor house then came into view through the fog sitting up on a hill near the bay of St. Mary's Isle.[21] Captain Jones and twelve armed crew men,[22] surprisingly obedient and probably expecting a treasure trove of Selkirk booty, beached their "Cutter"[23] on the sand and started up the path leading to the manor house. Armed with cutlasses and muskets, the landing party probably looked a lot more like the pirates that the British press was calling Jones and his deck hands. On the contrary, Jones knew that his noble intentions, once known, would overshadow any bad news reports.

Suddenly, the first potential derailing of his plan happened. Jones and the crew ran into the estate gardener on the path! In an example of typical quick thinking, Jones, even though bleary from lack of sleep,[24] said they needed to see the Earl because they were a British press gang there to "impress" (beat into unconsciousness and drag away to His Majesty's Royal Navy) the young men on the isle. Jones then knew the gardener would do exactly what he did: he took off running to warn all of the able-bodied men. The bad part was that just before turning and running, the gardener told Jones that unfortunately the Earl was not at home.[25]

Jones was dejected and told his men that they should all head back to the ship, when his men (predictably) said, "Hold on a minute. Not so fast." David Cullum, one of the men who had come ashore with Jones (and the one Jones had just threatened to blow his brains out for

20. From the captain's log of *Ranger*, Thursday, April 23, 1778; 142. The log entry mistakingly calls the Earl of Selkirk "Lord Murray."
21. St. Mary's Isle was not really an island, but rather a peninsula in Kirkcudbright Bay.
22. From the Log of *Ranger*, Thursday, April 23, 1778; 142.
23. Ibid.
24. Jones later recalled that he'd gone years with only a few hours' sleep per night from fear of his crews, even with a guard posted at his cabin door.
25. The gardener told Jones that Lord Selkirk was at Edinburgh; the Lord was actually at Buxton, Derbyshire, family records show.

mutiny) informed Jones that he and the others were not going back without some of the treasures they were sure were in the Selkirk mansion.

That put Jones in an awkward spot. He knew his men wanted to "pillage, burn, and plunder all they could."[26] Of course, who wouldn't? Captain Jones figured if he said no, the loyal crew would kill him on the spot, then pillage, burn, and plunder anyway. Aside from the probable destruction and death the crew would bring to the lord's manor house and occupants, Jones's *reputation* would also be in smoking ruins. He quickly came up with the only viable plan he had open to him. While he waited down on the path and out of sight (he didn't want to add to the pirate reputation he was being accused of), he would go ahead and allow the crewmen to loot - but with *strict* instructions that he laid down for the home invasion. The rules decreed by Jones, similar to those for trick-or-treating, were these:

- Only two men, the officers (Master Callum and Lieutenant Wallingford) were to knock on the door, introduce themselves, and "politely demand"[27] Lord Selkirk's family silver plate.[28]
- The other (dirty, dangerous and despicable) men were to wait politely nearby.
- Callum and Wallingford were to be "accepting what was given to them without further inquiry, returning without further search."[29]

Lady Helen Hamilton (Lady Selkirk), warned of the press gang, had sent the women and children to hide out on the third floor. She looked at the men outside; as she later wrote her husband, each of them was armed with "a musket, a bayonet, two large pistols and a hanger... "[30] Pirates, she must've thought! She may have been relieved when Lieutenant Wallingford (whom she described as "a civil young man in a green uniform, an anchor on his buttons")[31] politely introduced himself and said they were crewmen under orders from Captain Jones and his "frigate belonging to the States of America."[32] Wallingford said since the "Lord of the House" was not present, he was demanding "all your

26. "John Paul Jones's Memoir of the American Revolution," 19.
27. Ibid.
28. "Family silver plate" didn't mean a single plate. It was a term meaning any and all silver items owned by the family.
29. "John Paul Jones's Memoir of the American Revolution," 19-20.
30. Lady Selkirk to Lord Selkirk, April 24, 1778 in De Koven, *The Life and Letters of John Paul Jones*, 310.
31. Ibid.
32. Ibid, 309. Lady Selkirk incorrectly heard or wrote that Jones's ship was a "frigate." It was a sloop-of-war.

plate."³³ "Upon the whole," Lady Selkirk wrote confidentially, "I must say they behaved civilly."³⁴

The silver plate was collected into a bag of (according to Dr. Ezra Green, surgeon on *Ranger*) "as near as I can judge 160 lb. weight of Silver."³⁵

The band of gleeful blackguards came ambling down the sandy path to Captain Jones. Apparently, no one in the Selkirk household had been molested or killed, the manor house still stood, and the crew took some silver booty … *and* Jones's reputation was still somewhat intact. Everyone was happy. The men got to *Ranger* and "all sail was made to run down the Firth."³⁶

THE SELKIRK RAID AFTERMATH

Yet still, Jones's reputation (at least in the British Isles) had a growing stain. As news of vessel attacks, a fire raid on a British coast dock, and a home invasion, robbery, and an attempted abduction spread, the citizens, already jittery from rumors of a French invasion, were in full panic mode.

The alarms started flashing all the way to London. William Fraser, the British Undersecretary of State for the Northern Department, received an urgent dispatch from Philip Stephens, the Secretary of the Admiralty, complaining that, "the rebel privateer which plundered Lord Selkirk's house has thrown the whole western coast into consternation."³⁷ Four heavily-gunned frigates and men-of-war were dispatched to the Irish Sea to search for John Paul Jones, the privateer marauder.

Though Lady Selkirk wrote to her husband that the thieves "behaved civilly", she ironically has less kind words about their captain,

> It was immediately known that this Paul Jones is one John Paul, born at Arbigland, who once commanded a Kirkcudbright vessel belonging to Mr. Muir and others, a great villain as ever was born, guilty of many crimes and several murders by ill usage, was tried and condemned for one, escaped, and followed a piratical life, till he engaged with the Americans.³⁸

33. Ibid.
34. Ibid, 310.
35. "Diary of Dr. Ezra Green, Surgeon During the Cruise of the Continental Ship of War Ranger, From Nov. 1, 1777 to Sept. 27, 1778, From the original in the possession of the New England Historic Genealogical Society." Appendix A, *John Paul Jones and the Ranger*, 204.
36. Thomas, *John Paul Jones*, 127.
37. Philip Stephens to William Fraser, May 5, 1778, Admiralty Records, Public Records Office, Kew Gardens, England; and in Thomas, *John Paul Jones*, 133.
38. De Koven, *The Life and Letters of John Paul Jones*, 310-311.

THE SELKIRK-JONES PEN-PAL LETTERS

The complex character of John Paul Jones soon showed itself again, just two weeks after the silver pilfering at the Selkirk's place. As a naval captain, Jones was probably bothered by his own abdication of duty in allowing his unruly crew to rob Lord and Lady Selkirk of their family plate while he stood by at a distance. Jones was probably even *much more* bothered by how the whole episode would play out in the world press.

Jones wrote a letter to "the right honorable the Countess Selkirk"[39] from aboard *Ranger* at Brest, France on May 8, 1778 (and was sure to send copies of it to Benjamin Franklin, the American commissioner in Passy, France, and to the Marine Committee of Congress). In the strange letter, he started off by saying he was glad her husband wasn't home because (instead of saying he was ready to drag Lord Selkirk off as a war hostage), he wrote, "I wished to make him the happy instrument"[40] for a POW exchange. That's nice.

Jones also reiterated that looting the Selkirk silver hadn't been part of the plan. He wrote that he had to allow it since his "volunteers"[41] were "expressing their discontent"[42] of how it was so unfair the British soldiers in America got to loot but his men could not. That's when he disclosed to Lady Selkirk that he was planning on buying the silver back and returning it to her. "I have gratifyed my Men, and, When the Plate is sold, I shall become the purchaser, and will gratify my own feelings by restoring it to you."[43]

He then threw in some *extremely* vivid details emphasizing the fact that it was good that Lord Selkirk was not aboard *Ranger* the very next evening following the silver heist. Jones and his vessel were attacked by the "British ship of war Drake"[44] and Jones proceeded to describe "the awful pomp, and dreadful carnage,"[45] to probably paint for the Lady a breathtaking scene of bravery, danger and glory.

Jones then found the opportune time to make a pass at Lady Selkirk by subtly adding, "Nor am I in pursuit of Riches. My fortune is liberal enough, having no wife nor family"[46] and throwing in a reference to

39. "John Paul Jones's Memoir of the American Revolution," 90-92; also *John Paul Jones – Commemmoration at Annapolis*, 123-125.
40. "John Paul Jones's Memoir of the American Revolution," 90.
41. Ibid.
42. Ibid.
43. Ibid, 91.
44. Ibid.
45. Ibid.
46. Ibid.

"your gentle bosom."[47] He clinched it by saying, "I wage No War with the Fair. I acknowledge their power and bend before it with profound submission!"[48] He ended the letter with the friendly equivalent of "Drop me a line if you want to talk."

LORD SELKIRK GETS HOME AND READS JONES'S LETTER TO HIS WIFE

His Lordship was not amused. He dashed off a letter to "Monsieur J.P. Jones"[49] and in it spared few words, short of calling Jones a complete idiot. But first he warned Jones, as would happen in a modern get-even film, that had something happened to his family or "my Wife, then well advanced in her pregnancy,"[50] then "no quarter of the Globe should have secured you."[51]

Lord Selkirk then went on to recite why he had been such a poor choice to kidnap. First of all, King George III didn't even know him, since he had a "useless Scotch Title."[52] "With regard to the King's Ministers, I neither have nor can have an interest with them, as I have generally disapproved of most of their measures, and in particular of almost their whole conduct in the unhappy and illjudged American War."[53] In the final blow, Lord Selkirk revealed that he had always "been very friendly to the Constitutions and Just Liberties of America."[54] Whoops.

Over the next couple years occasional letters went back and forth between Jones and Lord Selkirk or through a third party. Selkirk eventually admitted he was grateful to Jones for the good discipline of his crew and for Jones's apparent honorable nature in trying to return the family's silver plate.

By February 12, 1784, Jones was able to write to Lord Selkirk from Paris to tell him that the transfer arrangements were being made to transport "your Plate" to "your Estate in Scotland."[55] Then, Jones being Jones, added at the end of the letter, "As you were so obliging as to say to Mr. Alexander, 'that my People beheaved with such decency at your House', I ask the favor of you to annonce that circumstance to the Public."[56]

47. Ibid, 92.
48. Ibid.
49. Lord Selkirk to J.P. Jones, June 9, 1778; *John Paul Jones – Commemmoration at Annapolis*, 127.
50. Ibid.
51. Ibid, 129.
52. Ibid, 128.
53. Ibid, 127-128.
54. Ibid, 128.
55. "John Paul Jones's Memoir of the American Revolution," 95.
56. Ibid, 96.

In a letter a year and one half later, dated August 4, 1785, a thankful Lord Selkirk acknowledged that the family silver had indeed arrived at Dumfries, very nearby "and I dare say quite safe."[57] He added, "I intended to have put an article in the News-Papers about your having returned it; but before I was informed of its being arrived, some of your friends, I suppose, had Put it in the Dumfries News-Paper; whence it was immediately copied into the Edinburgh Papers and thence into the London ones."[58] Imagine that.

Although someone beat His Lordship in announcing to the press that after seven years, John Paul Jones had returned every bit of the silver collection, Selkirk offered the best gesture of thank you that he knew "Monsieur Le Chevalier Paul-Jones"[59] would appreciate *the most*. He would instruct that London newspapers print Selkirk's accurate and honorable story of what happened that day at his Scottish estate on St. Mary's Isle. He ended the letter to Jones,

> Some of the English News-Papers, at that time, having put in confused accounts of your expedition to White-haven and Scotland, I ordered a proper one of what happened in Scotland to be put in the London News-Papers ... by which the good conduct and civil behavior of your officers and men was done justice to and attributed to your orders, and the good discipline you maintained over your people.
>
> I am, Sir your most humble Servant,
> Selkirk[60]

A few months after the successful publication of Lord Selkirk's corrected account of John Paul Jones's estate raid, Jones received a letter from Charles Hector, comte d'Estaing, the famous French general and admiral who spent much time in America during the Revolutionary War. D'Estaing had just finished reading Jones's memoir written for King Louis XVI. In a letter d'Estaing wrote to Jones, he summarized, "This lesson of military and naval heroism has, by your conduct to Lord and Lady Selkirk, also become one of generosity."[61]

John Paul Jones was probably quite happy with the letter from d'Estaing, and possibly considered making it available to global news outlets.

---

57. Ibid, 98.
58. Ibid.
59. Ibid, 99.
60. Ibid, 99.
61. Ibid, 104.

Admiral Rodney Ousts the Jews from St. Eustatius

❀ LOUIS ARTHUR NORTON ❀

An incongruous spectacle greeted a scorching Caribbean sun that shone upon a stone quay. Tall slim palms seemed to wave a mournful farewell while providing a much-needed cooling sea breeze. A crowd of darkly dressed Jewish men, their bearded faces hidden in the shadows of broad-brimmed dark hats, huddled on the pier. They were surrounded; prisoners of the British Marines, their menacing bayonets gleaming in the late morning light. On the nearby shore modestly dressed women, their heads covered in shawls, wailed and screamed out the names of their beloved fathers, husbands and sons. Children, confused and full of dread, added their refrain to the cacophony of the weeping chorus. This was the scene of a little-known anti-Semitic incident. It originated from a series of noteworthy incidents in the maritime history of the Revolutionary War ultimately presaging other far-reaching events.

A convoluted historical background is related to this scene. All Jews were expelled from Spain in 1492. Upwards of one hundred thousand immigrated to Portugal where they joined a centuries-old Jewish community already there, but their security was not long lasting. In 1496 the Portuguese King Manuel I delivered an edict allowing them to stay only if they converted to Christianity. Under duress, some became "New Christians" or "Conversos," or "Persons of the Nation" (*La Nación*), but approximately 20,000 Orthodox Jews sailed away from the country rather than convert. This Iberian Jewish subgroup became known as Sephardic Jews and spoke a Judeo-Spanish language known as *Ladino*.[1] In order to practice Judaism, some Sephardic congregations

1. When the Jews were expelled from Spain and Portugal they continued to speak Ladino in their communities to which they emigrated. Ladino therefore reflects the grammar and vocabulary of fourteenth and fifteenth century Spanish. Ladino's origins

immigrated to the Protestant centers of Amsterdam to avoid the Catholic Inquisition at other European hubs.

The Dutch established the West India Company in 1621 that was largely an Atlantic trading Company. In 1658 the Dutch Parliament recognized the Jews as Dutch citizens and supported their endeavors, particularly in the Caribbean zone. There they could escape the harsh winters of Holland and practice their faith openly. Thus a vibrant Jewish society was established, mostly of Jews of Spanish or Portuguese descent. Under the encouragement and protection of the Dutch West India Company, Jews started agricultural plantations. This enterprise alone did not meet the needs of the large families so they took up other occupations. The region had its share of Jewish ship owners, navigators, and merchants who often traveled with their ships and cargo. Their kinship and common language helped in the bargaining process.

The Spanish-Portuguese Jews took synagogue and religious life very seriously.

The planter refrained from working his laborers on the Sabbath and the sailor took his prayer shawl and kosher meat for his voyage. The Jewish festivals and holy days were observed, the Jewish law court was respected, and Jewish schools held a place of importance in communal expenditures. Contact was maintained with the Holy Land so that earth from the land of Israel could be placed on the eyelids of the dead before burial.

Jews had arrived in Colonial America starting in 1654. By the time of the American Revolutionary War there were fewer than two thousand or less than one tenth of one percent of a total American population at the time.[2] In the colonies, economic and religious discrimination noticeably lessened. Anti-Semitism existed in some quarters, but it did not thrive. The American colonies needed population, particularly an educated and skilled populace.

In 1753 the British Parliament had passed a Jewish "Naturalization Bill" to promote economic development in Great Britain and its colonies.[3] Foreign-born Jews who were awarded British citizenship were granted limited rights, including land ownership. The public reacted with an enormous outburst of anti-Semitism and Parliament repealed

are similar to those of Yiddish, a combination Hebrew and local languages, but Ladino was not as diverse as the various forms of Yiddish.

2. Ashkenazi Jews outnumbered Sephardic Jews by 1720.

3. Danby Pickering, *The Statutes at Large from the 26th to the 30th Year of King George II* (Cambridge, UK), Vol. XXI, 1766; also Carsten Schaprow, "Western Nations," in Alan T. Levenson, *The Wiley-Blackwell History of the Jews and Judaism* (Chichester, England: John Wiley & Sons, 2012), 327-342.

the bill in 1754.[4] Thus on the eve of the American Revolution, Jews were considered second-class citizens by the general population in Britain. The provisions of the original act were mostly upheld in Colonial America in spite of the bill's repeal in Britain, but they were dependent upon the domestic laws of each colonial legislature. In general, however, Jews were free to participate in colonial life, engage in commerce and practice their faith.

The Jewish American population was largely in support of the American Revolution.[5] They pledged their hearts and wealth for the possibility of even greater freedom and opportunity in an America that had thus far treated them fairly. Shortly after the Declaration of Independence was approved and signed in Philadelphia, a copy was sent to Amsterdam. Unfortunately the British intercepted the ship carrying the rebels' Declaration and a letter accompanying the historic document. Both were sent to London. It was assumed that the letter was seditious, because it appeared to be written in some secret code. The letter that needed to be deciphered was written in the Hebrew script—American Jews were simply communicating with their Dutch brethren.[6]

In order to secure their foothold in the Caribbean Islands, the Dutch colonial powers built bases on the islands of Martinique, Guadeloupe, Tobago, and Barbados that would serve as resupply stations and centers for the purchase of military armament. Arguably the most important was at St. Eustatius (also known as Sint Eustatius, Statius and more commonly Statia), a small island lying about 250 miles east-south-east of Puerto Rico. It has an area of 11.8 square miles with a natural port and dominated by an inactive 600-meter volcano known as "the Quill." In 1722, only 21 Jews lived on this small island. By 1750 the Jewish population had grown to more than 450 among the 802 free St. Eustatian citizens. They were mostly refugees of Recife-Brazil, Tobago, Surinam, North Africa, Curaçao, and Amsterdam. Several were Ashkenazi families from the community of Rotterdam. Although Jews had full civil rights, they were excused from serving in the Civil Guard to spare them from Sabbath military duty. In 1737 the community of *Honen Dalim* was

4. Diana Muir Appelbaum, "Jacob's Sons in the Bishop's Palace." Jewish Ideas Daily, November 14, 2012.
5. Jonathan D. Sarna, "The Impact of the American Revolution on American Jews," *Modern Judaism* (Baltimore MD: The Johns Hopkins Press, 1981), 1:149-160.
6. Laurence Busch, "July 4th: The Secret Code of the Declaration," *Jewish Currents, Activist Politics and Art*, July 3, 2011. The content of the letter, to whom it was intended or whether the letter was in Yiddish, a German-Hebrew linguistic mixture, or Ladino is not clear.

found, and in 1738 permission was given to build a synagogue on the Island.[7]

St. Eustatius became a significant commercial entrepôt of the Caribbean region. Sugar was exported from the French and Spanish colonies in the Caribbean to North America, meat was imported from North America and Canada, corn from Venezuela, flour from Scandinavia, largely with ships owned by St. Eustatius's Jews. By 1760, between 1,800 and 2,700 ships were recorded anchoring in St. Eustatius port each year.

Some American Jewish merchants had financial interests in small fleets of merchant vessels and established co-religious contacts especially in the Caribbean. Now that the United Colonies were at war, a few of these merchant traders converted their ships into privateers to harass the British at sea. Other Jewish merchant vessel owners engaged in the arms smuggling trade transporting weapons and powder from the West Indies, especially from the Dutch colonies; in May 1776 alone, eighteen ships from St. Eustatius reached the thirteen colonies. This dangerous venture was made easier because of ancestral and cultural ties between the Sephardic Jews of Dutch island colonies and those of the American colonies.

Holland had participated in several seventeenth and eighteenth century European wars, their navy was in decline and some in the government saw this as an opportunity to profit from being a nonaligned state. The Dutch set up free ports where all nations were welcome and St. Eustatius became the main North American conduit for trade with the nations of Continental Europe, principally France, and the New England maritime colonies.[8] Other countries that were forbidden by law from dealing directly with each other shipped their products to the neutral Dutch colonies of St. Eustatius.

In time many manifests appeared listing St. Eustatius as an intermediate port for goods produced elsewhere. At the time of the American Revolution the population of the island was an ethnic mosaic of about 8,000 Dutch, English and Jewish merchants. St. Eustatius became a vital port of call for American vessels where arms, although officially prohibited, could be purchased and smuggled into the northern climes of

---

7. Translation of Hebrew: He who is charitable (shows mercy) to the poor.
8. Barbara W. Tuchman, *The First Salute* (New York: Knopf, 1988), 7-10, 12, 22; Friedrich Edler, *The Dutch Republic and the American Revolution* (Baltimore, MD: Johns Hopkins Press), 1911; Nordholt Schulte, *The Dutch Republic and American Independence* (Chapel Hill, NC: University of North Carolina Press, 1981).

America. Several Dutch firms engaged in this clandestine traffic making St. Eustatius the cheapest source of European goods in the West Indies. Therefore this seemingly peaceful Caribbean island evolved into a serious economic and political threat to Britain.

Diplomatic relations had become strained between Holland and Great Britain, but the Dutch were members of the League of Armed Neutrality, an organization of nonaligned nations. The British prohibited the Royal Navy from search and seizure of the ships of non-belligerent countries. The Dutch took advantage of their neutrality and stockpiled arms on St. Eustatius for sale to any country with the funds to buy them. The colonial governor of the island, Johannes de Graaff, was personally sympathetic to the American rebel cause and at the same time profited from several island companies in which he had a financial interest.

On March 20, 1775 the Dutch parliament (the States General or *Den Stadhouder*), at the behest of the British, prohibited the export of munitions from all Dutch harbors, European and colonial, to any vessel that flew the English flag unless they had a special government issued license. This act was intended to prevent American ships, which were still technically British and thus allowed to fly the British flag, from purchasing arms for their rebellion. The six-month embargo was designed to cut America's supply of arms and to mollify the British. De Graaff and local Dutch traders, however, were astute businessmen and interpreted the States General's proclamation as an easily negotiated obstacle rather than a roadblock. American merchant ships sailed to and from St. Eustatius, frequently with Continental Navy vessels as escorts, but these ships were not effective against large enemy more formidable warships. They did however act as a buffer against ever-present privateers and occupied smaller British warships providing enough time for vulnerable merchantmen to escape.[9]

In a move to appease Great Britain, the Dutch government publically condemned the newly signed Declaration of Independence and expressed sympathy with Britain's efforts to extinguish the insurrection. American warships nonetheless carried secret communications and/or special cargo to or from the West Indies. On October 23, 1776 the Marine Committee of the Continental Congress of the United Colonies ordered the Continental Navy brig *Andrea Doria* to the Dutch colony of St. Eustatius with a dispatch to be forwarded to William Bingham at Martinico (currently the Dominican Republic). In June 1776 Bingham

9. The British Prohibition Act of December 22, 1775 was established in an attempt to stifle the American economy. Royal Navy vessels were ordered to seize any colonial ship engaged in commerce and impress its sailors.

had agreed to serve the Continental Congress in Martinique by gathering information about British naval and troop movements, arranging for weapons to be smuggled to the Continental Army, and recruiting privateers to prey on British shipping.

Flying the flag of Grand Union on its stern flagstaff, *Andrea Doria* arrived outside the harbor of St. Eustatius on November 16, 1776. Captain Isaac Robinson, the vessel's commander, decided to make a conspicuous entry into port. Robinson ordered the Grand Union of the Republic flag, the recently adopted American banner, dipped and a cannon salute fired from the vessel's deck. According to maritime custom, a return salute was the appropriate response of their host state.

Abraham Raven, the commander of the harbor's Fort Orange, assumed the unfamiliar flag might be that of a rebel American warship and realized that returning a salute would offend the British. Raven sent a message for instructions to Governor de Graaff and was ordered to answer the salute. Some minutes passed, then nine puffs of gray-white gun smoke arose from the walls of the fort followed by a salute of muffled thumps in cadence.[10] A historic moment transpired: the American colors had for the first time been publicly recognized by a European power.[11] These brief cannon reports turned out to be an expression of diplomatic indiscretion. This seemingly minor acknowledgment was contrary to Dutch foreign policy.

When news of the incident reached the neighboring island of St. Christopher (St. Kitts), its British governor, Craister Greathead, sent a vehement protest to Governor de Graaff, complaining "That … Supplies of all Sorts of Provisions and warlike Stores are almost daily & publickly furnished by the Inhabitants of St Eustatius to His Majesty's said rebellious Subjects," citing specific examples of ships from that port taking British vessels, and objecting to a salute being returned "with the Solemnity due to the Flags of Independent Sovereign States." A similar protest was made by Vice Admiral James Young, the senior British naval officer in the region. The governor responded to Young with justifications for some of the individual actions, but of the salute said only that "this Port always made and still makes distinction between Merchant or Private Vessells and the Ships of War belonging to Sovereign States: the latter receive constantly, when they honor its Fortress with a salute Gun for Gun, as a distinctive mark of Independancy."[12]

10. Louis Arthur Norton, "The Continental Navy Brig Andrew (Andrea) Doria," *The American Neptune*, 61, #1, 2001, 9-23.
11. Tuchman, *The First Salute.*
12. William B. Clark, et al. eds. *Naval Documents of the American Revolution* (Washington, DC: Government printing Office, 1964), 7:486-487, 508, 525.

Greathead officially reported the incident to the British Foreign Office, writing: "The Impartial World will Judge between us, whether a salute deliberately returned by a Dutch fort to the Rebel brigantine *Andrew Doria*, under Colours known to the Commandant of that Fort to be those of His Majesty's rebellious Subjects, be, or be not, a Partiality in Favor of those Rebels and a flagrant Indignity offered to his Majesty's Flag."[13] This complaint was sent from the British Foreign Office to the States General of the Netherlands.

The Americans viewed the incident as important.[14] Baltimore's *Maryland Journal* for January 22, 1777, commented that Governor de Graaff and the people of St. Eustatius had displayed their "partiality for the American States, now engaged in the Cause of all Mankind."[15] On February 21 Britain's Parliament sent a formal complaint to The Hague demanding that the Dutch government disavow the salute, dismiss Governor de Graaff and enforce the West Indies munitions embargo. If satisfaction was not received in a timely fashion, the British Parliament threatened to recall its ambassador to Holland.

The Dutch government called de Graaff home to answer the charges at a formal inquiry. In his defense, de Graaff claimed that he was unaware of the newly adopted American colors and had ordered *Andrea Doria's* salute returned out of normal courtesy, enforcing Dutch laws on the colonial island as he understood them.[16] As a result the governor was neither dismissed nor punished.[17] De Graaff was officially admonished, but essentially exonerated. He returned to his post at St. Eustatius in 1779.[18]

13. Ibid. The British anglicized the Italian ship's name Andrea to Andrew.
14. President Franklin Roosevelt visited the island on February 27, 1939 onboard the USS *Houston*. The plaque was given to the island's government that reads: *"In commemoration to the salute to the flag of the United States, Fired in this fort November 16. 1776, By order of Johannes de Graaff, Governor of Saint Eustatius, In reply to a National Gun-Salute, Fired by the United States Brig of War Andrew Doria, Under Captain Isaiah Robinson of the Continental Navy, Here the sovereignty of the United States of America was first formally acknowledged to a national vessel by a foreign official. Presented by Franklin Delano Roosevelt, President of the United States of America."*
15. Clark, *Naval Documents*, 7:1018-19.
16. Louis Arthur Norton, *Joshua Barney: Hero of the Revolution and 1812* (Annapolis, MD: The Naval Institute Press, 2000), 29.
17. The Dutch government did however reaffirm their earlier embargo order in the West Indies against the export of military stores to the Americans and formally disclaimed acts of their officials that might be interpreted as recognizing American independence.
18. On his return, de Graaff became somewhat of a hero of the American revolutionaries. Two American privateers were named for him and his wife, and a portrait of him hangs today in the New Hampshire Statehouse in gratitude for the salute he ordered and to honor the Dutch "armed neutrality" that gave one belligerent satisfaction and the other total discontent.

During the next few years St. Eustatius became more of a thorn in the side of King George III as additional arms reached the hands of the beleaguered Americans. Ships running contraband for the rebels became an even more profitable business for Dutch merchants. The British increased their patrols of the North American shipping lanes and by chance captured the American diplomat Henry Laurens at sea. A dispatch from the Continental Congress requesting a loan to help finance the Revolutionary War together with a proposal for a treaty of commerce with the Dutch was found in Laurens' possession. The evidence of subterfuge found in these seized documents became part of a pretext for the British to discontinue honoring Dutch neutrality. They would help themselves to the Dutch ships and cargo in the West Indies estimated at the time to be worth about five million pounds sterling. An Anglo-Dutch War was declared.

As a result, Royal Navy Adm. Sir George Brydges Rodney was ordered to interdict the supply of arms coming to the Americans through the Dutch colonies in the West Indies. Rodney had been promoted to Vice-Admiral in 1763 and made a Baronet in 1764. His penchant for gambling, living well and his run for Parliament in 1768 cost him much of his fortune. In 1771 he was appointed Commander-In-Chief at Jamaica, as well as given the honorary office of Rear Admiral of Great Britain. He held the Jamaica position until 1774, but became so far in debt that he settled in Paris instead of returning to London. In 1778, his friend Marshal Biron loaned him money to clear his debts. Returning to London, Rodney repaid Biron and was shortly promoted to Admiral. Rodney, now a rising fixture in the British aristocracy, became obsessed with securing his financial future.

Rodney and his fleet of fifteen heavily armed ships-of-the-line, several frigates and 3,000 land troops arrived at St. Eustatius on February 3, 1781. The garrison there numbered only fifty or sixty men.[19] The naval force in the harbor consisted of Dutch frigate of thirty-eight guns, and five smaller American vessels, of from twelve to twenty-six guns. The British naval force was an overwhelming threat. The port of St. Eustatius sheltered more than a hundred merchant vessels that flew the flags of many western countries including Britain's Union Jack. Apparently word of the new British policy of belligerency had not reached Governor de Graaff, but it was clear that the Dutch were militarily overmatched. In order to save lives and property, de Graaff surrendered unconditionally. Rodney declared that he would not leave the island until

19. Burke, in Hansard, XXII 221, 772.

"the *Lower Town*, that nest of vipers, which preyed upon the vitals of Great Britain, be destroyed."[20]

The rich prizes of ships in the harbor and the value of the goods in the warehouse would likely ensure that Rodney would be debt-free for the rest of his life. He attempted to maximize his prizes still further by leaving the Dutch flag flying over the fort and town, perhaps to lure unsuspecting ship captains to sail their vessels into his trap and add to the admiral's booty.

In his role of conqueror, Rodney now had to govern the citizens of a major foreign colony and many extraneously flagged prize vessels. His captives were citizens of many powerful European countries and it became diplomatically prudent to treat his prisoners with deference to avoid international repercussions. Nevertheless Rodney's orders were clear. He had to subdue the island's commerce, an active trade that had harmed the British effort to repress the American rebellion. Rodney seemed determined to make a show of Great Britain's power by punishing some of the inhabitants as an example.[21]

The execution of these decrees caused much hardship and the Dutch secretary of the island declared that the English acted like robbers.[22] The warehouses were locked, the merchants denied permission to take inventories, and all books, papers and cash were seized.[23] There were searches of portmanteaus and pockets, digging in gardens for hidden specie, damaging of houses, seizing of negro slaves, appropriation of riding-horses by the officers, and the daily work of shipping goods and sending away the inhabitants in companies, nation by nation.[24] The protests of to the assembly of St. Christopher on St. Kitts, presented to Rodney by its solicitor-general, were treated with contempt. Accounts vary concerning the details of what occurred, but after troops confiscated the stores on ships and the goods stowed in the island's warehouses, there was less cash and valuables than the admiral expected.[25]

20. To the Governor of Barbados, in Godfrey Basil Mundy, *The Life and Correspondence of the Late Admiral Lord Rodney* (London: John Murray, 1830), 2:29. The "Lower Town", as opposed to the "Upper Town", consisted in a double row of houses and warehouses down in the bay at sea level which had come into existence from 1760. It was not in fact destroyed, largely because Rodney's request to London for instructions never received a reply.

21. *American Historical Review*, Vol. 8 No. 4 (July 1903), 683 708.

22. Secretary A. Le Jeune to the greffier of the States General, June 27, in Corr. St. Gen., Sparks MSS., CIII. His arrival is noted in *Gazette de Leyde*, July 3, 4.

23. *Gazette de Leyde*, April 17, 1, May 8, 4; *Nederlandsche Jaerboeken*, 1781, 1225 1227, 1294; Hansard, XXII 221 223.

24. *Gazette de Leyde*, May 15, 5 6; *Nederlandsche Jaerboeken*, 1781, 807 813.

25. *Gazette de Leyde* of May 8, 3; they are commented on by Burke in Hansard, XXII 227-228.

Rodney then asked for a register of all local merchants and their religious affiliations. The hardest measure of all was meted out to the Jews. He ordered all male Jews to report at the weigh house where they were promptly and roughly searched for valuables.

Not only were they deprived of their property, they were sentenced to banishment, given only a day's notice for their departure, and were told that they were to go without their wives and children. The next day 101 men were confined in the weigh house and strictly guarded. They were then stripped, and the linings of their clothes ripped up in search of money. Approximately eight thousand pounds sterling was obtained in this way. Ironically one of these Jews had 900 johanneses (Dutch currency) sewn into his clothing.[26] Rodney suspected that the Jews may have concealed valuables in coffins to prevent them from becoming British conquest spoils, and directed his men to do some digging in fresh graves to see if what might be hidden there.

The British confiscated anything of worth in Jewish shops, offices, homes, and on their persons. On February 5, 1781 the majority of the Jewish male population of St. Eustatius was loaded upon transport vessels without family or property and scattered into exile, some to the nearby Island of St. Christopher and others farther afield.[27] No records exist concerning what became of deportees; where they finally went or whether they ever returned to their homes on St. Eustatius following the English occupation. Although the building was destroyed, the congregation *Honen Daliem* survived the ordeal, as related in a letter which Moses de Fonseca, a Statian Jew.[28]

Rodney was also hostile towards his countrymen who prospered from illicit wartime trade to the detriment of Great Britain. He was convinced that St. Eustatius was "an asylum for men guilty of every crime and a receptacle for outcasts of every nation."[29] The island's illegal trade allowed the rebellious Americans to extend the war and enabled the French to procure supplies for their own islands. This may explain why

26. Hansard, XXII 223 226. The *Gazette de Leyde*, June 5, 3, gives the name of this man as Moloch, surely an unlikely name for a Hebrew. Lord George Germain asserted that the treatment of the Jews was unknown to the commanders-in chief, but St. John declared himself ready to prove the opposite (ibid., 244, 247), and indeed it seems to be proved by the petition of the Jews of St. Eustatius, dated February 16, printed in the *Annual Register*, 308 310, and in *Nederlandsche Jaerboeken*, 1781, 817 820.

27. Ten months later the French, allies of the Dutch in this war conquered the island. The Dutch regained command over the island in 1784.

28. John Hartog, "The Honen Daliem Congregation of St Eustatius," *American Jewish Archives*, April 1967, 164-65.

29. Major-General G. B. Mundy, *The Life and Correspondence of the late Admiral Lord Rodney* (London, Murray, 1830), 2:43.

Rodney was so jubilant at the blow he had dealt to Holland. "It will teach them for the future not to supply the enemies of our country with the sinews of war: they suffer justly."[30] He believed his intervention affected a "just revenge of Britain" against not only the Dutch but also all the nation's enemies including France, America, and those English merchants who had put personal profit before the duty owed to their King and country. Rodney considered these British subjects guilty of treason that justly merited their own ruin.[31]

People of other nationalities were also harshly dealt with except for French agents and merchants. The Dutch governor of Martinique lodged a protest against the severity shown to his fellow countrymen, but Rodney felt that his treatment of Christian Dutch merchants was fair-minded and impartial, even though his personal opinion of Governor de Graaff was contemptuous.[32] He even showed reasonable deference to the sugar plantation owners whom he found were largely uninvolved in illegal practices. He treated the inhabitants of the other two Dutch islands captured in the operation, Saba and St. Maarten, well. Rodney felt that they would "prove to be loyal subjects."[33]

Rodney remained on the island ostensibly for its protection, but more likely he wanted to assure he found every pence his conquest produced. He then auctioned off the personal valuables seized from all the inhabitants and seamen, thus netting Rodney and the officers and crews serving under him a small fortune. The island's British subjects, most of whom lost property, later sued Rodney, questioning his behavior in Parliament.

The admiral stayed on St. Eustatius until the latter part of July 1781. During the intervening months he used part of his fleet to convey a substantial portion of the booty back to England. Ironically much of the spoils never arrived. A convoy laden with his treasures was intercepted in the English Channel by a French squadron and the cargoes, with an estimated value of more than three million pounds sterling, fell into French hands.[34]

There is evidence that Rodney spent time enriching himself on St. Eustatius rather than pursuing French Admiral François Joseph Paul compte de Grasse. On April 28, when de Grasse arrived off Martinique,

30. To Lady Rodney, February 12, 1781, in Mundy, *Life and Correspondence*, 2:25.
31. To the Governor of Barbados, in Mundy, *Life and Correspondence*, February 17, 1781, 2:29.
32. From the Marquis de Bouillé, February 27, 1781 in Mundy, *Life and Correspondence*, and Rodney's reply, 2:31-32
33. In Mundy, *Life and Correspondence*, 2:45.
34. William Laird Clowes, et al., *Royal Navy, A History from the Earliest Times to the Present* (London: Chatham Publishing, 1901), 3:480.

Rodney was in St. Eustatius apparently concerned with his financial problems. He gave the command to Rear Admiral Samuel Hood who did not know these treacherous waters and sailed with an inferior fleet. Neither Rodney nor Hood had any premonition that de Grasse was about to sail for the Chesapeake. Still, the poor result of Hood's foray was predictable. If Rodney had been in command of the fleet, perhaps the outcome of the Revolutionary War might have changed.[35] In September de Grasse sailed from the West Indies to arrive off Hampton Roads in early October 1781. The presence of de Grasse and his fleet of twenty-eight warships at the mouth of Chesapeake Bay prevented the British from providing support to Lord Charles Cornwallis's troops at Yorktown, Virginia. Cornwallis was forced to surrender on October 19, and this defeat led directly to the war's conclusion.[36]

News of Rodney's singling out the Dutch Jews for the harshest punishment reached Great Britain. Edmund Burke, a Member of Parliament, was an eloquent sympathizer of the American cause. Although in later years he became known for uncharitable statements toward Jews,[37] in 1781 he reproved Rodney for his mistreatment of them on St. Eustatius. Burke commented, "If Britons were so injured, Britons have armies and laws to fly to for the protection and justice. But the Jews have no such power and no such friend to depend upon. Humanity then must become their protector."[38] Recognizing Jewish vulnerability, Burke saw it as the responsibility of powerful nations like Great Britain to safeguard them. Burke may, however, have been more concerned with Rodney's actions seeming like an ethical lapse on the part of Great Britain, than with the plight of the Jews.

Edmund Burke's speech to Parliament in defense of the Jews of St. Eustatius was as partly follows:

> This island was different from all others . . . a magazine for all the nations of the earth. It had no fortifications for its defence; no garrison . . . Its inhabitants were a mixed body of all nations and climates . . . The Dutch commander yielded up the dominion . . . A general confiscation of all the property found upon the Island . . . without

35. Lee Bienkowski, *Admirals in the Age of Nelson* (Annapolis, MD: The Naval Institute Press, 2003), 63-7.
36. Ironically Rodney went on to decimate the French fleet and capture de Grasse at the "Battle of the Saints" in the West Indies on April 12, 1782. This historic British naval victory occurred a little over a year after Rodney's seizure of St. Eustatius and perhaps allayed the British condemnation of Rodney.
37. Edmund Burke became renowned as an anti-Semite. For example, in his "*Reflections on the Revolution in France,*" (1790) Burke deemed the Jews' financial dealings and their presence in Britain as a threat to Britain's national solidarity."
38. Records of Debate in the Parliament of Great Britain, November 30, 1781.

regard to friend or foe . . . and a sentence of general beggary pronounced in one moment upon a whole people. A cruelty unheard
of in Europe for many years . . . The persecution was begun with the
people whom of all others it ought to be the care and the wish of
human nations to protect, the Jews . . . the links of communication,
the mercantile chain . . . the conductors by which credit was transmitted through the world . . . a resolution taken (by the British con-
querors) to banish this unhappy people from the island. They
suffered in common with the rest of the inhabitants, the loss of their
merchandise, their bills, their houses, and their provisions; and after
this they were ordered to quit the island, and only one day was given
them for preparation; they petitioned, they remonstrated against so
hard a sentence, but in vain; it was irrevocable. They asked to what
part of the world they were to be transported: The answer was, that
they should not be informed . . . they must prepare to depart the island the next day; and without their families . . . The next day they
did appear to the number of 101, the whole that were upon the island. They were confined in a weigh-house . . . strongly guarded;
and orders were given that they should be stripped, and all the linings of their clothes ripped up, that every shilling of money which
they might attempt to conceal and carry off should be discovered
and taken from them. This order was carried into rigid execution,
and money, to the amount of 8,000 pounds was taken from these
poor, miserable outcasts . . . thirty of them were embarked on board
the Shrewsbury, and carried to St. Kitts. The rest, after being confined for three days unheard of, and unknown, were set at liberty to
return to their families, that they might be melancholy spectators of
the sale of their own property.[39]

Rodney's seizure of St. Eustatius, seemingly a footnote to the history
of the American Revolution, had significant wide-ranging consequences. It interrupted the rebel's supply of arms for the revolution, albeit rather late in the war. The opportunist admiral plundered the
island's assets and personal property, a distraction with unforeseen ram-
ifications affecting the outcome of the siege at Yorktown, Virginia and
the conclusion of the Revolutionary War. For the Jewish population of
St. Eustatius, the seizure of their little island by Admiral Rodney had a
much more immediate and disastrous impact.

---

39. "Debate on Mr. Burke's Motion relating to the Seizure and Confiscation of Private
Property in the Island of St. Eustatius," May 14, 1781, in *The Parliamentary History of
England*, 1754-1783, R.C. Simmons, and P. D. G. Thomas (Oxford, UK: Oxford Uni-
versity Press, 1983) vol. XXII, coll. 218-262.

North Carolina Patriot Women Who Talked Back to the Tories

❀❧ HERSHEL PARKER ❧❀

On January 10, 1776, the British governor of North Carolina, Josiah Martin, then bobbing on the HMS *Scorpion* off Wilmington, appointed just over two dozen Loyalists as colonels, nine of them Cross Creek Highlanders (notably Donald MacDonald) and at least six former Regulators (five in Guilford, one in Chatham).[1] These men, having raised companies of soldiers, were to seize from the rebels "arms, ammunition, provisions, horses and carriages," while taking "all possible care that the women and children" were left "unmolested." The colonels were to march their men to Wilmington where, joined to a formidable expected British force, they would subdue all the North Carolina rebels. Mac-Donald claimed to be distressed that some inhabitants were so afraid of him "as to fly before His Majesty's Army as from the most inveterate enemy." The Colonel's "determined resolution," he declared, was "that no violence shall be used to women and children."[2] Nevertheless, on February 14, according to Samuel Acourt Ashe, "many inhabitants of Wilmington moved out, carrying the women and children."[3] On February 5, 1776 MacDonald added that "private property" should not be violated.[4] He did not explain how he could seize horses and carriages without violating private property.

Despite these promises, the North Carolina Loyalists were cruel to Patriots from the outset, to go by the documents quoted here. Jesse Jones in his pension application said that about the time of a battle at the "widow Moores Creek" (February 27) he had reconnoitered near

1. Colonial and State Records of North Carolina, 10:441-443, docsouth.unc.edu/csr/index.html/volumes/volume_10.
2. Colonial and State Records of North Carolina, 10:429-430.
3. Samuel A'Court Ashe, *History of North Carolina* (Greensboro: Charles L. Van Noppen, 1908), 1:500.
4. Colonial and State Records of North Carolina, 10:443.

Wilmington "in order to keep the slaves in subjection and to protect the women & children of those who were engaged in the service of their country."[5] The Regulators called out by Governor Martin may have molested some rebels along their way to Cross Creek, for word quickly reached western North Carolina that the "Scotch & Tories" were said "to be committing great depredations in the Country around Cross Creek," according to my cousin John Sparks, who arrived too late for the battle.[6] Samuel Castle, who set out for Cross Creek from Wilkes County but also got there too late, thought that "the Scotch Tories" near Cross Creek had become "very troublesome, annoying the Whig settlement adjacent to where they lived very much."[7] Later, on May 12, a large British naval force carrying troops under Gen. Henry Clinton was off the North Carolina coast, and at Clinton's direction, Lord Cornwallis "ravaged and plundered" the American Maj. Gen. Robert Howe's plantation in Brunswick.[8] On May 13 a Wilmington man charged that a "few women, who lived in the house, were treated with great barbarity; one of whom was shot through the hips, another stabbed with a bayonet, and a third knocked down with the butt of a musket."[9] Then Cornwallis sailed away toward Charleston with Josiah Martin.

Despite the promises of Martin and MacDonald, brutality became commonplace. Throughout the war, bands of Tories in North Carolina sacked houses and farms of Whigs, most often when Patriots had left their households occupied only by women and children. In pension depositions transcribed on the *Southern Campaigns* website, at this writing, the word "depredation" (plural or singular, and however spelled) is used almost 700 times to describe the raids Tories made on Whig homes and farms. These were plunderings, pillagings. Robbery was compounded by wanton slaughter of livestock, destruction of crops, wrecking of kitchen and other household implements, shredding of clothing and beds, and intimidation or actual abuse of inhabitants. We know what the Tories looted. From Mrs. Elizabeth Forbis the Tories took "horses, except perhaps a colt that was unfit for work, her provisions, grain, cattle, and almost every thing on the plantation."[10] Mrs.

5. *Southern Campaigns Revolutionary War Pension Statements & Rosters*, revwarapps.org/; quotations have been verified against images of the original documents on Fold3.com.
6. Ashe, *History of North Carolina*, 1:498-500, describes the fast response of rebels in the west.
7. "Troublesome" meant something like "turbulent," and "annoying" meant "molesting."
8. John H. Wheeler, *Historical Sketches of North Carolina* (Philadelphia: Lippincott, Grambo and Co, 1851), 77.
9. *Virginia Gazette* (Dixon & Hunter), June 29, 1776.
10. E. W. Caruthers, *Interesting Revolutionary Incidents: And Sketches of Character* (Philadelphia: Hayes & Zell, 1856), 263.

Mary Morgan lamented that their feather-beds were "dragged into the yard, ripped open," their "blankets and other furniture," their "stock of every kind—horses, cattle, hogs, &c., driven off before their eyes—and the very bread and meat prepared for their next meal devoured in their presence by a set of voracious harpies in human shape."[11] My cousin William Sparks reported: "a party of tories, about 150 in number, robbed my Father, taking a horse saddle and bridle, six guns, all our pewter (we had no delft ware in those days) and whatever else they could carry." Thomas Shipp caught up with one gang about late 1781 at Chestnut Ridge and "killed three of the Tories," but the others fled, leaving "all their plunder, such as horses, Saddles, Blankets, some Guns &c &c." Dan Merrell told of being "repeatedly" called out to stop "some outrage & cruelty perpetrated" by Tories, "or upon some apprehension that they were organizing a force to do mischief; it was indeed a *Tory* warfare, when the summons to arms, might be & was often, the light of a dwelling house on fire, or women & children flying for safety, from Tory *cruelties*." Alexander Gray testified in support of William Clark's pension application: "Fannin & his troop made several private trips into this neighbourhood in one of which he murdered Colo. Belfour and Capt Bryant, each in his own house, with his family around him: and burnt several houses and barns where the man of the house was not at home." This was the May 10, 1782 raid, half a year after Yorktown.[12] There was little the Patriot women could do: resistance might cause the Tories to harm children or other women in the house.

Colin McRae, a boy during the war, told E. W. Caruthers that Tory raiders first seized the precious bag of meal. Having "been previously robbed," McRae recalled, "my mother had no bed clothes except one cotton sheet which was carefully wrapped round my infant brother John, by his mother's side. One of the company seized hold of the corner of this sheet and continued to jerk and shake it until the infant rolled out on the naked floor."[13] In 1844 William Whitfield's widow, Mary Whitfield, at age eighty-seven testified: "That when her husband left her and went to the war, she had to break up housekeeping & live with her father's family in Duplin county N. Carolina until the war closed. that they suffered a great deal, while her husband was out, her father & her three Brothers were frequently called out against the Brittish & Tory parties, & left her & her mother & four other sisters alone to keep house & support themselves, while the Tory party frequently came upon them,

11. Ibid., 271.
12. See my "Fanning's Bloody Sabbath as Traced by Alexander Gray," *JAR* (May 4, 2015).
13. Caruthers, *Interesting Revolutionary Incidents*, 236.

took their possessions, killed their cattle and stock, & burnt their smoke house & barn and stole her father's negroes & took them off & her mother, herself & family were frequently compelled to hide & secret themselves from fear of the ravages of these Tory parties." A Rowan County man, William Gipson, came home from a six months' enlistment to find that during his absence "his mother, a widow woman," had been "tied up & whipped by the tories, her house burned, & property all destroyed."

No history of the suffering of Patriot women in North Carolina in the Revolution can be anywhere near definitive. There were no newspapers in the state for several years, no diaries written by literate women and miraculously preserved from Tory house-burnings. There was no statewide push in 1783 and afterwards to document the war as it affected average people. More than a third of a century passed before two men, Archibald McBryde (or McBride) and Archibald D. Murphey, began to gather material for the history of the Revolution in North Carolina, and not until the 1830s and 1840s did David L. Swain, E. W. Caruthers, and others try to recover McBryde and Murphey's research and supplement it with fresh research and even interviews with some aged eyewitnesses.[14] Starting in 1832 a different kind of history was written in the pension applications by the surviving soldiers of the Revolution and sometimes by their widows—history from the ground up. These records, however, were hard to use until Will Graves and C. Leon Harris put their ongoing transcriptions into a great searchable modern archive.

All Patriot women in North Carolina suffered[15] and some stood up to the Tories. Perhaps the first story of defiance to reach print is Alexander Gray's in 1847. This passage takes up after Col. David Fanning has "called Bryan to the door, and shot him down while surrounded by his wife and children": "Fanning then proceeded with his troop to the house of William Bell, on Deep River, on the road which leads from Salisbury to Raleigh; Bell, having for safety repaired to the American camp, left none at home but his wife and negroes; but fortunately about 6 or 8 of the neighbors, armed as was usual, came in: when the Tories

14. See E. W. Caruthers's preface to *Revolutionary Incidents: And Sketches of Character* (Philadelphia: Hayes & Zell, 1854), not to be confused with his 1856 work of a similar title.
15. Robert O. DeMond in *The Loyalists in North Carolina during the Revolution* (Durham: Duke University Press, 1940) was so sympathetic to the suffering of Loyalists that he told twice (99 and 113) how Jean Dubois and Mrs. McNeill had to move away from Wilmington.

rode up within 30 or 40 yards and made a halt, the old Lady, who had the voice of a stentor and a spirit like that of a Washington or Lee, give orders (so loud that Fanning and his men could hear it,) to those within to throw open all the windows, take good sight, and not draw a trigger until they were sure of bringing a man down. This give Fanning a fright which caused him to retreat, without doing further mischief except burning Bell's barn."[16] A letter from Gray was Caruthers's source for this episode and other exploits of Martha Bell such as her spying for Richard Henry Lee and William Washington.[17] Her greatest triumph was in defense of her aged father, then visiting her. When Tories came at the old man with drawn swords she seized a broad-axe: "Raising that over her head, tightly grasped with both hands, she said to them, in the most positive manner, and with a sternness which was irresistible, 'If one of you touches him I'll split you down with this axe. Touch him if you dare!'" They "stood for a moment, abashed, confounded, and then left the house."[18]

Women could be brave even when life was not at stake. In his book on the Presbyterian minister David Caldwell,[19] Caruthers says that Mrs. Caldwell, after previous plunderings, still possessed the "very elegant table cloth" which her mother had given her when she set up house-keeping. She and a Tory were both tugging at it when she appealed to the thieves "with a woman's eloquence—asked them if they were not born of women, or if they had no wives or daughters whom they respected, and for whose sake they would treat others with more civility." Luckily for her, "a small man" stepped up and said she "should not be treated so rudely any more."

Caruthers in his 1856 book describes Mrs. Robert Rowan's behavior when Tories searched "every nook and corner" of her house for her husband. The Tories then told her "that she must tell them where he was, or they would kill her; but she told them that her husband did not hide in the cuddies, and dared them to hurt her; for, she said, if they did, they would see him before that time next day."[20] After "plundering the house and destroying everything they could not carry off, they went away," overpowered by her "womanly firmness and independence."

---

16. In *Newspapers.com* the Salisbury *Carolina Watchman* (June 4, 1847) is so blurred that I accept some punctuation from the Raleigh *Register* (September 11, 1847). "Give," twice used, is idiomatic for "gave."

17. Caruthers, *Interesting Revolutionary Incidents*, starting 308.

18. Ibid., 330.

19. *Life and Character of David Caldwell* (Greensborough: Swain and Sherwood, 1842), 243.

20. Caruthers, *Interesting Revolutionary Incidents*, 266.

Having been given a horse to replace what had been stolen, Mrs. Elizabeth Forbis faced down the Tory who was about to seize it: "she moved up right in front of him, with her hoe raised over her head; and, with a firm countenance and an earnest manner, told him if he touched the horse she would split his head with the hoe." They "left her with the horse."[21] She lived to tell Caruthers her stories.

Caruthers told of Margaret Caruthers (not one of his family) whose youngest son had been killed and scalped by neighboring Tories disguised as Indians. Later two Tories came to plunder the house, at first taking her only mare from the stable to a tree. Then they went into her corn crib, typically built so that anyone went in "somewhat longitudinally, head foremost," and had to back out one leg at a time. First moving the mare, she took a hickory stick drying by the chimney, one twice the size it would be when carved into an axe handle, and as the first Tory crawled out and the other was half out she cudgeled them severely. They crawled off "the best way they could" and did not return. Said Caruthers: "one act often furnished as good a test of native character as a whole life."[22]

Because some women filed for pensions after their husbands had died, we have more women's voices than Caruthers had. Elizabeth Ketner's (or Kitner), at eighty-six in 1840, made this declaration: "[her husband] went a tour of two months with a waggon load of Ammunition from Salem to Henry Courthouse in Virginia & from there to some place where the Main Army was & carried the powder to them, and while he was gone the British Army passed by her house coming from the Shallow ford on the Yadkin River to Houser Town & Rob'd her of all her corn, & small grain meat and every thing almost that her & family had to live on, even her Ducks & Chickens some of them asked her if she had a husband she said yes: Where is he they asked, She told them he was gone with a waggon to haul a load of Ammunition to the American Army to shoot you red coats that have rob'd me & my living[.]"

Few male North Carolina Patriots had been honored by 1856, Caruthers rightly said, while "the female portion of the Whig community, many of whom were, in their sphere, as patriotic, suffered as many privations and hardships, and made as resolute a resistance to oppression as the men, have been entirely neglected."[23] Although he drew his information from only in a few counties in the central portion of the

21. Ibid., 270.
22. Ibid., 289-291.
23. Ibid, 266-267.

state, Caruthers did more than anyone else to document the suffering of Whig women and children. He reflected on the larger implications of the stories he heard: "It would take a volume to record their virtues and their noble deeds; and all that the writer of the present work designs is merely to notice a few and show what may be done, or what abundant materials there are in the country, that others, who are more competent, may be excited to undertake the task and do the work to better purpose."[24] From the 1850s onward, historical study of the Revolution in North Carolina never faltered—but it gathered speed after almost all the witnesses were dead.

After the Centennial, the survivors of the Civil War turned fresh attention to the Revolution and recovered or embellished their local history. Around the turn of the twentieth century stories of women's bravery saw print, as on February 25, 1898, when Col. R. B. Creecy, the editor of the Elizabeth City *Economist* printed his "The Legend of Betsy Dowdy." Learning that the Virginia Governor Lord Dunmore was advancing on the Great Bridge, Betsy Dowdy of Currituck Banks late on December 9, 1775, had saddled Black Bess and set off to the nearest North Carolina militia. She and her horse waded and swam the Currituck Sound and "forded numerous small streams" and rode "more than 50 miles to reach the rebel militia commanded by General William Skinner." Isaac Dunn and his wife Mary star in an Anson County equine story. While galloping to escape a band of Tories, Dunn tossed their baby daughter (Susannah) to his wife, who caught her. A "group of Tories hunting for Isaac came . . . seeking information about her husband. She refused to give it and was struck on the head and face with a Tory saber. Fortunately she was wearing a bonnet with hickory splints which broke the thrust and saved her life. However, she carried the scar during her long life."[25]

This impulse to identify and celebrate local heroines did not lead to much new study of ordinary North Carolina Patriot women. Despite the scarcity of contemporary evidence, there may be more clues in the *Southern Campaigns* website, for example, and a rigorous search of North Carolina newspapers might turn up more stories of women who talked back to the Tories, and perhaps others who fought back.

24. Ibid, 267.
25. Mary Louise Medley, *History of Anson County, North Carolina, 1750-1976* (Charlotte: Anson County Historical Society, 1976), 53. In the Wadesboro *Messenger and Intelligencer* (February 20, 1913) Mary Dunn tosses the baby to Isaac. In the Charlotte *Observer* (December 27, 1931) Isaac tosses the baby to Mary.

Major Patrick Ferguson—A Fresh Look

❊ WAYNE LYNCH ❊

Journal of the American Revolution has published many articles reappraising certain participants involved with the southern campaign. One personality who gets frequent mention but little detail is Maj. Patrick Ferguson. In order to supplement that information and provide a slightly more complete analysis of the major, here are a few thoughts dedicated to him. We start by looking at what a few prominent historians have indicated before getting into some evidence.

First, Dr. J. B. O. Landrum of South Carolina wrote a history of the southern campaign in 1897 that was largely based upon traditions in the back country. These traditions would come from the same people who would otherwise be most likely to despise Ferguson. Instead of critical comments, Landrum describes Ferguson as "a finished soldier and his bearing throughout his military career proved him as brave as a lion." Ferguson was also an intelligent man of "eminent literary talents who was deemed by other writers and contemporary sages equal to the best authors of the Scottish Augustan age." "Possessing a vigorous mind and brilliant parts," he "early displayed inventive genius, sound judgment and intrepid heroism . . . He was pleasant and conciliatory in manner, and was well calculated to gain friends." During the British occupation of Ninety-Six in June 1780, Ferguson told the inhabitants, "We come not to make war upon women and children, but to give them money and relieve their distresses."[1]

The next historian reviewed was actually a very reputable officer who served with Ferguson, Charles Stedman. He provided a nice summary: Ferguson's "zeal in the service of his king and country was equal to his other great qualities as an officer." Stedman also described the

1. Dr. J. B. O. Landrum, *Colonial and Revolutionary History of Upper South Carolina* (Greenville, SC: Shannon & Co, 1897), 234–235.

Major as a "gallant officer" possessed of an "unconquerable spirit" that "refused to surrender" and was therefore killed at Kings Mountain.[2]

After reviewing those incredibly positive descriptions of Major Ferguson, one almost feels like the man might qualify for sainthood. However, there are a few more realistic historians whose judgments come across favorably but do, at least, admit to a few faults. In his very popular and well thought of history of the British occupation, John Buchanan mentioned that Ferguson's letters displayed an "almost cavalier recommendation to burn and destroy on a wide scale," thereby leaving the civilian population to starve. Buchanan also described Ferguson's attitudes toward the militia and his own capabilities as "overly optimistic," He emphasized the negative opinions of British officer Nesbit Balfour admitting that Ferguson had a "good mind, especially for technical subjects" but Buchanan openly doubted descriptions of Ferguson as a "brilliant soldier". Overall, Buchanan seems to regard Ferguson as a good soldier and decent enough fellow but one overstated by history.[3]

On the other side of prominent twentieth century historians, we find the Wickwire biography of Lord Cornwallis which contains very positive descriptions of Patrick Ferguson. "A brilliant man aware of his brilliance, the inventor of a superior rifle that the authorities ignored, he was by 1780 a mere major, though his seniority and birth might have entitled him to the command of a regiment. Under these circumstances, he was understandably a willful and impatient subordinate. In his eyes, his appointment in 1780 as inspector of militia now gave him a semi-independent command. Having secured the position at his own request, he intended to use it to prove himself to his superiors. . . . Some qualities worked in his favor. Haughty he might look, but he cultivated a familiarity with loyalists unusual among British officers, who tended to treat American civilians of whatever political persuasion with contempt. . . . Ferguson was, furthermore, humane and chivalrous, merciful and gentlemanly, with a nice sense of duty and honor. 'We came not', he said, 'to make war on women and children, but to relieve their distress.' . . . Such a man naturally attracted loyalist militia to his cause. Had prudence and discretion balanced his noble qualities, he might in the end have achieved what Cornwallis's army could not. But Ferguson was willful, impatient, and headstrong."[4]

2. Ibid., 223.
3. John Buchanan, *The Road to Guilford Courthouse* (New York: John Wiley & sons, 1997), 195—203.
4. Franklin and Mary Wickwire, *Cornwallis and the War for Independence* (London: Faber and Faber, 1971), 204. The Wickwire text relies heavily on the manuscripts of Lyman Draper and provides examples from him and Charles Stedman of Ferguson's gallant and proper conduct toward women.

Those descriptions all sound fine and wonderful, mostly positive comments. Even so, the reader is left wondering what might be underneath these descriptions. And perhaps going just a step further, one might also take a closer look at what evidence may have led the one historian to question these glowing conclusions.

First, Major Ferguson is highly praised for his bravery and military skill. There are several examples of this. As most fans of the revolution are aware, Ferguson spent much of 1775 and 1776 in Britain working on improvements to a breech loading rifle. His design came to be known as the Ferguson Rifle and, in a famously reported field trial, Ferguson maintained a pace of four shots per minute (up to six) while pouring in a steady stream of hits at the one hundred yard target. Even with rain and high winds, the major proved deadly with his new weapon. He was rewarded with a patent and a special corps of marksmen picked from regular regiments that would test the new rifle in combat. Unfortunately, the rifle corps' first real combat was at Brandywine and Ferguson was wounded before having an opportunity to impress. General Howe disbanded the corps while Ferguson recovered, the explanation being that his rifle was too difficult for most enlisted men and, since Patrick himself now had a bad arm and would be unable to use the weapon, the corps was not viable.[5]

While Ferguson recovered from his wound, he spent time around New York inspecting defenses and writing letters to Sir Henry Clinton. Many of those letters go into great detail about improvements to the various military facilities around New York. Later on he made similar observations concerning defenses in the south. The letters also contain detailed plans about using a total force of 27,000 men acting as light troops to subdue the colonies. They would divide into four army groups and travel about, living off the land while setting up temporary bases to disarm the rebels and bring them back to the Crown.[6] Unfortunately, this is likely where historians start to doubt his military abilities. The first and immediate fatal flaw in such a plan is that no such numbers of light troops existed in the British Army of North America. Light troops in the revolution represented the best of the infantry rank and file and the British Army was just not that large. His plan would require virtually one hundred percent of all troops in North America fight as light troops, thereby completely ignoring that not all soldiers were up to that

5. Hugh Rankin, "An Officer out of his Time," in Howard H. Peckham, *Sources of American Independence* (Chicago: University of Chicago Press, 1978), 2:288.
6. Ferguson to Clinton, August 1, 1778, in Peckham, *Sources of American Independence*, 2:301.

type of duty. As if that flaw were not enough, Ferguson's notion that 27,000 troops should live off the land in army groups of 6,000 men each seems incredibly risky. At least one detractor considered Ferguson's ideas "ridiculous."[7]

And that brings up a second trait to examine. Most historians consider the major to be a gallant and chivalrous man who treated people well on a personal level. His letters to Clinton sort of fly in the face of that description. Just as the 27,000 light troops were to live off the land, their mission would be to move into a "particular district, to gather up all the enemy's partys, collect carriages, provisions or forage, disarm the inhabitants, take hostages or, if necessary, lay waste to the country." After all, it was now time to "exert a degree of severity which would not have been justifyable at the beginning."[8] This was not a single reference. In his plans to raid coastal towns, Ferguson recommended the "burning of their grains & the depriving their cattle of all means of subsistence during the hard winter of that country." The rebels "would be obliged to beg for bread."[9]

The letters to Clinton do not represent the only black marks to Ferguson's humanity. In October of 1778, he raided Little Egg Harbor in New Jersey and caught Count Pulaski's infantry companies sleeping. His men, under orders to give no quarter, killed them all. Reports range from 50 to 250 dead rebels with the British loss limited to one man. There were only five prisoners taken. Ferguson justified the action by incorrectly claiming that Pulaski had posted orders that no quarter was to be given to the British. Also that, being a night action, it wasn't practical to give any quarter to the sleeping enemy.[10] The explanation may have seemed more sincere if Ferguson had not just witnessed John Graves Simcoe's ranger unit win great praise for a similar action at Hancock House. It probably should be noted that the letters suggesting severity and the Little Egg Harbor action took place right after Ferguson's wound and subsequent recovery. There is a bitter tone during that period that doesn't really seem to carry over to his time in the south.

Which brings up the incidents that give evidence of Ferguson's good character. Historians point to his harsh reaction to rapes committed by

7. Balfour to Cornwallis, June 20, 1780, in Ian Saberton ed., *The Cornwallis Papers: The Campaigns of 1780 and 1781 in the Southern Theatre of the American Revolutionary War* (Uckfield: The Naval & Military Press Ltd, 2010), 1:98.
8. Ferguson to Clinton, August 1, 1778, in Peckham, *Sources of American Independence*, 2:301.
9. Ibid., 307.
10. Ferguson to Clinton, August 15, 1778, in Peckham, *Sources of American Independence*, 2:313.

members of the British Legion during the siege of Charleston. Another strong point to be made in his favor is that, once given a measure of command independence in the southern campaigns, Ferguson does not seem to have been guilty of many hangings or other atrocities.[11] Unfortunately, his men were a different matter: they were often undisciplined and Ferguson was unable to control them. In letters to General Cornwallis, Ferguson indicated that, if he tried to discipline them, the new royal militia would simply desert and go home.[12] As a result, his men freely plundered the rebel population and sought private retributions at will. However, the same back country historians that freely demonize Banastre Tarleton, James Wemyss, and Thomas Brown, seem to understand his predicament and have very positive things to say about Patrick Ferguson.[13] It appears that, outside of the Little Egg Harbor incident, Ferguson's severity is really just a bunch of talk in some letters and was not how he operated when actually put in the position to do so.

Talk of Ferguson's character should not stop without at least some mention of his gallantry in restraining himself at Brandywine from shooting George Washington. Even though good reason exists to think Washington was not the officer in question, Ferguson's act in passing up the shot remains in good standing. Almost ironic, in fact, is that James Delancey later identified the officer "dressed in Hussar" garb as Count Pulaski, the same man whose men were killed at Little Egg Harbor.[14]

A third aspect of Ferguson's character often discussed by historians is ambition and overconfidence. In Major Ferguson, the two traits seem hopelessly intertwined and should be looked at together. One can clearly see from the history of Ferguson's life that his ambition was to be a career soldier and he sought notice for his military ability. His lengthy and detailed letters to Clinton show dedication but also ambition. A real gung-ho type who volunteered his advice to superiors and always remembered to point out how he could accomplish his goals, "at small expense," even to the point of personally guaranteeing to pay

11. There is at least one reference to hanging a patriot named Smith for breaking parole after Musgrove's Mill. the Diary of Anthony Allaire, entry for August 20, 1780, in Lyman Draper, *Kings Mountain and Its Heroes* (Cincinnati: Peter G. Thomson, 1881), 505.
12. Ferguson to Cornwallis, July 24, 1780, in Saberton, *The Cornwallis Papers,* 1:293.
13. Referring primarily to Draper and Landrum.
14. Buchanan, *The Road to Guilford Courthouse,* 198 quoting James Fenimore Cooper who said that Delancey "constantly affirmed that his commander was mistaken ... It was his opinion from some particulars of dress and stature that it was the Count Pulaski."

Death of Major Ferguson at King's Mountain. (*New York Public Library*)

any excess out of his personal pocket—which was likely not to be taken seriously since Patrick Ferguson did not have a deep pocket on which to draw.

Even the questionable incident at Little Egg Harbor reflects the ambition of Major Ferguson. Only a few months prior to the raid, Ferguson saw his friend, Capt. James Dunlop, gain great accolades for a violent night assault at Hancock's House where the rebels were killed rather than taken prisoner. Ferguson was likely eager to show his own ability to lead raids and quell the rebellion.

These same traits appear complicit in Ferguson's death. Near the end of the Kings Mountain campaign, Ferguson clearly saw the danger posed by the Overmountain Men and requested "3 or 400 hundred good soldiers, part dragoons" in order to defeat the rebels. Even with that request, he still reflected desperation to retain his independent command. Risking his entire army, Ferguson remained at Kings Mountain instead of rejoining Cornwallis; his last request on the 5th was that the general not "supersede me by sending a superior officer."[15]

In those last movements we don't just see the ambition but also the overconfidence. Ferguson evidently believed his eighty regulars and the newly formed Royal militia were ready to go into battle. A review of his correspondence with Cornwallis and the lack of any training time

---

15. Ferguson to Cornwallis, October 5, 1780, in Saberton, *The Cornwallis Papers*, 2:164.

reflects a military force nowhere close to battle readiness. Instead of heeding the instructions of Lord Cornwallis, Ferguson chose to dig in at Kings Mountain where he had "taken a post where I do not think I can be forced by a stronger enemy than that against us." Of course he was wrong and the result was Major Ferguson's death at Kings Mountain.[16]

Having droned on long enough here, I conclude with a few thoughts of my own about Major Ferguson. I found no reason to believe him personally unpleasant or inappropriate in his relations with the rebel population. I find his good reputation among the rebel population highly persuasive. His harsh letters during the time of wound recovery should likely be taken with a grain of salt as something he never acted upon. The records from the southern campaigns that I have read do not show Ferguson among the British officer group that engaged in frequent hangings or other depredations. In his various explanations for the brutal actions at Little Egg Harbor, I think there is a hint of regret for those results and I think he should be allowed the error in judgment.[17] It is difficult for soldiers faced with an enemy unprepared to receive them yet motivated to kill.[18] All that said, I agree with John Buchanan's assessment concerning the major's military skills. Even though I see an active and enthusiastic soldier, I do not see military genius. His plans for conquest are woefully unrealistic and his decision to remain at Kings Mountain shows little military skill in establishing a defensive position or assessing his situation. Instead, I see a young officer desperate to gain glory and accolades, even to his own detriment and death. I believe he was a probably a good officer at times but not really the stuff of independent command.

---

16. Ferguson to Cornwallis, October 6, 1780, in Saberton, *The Cornwallis Papers*, 2:165.
17. Possibly just my imagination.
18. A very similar situation to that of Pyle's Defeat by Henry Lee in March of 1781.

George Washington Tells a Lie

❦ BENJAMIN L. HUGGINS ❦

In June 1780, Gen. George Washington told a lie. In fact, he planned a major deception. But as it was intended to deceive the British high command during the midst of the Revolutionary War, most Americans would likely forgive him. General Washington, with the aid of Major General Lafayette, wanted the British to believe that the French army under the command of Lieutenant General Rochambeau, soon expected to arrive in North America, was intended to help the Americans liberate Canada from the British yoke.

Washington and Lafayette designed a proclamation that they planned to have printed in Philadelphia. "We talked of a Proclamation to the Canadians," Washington wrote to Lafayette in May, "If it is not already done, I think it ought not to be delayed. It should be in your own name, and have as much as possible an air of probability." Washington wanted to use the document (to be written in French) to propagate an elaborate ruse. The proclamation, the American commander wrote, "should contain an animating invitation [to the Canadians] to arrange themselves under the allied banners. ... you should hold yourself up as a French and American officer charged both by the King of France and by Congress with a commission to address them upon the occasion. It may indeed be well to throw out an idea that you are to command the corps of American troops destined to cooperate with the French armament. The more mystery in this business the better. It will get out and it ought to seem to be against our intention."[1]

In late May Lafayette was busy drafting the proclamation. He explained to the Chevalier de La Luzerne, French minister in Philadelphia, who was to be in on the secret of the deception, that the purpose of the missive was to "mislead the enemy" on the aim of the Continental

---

1. Washington to Lafayette, May 19, 1780, U.S. Library of Congress, George Washington Papers (DLC:GW).

army's joint operations with Rochambeau's force. "This document will be printed in the greatest secrecy, but we shall take care to pass it on to New York," he explained. (British headquarters in North America was located in New York City.) Once the French army actually arrived, the documents would be "thrown in the fire."[2] The whole purpose was for the "secret" printing of the document, and it contents, to leak out in Philadelphia and make its way to Gen. Henry Clinton, the British commander in chief, who would then hopefully direct his efforts to defending that province instead of Washington's real objective, New York City. Lafayette even asked La Luzerne for a stamp with the arms of Louis XVI, King of France. If he could place the king's arms on the proclamation "it could help to deceive the enemy's spies even more."[3]

By early June, Lafayette had a draft of the proclamation finished, and Washington forwarded it to the military commander in Philadelphia. The chief Continental officer in that city at the time happened to be Maj. Gen. Benedict Arnold. On the 4th of June, Washington wrote to Major General Arnold from his headquarters at Morristown, New Jersey: "Dear Sir . . . You will be pleased to put this into the hands of a printer whose secrecy and discretion may be depended on and desire him to strike off a proof sheet with the utmost dispatch . . . The importance of this Business will sufficiently impress you with the necessity of transacting it with every possible degree of caution."[4] Although the American commander had no inkling at this time that Arnold was a traitor, his caution in not revealing the "secret" led Arnold to believe the proclamation was genuine. In a few days, Arnold, after some difficulty finding a printer who could be trusted, had a proof sheet of the proclamation printed and sent it to Washington's headquarters for final corrections. At the end of June, the American commander returned the proof sheet, with corrections (presumably done by Lafayette) to the printer.[5]

---

2. Lafayette to the Chevalier de La Luzerne, May 25, 1780, in Stanley J. Idzerda et al, eds., *Lafayette in the Age of the American Revolution Selected Letters and Papers, 1776-1790*, 5 vols. (Ithaca and London: Cornell University Press, 1977-83), 3:35.

3. Ibid. Idzerda notes that although La Luzerne agreed to the request, the king's arms did not appear on the printed proclamation.

4. Washington to Arnold, June 4, DLC:GW. The enclosed draft of this proclamation has not been identified.

5. Arnold to Washington, June 7, 1780, Pennsylvania Historical Society: Gratz Collection. The corrected proof sheet that Washington sent to the printer has not been identified; but there is a hand-corrected proof sheet of the proclamation (in French) in the Nourse Family Papers (3490-a) at University of Virginia's special collections library.

Arnold had been in communication with Maj. John André, Clinton's adjutant general, for over a year. Arnold sent his letters to André through a system of intermediaries. Loyalist Joseph Stansbury acted as Arnold's chief contact in Philadelphia, and the Loyalist Rev. Jonathan Odell received them in in New York City for André. While André was with Clinton on an expedition to capture Charleston, South Carolina, in the spring of 1780, Capt. George Beckwith, aide to the acting commander in New York City, received Arnold's missives.[6]

Arnold, in addition to having the proof struck, immediately advised Beckwith of the proclamation and sent him the text of the document. On June 7, Arnold, using his code name "Mr. Moore" wrote the British captain (via Stansbury): "I have received from The Commander-in-Chief a Proclamation in order to have a number of Copies printed, the purport of which, will be transmitted to you by J:S: [Stansbury] to whom I have communicated it. . . . The American Army intended to cooperate with the French will probably go up Connecticut River to Number Four and cross the Country to St Johns."[7]

Other elements of the deception transpired just as Washington and Lafayette hoped (though they had no idea Arnold would be the vehicle). The French ambassador played his role perfectly. Arnold wrote Beckwith: "The Minister of France this day assured me that the French Troops destined for Canada amount to Eight Thousand."[8] Stansbury converted Lafayette's proclamation to code and sent it, with Arnold's letter, to Beckwith, commenting that the proclamation "must be a profound secret."[9]

Arnold thus unwittingly served Washington's purpose: to get the proclamation into the hands of the British commander in chief and create the impression that the expected French army was intended for an attack on Canada. Thanks to Arnold's treachery, Washington's deception had succeeded.

---

6. For more on this chain of communication, see Carl Van Doren, *Secret History of the American Revolution: An Account of the Conspiracies of Benedict Arnold and Numerous Others drawn from the Secret Service Papers of the British Headquarters in North America now for the first time examined and made public* (New York: The Viking Press, 1941), 196-201.
7. Arnold to Beckwith, June 7, 1780, in Van Doren, 459-60.
8. Ibid.
9. Ibid.

The French Bread Connection

TOM SHACHTMAN

It was the letter that forced Washington to give up his dream of recapturing New York.

Gen. Jean-Baptiste Donatien de Vimeur, comte de Rochambeau, encamped with his French army at Phillipsburg on the Hudson River, received it on August 14, 1781 and showed it immediately to Gen. George Washington, whose headquarters was nearby. Written on July 28 by Adm. François Joseph Paul de Grasse, leader of the French naval force in the Caribbean, who had sent it by fast cutter to Newport, whence it had been forwarded to Rochambeau, it announced that de Grasse and his formidable fleet were en route to Chesapeake Bay, "the spot which seems to be to be indicated by you, M. le comte, and by MM Washington, de La Luzerne [French minister to the U.S.] and de Barras [leader of the French naval contingent in Newport] as the surest to effect the good which you propose."[1]

That "good" was the capture or destruction of a British force sizeable enough to bring the Revolutionary War to a successful end. Ever since the fall of 1776, when Washington had been forced to abandon New York City to the British, he had been convinced that New York was the only such target whose recapture could win the war – but the news that de Grasse and his fleet was going to the Chesapeake forced Washington to give up the dream of recapturing New York.

He did so in a way that illustrates, as well as any moment in his career, his pragmatic approach to leadership. On being informed of de Grasse's destination, Washington did not fight the decision or try to change it; rather, he channeled his energies toward moving the combined Franco-American forces to the Yorktown peninsula in time to meet de Grasse there. He very quickly laid out a comprehensive, day-

1. De Grasse to Rochambeau, et al., July 28, 1781, in Henri Doniol, *Histoire de la participation de la France a l'établissement des États-Unis d'Amérique* (Paris: Imprimerie Nationale, 1886-1892), 4:650-651.

by-day marching plan, explaining to Rochambeau, "I have named no halting day because we have not a moment to lose."[2] And he sent off a flurry of letters to his commanders nearer Yorktown to ready them, instructing Lafayette,

> You will immediately take such a position as will best enable you to prevent [the enemy's] sudden retreat thro' North Carolina, which I presume they will attempt the instant they perceive so formidable an Armament [as de Grasse arriving]. . . . You will be particularly careful to conceal the expected arrival of the Count, because if the enemy are not apprised of it, they [will stay] on board their transports in [Chesapeake] Bay, which will be the luckiest Cercumstance in the World.[3]

Washington also had another thing to conceal. As his trusted chief engineer, the Frenchman Louis Duportail, advised him, "If the enemy perceive that we give up the idea of attacking New york they will reinforce Portsmouth Virginia may be before we can get there."[4] Washington and Rochambeau agreed: to prevent Gen. Henry Clinton in New York from sending reinforcements to Lt. Gen. Charles, Earl Cornwallis, whose troops and ships then controlled the Yorktown peninsula, they had to deceive Clinton into thinking they were still focused on assaulting New York.

After six years at war, the ruse that Washington had so often used to fool the British—constructing extra tents and lighting extra fires to make it seem that more troops faced them than actually existed—was shopworn. A new stratagem was needed. The key to it lay in recent British actions on the North (Hudson) River.

In mid-July, shortly after the French had trekked to the Hudson from Newport, Baron Ludwig von Closen, a Rochambeau aide-de-camp, noted in his diary that five British ships led by the sloop *Savage* had sailed near to Tarrytown, and "we feared immediately that their object was the seizure of some bread . . . that we were expecting to come from Peekskill," where ovens had been built. Later that day von Closen learned that his fear was justified, as those British ships fired on three "little covered boats laden with bread for our army," and from a nearby

2. Washington to Rochambeau, August 17, 1781, founders.archives.gov/documents/Washington/99-01-02-06713.

3. Washington to Lafayette, August 15, 1781, founders.archives.gov/documents/Washington/99-01-02-06693.

4. Duportail to Washington, August 15, 1781, in E. S. Kite, *Brigadier General Louis Lebegue Duportail, Commandant of Engineers in the Continental Army, 1777-1783* (Baltimore: The Johns Hopkins Press, 1933), 202.

French warehouse took more bread and other items.[5] But two days later, as the British ships were returning down the river with their booty, the French targeted them: "Our howitzers paid them such a tender adieu that the *Savage* . . . was seriously set on fire and half the crew threw themselves overboard," Closen wrote, adding, "You can be sure that this little lesson will give these gentlemen a distaste for this kind of amusement, and that they will no longer crave our white bread."[6]

Washington's plan called for French and American armies to cross the Hudson from east to west, well north of New York City, and then to turn southward and course in parallel through New Jersey to Philadelphia. The plan of march suggested a stopping place for the French Army at Chatham, New Jersey, that was perfect for Washington and Rochambeau's deceptive purposes. Chatham was twenty-five miles directly west of New York City and an equivalent distance from Staten Island and Sandy Hook, the most accessible water approach to New York's harbor. Washington noted in his diary why they were going to Chatham: "Hazens regiment being thrown over [crossed the Hudson River] at Dobbs's ferry was ordered with the Jersey Troops to March & take Post on the heights between Spring field & Chatham & Cover a french Battery at the latter place to veil our real movement & create apprehensions for Staten Island."[7]

Washington and Rochambeau believed that the British would reason thusly: If the French and Continental armies were going to attack New York or Staten Island, they would make a more-or-less permanent base at Chatham, but if those armies were headed further south, the base would be temporary.

How to make the British think the Chatham base was a permanent one? The answer—as Rochambeau would note a few months later, in a pamphlet—was "to establish a *boulangerie* at Chatham," a set of ovens for baking bread.[8] He dispatched his quartermaster to the banks of the Raritan River area to buy up whatever bricks could be obtained – the French predilection for brick ovens was well known, and Rochambeau hoped that buying up bricks, which could have no other military pur-

5. Ludwig Von Closen, *The Revolutionary Journal of Baron Ludwig von Closen,* translated by Evelyn Acomb (Chapel Hill: University of North Carolina Press, 1958), 95.

6. Ibid, 97.

7. Washington Diary entry, August 19, 1781, founders.archives.gov/documents/Washington/01-03-02-0007-0004-0013.

8. John Baptise Donatien de Vimeur, Comte de Rochambeau, *Relation, ou Journal des opérations du Corps Français sous le commandement de Comte de Rochambeau, Lieutenant-Général des Armées du Roi, depuis le 15 d'Août 1781* (Philadelphia: Guillaume Hampton, 1781).

pose than to prepare ovens, would be noted by local Loyalists who would report it to Clinton. Washington for his part dispatched a Continental guard unit to watch over the French advance corps as they constructed the ovens, and he had some thirty boats on carriages accompany the troops. Washington aide-de-camp Col. Jonathan Trumbull, Jr. noted in his diary:

> French ovens are building at Chatham in Jersey. Others were ordered to be prepared at a place near the Hook. Contracts are made for forrage to be delivered immediately to the French Army on their arrival at the last mentioned place. Here it is supposed that Batteries are to be erected for the security and aid of the Fleet, which is hourly expected. By these maneuvres and the correspondent march of the Troops, our own army no less than the Enemy are completely deceived.[9]

When Rochambeau's forces arrived at Chatham, the ovens were in operation in a sixty-five-foot shed, and producing 3,000 loaves of aromatic, crusty French bread per day.[10]

The ruse worked like a charm. Although Clinton may have had a suspicion that the Chatham installation was meant to deceive him, he could not be certain; and furthermore, since he had no information on the whereabouts of de Grasse other than the knowledge that he had headed north from the Caribbean, Clinton could not risk sending troops to help Cornwallis, either by land or aboard warships, needing to keep both soldiers and ships in place in New York in case the French fleet suddenly appeared off Sandy Hook.

"This [boulangerie] maneuver prevented General Clinton from sending forces to the rescue of Cornwallis," Rochambeau would definitively state.[11] And Washington would much later recall,

> That much trouble was taken and finesse used to misguide & bewilder Sir Henry Clinton in regard to the real object, by fictitious communications, as well as by making a deceptive provision of Ovens, Forage & Boats in his Neighbourhood, is certain. Nor were less pains

9. "Minutes of Occurrences respecting the Siege and Capture of York in Virginia, extracted from the Journal of Colonel Jonathan Trumbull, Secretary to the General, 1781," *Proceedings of the Massachusetts Historical Society* 14 (1875-76): 331–38.
10. Although the exact location of the ovens is not known, the French encampment was in the area of what is today Shephard Pollock Park in Chatham.
11. Rochambeau, *Relation.*

taken to deceive our own Army; for I had always conceived, when the imposition did not completely take place at home, it could never sufficiently succeed abroad.[12]

Through the final week of August, Clinton continued to believe that the French and Americans were still in Chatham; on August 30, he wrote to Cornwallis, "Mr. Washington's force still remains in the neighbourhood of Chatham, and I do not hear that he has as yet detached to the southward," and in a post-script written on September 1, he added, "Unless Mr. Washington should send a considerable part of his army to the southward, I shall not judge it necessary until then to detach [some of my forces] thither."[13]

And Washington kept up the deceit even as the armies departed Chatham, leaving behind not only the ovens, which continued to operate, but also American units to guard them. He wrote ahead to deputy quartermaster Col. Samuel Miles, near Trenton, directing him to collect and prepare boats to take the troops over the Delaware River from Trenton to Philadelphia, advising Miles,

> I have delayed having these preparations made until this Moment, because I wished to deceive the Enemy with regard to our real object as long as possible – our movements have been calculated for that purpose and I am still anxious the deception should be kept up a few days longer, until our intentions are announced by the Army's filing off towards the Delaware.[14]

Even on September 2, when Clinton informed Cornwallis, "Mr. Washington is moving an army to the southward, with an appearance of haste, and gives out that he expects the co-operation of a considerable French armament," and the British fleets then in New York prepared to sail for the Chesapeake, Clinton still reassured Cornwallis "that your Lordship will have little to apprehend from [the fleet] of the French."[15]

The alarm was raised too late, and the braggadocio was misplaced. Days earlier, de Grasse's fleet had made the outskirts of Chesapeake Bay, just as Generals Rochambeau and Washington were entering

12. Washington to Noah Webster, July 31, 1788, founders.archives.gov/documents/Washington/04-06-02-0376.

13. Clinton to Cornwallis, August 30-September 1, 1781, *Correspondence Between His Excellency General Sir Henry Clinton, K.B., and Lieutenant General Earl Cornwallis* (New York, 1781), 45-46.

14. Washington to Samuel Miles, Aug. 27, 1781, founders.archives.gov/documents/Washington/99-01-02-06801.

15. Clinton to Cornwallis, *Correspondence*, 46-47.

Philadelphia ahead of the main body of their troops, and as Duportail was being rowed out to de Grasse's flagship, *Ville de Paris* to convey the news that the French and American armies were en route down the Atlantic seaboard to link with his ships and begin the encirclement of Cornwallis and the battle of Yorktown. By the time Cornwallis received his superior's note, his fate had already been sealed.

Neither then nor later did General Clinton ever acknowledge that he had been effectively tricked into complacency and into remaining with his forces in New York, rather than going to the relief of Cornwallis at Yorktown, by the British taste for French bread.

We Have Sacrificed Our All

❦ CONNER RUNYAN ❦

"We Have Sacrificed Our All." Thus, stated eleven loyalist officers from Ninety-Six and Camden Districts of South Carolina in a petition intended for the King of England. What happened to them, and the three hundred more named in the petition, is part of the equation leading to the question of how many families lost husbands and fathers in District Ninety-Six. Should the Loyalist families of these three hundred murdered men—or is it more like nine hundred?—be considered an addition to the fourteen hundred widows and orphans thought to have lived in Ninety-Six District? If so, is it conceivable that an unbearable one in five families came out of this horrific civil war made up only of widows and orphans? In truth, all we will ever know is that a murderous civil war, tightly coiled inside a revolution, sprang forth along the frontier of South Carolina.

In August 1783, Francisco De Miranda, one of several liberators of Venezuela, visited Charleston, South Carolina, as part of his worldwide tour of countries that interested him. Miranda, an aristocrat who disliked anyone who thought noble birth conveyed worthiness, mingled effortlessly with Charleston's elite. He met and conversed with such notables as generals Nathanael Greene and William Moultrie. In the weeks that followed, Miranda made good his pledge to learn as much as he could about the American Revolution, even if it meant he must speak to every woman in Charleston, a promise Miranda had already made good on when in Russia, chatting with no less than Catherine the Great, and conversing so well he became her lover. Miranda, in his travels, never failed to collect a souvenir "inamorata"[1] as a memento.

In his tour about Charleston, viewing charred buildings, meeting maimed men, inspecting foreboding deserted fortifications, Miranda be-

---

1. Karen Racine, *Francisco de Miranda, Transatlantic Life in the Age of Revolution* (Wilmington, DE: Scholarly Resources, Inc, 2003), 36.

came impressed by something he heard, perhaps from someone of "good judgment, considerable education and a love of the sciences, society and humanity" (was this David Ramsay, author of *The History of the American Revolution?*).[2] Miranda was told that in the distant, remote backcountry of South Carolina, in the Ninety-Six District, the Revolutionary War made eighteen hundred widows and orphans.

Two years later, historian Dr. David Ramsay wrote: "The single district of Ninety-Six, which is only one of six districts into which the state of South Carolina is divided, has been computed, by well-informed persons residing thereon, to contain within its limits fourteen hundred widows and orphans, made so by the war."[3] This would have been out of an estimated population of 24,677[4] women and children. Ramsay's referring to Ninety-Six district as one of six districts tells us he was writing about the area that became the eight modern counties of Abbeville, Edgefield, Spartanburg, Greenville, Laurens, Newberry, Pendleton and Union.

The simple fact is, neither Ramsay nor Miranda told us how they came to know their numbers; yet their estimates were not viewed by the better informed about them as wildly exaggerated. We do know that Ramsay got his number of fourteen hundred from "well informed persons residing"[5] within Ninety-Six District, and that he "had access to a vast number of historical records,"[6] many of which are no longer available.

Years later Patriot Maj. Gen. William Moultrie, who certainly would have, along with Ramsay, talked with Miranda about the war, continued to have on his mind the inhumanity of the backcountry conflict. It is not known if Moultrie used Ramsay as a source or if there is a common source from which both men drew the same conclusion. Moultrie wrote in his memoirs that "It is generally said, and believed, that in the District of Ninety-Six alone, fourteen hundred unhappy widows and orphans were left to bemoan the fate of their unfortunate fathers, hus-

---

2. Robert D. Bass, *Ninety Six: The Struggle for the South Carolina Back County* (Lexington, SC: The Sandlapper Store, 1978), 9; Racine, *Miranda*, 34-36.
3. David Ramsay, *The History of the Revolution of South-Carolina, From a British Province to an Independent State, Volume II* (Trento: Isaac Collins Publisher, 1785), 275.
4. United States Bureau of the Census, "Population in the Colonial and Continental Period," www2.census.gov/prod2/deconnial/documents/00165897chol.pdf., 7.
5. David Ramsay, *Ramsay's History of South Carolina, from its first settlement in 1670 to the year 1808* (Charleston, SC: Walker, Evans & Co., 1858), 258.
6. Robert H. Brunhouse, ed. *David Ramsay, 1749-1815: Selected from his Writings,* American Philosophical Society, Transactions, New Series, 55 (1965), Part IV, 139-140. Ramsay makes this observation in a letter: Ramsay to Belknap, March 11, 1795.

bands and brothers, killed and murdered."[7] How Moultrie chose to frame this sentence suggests he likely used Ramsay as his source. Regardless, it is clear General Moultrie did not find such numbers extreme.

In January 1776, Col. Richard Richardson, commanding the largest army yet in South Carolina, wrote an exuberant letter to the Council of Safety in Charlestown. Having tramped through snow in Ninety-Six and Orangeburg Districts, rooting out loyalists, a somewhat immodest Richardson made what appeared to be an extraordinary claim. A less humane man, he wrote, could have "on the rivers, had I burnt, plundered, and destroyed, ten thousand women and children must have been left to perish."[8] Within a few years, a less humane man than Richardson, as will be seen below, paid the widow of Richardson a visit, giving a whole new meaning to the phrase "rooting out" an enemy.

Perhaps the number—was it fourteen hundred, eighteen hundred, or something else?—or the reliability—how could anyone really know the true number of widows and orphans, without some type of census?[9]—is equally important to the fact men such as Miranda, Ramsay and Moultrie continued for years to be impressed, and to single out this one South Carolina district, far distant and removed from Charleston. I contend, regardless of what the real number may be, what took place in the Revolutionary War era in the Ninety-Six District, was a civil war, a social upheaval that obliterated the social and cultural fabric of numerous families to the point that many lived for a time in stone age conditions.

Certainly Nathanael Greene thought what took place in the South Carolina backcountry, if not stopped, would result in the near annihilation of many families and small settlements: "Nothing but blood and slaughter has prevailed among the Whigs and Tories, and their inveteracy against each other must, if it continues, depopulate this part of the Country."[10] Greene, writing to his wife, perhaps thinking of his own home, told her, "You have nothing but the mournful widow and the plaints of the fatherless child; and behold nothing but houses desolated

7. William Moultrie, *Memoirs of the American Revolution, Volume II* (New York, NY: David Longworth, Printer, 1802), 242.

8. Bass, *Ninety Six*, 122.

9. Paul R Sarrett, Jr, *America online,* Files.usgwarchives.net/sc/Spartanburg/census/1790/1790spar.txt; Daniel Wright, Assistant U.S. Federal Marshall, *1790 Federal Census of the United States, returned April 15, 1791.*

10. George Washington Greene, *The Life of Nathanael Greene, Volume II* (Bedford, MA: Applewood reprint, 2009), 208.

and plantations laid waste. Ruin is in every form and misery in every shape."[11]

What is curious in the numbers given by these men in far-away Charleston is they suggest attention was mainly being given to widows and orphans of rebels; loyalist families without husband or father do not seem to be of much concern, although given the fact so many families switched from one side to the other, it is inconceivable some loyalist families are not included in this fourteen hundred.

It takes a careful reading of Ramsay to support this conclusion. Ramsay often spoke of the widows and orphans resulting from the "careless" concern of the British toward "the civil rights of the inhabitants. They conducted as tho interior order and police were scarcely objects of attention. The will of the strongest was the law."[12] He then added a clue that his interest was in what happened to rebel families: "Such was the general complexion of those who called themselves royalists, that nothing could be expected from them but outrages against the peace and order of society."[13]

For this reason—the possibility Ramsay and Moultrie were talking mainly about rebel wives and children—causes me to suggest my imperfect ballpark estimate of one in twenty families left without husband and father may be too low. A better estimate would come if we knew to what extent loyalist widows and orphans were included in this fourteen hundred. For the moment, this is the best that can be done, using rough population numbers,[14] along with the "first attempt within the knowledge of the census authorities,"[15] to project populations prior to the first Federal census in 1790.

What would happen, I wonder, if included where the loyalist families who also lost husband and father, forced to leave Ninety-Six District and not known or considered by Ramsay's source? When I reflect on this possibility, I reach the sad, startling conclusion that in the Ninety-Six District was not only a civil war within a revolution, but an effort to eliminate, by murder, intimidation, starvation and death by exposure,

11. Ibid., 351.
12. Ramsay, *The History of the Revolution of South-Carolina*, 259.
13. Ibid.
14. George Bancroft, *History of the United States of America, From the Discovery of the American Continent, Vol IV* (Boston, MA: Little, Brown, 1856), 128.
15. S.N.D. North, Director Bureau of the Census, *A Century of Population Growth: From the First Census of the United States to the Twelfth, 1790-1900* (Washington, DC: Government Printing Office, 1909), 9.

all opposition to either King or a new nation, depending on what side was the strongest at the moment. What took place in Ninety-Six District would get a name nine years later, in another revolution. The French came to see what happened to them as populicide, a "slaughter of the people."[16]

It was more than just slaughter. What happened to women and children at the slightest sign of opposition often resulted in slow starvation and death by exposure. Hesitation in signing a loyalty oath—either for or against the King—brought about destruction of everything needed for family survival—shelter, clothing, blankets, food, tools and livestock. Sometimes just the absence of a militia-age male about the farm, a suggestion that a male family member was off fighting for or against either side, was reason enough to destroy. Then again, sometimes the presence of a male at home, not with the right militia command at that moment, got him murdered. Sometimes wives and children were punished for something done by husbands and fathers. One of the more curious aspects of this backcountry civil war are accounts of men leaving behind their families, fleeing upon sight of an approaching enemy. These husbands and fathers would hide nearby, watching what happened to their families. I have come to realize this was the last, most imperfect strategy of survival left to these men. There was zero chance if a husband or father remained; but some chance his family might make it out alive if he were not there. This kind of desperate thinking is beyond my reckoning.

Even the dead and buried were not immune to savagery. Old Colonel Richardson, the man above who could have made ten thousand widows and orphans if he were less humane, now a general, died in 1780. British Lt. Col. Banastre Tarleton, today undergoing a revision by historians who suggest his reputation for brutality is undeserved because he did not conduct himself outside the norms of these times, allegedly had his men dig up the grave so he might gaze upon the face of a despised enemy. James Piecuch, a very good readable historian, says this never happened: "South Carolina Governor Rutledge wrote that the British claimed to be seeking the recently deceased Richardson, but that if they really wanted to find him all they would have had to do was dig up his grave near the front door."[17] The fact that Tarleton had an interest in the grave of a dead rebel general has, to me, a ghoulish intrigue about it, even if the grave was not opened. Tarleton, an example

16. Websters1913.com/words/Populicide.
17. Jim Piecuch, bantarleton.tumblr.com/post/118130184025/i-like-the-tale-of-how-banastre-tarleton-allegedly.

to his men, was not above thinking about plundering the dead. After gazing, or not, on the face of the dead general, Tarleton had every animal on the plantation, even the chickens, rounded up and put in a barn which was burned.[18] Another widow was made even more destitute.

The methods of killing in the Revolutionary War were medieval, but the kinds of atrocities committed on those who happened to be at the wrong place at the wrong time, and for the most innocuous of reasons, such as carrying or reading a Presbyterian Psalm book, suggest a determined effort was being made by both Whigs and Loyalist to exterminate all signs of opposition.

Certainly many of the old men who survived the war thought so. They used words such as "butchery," "massacre," "inhuman," "cruel," and a term particular to the times, "breaking up"[19] to describe what happened to families. In discussions of the revolutionary war in the backcountry, historians such as Lambert repeatedly used the word "savage."[20] Nathanael Greene said, "The Whigs and Tories pursue one another with the most relentless fury, killing and destroying each other whenever they met . . . The great bodies of militia . . . employed against the enemy and in quelling the Tories have almost laid waste the country."[21] What Greene was telling us was the war in the South was not like the one he experienced in the North. "The war here," he wrote, "is upon a different scale to what it is to the northward. It is a plain business here."[22] My sense is that Greene meant "plain business" as in brutal, relentless, and savage.

Neither Patriot Greene nor British Southern Commander Cornwallis ever came to grips with what took place in and around Ninety-Six District. Almost every major figure who went there, British or rebel, remarked upon this "breaking up" of families. Lord Rawdon, a man who encouraged inhabitants of the backcountry to commit atrocities by offering "ten guineas for the head of any deserted . . . and five guineas' only if they bring him in alive,"[23] wrote to Lord Cornwallis that, in the

18. Patrick O'Kelley, *Nothing but Blood and Slaughter Volume Two* (United States: Blue House Tavern Press, 2004), 354.

19. Ian Saberton, ed., *The Cornwallis Papers* (Uckfield, East Sussex: The Naval & Military Press, 2010), 1:151.

20. Robert Lambert, *South Carolina Loyalists in the American Revolution,* (Columbia, SC: University of South Carolina Press, 1987), 142.

21. Lambert, *South Carolina Loyalists,* 141.

22. Scott Aken, *The Swamp Fox: Lessons in Leadership from the Partisan Campaigns of Francis Marion* (Annapolis, MD: Naval Institute Press, 2012), 277n67.

23. Michael J. O'Brien, *A Hidden Phase of American History* (New York, NY: Dodd, Mead and Company, 1919), 193.

dead of winter, one of his patrols came upon a dazed woman "left standing in her shift," beside her "four children stripped stark naked." Her home had been "stripped of everything that could be carried off."[24] Unfortunately, Rawdon failed to tell us which side committed this atrocity, or what became of a mother and her four naked children in the dead of winter.

Reading the pension applications of these old veterans is often a melancholy journey to the past. Thomas Witten states he took part "in several little skirmishes, and was an eye witness to some of the many instances of inhuman butchery and massacre committed upon the frontier families within the range of his marches."[25] Ezekiel Croft told of how the "numbers & butcheries had multiplied"[26] among the settlers, following the defeat of Gates at Camden in August 1780, an event considered the start to British control of the Backcountry.

Historian Lambert concluded, "the British reputation for pillaging, giving no quarter in battle, and for mistreating prisoners was well established by the end of the summer of 1780."[27] But then came Autumn, and Kings Mountain. The pendulum swung, and the rebel reputation for pillaging, giving no quarter and mistreatment of prisoners became equally earned but often glossed over by those of us on the western side of the Atlantic who now look at these things.

Following years of relative calm in the Ninety-Six District, after the British took Charleston, there was a brief ascendency of about two or three months in the summer of 1780, and more hopeful than reality, where the British attempted half-heartedly to restore civil government. They failed to do so miserably, in part because no one appeared to accept civilized "standards of behavior."[28] Lord Cornwallis assumed too quickly, "from every information I receive, and numbers of the most violent rebels hourly coming in to offer their services, I have the strongest reason to believe the general disposition of the people to be not only friendly to Government but forward to take up arms in its support."[29] This optimism of Cornwallis was part of the failure of the British strategies—there was more than one—in the South, and a contributing reason to why things quickly got out of control. The British were interested

24. Rawdon to Cornwallis, December 5, 1780, Papers of Charles, First Marquis Cornwallis, PRO 30/11/14, 140, British National Archives.
25. Leon C. Harris, transcriber. Thomas Witten Pension Application S6407, *Southern Campaigns Revolutionary War Pension Statements & Rosters*, revwarapps.org, as of 2016.
26. Graves, Ezekiel Croft S16739.
27. Lambert, *South Carolina Loyalists*, 142.
28. Saberton, *Cornwallis Papers*, 1:33.
29. Ibid., 1:54.

in restoring government—justices, courts, rule of law—only to the extent their eastern flank was secured. The Carolinas were little more than a march route to be used to close the gap between Charleston and New York.

I have come to regard this as one of Cornwallis's greatest strategic mistakes: failing to recognize the extent to which a potential slaughter smoldered in the Backcountry, waiting for the smallest breeze to burst into flame. Rather than walking around a hornet's nest, Lord Cornwallis bumped his head against it.

The inability of the British to control "men cloathed in green"[30] and newly formed, barely disciplined provincial loyalist companies—all plundering opportunists—were circumstances leading to the only type of justice found in this backcountry anarchy: revenge, retribution, hatred, plundering and the rule of the momentary mighty. Time and again, Cornwallis and his officers wrote about the vulnerably of loyalists who sought British protection, and what would happen if regular British troops moved too quickly from one area to another in their haste to move north. The British never created the structures permitting vulnerable groups to have genuine access to the King's protection. I find it remarkable that British Lt. Col. Nisbet Balfour, even before he arrived at Ninety-Six, made an observation similar to that of Greene. Balfour, within a month of the fall of Charleston, wrote to Cornwallis, "Allowing rebels on parole to return to their homes is something I confess I think ought immediately to be stopped, for this will be otherwise a constant dissatisfaction and these gentry will throw every impediment in the way of settling the country."[31] Then, completing his frustration, he added this postscript: "Some stop ought to be put, *if possible,* to the depredations of the cavalry, who in small partys and as expresses commit every enormity."[32] Balfour placed the emphasis on *if possible.* (Poor Colonel Balfour soon got out of this hornet's nest and back to the civilized war of Charleston, only to hit his own head against another hornet's nest, embroiled in what was considered one of the greatest British war crimes of the revolution, the execution of Isaac Hayne.)

On the other side of the coin was that most peculiar sense of backcountry honor, never understood by the British, that allowed "violent, persecuting men"[33] to find cracks in their paroles. I, for one, consider as a factor in the subsequent violence the understanding that men like Andrew Pickens had of their promise to remain out of the war. "My honor

30. Ibid., 1:40.
31. Ibid., 1:80.
32. Ibid.
33. Office of the UN Special Advisor on the Prevention of Genocide, 2.

is pledged," he stated, "I am bound by the solemnity of an oath not to take up arms, *unless* . . ."[34] This "*unless*," emphasis added by me, was either an invitation or awareness that no one could avoid this savagery. It would only be a matter of time for Andrew Pickens. Cornwallis understood how men like Pickens viewed honor, but failed to do much with this understanding other than refuse to be "godfather to any man's honesty in this province."[35] Failure to remove "violent, persecuting men" and thereby reduce the capacity of influential men to control others by violence and brutal intimidation was a most serious omission in the British strategy to restore the King's rule. All of Lord Cornwallis's work to persuade leading men like Pickens to help restore control in the backcountry was undone ever so conveniently by the British themselves. Yet, in kindness to Cornwallis's understanding of the situation, I note that whatever the British policy toward leading men in the backcountry might have been, other men, equally violent and persecuting, if not more so, would have taken their place, acting as government officials dispensing frontier justice. There was just too much "existing and past conflicts over land, power . . . language, religion and culture"[36] in the different settlements to not have targeted groups and families, with no real protection or system of justice except what the powerful, at that moment, thought right.

In considering when a revolution becomes a civil war, I have had to rely upon soft, squishy sources, prejudiced toward the American side. There is, however, a most remarkable document sent to Lord George Germain in April of 1782.[37] It was a petition signed by eleven well-known loyalists, living as refugees in Charleston, who were greatly offended by the reaction in Britain to the execution of Isaac Hayne. The list contains the names of more than three hundred loyalists killed in the Ninety-Six and Camden Districts. Although the list was not exclusive to the Ninety-Six District, most of the focus was on this area.

The petitioners made a rather amazing claim: a more complete list would contain "thrice that number" of "butchered and hanged."[38] Should these men and their families, I wonder, be added to the fourteen hundred widows and orphans claimed by Ramsey and Moultrie, or should they be considered already included? If added, the number of

---

34. William R. Reynolds, Jr, "The Parole of Andrew Pickens," *Southern Campaigns of the American Revolution*, Vol. 10, No. 1.0 Spring 2014, 13.
35. Saberton, *Cornwallis Papers*, 1:33.
36. Ibid.
37. "Petition to Lord Germain Dated 19 April 1782", freepages.genealogy.rootsweb.ancestry.com/~eazier1/Young/LoyalistList.pdf.
38. Lambert, *South Carolina Loyalists*, 211.

widows and orphans would push the ratio of families without a head of household to one in ten families. If "thrice that number" murdered is a reliable claim, this ratio would become an unbearable one in five, making the Revolution in the South Carolina backcountry comparable to what happened in the next civil war, eighty years later.

If most of the murdered Loyalists in the Germain petition were already in Ramsay's and Moultrie's estimate, much support is given to my claim that, at a minimum, one in twenty families in the South Carolina Backcountry lost their head of household. My suspicion is that many of these loyalist families were not being thought of by Ramsay and Moultrie; the real ratio is probably at least twice what I am unwilling to claim at this point.

On the Germain petition is the name of Col. Ambrose Mills. Mills was at the skirmish of Earle's Ford and commanded the loyalist militia who brutally murdered two defenseless teenage boys, awakened and still in their tent. A few months later, he was the first of nine loyalists hung at Biggerstaff Farm, following Kings Mountain, and after a convoluted mock trial. Four months later, the man who hung Mills, Patriot William Merrill, was dragged from his home and taken back to Biggerstaff Farm. There he was hung from the same tree limb as had been Ambrose Mills. William, the son of Ambrose, just recovered from wounds so severe he had been left for dead at Kings Mountain, hung Merrill. Thus, one name on this petition, Ambrose Mills, selected by me from three hundred murdered men, not quite at random but simply by catching my eye because I am familiar with him, lead to twelve atrocities. Probably each of these men had a wife and at least one child, struggling to survive at barely subsistent levels.

Also on the list is "_____ Dunlap, Major of Dragoons." James Dunlap shared the command with Mills at the Skirmish of Earle's Ford, where the two sleeping boys were murdered. Dunlap, not from the area and somewhat vaguely remembered by those who wrote this petition, did not leave behind his own widow and children in Ninety-Six District, but he left several dozen local families without husband and father. He also left one man without hope of a new wife. Mary McRea, a young woman who was kidnapped by Dunlap, died still his prisoner, and euphemistically was the object of his "amorous advances,"[39] needs to be added to this seemingly endless list of settlers who sacrificed all.

39. Wayne Lynch, "Major James Dunlap: Was He Murdered Twice?" *Journal of the American Revolution,* January 14, 2016, allthingsliberty.com/2016/01/major-james-dunlap-murdered-twice/.

Lord Cornwallis was himself not above adding fuel to the raging backcountry fire. In a blundering, ill-conceived order, he commanded Dunlap to destroy Pickens' home and, upon finding Pickens, to hang him "instantly."[40] Pickens' *"unless"* came full circle.

When the pendulum swung back, Pickens ordered that, should any of Dunlap's men be captured, to "not spare" any "that needed killings."[41] Those needing killing was left to the discretion of the captors.

The Germain Petition needs more study. On the list of murdered loyalists are the names of several suggesting that we do not have a full understanding of what happened to women and children along the frontier: "John Atkinson (aged 65)," "Arthur Carradyne (aged 76)," "James Clark, and a youth, his son," "John Donahoe, aged 78," "Thomas Keating, Major, aged 80," "James Kane, and his son," "Richard Love (killed while asleep and another man)," "Emanuel Miller—aged 70."[42] Where these men, many with elderly wives now elderly widows, along with hundreds more, known to Ramsay and Moultrie?

In 1782, as the British army prepared to leave America, Gen. William Moultrie traveled from Philadelphia back to South Carolina. His journey took him through shattered country. "It was the most dull, melancholy, dreary ride . . . not the vestiges of horses, cattle, hogs, or deer, &c. was to be found. The squirrels and birds of every kind were totally destroyed . . . no living creature was to be seen, except now and then a few camp scavengers [turkey buzzards], picking the bones of some unfortunate fellows."[43]

How many widows and orphans came from this backcountry Ninety-Six District, in their civil war we know as the American Revolution? Each time I looked at an individual who crossed my path in the investigation of this question, I discovered in their life multiple occurrences of murder, brutality and savagery.

---

40. Ibid.
41. Ibid.
42. Petition to Lord Germain, 2-3.
43. William Moultrie, *Memoirs of the American Revolution, so far as it relates to the states of North and South Carolina, and Georgia, Volume I* (New York, NY: David Longworth, 1802), 354-55.

Terror on the Frontier: The Grim Ordeal of Delilah Corbly

JOSHUA SHEPHERD

More often than not, the horrific realities of warfare are shielded by bland accounts and cold statistics. When it comes to the Revolutionary War, affairs on the frontier suffer egregiously in that regard, and the grim cost of the conflict is often overshadowed by the epic sweep of affairs on the eastern seaboard. But in the hinterlands of the west, the war was a very personal and brutal affair which left seared memories—and scarred lives—on both sides of the conflict. Those horrors are tragically humanized by the experiences of a single little girl from western Pennsylvania: seven-year-old Delilah Corbly.

Her story would likely have been lost to history had it not been for the Rev. William Rogers, a Philadelphia minister who contacted the *Pennsylvania Packet and Daily Advertiser* in 1785. Rogers submitted a letter from fellow Baptist minister John Corbly, whose family had experienced a nightmarish ordeal three years earlier. By Rogers' reckoning, such accounts needed to be recorded "so that our posterity may not be ignorant of what their ancestors underwent, at the trying period" of the Revolution. In the aftermath of the conflict, it was likewise obvious that Rogers harbored no small resentment toward the British, who, he thought, "basely chose to encourage, patronize, and reward, as their most faithful and beloved allies, the savages of the wilderness."[1]

Since the outbreak of hostilities in the spring of 1775, the western frontiers of Pennsylvania and Virginia had, somewhat surprisingly, escaped an all-out war. Clearly frustrated by the course of the conflict and determined to throw all available means at the Rebels, American Secretary Lord George Germain changed all of that early in 1777. In written orders for British officers at Detroit, Germain observed that "it is His

---

1. *The Pennsylvania Packet, and Daily Advertiser*, August 3, 1785, 2-3.

Majesty's resolution that the most vigorous Efforts should be made, and every means employed that Providence has put into His Majesty's Hands, for crushing the rebellion."[2] It was high-flown language which would contribute to widespread suffering in American settlements and Native villages across the frontier.

Germain was specifically authorizing the arming of Indian allies. Because a number of the northwestern tribes—the Chippewa, Wyandot, Shawnee, Seneca, Delaware, and Pottawatomie—possessed an inclination "for war," Germain ordered that they be supplied for "making a Diversion and exciting an alarm upon the frontiers of Virginia and Pennsylvania." It would be best, Germain instructed, for Indian war parties to have a "proper" white officer placed at their head in order to protect Loyalist civilians, or as he put it, to "restrain them from committing violence on the well affected and inoffensive Inhabitants." At least in his official orders, Germain expressed no similar concern for Rebel civilians.[3]

For gentlemen officers steeped in the conventions of European warfare, the ugly realities of frontier bush fighting constituted a double-edged sword that could nettle the conscience. Vincennes Lt. Gov. Edward Abbott, although he had previously offered to raise Indian war parties to the Crown's standard, later experienced second thoughts. Although greatly underestimating the tribes' ability to confront conventional forces in pitched battle, he nonetheless observed that the norm for frontier warfare constituted small-scale strikes against civilians. In a letter to Sir Guy Carleton, Abbott particularly lamented the plight of Loyalist families and observed that "it is not people in arms that Indians will ever daringly attack, but the poor inoffensive families who fly to the deserts to be out of trouble and who are inhumanely butchered sparing neither women or children."[4]

When the Continental Congress began receiving reports of a complete destabilization of the frontier over the summer of 1777, they were aghast at the depredations perpetrated "by some savage tribes of Indians, wherein a number of helpless people have been cruelly massacred, and the peaceable inhabitants driven from their homes and reduced to great distress."[5] The western war sparked during the summer of 1777

2. Letter, Lord George Germain to Henry Hamilton, March 26, 1777, in M. Shoemaker, et al, eds., *Report of the Pioneer Society of the State of Michigan* (Lansing: Wynkoop Hallenbeck Crawford Co., 1908), 9:347.
3. Ibid.
4. Letter, Edward Abbott to Guy Carleton, June 8, 1778, in *Report of the Pioneer Society of the State of Michigan*, 9: 488-489.
5. Worthington Chauncey Ford, ed., *Journals of the Continental Congress* (Washington: Government Printing Office, 1907), 9:942.

would continue through the end of the Revolution and beyond. It was a conflict characterized by exceedingly brutal acts of revenge and reprisal in which neither side would maintain clean hands. The Revolution may have begun in the east over grand themes of liberty, but on the far reaches of the western frontier the war could fall with irrevocable tragedy on the lives of common settlers. Due to a woeful lack of primary documents, most casualties of the war in the west remain nameless, faceless victims.

However, one family's tragic story, that of the Rev. John Corbly, can be told in frightening detail. By profession, Corbly was a Regular Baptist minister and farmer. After initially settling in Virginia, Corbly underwent a conversion to evangelical Christianity of the nonconformist evangelical stripe, became an itinerant preacher, and quickly ran afoul of Virginia's Anglican establishment. In July of 1768 he was jailed in Culpeper along with three other men as "Vagrant and Itinerant Persons for Assemblying themselves unlawfully" and "for teaching and preaching Schismatic Doctrines."[6]

By 1770 Corbly was on the frontier of modern-day Pennsylvania, continuing to plant churches, and farming his own ground on Whitely Creek, just north of the stockade of Garard's Fort. The widowed Corbly, who had fathered four children with his first wife, married Elizabeth Tyler about 1773. Over the following decade, five more children followed. Settler John Crawford recalled Corbly as thoroughly Whig in his political sentiments. "His preaching was attended by large assemblies," claimed Crawford, "many would come ten miles to hear him. He represented our cause as the cause of heaven."[7]

On Sunday morning, May 12, 1782,[8] Corbly headed out for services at his primary congregation at Goshen Meeting House, which was about a mile's walk from the family home.[9] Corbly, "meditating", as he

---

6. Howard L. Leckey, *The Tenmile Country and Its Pioneer Families* (Apollo, PA: Closson Press, 1993), 581.

7. John Crawford's Narrative, in John and Jennings Crawford, eds., *The William Crawford Memorial* (Brooklyn: Eagle Book Printing, 1904), 54.

8. A number of accounts of the incident record May 10 as the date of the attack; Corbly indicated that the event took place on the second "sabbath," or Sunday, of May 1782, which fell on May 12.

9. The following description of the attack and its aftermath comes from Corbly's own account, penned three years after the incident, which first appeared in print in the *The Pennsylvania Packet and Daily Advertiser*, August 3, 1785, and later in Letter, John Corbly to William Rogers, July 8, 1785, in Mathew Carey, ed., *Affecting History of the Dreadful Distresses of Frederic Manheim's Family to which are Added the Sufferings of John Corbly's Family* (Philadelphia: D. Humphreys, 1794), 7-8. Nineteenth century family lore and local oral tradition purport to flesh out further details of the attack, but are uncorroborated by primary sources. For such additional perspectives, see Nannie L. Fordyce,

said, on his sermon for the day, walked about 200 yards behind the rest of his family. The pastor carried his Bible, but was unarmed. Mrs. Corbly led the rest of the family; in her arms was infant Nancy, not a year old. Close in tow were the remainder of Corbly's minor children: Delilah, just shy of her eighth birthday, Elizabeth, seven, Isaiah, six, and Mary Catherine, about two.[10]

Before the family reached the meeting house, bedlam erupted. An Indian war party which had been concealed in the forest burst from cover and rushed Mrs. Corbly and the children. The pastor, immediately realizing what was happening, ran through the forest "vainly hunting" for a club while he listened to "the frightful shrieks of my dear family." When he was about forty yards from the scene of the attack, Mrs. Corbly caught a glimpse of him and, no doubt sensing the utter hopelessness of the situation, frantically shouted for her husband to make his "escape."

A warrior immediately saw Corbly and raised his piece to take aim, but Corbly sprinted off before he could fire. The Indian set out in pursuit but quickly gave up the chase and returned to the scene of the ambush. By his later description of events, it seems likely that Corbly, though out of range, was nonetheless close enough to hear some of the horrifying events that followed.

It was over in a few terrifying minutes. When the attack began, seven-year-old Delilah scampered, apparently undetected, about twenty yards into the forest and hid in a tree, where she "saw the whole proceedings." As she watched, the war party wasted little time. The infant Nancy was jerked from her mother's arms, killed and scalped, as was the toddler Mary Catherine. Five-year-old Isaiah was scalped and received a tomahawk blow to the head.[11] Seven-year-old Elizabeth was scalped and left for dead.

The Life and Times of Reverend John Corbly and the John Corbly Family Geneology (Washington, PA: by the author), 27-30.

10. Because frontier births were often never officially recorded, the ages of the Corbly children are approximate. John Corbly described Isaiah as "about six" at the time of the killings. Although most accounts cite Delilah's birthdate as July 19, 1774, it's likely that she was born slightly earlier. The date of death on Delilah's fading tombstone appears as January 10, 1839, and her age at time of death appears as 64 years, 7 months, and 11 days, rendering a possible birthdate around May 30, 1774. Much thanks to Patrick Kennedy of the Troy-Miami County Local History Library for information on Delilah's age.

11. Later accounts claimed that Isaiah lived for twenty-four hours following the attack. Corbly's letter describing the incident, however, simply states that the Indians "sunk the hatchet into his brains, and thus dispatched him." Corbly Letter, 7.

The warriors had slightly more trouble with Mrs. Corbly. After shouting warnings to her husband, she sustained repeated tomahawk blows but remained on her feet. When the warrior who had pursued Corbly returned to the scene, he levelled his piece and shot her dead; she was scalped with the rest.

When she finally heard her family's screams subside, Delilah, assuming that the Indians had fled the scene, "got up, and deliberately crept out from the hollow trunk." She was tragically mistaken. One of the warriors noticed her, quickly ran her down, knocked her to the ground, and scalped her.

Pastor Corbly thought that the entire affair lasted no more than ten minutes. "At the time I ran round to see what was become of my family," he later wrote, "and found my dear and affectionate wife, with five children, all scalped in less than ten minutes . . . no one . . . can conceive how I felt." After viewing the sight, he fainted.

While the Indian party sped off to the west, a pursuit party was organized at Garard's Fort. The men followed the Indians' trail for some time but eventually gave up the chase. It was never recorded what tribe was thought to have been involved in the attack, or how many warriors participated. Back at Garard's Fort, a devastated John Corbly struggled to regain his senses. "Would to God I had died for them," he cried out, "would to God I had died with them."

Amazingly, both Delilah and Elizabeth survived the incident. Delilah had suffered a scalping to the crown of her head but was otherwise unhurt. Elizabeth's wound was simply ghastly. Corbly later explained that a piece of her skull had been cut away during the attack and that not more "than one inch round, either of flesh or skin, remained on her head."

Although it was not terribly uncommon for a scalping victim to survive such an injury, the medical procedures needed to treat such a wound would have been simply terrifying for little girls not yet ten years old. Although we don't know for certain what specific treatments the girls were forced to endure, it was generally customary to treat a scalp wound by boring a number of small holes, in a grid pattern, into the skull.[12] In a letter to William Rogers three years after the attack, Corbly expressed thankfulness that Delilah and Elizabeth had been "miraculously preserved," but indicated that he was full of "anxiety" over their future. "I am yet in hopes of seeing them cured," he wrote, "they still,

---

12. For a thorough and readily-accessible treatment of the topic, see Hugh T. Harrington, "How to Treat a Scalped Head", *Journal of the American Revolution*, May 14, 2013.

blessed be God, retain their senses, notwithstanding the painful operations they have already and must yet pass through." Paying for the medical treatment, Corbly explained, had "almost ruined" him financially.

Fellow Baptist minister Robert Semple recorded that during the
wake of the horrific experience an inconsolable Corbly somewhat understandably "fell into a melancholy state of mind; during which, he
could not preach, or scarcely do anything else."[13] For Delilah and Elizabeth, the physical pain and mental trauma of witnessing the murder
of their family, enduring scalpings, and then facing adolescence, can
only be imagined. Elizabeth lived to the age of twenty-one before dying
suddenly, so her family maintained, from an infection to her scalp
wound, which never entirely healed.[14]

Delilah Corbly would remain the only long-term survivor of the
massacre and, despite the tremendous adversity that her injury clearly
presented, went on to live a fulfilled and productive life. Married young,
she received little schooling and remained illiterate.[15] About the age of
sixteen, Delilah wed Levi Martin, who was no stranger to the dangers
of the frontier. During the Revolution Martin had served several stints
as a militia ranger. In such a capacity he had escaped seeing any large-
scale battles but, he said, participated in "frequent skirmishes with the
Indians."[16]

The Martins eventually moved farther west and settled in Ohio's
Miami Valley, raising a family of ten children. According to family oral
tradition, Delilah was plagued by chronic headaches, a condition attributed to her old wound. For decades, she concealed the scars as best
she could. Her hair "grew thriftily around the edge of the scalped surface, which, by careful training, grew upward, and served as a protection
to the exposed parts."[17] To her dying day—January 10, 1839—Delilah
Corbly Martin was left with a healed but bare scalp, a grim reminder
that the Revolution in the west often drew little distinction between
soldiers and non-combatants.

---

13. Robert Semple, *A History of the Rise and Progress of the Baptists in Virginia* (Richmond:
John O'Lynch, 1810), 429.
14. Fordyce, *Life and Times of Reverend John Corbly*, 29.
15. Will of Delilah Martin, in *The Tenmile Country*, 590-591. Delilah Martin signed her
will with a mark.
16. Pension Application of Levi Martin, in Don Corbly, *The Families of Elizabeth Betsy
Tyler Corbly* (By the author, 2014), 144.
17. *The History of Miami County, Ohio* (Chicago: W.H. Beers and Company, 1880), 221.

Benedict Arnold's Phantom Duel

JOHN KNIGHT

Though he was just twenty-two years of age, Walter Stirling already possessed enviable social advantages. He had powerful family connections and enormous personal wealth. A successful banker himself, his renowned father was on the verge of being raised to one of the most prestigious posts in the Royal Navy as Commander-in-Chief, The Nore.[1] If he was considered by many a boorish social climber, his connections, ambition and wealth were compensation enough to make him a much sought-after patron.[2] For those wishing admission to the exclusive court soirees and levees distracting London's aristocracy during a long and failing war, his acquaintance was considered invaluable.

Yet even with his influence, the Philadelphia-born Stirling must have felt unusually apprehensive as he waited in line outside the Throne Room at St. James Palace to present his respects to King George III. For the man standing alongside him, dressed in the cochineal scarlet of a British general officer, was not just the husband of his cousin Peggy Shippen, but also the most notorious officer of the war, Benedict Arnold.[3]

Stirling's fleeting anxieties about introducing such a pariah to his sovereign, however, were quickly appeased. George III, a stubborn but immensely faithful man, immediately took to both the "Loyalist" Arnold and his charming wife Peggy, whom he declared "the most beautiful woman he had ever seen."[4] Though the British government

1. www.clanstirling.org/com.
2. For an amusing if caustic assessment of Stirling from among others the future Prime Minister George Canning, see www.historyofparliamentonline.org/volume/1790-1820/member/stirling-walter-1758-1832
3. Milton Lomask, "Benedict Arnold: the Aftermath of Treason," *American Heritage*, October 1967, www.americanheritage.com/content/benedict-arnold-aftermath-treason?page=3
4. Ibid.

had already amply rewarded his treachery, the King granted Arnold a gratuity of £500, while his enamoured consort Queen Charlotte awarded Peggy a further annuity of £100.[5] Through early 1782 George was often to be seen wandering the Royal Parks in deep conversation with Arnold and his Secretary of State Lord George Germaine, even commissioning a paper from him on his "Thoughts on the American War."[6]

Though Arnold received only cordiality and favour from the King, he was not nearly so highly regarded by his subjects.[7] One morning George was strolling with Arnold when he spied his Aide-de-Camp Lord Balcarres.

"My Lord do you know General Arnold?"

Balcarres, a veteran of the American war, stiffened, drew himself to his full height and spluttered, "what Sire? Do you mean the traitor Arnold?!" He pointedly turned his back and retreated. Needless to say, the fiery and volatile Arnold regarded such a tart response as an unforgivable attack on his reputation, and a duel of honour was swiftly arranged.

On the prescribed morning Arnold stood just twelve paces from an adversary he had last faced amongst the wheat fields of Saratoga. At his second's command, Arnold drew his pistol and fired, but wide. He stood, nervously awaiting Balcarres's riposte, but it never came. The Earl turned on his heel and nonchalantly began to stroll away. Incensed at a further challenge to his honour Arnold called out,

"Sir will you give me no satisfaction?"

The Earl replied without breaking step, "Sir, I leave that task to the Devil."

It is an excellent tale free from any moral ambiguity. Two heroic champions are thrown together on battlefield and duelling ground clean across two continents, both men the personification of loyalty and treachery, their lives fated to be entwined in a tragedy of Shakespearian proportions. There is only one inconvenient problem with this epic tale. It never happened.

It is not difficult to understand why this oft-reported story has been misrepresented in histories for nearly two hundred years and is regularly repeated today. Its first appearance was not until 1833, long after the

5. Charles Burr Todd, *The Real Benedict Arnold* (New York: A.S. Barnes, 1903), 22.
6. Peter de Loriol, *Famous and Infamous Londoners* (Charleston, SC: The History Press, 2004), 31.
7. For a contemporary assessment of Arnolds' career that ends with a stinging and vitriolic conclusion, see *The European Magazine and London Review*, February 1783.

death of both protagonists, in the book *Three years in North America* by James Stuart.[8] In many ways a gem of a book, this gossipy, opinionated travelogue is unfortunately wholly unreliable as a historical source. This has not stopped both American and British academics referencing it in varying guises ever since. Indeed so compelling is the tale even the current Earl Balcarres insists it to be fact.[9]

The Lord Balcarres was born into one of Scotland's mightiest aristocratic Clans, the Lindsays, and after a first-class education in England and Germany he followed a long family tradition by joining the Army. By 1777 he was a major in a light infantry battlion at the age of just twenty-five.[10] A down to earth, outspoken man with a tendency towards sarcasm, Balcarres proved to be an able and vigorous officer in action if a lazy and disinterested administrator.[11] Like Arnold, he possessed an almost demonic personal bravery. At the battle of Hubbardton, his clothing was shot through in thirteen different places, yet Balcarres suffered only a minor wound in the British victory. At Saratoga, only his foresight in engineering the formidable redoubt that still bears his name saved Burgoyne's army from complete destruction.[12] It is not too fanciful to suppose that Arnold, whipping the troops of Enoch Poor's Brigade Into a frenzy beneath the sharpened stakes at the base of this redoubt, must have been just yards from him.[13]

Though his prudence saved Burgoyne's army from annihilation, it could not save it from defeat, and for two years he was a "Convention"

8. James Stuart, *Three Years in North America* (Edinburgh: R. Cadell, 1833), 1:461.
9. There are countless references to the supposed Balcarres-Arnold duel both online and in print many by sophisticated historians. None give reliable sources earlier than the James Stuart book. All have slightly different details but end with the same tag line of an irate and humiliated Arnold and a nonchalant and caustic Balcarres. Examples include: "Today in history Alexander Lyndsey 6th Earl Balcarres passes away," Masonry Today, www.masonrytoday.com/index.php?new_month=3&new_day=27&new_year =2016; A. P. Kup, "Alexander Lindsay, 6th Earl of Balcarres, Lieutenant Governor of Jamaica 1794-1801," Manchester University, www.escholar.manchester.ac.uk/api/datastream?publicationPid=uk-ac-man-scw:1m2767&datastreamId=POST-PEER-REVIEW-PUBLISHERS-DOCUMENT.PDF; "I'd rather take a bullet than apologize," www.sorrywatch.com/2015/05/01/id-rather-take-a-bullet-than-apologize/Sorrywatch.com The Scottish Nation: Balcarres, www.electricscotland.com/history/nation/balcaress. htm; Joe Craig, "Duel Personalities," friendsofsaratogabattlefield.org/duel-personalities/
10. Lord Lyndsay, *Lives of the Lyndsays: A memoir* (London: J. Murray, 1858), 343.
11. F. Cundell, *Lady Nugent's Journal*
12. Nickerson Hoffman, *The Turning Point of the Revolution* (New York: Houghton Mifflin, 1928), 365. Hoffman also repeats the myth of the duel later in the book.
13. John Luzeder, *Saratoga, a Military History* (New York: Savas Beattie, 2008), 289.

prisoner in New England and Virginia.[14] On his return to Britain in 1779, he entered into manufacturing and helped establish the famous Haigh Ironworks in Lancashire, while all the time maintaining an active military career, first as commander in Gibraltar then as Lieutenant-Governor in Jamaica. There is no evidence that Balcarres ever met Arnold either as a prisoner in America or as a fellow officer in Great Britain.

As for Arnold, it is true that the pugnacious Connecticotian fought many duels before, during and after the war, and that one of them was against a Scottish Earl. However, that man was Lord Lauderdale, not Balcarres, whom Arnold believed, quite wrongly, had slighted him during a Parliamentary speech. Both men survived the duel.[15]

Though it was officially a secret, the affair was widely reported by the newspapers of the day and featured melodramatically in a letter Peggy sent back to her father in Philadelphia. "The time appointed was seven o clock the morning of Saturday last . . . It was agreed they should fire together which the General did without effect . . . Lord Lauderdale refused to fire." She concluded rather too optimistically, "It has been highly gratifying to see the Generals conduct so much applauded."[16] A voracious letter writer, she never again mentioned any past or extant duels in her correspondence, something her dramatic temperament would have been unlikely to have let pass without comment. In contrast, the supposed Balcarres duel is not reported in any contemporary newsprint or aristocratic correspondence. It's details, however, bear a remarkable similarity to the contest involving Lauderdale.

In fact, despite the late eighteenth century being looked upon in popular imagination as an age of duelling, only a handful of well-documented cases concerning nobles took place during Arnold's time in England. Had Arnold challenged an aristocrat like Lord Balcarres in the claustrophobic and febrile society of Georgian London, it would not have gone unnoticed.

Perhaps most damning of all, there is the unlikely circumstance that the insult was delivered in the direct presence of the King. Balcarres was never Aide-de-Camp to George III, and it is improbable that any respectable aristocrat would have snubbed an introduction from his sovereign in a way that placed him in such an invidious position. To have done so would have been more an insult to the King than to

14. Lyndsay, *Lives of the Lyndsays*, 344.(London: West India Committee for the Institute of Jamaica, 1939), 18, 19, 22, 33.
15. Issac Newton-Arnold, *Life of Benedict Arnold: His Patriotism and Treason* (Chicago: Jansen Co., 1880), 367.
16. Lomask, "Benedict Arnold."

Alexander Lindsay, 6th Earl of Balcarres.

Arnold, and would have assuredly destroyed his career. There were many occasions when both Benedict and Peggy were slighted during their time in London, but strict social etiquette prevented any of them from being delivered in the presence of the Monarch.

What is left is undoubtedly more a parable than a historical narrative. It is hard not to suspect that it is still given credence today because so many long for it to be true. But false it assuredly is.

Nevertheless, there is some consolation for those who wish to study the associated lives of Arnold and Balcarres. If a close inspection of the duel's circumstances exposes an account that cannot be verified, it unearths an even more tragic story that has passed by virtually unremarked.

Benedict Arnold's eldest son, Benedict VI, did not share his father's manufactured loyalty for the British; it was undoubtedly genuine. Like his father, he could be violent and headstrong, and twice he directly defied him by taking up a commission in the British army, even spending two years in France as a prisoner of war.[17] At twenty-seven as a captain in the Royal Artillery, he was assigned to the West Indies, where the British were having great trouble suppressing a rebellion of Maroons on the economically precious Island of Jamaica. The Jamaican Maroons were descendants of escaped African slaves who had formed indepen-

17. Willard Sterne Randall, *Benedict Arnold Patriot and Traitor* (New York: William Morrow, 1990), Ch9.

dent free settlements in the Islands interior. For over fifty years they had been fighting a sporadic guerrilla war the British seemed incapable of quelling.[18] Attacking in well trained small bands from behind the rocks and dense undergrowth of the "cockpit" country, their hit and run tactics ground down and demoralised the completely unprepared British. In 1795 during one such maroon ambush, Benedict Arnold VI was mortally injured after a flesh wound in his leg turned gangrenous. Poignantly like his father at Saratoga, he stubbornly refused amputation of the limb, this time with tragically different consequences.

Back in England Benedict, already ailing with dropsy, received the devastating news of the loss of his son stoically but confessed, "his death is a very heavy stroke to me."[19] He found some consolation when George Grenville, Earl Temple visited him in London and handed him his son's sword and personal condolence letters, the latter affirming the regard and love Benedict VI had been held in by his fellow officers.[20] (25) Reading them, he must have also found solace in the detail that the general commanding the British forces in Jamaica had marked him out for commendation and future promotion.

That general, Benedict VI's last commanding officer and would-be patron, was Alexander, 6th Earl of Balcarres.

18. The Hon, John Fortescue, *A history of the 17th Lancers* (London: MacMillan Co., 1895), 73.
19. Randall, *Benedict Arnold Patriot and Traitor*, Ch9.
20. Ibid., v, though wrongly addressed as Grenville Temple.

Benjamin Franklin and Judaism

ᓚᔰ SHAI AFSAI ᖇᖇ

Though not always able to offer definitive evidence of a link between the two men, since the nineteenth century Jewish scholars have affirmed that *Sefer Heshbon Ha-nefesh* (*The Book of Spiritual Accounting*)—a Hebrew work published in 1808[1] by the early Eastern European *maskil* (Jewish enlightener)[2] Rabbi Menahem Mendel Lefin of Satanow (1749-1826)[3]—is based on the writings of Benjamin Franklin (1706-1790). Certain scholars have been more specific in their source attribution, noting that the method for self-examination and character improvement presented at greater length by Lefin in *Spiritual Accounting* is similar to one the American founding father outlined earlier in his famous *Autobiography*.[4]

Both the *Autobiography* and *Spiritual Accounting* put forward year-long, quarterly-repeated self-reform programs that focus on thirteen character traits. Each trait is given a week of close attention, and daily journaling—in a grid chart that has the seven days of the week running horizontally and the thirteen desired traits running vertically—is used

---

1. Israel Zinberg, *A History of Jewish Literature*, trans. and ed. Bernard Martin (New York: Ktav Publishing, 1975), vol. 6, 279.
2. The adherents of the Jewish Enlightenment, or Haskalah, were known as *maskilim* (singular: *maskil*). As described by Immanuel Etkes ("Haskalah," *The YIVO Encyclopedia of Jews in Eastern Europe*, yivoencyclopedia.org/article.aspx/Haskalah.): "The Jewish Enlightenment, or Haskalah, was an ideological and social movement that developed in Eastern Europe in the early nineteenth century and was active until the rise of the Jewish national movement in the early 1880s . . . Essentially, Haskalah sought to exploit the new possibilities of economic, social, and cultural integration that appeared to become available to Jews in the late eighteenth century with the removal of legal discrimination [against them]."
3. Lefin's surname has also been spelled or pronounced as Leffin, Leffins, Levi, Levin, Levine, Lewin, and Lapin.
4. Benjamin Franklin, *The Autobiography and Other Writings*, ed. Kenneth Silverman (New York: Penguin Books, 1986), 90-103.

to monitor growth and progress. After thirteen weeks the cycle is begun again, so that over the course of a year each trait can be carefully worked on for four weeks.[5] Franklin focused on temperance, silence, order, resolution, frugality, industry, sincerity, justice, moderation, cleanliness, tranquility, chastity, and humility. The traits outlined for improvement in both texts, though not identical, largely overlap, as does the emphasis on acquiring positive habits and overcoming undesirable ones gradually and systematically.

Temperance.							
Eat not to Dullness. *Drink not to Elevation.*							
	S	M	T	W	T	F	S
T							
S	**	*		*		*	
O	*	*	*		*	*	*
R			*			*	
F		*			*		
I		*					
S							
J							
M							
Cl.							
T							
Ch.							
H							

The form of Franklin's weekly chart in his *Autobiography*.

Franklin devised his moral-improvement method when he was in his twenties and had originally intended to compose a book elaborating on it. In the *Autobiography*, he laments that due to his many other concerns, this task was never accomplished: "I should have called my BOOK the ART *of Virtue* . . . But it so happened that my Intention of writing & publishing this Comment was never fulfilled . . . the necessary close Attention to private Business in the earlier part of Life, and public Business since, have occasioned my postponing it . . . [and] it has hitherto remain'd unfinish'd."[6]

5. Franklin, *Autobiography*, 91-95; Rabbi Mendel Lefin, *Sefer Heshbon Ha-nefesh* [Hebrew] (Jerusalem: Merkaz Ha-sefer, 1988), 32-36.
6. Franklin, *Autobiography*, 101-102.

Producing this book was integral to "a *great and extensive Project*"[7] Franklin had envisioned: the formation of an international secret fraternity and mutual-aid society, "the Society of the *Free and Easy*," whose initiates would profess a belief in a generic religious creed—so that people of all religions would be able to join[8]—and follow "the Thirteen Weeks Examination and Practice of the Virtues." Together, these men were to comprise a "united Party for Virtue":[9]

> My Ideas at that time were, that the Sect should be begun & spread at first among young and single Men only . . . that the existence of such a Society should be kept a Secret till it was to become considerable, to prevent Solicitations for the Admission of improper Persons . . . [and t]hat the Members should engage to afford their Advice Assistance and Support to each other in promoting one another's Interest, Business and Advancement in Life.[10]

As Norman Fiering notes in "Benjamin Franklin and the Way to Virtue" (1978), Franklin's party for virtue easily calls the Masonic fraternity to mind: "One thinks of a quasi-religious society, like the Freemasons, perhaps—of which Franklin was a member—as the basis for this idea."[11] Franklin's vigorous participation in the Masonic fraternity, which he joined after coming up with his party for virtue plan, may also have been a factor in the project's prolonged postponement, since the existing fraternity already satisfied some of the same functions as the new society he had hoped to form. According to Franklin biographer Gordon Wood, Franklin "discovered just the organization he was looking for" in Freemasonry and had no pressing need to create a new one of his own:[12]

> Freemasonry more than fulfilled Franklin's Enlightenment dreams of establishing a party for virtue, and he became an enthusiastic and hard-working member of the fraternity . . . Eventually he became the grand master of all the lodges in the colony of Pennsylvania. No organization could have been more congenial to Franklin, and al-

---

7. Franklin, *Autobiography*, 101.

8. Franklin explains that the creed he composed for the intended members of "the Society of the *Free and Easy*," which he reproduces in the *Autobiography*, is one "containing as I thought the Essentials of every known Religion, and being free of every thing that might shock the Professors of any Religion" (*Autobiography*, 104).

9. Franklin, *Autobiography*, 104-105.

10. Franklin, *Autobiography*, 105.

11. Norman S. Fiering, "Benjamin Franklin and the Way to Virtue," *American Quarterly* 30 (1978): 223, note 63.

12. Gordon S. Wood, *The Americanization of Benjamin Franklin* (New York: Penguin Press, 2004), 43.

though he seldom mentioned the organization in his correspondence, he remained a Mason throughout his life. Not only was Masonry dedicated to the promotion of virtue throughout the world, but this Enlightenment fraternity gave Franklin contacts that helped him in his business.[13]

Whether Freemasonry initially inspired his vision of a party for virtue, as Fiering suggests it may have, or whether his Masonic involvement ultimately hindered the party's formation, as Wood implies—both may be correct—in the end Franklin neither completed his book nor created his party. In the *Autobiography* he reconciles himself to the fact that he is unlikely to carry out his plan at his now more advanced age: "my multifarious Occupations public & private induc'd me to continue postponing, so that it has been omitted till I have no longer Strength or Activity left sufficient for such an Enterprise."[14]

Nearly twenty years after Franklin's death and half way across the world from Philadelphia, Rabbi Lefin of Satanow published his own book based on the *Autobiography*'s self-improvement method. However, instead of this being a broad work to be used by the "Virtuous and good Men of all Nations,"[15] whom Franklin had envisioned as the members of his party for virtue, Lefin's *Spiritual Accounting* was written for the religious and moral edification of his fellow Jews.[16] As a *maskil*—a Jewish enlightener and a supporter of the Haskalah movement—Lefin "saw European governments and/or non-Jewish thinkers as having a positive role or potentially positive influence on the Jewish people."[17] He seized the opportunity to reset Franklin's self-improvement method within the framework of a Jewish religious tract in Hebrew.

Lefin's work received the approbation of prominent rabbis, was embraced by Judaism's Mussar movement,[18] and continues to be studied

---

13. Wood, *Americanization of Benjamin Franklin*, 44.

14. Franklin, *Autobiography*, 105.

15. Franklin, *Autobiography*, 104.

16. Nancy Sinkoff, "Benjamin Franklin in Jewish Eastern Europe: Cultural Appropriation in the Age of the Enlightenment," *Journal of the History of Ideas* 61 (2000): 142.

17. Shimon S., "What's a 'maskil'?," *On the Main Line*, September 3, 2009. onthemainline.blogspot.com/2009/09/whats-maskil.html.

18. Rabbi Bernie Fox offers a useful and concise definition of *mussar* (Jewish ethical teachings) and the movement surrounding its instruction: "At a basic level, mussar is study directed towards motivating the student to conduct himself in everyday life in a manner consistent with the Torah [i.e., the Five Books of Moses, and by extension, the Jewish religion that is based upon them]. In other words, mussar responds to a specific problem. Knowing how to behave does not necessarily translate into proper behavior ... Mussar is designed to address this issue." ("Parshat Korach: What Could Be Wrong With Mussar?," ou.org/torah/parsha/rabbi-fox-on-parsha/parshat_korach_2/.)

and put to practical use. As such, Franklin may well be said to have had an impact on Jewish thought and practice by way of his *Autobiography*.

רמ״ם	א	ב	ג	ד	ה	ו	ז
מנוחת							
סבלנות							
סדר							
חריצות							
נקיות							
ענוה							
צדק							
קמוץ							
זריזות							
שתיקה							
ניחותא							
אמת							
פרישות							

The form of Lefin's chart in *Spiritual Accounting*.

However, given *Spiritual Accounting*'s relative obscurity in comparison to Franklin's widely popular *Autobiography*, it is not surprising that many of Franklin's admirers, as well as many students of Judaism, remain unaware that in addition to being an author, editor, inventor, natural philosopher, scientist, Grand Master, businessman, musical-innovator, abolitionist, diplomat, statesman, and American founding father, Franklin also managed to posthumously impact Jewish religious thought and practice.

Nonetheless, rabbis and Jewish scholars have noted the connection between Franklin and *Spiritual Accounting*, often commenting approvingly on its source and content. In a Hebrew letter written to a colleague in 1815, for instance, the prominent *maskil* Jacob Samuel Bick described the self-improvement method of *Spiritual Accounting* as

> a wonderful technique invented by the sage Benjamin Franklin from the city of Philadelphia in North America. This scholar is renowned in all corners of the earth . . . Thus Rabbi Mendel [Lefin] has prepared a delicacy for his nation . . . and taught a simple and clear solution for the broken but still precious soul to speedily return from the bad to the good. In their approbation, the rabbis of the generation said that this thing is beneficial and new. And the nation replied in turn: Sanctified! Sanctified![19]

19. Jacob Samuel Bick, "Letter 28," in *Sefer Kerem Hemed* [Hebrew], ed. S. Y. L. Goldenberg (Avien: Anton Schmid Buchdrucker und Buchhandler, 1833), vol. 1, 97.

Another early example of such recognition is found in Rabbi Meir Halevi Letteris's 1863 Hebrew biography of Rabbi Nahman Krochmal,[20] a disciple of Lefin. Letteris mentions "the famous, illustrious sage, our teacher and rabbi, Menahem Mendel Levin," and provides a lengthy footnote listing and describing some of his works, including *Spiritual Accounting*: "The book *Heshbon Ha-nefesh* teaches *mussar* and good conduct according to the way of the English sage Mister Franklin, whose approach [Lefin] often embraced in his manner of inquiry and acquisition of wisdom."[21]

Still, while the fact of Franklin's influence on Lefin has been known among rabbis and Jewish scholars, there has been much confusion about which of Franklin's texts Lefin utilized, and about whether Lefin had translated that text, adapted it, or more loosely based his book on its self-improvement method. For example, in his five-volume Hebrew history of the Mussar movement, *Tenuat Ha-mussar* (first published in 1945), Rabbi Dov Katz mentions *Spiritual Accounting* and then adds in a footnote: "By the way, it must be noted that the book 'Heshbon Ha-nefesh' was written according to the gentile scholar Benjamin Franklin's book for perfecting character traits."[22] As we have seen, however, despite his intention to do so, no such book by Franklin was ever written.

Much of the misunderstanding and uncertainty that has persisted in this matter has been the result of Lefin's decision not to include Franklin's name or to mention the *Autobiography* within *Spiritual Accounting*. Lefin did not claim that the moral technique presented in *Spiritual Accounting* was his own invention, and actually informed his readers that the method preceded him and originated elsewhere, but he did not cite its source:

> Indeed, a few years ago a new technique was discovered, which is a wonderful innovation in this task [of overcoming one's animal nature], and it seems its mark will spread as quickly, God willing, as that of the innovation of the printing press, which has brought its light to the world.[23]

This raises the question of why, having already acknowledged that the "new technique" and "wonderful innovation" was not his own, Lefin did not simply mention Franklin or the *Autobiography*. With a particu-

20. See Meir Halevi Letteris, "Toledot Nahman Hacohen Krochmal," a biography published as an introduction to the posthumous second edition of Nahman Hacohen Krochmal's *Moreh Nevuche Ha-zeman* [Hebrew] (Lemberg: 1863), 11-29.
21. Letteris, "Toledot Nahman Hacohen Krochmal," 13, note 2.22. Dov Katz, *Tenuat Ha-mussar: Toledoteha, Isheha, Ve-shitoteha* [Hebrew] (Tel-Aviv: Betan Ha-sefer, 1952), 282, note 15.
23. Lefin, *Heshbon Ha-nefesh*, 31.

larly traditional Jewish readership in mind, Lefin appears to have settled on a compromise in *Spiritual Accounting*. He never inaccurately implies that the book's method is of Jewish origin, and also steers clear of plagiarism by affirming that he is not the discoverer of the method, but he does not cite Franklin or the *Autobiography* as its source, and thereby avoids possibly alienating or perplexing some of his intended audience. If this was his motivation, he may have felt confident that the enlightened portion of his readers would be able to recognize the method as Franklin's even without explicit mention of his name. The rest, for their part, could remain happily unaware of its precise source.

One of the most fascinating and important records of the *Autobiography*'s influence on Lefin's thought is found in a serialized biographical essay on him written by Israel Weinlos, which appeared in installments in the World Zionist Organization's weekly Hebrew newspaper, *Haolam* (*The World*), during 1925. In the course of this biography, Weinlos describes his discovery of two unpublished and forgotten copies of a German work by Lefin:

> This book *Nachlass eines Sonderlings zu Abdera* (The Estate of a Loner from Abdera) includes R[abbi] Mendel Lefin's views on life and the world, and is the fruit of his examination and study of philosophy and the sciences. But he was unable to publish it and it remains stored until this day in Joseph Perl's[24] library in Tarnopol, which is where I found it among his other stored writings.[25]

According to Weinlos, this book represents the author's life work: Lefin labored on it over the course of twenty-nine years, completing two editions. (The first was completed in 1806, followed by a corrected edition in 1823.) Weinlos transcribes the table of contents of this previously unknown work, which includes this section: "Sittenverbesserungskunst, oder Kunst die menschliche Animalitaet nach der franklinischen vierteljaehrlich wiederkehrender Uebungsmethode abzurichten"—"Art of moral improvement, or the art of adjusting human animalness according to Franklin's cyclical, quarterly-scheduled method of practice." In addition, Weinlos transcribes part of a German letter written by Lefin, in which the rabbi lists his published works, including his Hebrew book of "Franklin's art of character improvement," i.e., *Heshbon Ha-nefesh*.[26] Thus, since the 1920s, evidence that Lefin himself gave Franklin credit has been publically available.

24. Perl was a disciple of Lefin.
25. Israel Weinlos, "R. Mendel Lefin" [Hebrew], *Haolam* 13 (1925): 800.
26. Weinlos, "R. Mendel Lefin," 819.

Nonetheless, subsequent editions of *Spiritual Accounting* still make no mention at all of Franklin. The 1995 Feldheim Hebrew-English edition[27] is not only silent about Franklin's influence, but its back cover offers a rather misleading depiction of *Spiritual Accounting*'s character-improvement method, suggesting—contrary to Lefin's own words in the book, which acknowledge that the method preceded him—that it is unique to *Spiritual Accounting*, was formulated by Lefin, and was designed specifically for Jews:

> CHESHBON HA-NEFESH, first published in Lemberg in 1812, presents a unique system for self-improvement and the development of positive character traits. Employing sophisticated psychological techniques and charts to monitor one's progress, this method was designed specifically for *bnei Torah* [i.e., those engaged in the study of Torah] and is as applicable today as it was when it was first formulated, nearly 200 years ago.

That and other editions of *Spiritual Accounting* also contain very little biographical information on Lefin, who has ceased to be a widely known rabbinic figure. Today, even those Orthodox *yeshiva* students and learned laymen who have heard of *Heshbon Ha-nefesh*, and possibly studied portions of it, are not certain to recognize its author's name, let alone be familiar with details of his life and the sources of his writings. To a different degree, this trend can also be seen in Ira F. Stone's *A Responsible Life: The Spiritual Path of Mussar* (2007) and Alan Morinis's *Everyday Holiness: The Jewish Spiritual Path of Mussar* (2007), neither of which cites the connection between Franklin and Lefin. Responding to a review of these books in *The Forward*,[28] Nancy Sinkoff tries to call attention to such lacunae, emphasizing the fact that one of the *mussar* methods described in *Everyday Holiness* originated in Franklin's writing:

> Detailed explicitly—with a chart!—in Franklin's French Memoirs, this guide to individual moral self-improvement found its way to Jewish Eastern Europe via an enlightened Polish aristocrat and freemason, Adam Kazimierz Czartoryski, who financially supported a Jewish enlightener (*maskil*), Mendel Lefin of Satanow, in his efforts to reform traditional Jewish society. . . . To this day, [Rabbi Israel] Salanter's reprinting of Lefin's book has found a home among tradi-

---

27. Mendel of Satanov, *Cheshbon ha-Nefesh*, eds. Dovid Landesman and Shraga Silverstein (Jerusalem: Feldheim, 1995).
28. Jay Michaelson, "The Path of the Just: Is Mussar the 'New Kabbalah'?," *The Forward*, March 7, 2008. forward.com/articles/12792/.

tionalist Jewish circles . . . Work on Franklin, Lefin, and Salanter is readily available in English, Yiddish, and Hebrew.[29]

Sinkoff's response asserts that the conduit between Franklin's *Autobiography* and Lefin's book was a Freemason: Adam Kazimierz Czartoryski (1734-1823). Elsewhere, she addresses this Masonic role in greater detail, describing Czartoryski as "the connective tissue between the American and the East European Jew."[30] Not only did Czartoryski hire Lefin to tutor his sons, but he later assisted Lefin in publishing his books:[31]

> While Mendel Lefin may have encountered Benjamin Franklin's writings when he was still in Berlin, Czartoryski's esteem for the American natural philosopher no doubt sealed Lefin's interest . . . Czartoryski knew Franklin personally; both men were freemasons, belonging to the Parisian Lodge, "Les Neuf Soeurs," which, established in 1776, elected Franklin as "Venerable" in 1781.[32]

Fiering argues in "Benjamin Franklin and the Way to Virtue" that when it comes to his self-improvement method, Franklin should not be given too much credit for originality, nor should the method be situated too specifically within the context of the American Enlightenment:

> Franklin's method, insofar as it was a system for achieving perfection through reiterated small acts, was part of a general enthusiasm at the time for applying a technique of great antiquity [i.e., the ancient idea of acquiring virtue through habit] that had only recently come into its own. It is tempting to believe that conditions in Franklin's America were peculiarly conducive to practicality and meliorism, but the trend was much grander than any mere American phenomenon. Franklin's thinking was simply representative of developments found elsewhere at the same time, particularly among the British associationists.[33]

Fiering grants that Franklin may have been innovative in having his "ethical program . . . break down the virtues into relatively small units

29. Sinkoff, "Benjamin Franklin and the Virtues of Mussar," *The Seforim Blog*, March 25, 2008, seforim.blogspot.com/2008/03/nancy-sinkoff-benjamin-franklin-and.html. *The Forward* did not publish Sinkoff's response to the review, but see my short online article "Benjamin Franklin, Mussar Maven," *The Forward*, January 17, 2011, forward.com/opinion/134721/benjamin-franklin-mussar-maven.
30. Sinkoff, "Benjamin Franklin in Jewish Eastern Europe," 136.
31. Sinkoff, "Benjamin Franklin in Jewish Eastern Europe," 138.32. Sinkoff, "Benjamin Franklin in Jewish Eastern Europe," 140.
33. Fiering, "Benjamin Franklin and the Way to Virtue," 213.

of behavior."[34] This aspect of Franklin's method was certainly significant to Lefin, as it turned the daunting task of self-transformation into a more manageable, step by step process. Sinkoff observes that Lefin was drawn to Franklin's method for the very reason that Franklin had originally been compelled to devise it himself. Both the American philosopher and the Eastern European rabbi had "come to the conclusion that a practical program of behavior modification was necessary to effect individual change . . . [and] that self-improvement required a structured plan of behavior modification."[35]

Explaining why he had thought up his program, Franklin writes: "I concluded at length, that the mere speculative Conviction that it was in our Interest to be completely virtuous, was not sufficient to prevent our Slipping, and that the contrary Habits must be broken and good ones acquired and established, before we can have any Dependence on a steady uniform Rectitude of Conduct."[36] Finding that no practical method for breaking bad habits and inculcating better ones had been formulated to his satisfaction, Franklin developed his own. Likewise, explaining his decision to embrace Franklin's method, Lefin writes:

> [T]he educational work that we are dealing with here [in *Spiritual Accounting*] is very valuable, because it is necessary for every person . . . [but] the wise men of preceding generations bequeathed us exceedingly little concerning it . . . . So too with the wisdom of *mussar* itself . . . even though [the sages of blessed memory] were themselves tremendously righteous and pious . . . they only addressed the intellectual soul [in their instruction]; but where will we take advice for controlling our animal soul, and subordinating it to our direction?[37]

Lefin wished that the rabbis of the past had provided more detailed explanations of the practical methods they had used in refining themselves: "Would that those admonishing righteous ones of blessed memory, or at least their students who served them, had also left us the details of their life stories [i.e., their autobiographies or biographies], and made us wise to those wonderful techniques that they invented for themselves."[38] Whereas they hadn't done so, Franklin's *Autobiography* furnished just such an account, and Lefin believed that his method could benefit all who were interested in self-improvement.

However, Lefin modified Franklin's method as he saw fit. Because Franklin had envisioned his program as universally applicable and as

---

34. Fiering, "Benjamin Franklin and the Way to Virtue," 214.
35. Sinkoff, "Benjamin Franklin in Jewish Eastern Europe," 141.
36. Franklin, *Autobiography*, 91.
37. Lefin, *Heshbon Ha-nefesh*, 30-31.
38. Lefin, *Heshbon Ha-nefesh*, 31.

forming the basis of an international fraternity, he needed a set of traits that could be focused on by all its prospective members. Franklin compiled his fixed list of thirteen virtues deliberately, and arranged it cumulatively so that improved mastery of the first behavioral trait might make it easier to master the second, and so on, telling his readers: "And as the previous Acquisition of some might facilitate the Acquisition of certain others, I arrang'd them with that View as they stand above."[39] Lefin, on the other hand, had no such concerns. Disregarding these aspects of Franklin's program, Lefin instead urged his readers to select and focus on behavioral traits relevant to their own unique circumstances and personalities, rather than on the specific ones he outlined as examples.[40]

Although Lefin still instructed his readers to select thirteen traits— so that they wouldn't exhaust themselves by focusing too closely on a smaller number—the order of the traits could be shuffled as needed, and practitioners might dwell on a trait for more than one week of a thirteen-week cycle if they felt it required their special attention. Lefin also expected that as they mastered certain behaviors and became ready for new challenges, practitioners would amend the list of traits they focused on.[41] In general, *Spiritual Accounting* offered a more individualized and malleable method than the one Franklin had presented in his *Autobiography*.

David Morgan argues in "Benjamin Franklin: Champion of Generic Religion" that "no one to this very day is quite sure of Franklin's religious beliefs."[42] He surmises that "Franklin can best be described as a Deist, though with personally tailored modifications of the Deist creed."[43] His personal creed notwithstanding, "all religions were essentially the same"[44] to Franklin, who was "a proponent of all religions and sects."[45] Since he viewed any religion as potentially useful, he "treated all religions alike, making him in all probability the first American champion of generic religion."[46] This championing can be seen in the *Autobiography*, where Franklin explains his original intention to make his system for self-betterment (as well as the international fraternity whose members would adhere to it) universally accessible:

---

39. Franklin, *Autobiography*, 93.
40. Lefin, *Heshbon Ha-nefesh*, 36, 88, 123-124. 41. Lefin, *Heshbon Ha-nefesh*, 36.
42. David T. Morgan, "Benjamin Franklin: Champion of Generic Religion," *The Historian* 62 (2000): 723.
43. Morgan, "Benjamin Franklin," 728.
44. Morgan, "Benjamin Franklin," 728.
45. Morgan, "Benjamin Franklin," 729.
46. Morgan, "Benjamin Franklin," 723.

It will be remark'd that, tho' my Scheme was not wholly without Religion there was in it no Mark of any of the distinguishing Tenets of
any particular Sect. I had purposely avoided them; for being fully
persuaded of the Utility and Excellency of my Method, and that it
might be serviceable to People in all Religions, and intending some
time or other to publish it, I would not have any thing in it that
should prejudice any one of any Sect against it.[47]

Since Franklin took a generic religious approach for the moral
method outlined in the *Autobiography*, there were no philosophical or
religious obstacles preventing its development within a Jewish context.
Lefin was able to adapt Franklin's system, to expand upon it, and to
publish it as a book—something Franklin had intended to do, but never
carried out—for Jewish readers. *Spiritual Accounting* received the approbation of prominent rabbis, was embraced by the Mussar movement,
and became one of the many Hebrew texts studied in *yeshivot*, furthering Franklin's initial goal of making his system for self-examination and
character improvement "serviceable to People in all Religions."

The notion that Franklin was antisemitic first emerged some eighty
years ago, in 1934, with the publication of a fraudulent and since then
repeatedly discredited text commonly known as "Franklin's Prophecy."
On February 3, 1934 William Dudley Pelley, the occultist head of the
pro-Nazi Silver Legion of America and publisher of the fascist *The
Weekly Liberation*, ran an article in his paper ("Did Benjamin Franklin
say this about the Hebrews?") containing a supposed excerpt from the
previously unknown diary of Charles Coatesworth Pinckney, South
Carolina's delegate to the Constitutional Convention. As presented by
Pelley, "Charles Pinckney's Diary" contained the record of a diatribe
(or "prophecy") by Franklin against Jews during the Convention, including a description of Jews as "a great danger for the United States of
America" and as "vampires," as well as an admonition to have the Constitution bar and expel them from the country lest in the future they
change its form of government.[48] By August 1934 "Franklin's Prophecy"
had been published in Nazi Germany. Nazi leaders and sympathizers
helped disseminate the fraud in German, French, and English, and in
Germany, Switzerland, and the United States.[49]

---

47. Franklin, *Autobiography*, 100.
48. William Dudley Pelley, "Did Benjamin Franklin say this about the Hebrews?," *Liberation*, February 3, 1934, 5.
49. Charles A. Beard, *Charles A. Beard Exposes Anti-Semitic Forgery about Benjamin
Franklin (The Jewish Frontier Reprints No. 4)* (New York: The League for Labor Palestine,
1935), 3.

In September 1934 "Franklin's Prophecy" reached American historian Charles A. Beard, best known for his 1913 *An Economic Interpretation of the US Constitution.* Beard began a search for the source of "Franklin's Prophecy," in the process consulting with other scholars such as John Franklin Jameson, chief of the Manuscripts Divisions of the Library of Congress. Six months later (in March 1935) his conclusions were published in an essay in *The Jewish Frontier,* which then reprinted them as a pamphlet titled *Charles Beard Exposes Anti-Semitic Forgery about Benjamin Franklin.* Summing up the results of his investigations, Beard wrote:

> All these searches have produced negative results. I cannot find a single original source that gives the slightest justification for believing that the "Prophecy" is anything more than a bare-faced forgery. Not a word have I discovered in Franklin's letters and papers expressing any such sentiments against the Jews as ascribed to him by the Nazis—American and German. His well-known liberality in matters of religious opinions would, in fact, have precluded the kind of utterances put in his mouth by this palpable forgery.[50]

Henry Butler Allen, the director of the Franklin Institute in Philadelphia, also weighed in on the imaginariness of "Charles Pinckney's Diary," stating: "Historians and librarians have not been able to find it or any record of it having existed."[51] The responses of Beard, Allen, and several others were collected into the pamphlet *Benjamin Franklin Vindicated: An Exposure of the Franklin "Prophecy" by American Scholars,* issued jointly by the International Benjamin Franklin Society, the American Jewish Committee, the American Jewish Congress, and the Jewish Labor Committee in 1938.[52]

A more recent discussion of the emergence and debunking of "Franklin's Prophecy" may be found in Nian-Sheng Huang's *Benjamin Franklin in American Thought and Culture, 1790-1990.*[53] Huang shows

---

50. Beard, *Beard Exposes Anti-Semitic Forgery,* 8.

51. Henry Butler Allen, "Franklin and the Jews," in Beard et al., *Benjamin Franklin Vindicated: An Exposure of the Franklin "Prophecy" by American Scholars* (New York: American Jewish Congress, 1938), 10.

52. Jewish Telegraphic Agency, "7 Scholars Refute Franklin Anti-semitism Allegation," January 3, 1939. jta.org/1939/01/03/archive/7-scholars-refute-franklin-anti-semitism-allegation. As stated within the pamphlet, most of its material was reprinted from the November 1938 issue of the *Contemporary Jewish Record.*

53. Nian-Sheng Huang, *Benjamin Franklin in American Thought and Culture, 1790-1990* (American Philosophical Society, 1994), 174-180. See also Claude-Anne Lopez, "Prophet and Loss," *New Republic,* January 27, 1997, 29-31, and Lopez's chapter on "Franklin,

"Franklin's Prophecy" to be an extreme case of exploiting, vulgarizing, and distorting Franklin's image. The ease with which the "Prophecy" has spread and its staying power demonstrate how successful bigots world-wide have been in misappropriating the American founding father's good name and fame for their vile purposes. However, despite his famous liberality in matters of religious opinions, Franklin actually did on several occasions use anti-Jewish language in his letters.[54] Though this offensive language does not come near the vitriol Franklin is purported to have publicly uttered in the "Prophecy," Franklin, who also owned slaves and featured slaves for sale in his newspaper prior to becoming an abolitionist, was not always a man free of prejudice.

Nonetheless, Franklin did eventually become an anti-slavery activist. In 1788, he also gave money to Congregation Mikveh Israel, the oldest formal Jewish congregation in Philadelphia. This occurred during a time when the small congregation was overburdened with debt and had turned to its neighbors, "worthy fellow Citizens of every religious Denomination," for assistance. Among those stepping forward to help was Franklin, who gave five pounds, a donation very much in line with his attitude toward religion. As the editors of *The Papers of Benjamin Franklin* note, "the archives of Congregation Mikveh Israel in Philadelphia contain a subscription paper dated April 30, 1788, in which Franklin, together with forty-four other citizens of all faiths, contributed towards relieving the Congregation's debt incurred in building a synagogue. Franklin's donation and those of two others are the largest on the list."[55] It is not surprising that Franklin, with his encouragement of all religions and sects, and his interest in works that would be "serviceable to People in all Religions," would assist in alleviating Congregation Mikveh Israel's debt and ensuring a Jewish presence in Philadelphia.

Hitler, Mussolini, and the Internet" in her *My Life with Benjamin Franklin* (New Haven: Yale University Press, 2000), 3-16. Though Lopez does not reference Huang's work at all in "Prophet and Loss," it is mentioned in *My Life with Benjamin Franklin*.

54. For a discussion of two of these letters, see Lopez's "Prophet and Loss," 30, and *My Life with Benjamin Franklin*, 11-12.

55. *The Autobiography of Benjamin Franklin*, eds. L. W. Labaree, R. L. Ketcham, H. C. Boatfield, and H. H. Fineman (New Haven: Yale University, 2003), 147, note 1. See also "Our History," at the website of "Congregation Mikveh Israel: Synagogue of the American Revolution," mikvehisrael.org/e2_cms_display.php?p=past_our_history.

Anti-Indian Radicalization in the Early American West, 1774–1795

✵ DARREN R. REID ✵

Setting aside the question of whether or not the American Revolution was as radical as Gordon Wood famously argued that it was, at least two fundamental changes occurred west of the Appalachian Mountains in the last quarter of the eighteenth century that had little to do with the political revolution in the east.[1] Stephen Aron, in his study of the Kentucky frontier, touched upon one such revolutionary shift which, from the perspective of its participants, was significantly more radical in nature than those events concerning the thirteen colonies. The transformation of the Shawnee and Cherokee from long term enemies into staunch allies was, as Aron correctly highlighted, a seismic shift that turned relations in Indian country upon their head.[2] It completely changed the aboriginal map of the American interior, transforming Kentucky, once a buffer zone between those antagonistic tribes, into a symbol of cooperation and mutual support. It became the centre of a new

1. For a very brief overview of the interpretive dissonance concerning the revolution see Gordon S. Wood, *The Radicalism of the American Revolution* (New York: Random House, 1993); Bernard Bailyn, *The Ideological Origins of the American Revolution: Enlarged Edition* (Cambridge: Harvard University Press, 1992); Gary B. Nash, *The Unknown American Revolution: The Unruly Birth of Democracy and the Struggle to Create America* (New York: Penguin Books, 2005); John Ferling, *A Leap in the Dark: The Struggle to Create the American Republic* (Oxford: Oxford University Press, 2003); Staughton Lynd and David Waldstreicher, "Reflections on Economic Interpretation, Slavery, the People Put of Doors, and Top Down versus Bottom Up," *The William and Mary Quarterly*, Vol. 68 (2011): 649-656; Michael A. McDonnell, "Men Out of Time: Confronting History and Myth," *The William and Mary Quarterly*, Vol. 68 (2011): 644-648; and Alfred F. Young, *Liberty Tree: Ordinary People and the American Revolution* (New York: New York University Press, 2006), 215-261.
2. Stephen Aron, *How the West was Lost: The Transformation of Kentucky from Daniel Boone to Henry Clay* (Baltimore: Johns Hopkins Press, 1999), 37-38.

relationship which was built around a common identity that was defined in opposition to the European Americans who were increasingly encroaching upon their lands.[3] That was not, however, the limit of the fundamental changes which were occurring in the Trans-Appalachian country.

By resisting European American settlement as effectively and as determinedly as they did, the Shawnee, Cherokee, and their numerous allies set off a conceptual revolution among their enemies. Faced with one of the bloodiest and most prolonged frontier wars in North American history, European Americans in the Trans-Appalachian country discarded the nuance of past world views in order to adopt a hard, racialized construct of the region's Indian population. Prior to the 1770s, a meaningful middle ground, as Richard White paradigmatically put it, existed between European Americans and Native Americans.[4] The war for the Trans-Appalachian country, however, destroyed that theoretical space; middle ground became battle ground. Anti-Indian prejudices had certainly existed before the 1770s but events during and after that decade turned what had been a divisive and inconsistent philosophy into a widely held, deeply pejorative belief which appeared, to those cultures which developed in the west, to be a self-evident truth. Before the 1770s, there were cultures which accommodated Indian haters; after that period, however, there was, in the west, a culture which promoted and even demanded Indian hatred. To put that another way, and to borrow a theoretical framing device from Ira Berlin, there were cultures with Indian hatred and there were Indian hating cultures.[5] Whatever can be said about the American Revolution, the changes occurring between the Appalachian Mountains and the Mississippi River in the late eighteenth century were radical indeed.

3. For Kentucky as buffer between the Shawnee and Cherokee see James Mooney, "The Old Cherokee Country [Map]" and "The Cherokee and their Neighbours [Map]" in James Mooney, *Myths of the Cherokee: Extract from the Nineteenth Annual Report of the Bureau of American Ethnology* (Government Printing Office: Washington, 1902), 15, 23.
4. For theoretical spaces of interaction and cooperation between European and Native Americans see Richard White, *The Middle Ground: Indians, Empires, and Republics in the Great Lakes Region, 1650-1815* (Cambridge and New York: Cambridge University Press, 1991); Michael N. McConnell, *A Country Between: The Upper Ohio Valley and its Peoples, 1724-1774* (Lincoln and London: University of Nebraska Press, 1992); and James H. Merrell, *Into the American Woods: Negotiators on the Pennsylvania Frontier* (New York and London: W.W. Norton and Company, 1999).
5. Ira Berlin, *Many Thousands Gone: The First Two Centuries of Slavery in North America* (Cambridge and London: The Belknap Press of the Harvard University Press, 1998), 8-14.

The shift in world views that was occurring in the west was rooted in a crisis brought about by a clash of evolving ideas and a rapidly changing set of external circumstances. In the backcountry, European American views of the Indians had suffered during the Seven Years War, becoming increasingly negative as a result of that conflict.[6] From 1774 until 1795, however, European American inhabitants of the Trans-Appalachian country were confronted by two decades of almost unbroken, deeply violent, and intensely bitter conflict—their pre-existing negative bias, exposed to those conditions, was transformed into a negative certainty. Historians who have examined the re-framing of the Indians into a racial group have failed to settle upon a consensus as to when that event occurred, identifying eras as divergent as the late seventeenth and late eighteenth centuries as the moment of that transformation. Of these it is Patrick Griffin's argument, that the period of the American Revolution marked the greatest change, which bears the most weight.[7] Griffin identified that era as a type of theoretical "frontier"—following the Frederick Jackson Turner model—in American history, a watershed; but it was more than a national shift in anti-Indian consciousness.[8]

It was a turning point mired in the specific experience of the region in which it occurred. It was a conceptual revolution which marked a philosophical splintering of western and eastern world views that would not be reconciled until western anti-Indian views found national acceptance in the context of the Indian wars of the mid-late nineteenth century. In 1832 and 1833, Black Hawk, the leader of this period's eponymous war, would be celebrated as an ennobled sensation in the east; in the west, he would be antithetically burned in effigy.[9] The ide-

6. See Matthew C. Ward, *Breaking the Backcountry: The Seven Years War in Virginia and Pennsylvania, 1754-1767* (Pittsburgh: University of Pittsburgh Press, 2003), 3-4; and Stephen Brumwell, *White Devil: A True Story of War, Savagery, and Vengeance in Colonial America* (Cambridge: Da Capo Press, 2004); for a broader discussion of the Seven Years War as a key turning point in American history see Lawrence Henry Gipson, "The American Revolution as Aftermath of the Great War for the Empire, 1754-1763," *Political Science Quarterly*, Vol. 65 (1950): 86-104.

7. See Alder T. Vaughan, *The Roots of American Racism: Essays on the Colonial Experience* (Oxford and New York: Oxford University Press, 1995), 13-33; Jill Lepore, *The Name of War: King Philip's War and the Origins of American Identity* (New York: Vintage Books, 1999), 173-225; John Grenier, *First Way of War: American War Making on the Frontier* (Cambridge and New York: Cambridge University Press, 2005), 11-12; Jane T. Merritt, *At the Cross Roads: Indians and Empires, 1700-1763* (Chapel Hill and London: University of North Carolina Press, 2003), 285-295; and Patrick Griffin, *American Leviathan: Empire, Nation, and the Revolutionary Frontier* (New York: Hill and Wang, 2007), 12-14.

8. Griffin, *American Leviathan*, 15.

9. Kerry A. Trask, *Black Hawk: The Battle for the American Heart* (New York: Henry Holt and Company, 2007), 301-302.

ological break which was reflected in that contrast was rooted in the Trans-Appalachian country's anti-Indian revolution. Twenty years of psychological warfare, sieges, and wilderness domination failed to drive European Americans out of that country, but it did succeed in fundamentally souring western perspectives of the Indians and, as a result, drew a conceptual line down the spine of the Appalachians.[10] Unlike in the east, where writers such as James Fenimore Cooper could comfortably romanticise and ennoble the Indians, European Americans in the west experienced almost an entire generation of warfare and, as a result, came to self-identify as victims of the Indians; and it was through that lens that they constructed their particular understanding of the peoples against whom they were fighting.[11]

Since the first regular settlement was founded in Kentucky in 1775, warfare with a spectrum of tribes, including the Shawnee, Cherokee, Mingo, Miami, Wyandot, and Delaware had been a constant and defining feature of the region. By 1783 approximately seven percent of Kentucky's population had been killed in combat with Native Americans; to put that number into perspective, the thirteen rebelling colonies had lost just one percent of their population during the Revolutionary War.[12] Such a high casualty rate hints at the broad impact violence had upon the region and, in particular, the ordeal faced by those who survived. Bodies—and there were many—were routinely mutilated; women and men had watched as their spouses were brought down by tomahawk and musket ball; and entire communities were besieged and assaulted, enduring, as a collective, military actions designed to drive them back east; and for those not directly involved, a vibrant and long lived oral culture ensured that they were exposed to many of the macabre details. Therein lay the root of the western revolution in anti-Indian thought. Bodies, real and imagined, the latter just as potent as the former, piled up on the frontier and, as a result, world views shifted in order to ac-

10. Griffin identifies the era of the American Revolution as a turning point but that period is too restrictive. The total duration of the war during this period, which extended long past the conclusion of the Revolutionary War, must be accounted in any analysis of this period. The continuation of the war for the Trans-Appalachian country beyond 1782 allowed the region to be exposed to the violence of wilderness warfare for another thirteen years, a period which, even considered in isolation, eclipsed the exposure of the Seven Years War in terms of its capacity to spread the experience of warfare and underline any sense of self-identified victimisation. Griffin, *American Leviathan*, 15.

11. For an example romanticised literary Indians in the east see James Fenimore Cooper, *The Last of the Mohicans: A Narrative of 1757* (New York: W.A. Townshead & Company, 1859).

12. John Mack Faragher, *Daniel Boone: The Life and Legend of an American Pioneer* (New York: Henry Holt and Company, 1992), 144.

commodate that reality. When Simon Kenton narrowly escaped being burned alive, he reflected the potential of past violence to change future expectations and aspirations: "I felt determined to avenge myself of the wrongs that had been inflicted on me. I joined myself to the garrison and went with almost every expedition that was sent out [against the Indians]. . . whenever there was a party going out, I was ready to go with them."[13] Through prolonged exposure to one of the bloodiest frontier wars in US history, anti-Indian thought and action was thoroughly normalised; moderation gave way to radicalisation.

Violence during this period was more than an incidental detail. It was a process, an experience, the importance of which was captured in the surviving record of the region's fundamental oral culture. Through recorded oral testimony, that which gave a voice to those typically denied a detailed or meaningful presence in the historic record, memories of horror and revulsion were captured and revealed to be common, a key part of the Trans-Appalachian experience.[14] When the recorded oral collection of Presbyterian minister John Shane is analysed, it demonstrates an almost overwhelming obsession with the memory of the war. In spite of Shane's attempt to record a tradition which would have served as the basis for a history of the Presbyterian Church in Kentucky and Southern Ohio, he found that virtually all of those with whom he spoke dwelt disproportionately upon the conflict with the Indians.[15] The unguided nature of the accounts which Shane recorded gave his subjects freedom, but almost all roads seemed to lead back to the Indians and their means of making war. In the resultant collection, which comprised more than three hundred separate interviews, seventy-five percent of all the individuals mentioned were actively engaged in, or victims of, the war.[16] When Shane spoke with an early settler

13. Jonathan Alder and Larry L. Nelson, ed., *A History of Jonathan Alder: His Captivity and Life with the Indians* (Arkon: University of Arkon Press, 2002), 174-175.

14. For a discussion on the critical opportunities and limits of the Shane collection see Elizabeth A. Perkins, *Border Life: Experience and Memory in the Revolutionary Ohio Valley* (Chapel Hill: University of North Carolina Press, 1998), 7-39.

15. For Shane's oral record as the basis of an attempt to write a history of Presbyterianism in Kentucky and southern Ohio see Perkins, *Border Life*, 9 and Unknown Author, "Early Indiana Presbyterianism excerpt [excerpt—pages removed from original source]," John D. Shane Papers 63M289, University of Kentucky Archives.

16. A survey of Shane's interviews was turned into a database of 11,179 individual European American settlers. Not included were individuals who fell out with the date (1774-1795) or geographic (Kentucky, western Virginia, and southern Ohio) ranges of this survey. Of the 11,179 records created, 6,148 (fifty-five percent) were classified as being directly involved in combat through participation in a confrontation with the Indians, suffering an attack, experiencing a siege, or being reported as dead, etc. A further

named John Wilson, for instance, he gained no insight into the evolution of the church, but obtained instead a potent glimpse into the human cost of the fighting. Recalling the day when the body of one of his fellows, recently killed by the Indians, was returned to his wife, Wilson reported to Shane that the newly widowed woman had "examine[d] all the wounds of her husband . . . very carefully, fondly, at first without a tear [and] the[n] suddenly gave way to her grief."[17] In another account, Shane was vicariously exposed to Sally Wilcox's terror on the day she had witnessed the pursuit of her husband by a band of Indian raiders: "Run, Daniel, Run!'" she had "hallooed to him as hard as she could."[18] In another such account, Shane was again exposed by proxy to the emotional turmoil caused by spouses who disappeared. When John Hayden apparently vanished, Shane was told that his wife "looked like she would go distracted" from worry.[19]

In another of Shane's recollections, typical in its candour and its subject matter, his interviewee, William Niblick, described the day he, as a child, had witnessed the recovery of John Wymore's body—sans scalp—from the wilderness. "[I was] hanging on to my mother's apron and heard the women crying . . . I saw them bring Wymore in [on] a sheet that was all bloody; he [had been left by the Indians] hanging on a pole."[20] When George Fearis spoke about the early settlement of the country, memories of horror and distress were not far away. One of the incidents he described concerned the day he and a friend "saw the hog at something." Investigating the odd sight, Fearis's companion discovered that the pig had in fact been feasting upon the remains of one of his recently scalped children. According to Fearis, the child's father "gathered what of it he could, and took it along and buried it."[21] Such incidents made deep impressions. When Shane interviewed Mr. Spence, a comparative latecomer to the Kentucky country who arrived in the 1790s, his short account of his brother's death contained several telling details. Though the incident was, in the broader context of the war, fairly unremarkable—his brother stepped out of his house and was

2,236 (twenty percent) were described as joining an anti-Indian militia parties but werenot recorded as engaging the Indians directly. Database compiled from John D. Shane 'Interviews' located in the Draper Manuscripts 11CC, 12CC, 13CC, 16CC, 17CC.
17. John D. Shane, "Interview with Captain John Wilson," Draper Manuscripts 17CC6-25.
18. John D. Shane, "Interview with an Unnamed Subject," Draper Manuscripts 11CC177.
19. John D. Shane, "Interview with a Unnamed Person in Cincinnati," Draper Manuscripts 11CC279-283.
20. John D. Shane, "Interview with William Niblick," Draper Manuscripts 11CC84-85.
21. John D. Shane, "Interview with George Fearis," Draper Manuscripts 13CC238-244.

shot—to Spence it was worthy of deep and long lasting investigation and reflection. Because of the tracks discovered near his brother's home, Spence had deduced that three Indians had been involved in his death, one of whom had "stood off at a distance and held a horse;" according to Spence, such an animal had been stolen "from a young man about 2 miles in," suggesting that his brother's death was one part in a longer chain of events. The actual death had been, according to Spence's investigation, a sudden and close range affair: "He was not more than 10 steps from the Indians when they shot him." To underline the episode's personal importance, he then added that "I have measured it many a time."[22] The recorded oral testimony of the region reflected the visceral nature of the war, the ways in which it intersected with daily life and routine, and the depth of the memories it helped to forge as well as causative links between experiences of violence and later actions and attitudes.

When, in 1777, Hugh McGary had found the Indian who had killed his stepson, he was moved not only to take the life of the perpetrator but to carry out a morbid form of post-mortem retribution. Rather than scalping the Indian, or committing some other act of hasty mutilation, McGary had instead set about the lengthy and gory task of butchering, slicing, dicing, and ultimately feeding the body to the dogs at the township in which he lived.[23] When John Wymore was killed, the men of his settlement had set out in pursuit of his killer; they had found an Indian, upon whom they presumed guilt, severed his head, and "cut up" the remains "for the dogs."[24] In 1782 a band of European Americans, from a settlement which had recently survived an Indian attack, discovered two Indian bodies in the nearby wilderness. With the first body sunk to the bottom of a pond, and thus inaccessible, they instead turned upon the second, a young man around "17 or 18" years of age they discovered in a thicket, wrapped carefully in a blanket. The body, which they brought back to their settlement, elicited sympathy from many of the town's women who commented upon its "fine [and] tender hands and feet." Many of them then "begged that he might be buried" but, unmoved, the men of the township laid the corpse out in a public space where it "made a greater smell than a hundred horses" as it was graphically consumed by the town's livestock. As one of the settlement's inhabitants would later recall, "I saw my sow in his belly more than a

22. John D. Shane, "Interview with ——— Spence," Draper Manuscripts 13CC198-199.
23. John D. Shane, "Interview with Jacob Stevens," Draper Manuscripts 12CC135.
24. John D. Shane, "Interview with —— Wymore," Draper Manuscripts 11CC128-132.

dozen times."[25] Sympathy was not alien on the increasingly violent frontier, but it was overpowered by those who were determined to extract revenge, symbolic or otherwise, from their enemy.

The experience of war changed people. In 1783, for example, the Davis family of Fisher's Station was attacked by an Indian raiding party who killed the family patriarch and kidnapped the four children present. Mrs. Davis, who had "gone out in the night to bring in some clothes" was, by virtue of her location, saved from either death or captivity but, from her vantage point, witnessed the death of her husband. Davis was, at that moment, caught by indecision, pressured between her desire to go to her family and her fear that a similar fate to her husband's awaited her. According to one of her acquaintances, "There she stood in agony, saying 'I must go in,' and then her heart would fail her, and she would turn back, and then go again." The pressure and distress of that moment was not soon in passing: "After this tragedy her countenance put on a change, and she got all her sleep alone in the daytime. She would be up and walk the room all night."[26] Peter Silver has argued that the Indians of this period were perceived to have acted in a "terroristic" manner, fostering a sense of fear that preceded and, in some cases, negated the need for their actual presence.[27] Certainly, they were effective at spreading anxiety, and not always through the direct use of violence. On one occasion they "came along and stole all of John Smith's bed clothes" and, on another, "threw a couple of frogs" into an unattended pan of boiling sugar, subtle acts of psychological warfare that told their intended victims they were, at all times, in danger.[28] Fear was a weapon that the Indians wielded expertly; when Tom Berry's family received word that an Indian raiding party *might* be in the vicinity, they reportedly "began to cry as if the Indians were at the door."[29] In spite of the panic they instilled, however, the Indians were unable to shift, through threat or terror, those who had come to claim their country. By delib-

---

25. John D. Shane, "Interview with Mrs. Arnold," Draper Manuscripts 11CC241-245.
26. John D. Shane, "Interview with Sarah Graham," Draper Manuscripts 12CC45-53.
27. Peter Silver, *Our Savage Neighbours: How Indian War Transformed Early America* (New York: W.W. Norton and Company, 2008), 41-42.
28. John D. Shane, "Interview with Benjamin Stites," Draper Manuscripts 13CC56-57. For a broader discussion on the role played by psychological warfare in this conflict see Darren R. Reid, "Soldiers of Settlement: Violence and Psychological Warfare on the Kentucky Frontier, 1775-1783," *Eras*, Vol. 10 (2008): arts.monash.edu.au/publications/eras/edition-10/reid-article.pdf.
29. John D. Shane, "Interview with Nathaniel Hart," Draper Manuscripts 17CC209-213.
30. For fear as a reason to leave the west see "Journal of William Calk, 1775," Calk Family Collection 2005M14, Box 7, Folder 96, Kentucky Historical Society; and John D. Shane, "Interview with Benjamin Allen," Draper Manuscripts 11CC67-69.

erately using non-direct violence, or psychological tactics, the Indians had theoretically reduced the need to use direct (physical) violence but their imaginary sword was double edged. It did inspire some European Americans to abandon the west, but the allure of apparently free land was strong and many of their victims stayed regardless, responding to threat, fear, and suffering through other means.[30]

By the 1780s, anti-Indian sentiment in the west was, generally, serving to unite rather than divide communities. In 1764 the march of the Paxton Boys, a vigilante group determined to avenge themselves on the local—peaceful—Indian community, had highlighted how divisive anti-Indian radicalism could be, even in the aftermath of the Seven Years War. In spite of their willingness to tar all Indians with the same proverbial brush, they encountered a not insignificant amount of resistance from many of their peers.[31] That was not the case in 1780 when, in the wake of a successful incursion by a multi-tribal Indian force, between eight hundred and one thousand Kentuckians, approximately eighty percent of the adult male population of the country, gathered to march upon the northern tribes. Even those who had remained behind had done so with an air of martial responsibility, to "protect the settlements," whilst those unable to take part directly in the operation—women and children—also played a role as they "scraped up corn . . . and made bread" and prepared other necessary provisions.[32] Prior to 1780, the community of early Kentucky had been united in defence, enduring numerous sieges and assaults during the country's first half-decade of European American settlement but, by the turn of the next decade, their unity was such that they were now willing to proactively seek, though not necessarily accomplish, a reckoning.[33] Following five years of con-

31. For examples of works dealing with the Paxton Boys see Kevin Kenny, *Peaceable Kingdom Lost: The Paxton Boys and the Destruction of William Penn's Holy Experiment* (Oxford and New York: Oxford University Press, 2009); James Kirby Martin, "The Return of the Paxton Boys and the Historical State of the Pennsylvania Frontier," *Pennsylvania History*, Vol. 38 (1971): 117-133; and Brooke Hindle, "The March of the Paxton Boys," *The William and Mary Quarterly*, Vol. 3 (1946): 462-486.

32. John D. Shane, "Interview with Ephriam Sandusky," Draper Manuscripts 11CC141-145; and John Bradford, "Notes on Kentucky," in Thomas D. Clark, ed., *The Voice of the Frontier: John Bradford's Notes on Kentucky* (Lexington: University Press of Kentucky, 1993), 37. See also William Hayden English, *Conquest of the Country Northwest of the River Ohio, 1778-1783 and Life of General George Rogers Clark* (Indianapolis: The Bowell-Merrill Company, 1896), 2:697-733; and Lowell Hayes Harrison, *George Rogers Clark and the War in the West* (1976; reprint, Lexington: University of Kentucky Press, 2001), 69-76.

33. The principle exception to the rule of defensive collection action in Kentucky prior to 1780 was George R. Clark's march against the British in Illinois, but the fear of Indian

tinuous raids and assaults, retribution, the death of Indians, was, by 1780, seen as their "only hope."[34] In 1782, following a second successful mass strike by the northern tribes, one thousand Kentuckians again gathered to make war upon the Indians whilst, in 1786, following another four years of conflict and violent intercourse, another comparable campaign was launched.[35] On that latter expedition Hugh McGary, the same who had diced up the body of his step-son's killer and fed the remains to his dogs, murdered an elderly Shawnee chief who had surrendered peacefully to the invaders, burying a tomahawk in his head as he cried "d— n you, I'll show you Blue Licks play."[36] The "Blue Licks" in question was the site of a disastrous defeat the Kentuckians had suffered four years earlier. As there was no credible reason for McGary to suspect that the elderly man before him had had anything to do with the defeat at the Blue Licks (he had not), it seems that McGary's desire to extract revenge by killing practically any Indian had diminished not at all over the course of almost half a decade.[37]

Faced with military defeats, ongoing assaults, and the mutilated remains of those they held dear, European Americans responded to the war by dehumanising and homogenising their enemy. In 1782, when colonel William Crawford was executed in retaliation for the Gnadenhutten massacre—in which over ninety pacifist Indians were systematically butchered at a Moravian mission town—Hugh Henry Brackenridge quickly arranged for the publication of two captivity narratives which described, in lurid detail, the failed expedition that had led to Crawford's death.[38] One of those accounts, by Dr. John Knight, provided a particularly grim and macabre description of Crawford's tor-

raids served to limit participation in that campaign rather than encourage it. European American settlers were unwilling to march north when, so doing, they would leave their homes vulnerable to further raids. For Clark's march on Illinois see "Letter from George R. Clark to Colonel George Mason, November 19th, 1779," Microfilm B/C 593m, Filson Historical Society, 1-6; and John D. Shane, "Interview with Josiah Collins," Draper Manuscripts 12CC68.

34. Bradford, "Notes on Kentucky," 37.

35. John D. Shane, "Interview with Isaac Clinkenbeard," Draper Manuscripts 11CC3; and Larry L. Nelson, *A Man of Distinction Among Them: Alexander McKee and the Ohio Country Frontier, 1754-1799* (Kent: Kent State University Press, 1999), 127.

36. John D. Shane, "Interview with Isaac Clinkenbeard," Draper Manuscripts 11CC3.

37. For a broader discussion on McGary's actions see Faragher, *Daniel Boone*, 254.

38. For Gnadenhutten see Harper, "Looking the Other Way: The Gnadenhutten Massacre and the Contextual Interpretation of Violence," 621-643; and Leonard Sadosky, "Rethinking the Gnadenhutten Massacre: The Contest for Power in the Public World of the Revolutionary Pennsylvania Frontier" in David Curtis Skaggs and Larry L. Nelson, eds., *The Sixty Years War for the Great Lakes, 1754-1814* (East Lansing: University of Michigan Press, 2001); for the Brackenridge's publication see R.W.G Vail, *Voice of the Old Frontier* (1949, reprint; New York: Octagon Books, 1970), 44.

ture and eventual execution, dwelling upon the colonel's slow roasting as a means to "induce our government to take some effectual steps to chastise and suppress" the Indians.[39] In that publication the massacre of over ninety pacifist Indians at the Moravian mission town of Gnaden-hutten, the necessary context of that episode, was ignored. Instead, the pamphlet used the language of atrocity to create an image of victimisation, emphasising the brutality of the Indians whilst painting a deeply misleading portrayal of European American innocence. In Knight's narrative, the wilderness came alive with hidden, unseen threats which snatched the unsuspecting away: "The old man lagged behind . . . While we were preparing to reprimand him for making a noise, I heard an Indian halloo . . . After this we did not hear the man call again, neither did he ever come up to us anymore."[40] It is the scene of Crawford's execution, however, where the greatest care was made to assassinate the collective character of the Indians: "When we went to the fire the Col. was stripped naked, ordered to sit down by the fire and then they beat him with sticks and their fists . . . The Indian men then took up their guns and shot powder into the Colonel's body, from his feet as far up as his neck . . . Three or four Indians by turns would take up, individually, [a] burning piece of wood and apply it to his naked body, already burnt black with powder . . . Some of the squaws took broad boards, upon which they would carry a quantity of burning coals and hot embers and throw on him, so that in a short time he had nothing but coals of fire and hot ashes to walk on."[41]

Such sensational language was certainly evocative, simultaneously capturing and informing the shape of the west's emerging hatred of the Indians.[42] Brackenridge was identifying the Indians as a broad group

39. "A Letter from Hugh Henry Brackenrige to 'The Public,' August 3rd, 1782," in Hugh Henry Brackenrige, ed., *Indian Atrocities: Narratives of the Perils and Sufferings of Dr. Knight and John Slover, Among the Indians, During the Revolutionary War, with Short Memoirs of Colonel Crawford and John Slover* (Cincinnati: U. P. James, 1867), 5-6.

40. John Knight, "The Narrative of Dr. Knight," in Brackenrige, *Indian Atrocities*, 16.

41. Knight, "The Narrative of Dr. Knight," 23.

42. That being said, there is evidence which suggests the later popularity of those narratives in locations deeply affected by the violence, though it seems unlikely that pamphlet was the specific cause of further anti-Indian sentiment. Rather, if the document played a role it was likely that it provided confirmation bias, seemingly demonstrating the truth of assumptions and ideas already widely held by the community. For the popularity of Knight's account see Daniel Trabue, "The Narrative of Daniel Trabue: Memorandum Made by me D Trabue in the Year 1827 of a Jurnal of Events from Memory and Tradition," in Chester Raymond Young, ed., *Westward into Kentucky: The Narrative of Daniel Trabue* (Lexington: University of Kentucky Press, 1981, Reprinted 2004), 142-143; and John D. Shane, "Interview with Captain Marcus Richardson," Draper Manuscripts 12CC126-127.

who could be collectively characterised by violence and brutality, in effect articulating a framework of cruelty as a framework of understanding. By virtue of omission, Brackenridge's publication implied the opposite was true of European Americans. In contrast, Thomas Jefferson, in his *Notes on the State of Virginia*, articulated an interpretation of the Indians that was wholly incompatible with Brackenridge's, assigning to them the same potential for good and evil as his own ethnic peers.[43] Such an interpretation was diametrically opposed to Brackenridge's and, as a result, Jefferson drew a theoretical line not only between the pair, but between himself and the denizens of the west. Jefferson recognised plurality in the Indians, not just tribally, but on a fundamental and individual level; Brackenridge, on the other hand, ignored nuance in favour broad stereotypes supported by a particular and prejudiced interpretation of the evidence available. Writing in 1792 in an open letter which was printed prominently in the *Kentucky Gazette* he stated, rather bluntly, that "men who are unacquainted with the savages are like young women who have read romances, and have an improper idea of the Indian character in one case as the female mind has of real life in the other."[44] In other words, the experience of the west had taught European Americans living in that country to think about the Indians in a way that was alien to those who were separated from them by distance and, as Brackenridge characterised it, the naivety of circumstance.

After the fighting had come to an end in the mid-1790s, the prejudices of war continued to inform the attitudes of peace. One month after the climactic battle which crippled the northern Indian war effort, European Americans in Cincinnati started a race riot, demonstrating in the process that even friendly, allied tribes were perceived through a lens that had been shaped by conflict.[45] It mattered little that the Choctaws, whom they targeted, were known allies of the American cause.[46] Nor did it matter that they had served as scouts for General

43. Thomas Jefferson, *Notes on the State of Virginia: A New Edition, Prepared by the Author* (Richmond: J.W Randolph, 1853), 63-69.
44. "Farther and Concluding Thought on the Indian War by H. H. Brackenrige of Pittsburgh," *Kentucky Gazette* (Bradford), May 19, 1792.
45. "Letter from Secretary Sargent to Captain Pierce, September 8th, 1794" and "Secretary Sargent to Judge McMillan, September 8th, 1794," in William Henry Smith, ed., *The St. Clair Papers: The Life and Public Services of Arthur St. Clair, Soldier of the Revolutionary War; President of the Congress; and Governor of the Northwest Territory with his Correspondence and Other Papers, Volume II* (Cincinnati: Robert Clarke and Company, 1882), 327-328.
46. *Kentucky Gazette* (Bradford), April 27, 1793.

Anthony Wayne, and thus helped to bring about the final victory that had ended the war. What mattered to those who started the riot was the ethnicity of their prey and, most importantly, the characteristics they associated with it. When one of the rioters asked the local proprietor who had allowed the Choctaw to drink in his establishment, "is this the kind of Company you keep," he was not asking a question; he was making a statement.[47] The Cincinnati rioters were expressing a sentiment, a blanket and pejorative bigotry that had become common and, though not universal, was now widely accepted throughout much of the west, particularly south of the Ohio River where the fighting had gone on longest. When, in 1811, Indiana Gov. William Henry Harrison required an army to attack the pan-Indian movement that was coalescing around two Shawnee brothers at Prophetstown he was able to rely upon the support of Kentuckians whose staunch anti-Indian world view, alongside their willingness to kill Indians, had remained firmly intact.[48] During the subsequent War of 1812, Kentuckians and other westerners once again found ample opportunity to fight their old enemies while the actual fighting, and the losses they suffered, served to replenish the anti-Indian cultural coffers of the region.[49] When Black Hawk led an armed resistance in northern Illinois in 1832 it should perhaps come as no surprise that, in response to the five hundred warriors he was able to mobilize, Illinois raised a volunteer army nine thousand strong. When Black Hawk, recognizing the futility of his position, had attempted to surrender to the militia on May 14, the party he dispatched bearing the white flag was fired upon and forced to retreat.[50] As one

47. "Testimony of N.R. Hopkins, September 18th, 1794," Arthur St. Clair Papers, Roll 4, Folder 7 MIC 96 Series 10, Ohio Historical Society.
48. Robert M. Owen, *Mr. Jefferson's Hammer: William Henry Harrison and the Origins of American Indian Policy* (Norman, OK: University of Oklahoma Press, 2007), 214-215.
49. Elias Darnall, *A Journal, Containing an Accurate and Interesting Account of the Hardships, Sufferings, Battles, Defeat, and Captivity, of those Heroic Kentucky Volunteers and Regulars, Commanded by General Winchester, in the Years 1812-1813. Also, Two Narratives by Men that were Wounded in the Battles on the River Raisin, and Taken Captive by the Indians* (Paris: Joel R. Lyle, 1813).
50. Patrick J. Jung, *The Black Hawk War of 1832* (Norman: University of Oklahoma Press, 2007), 87-89; and James E. Davis, *Frontier Illinois* (Bloomington and Indianapolis: Indian University Press, 1998), 193-198.

Illinoisan put it, his fellows acted with a "cowardly vindictiveness."[51] Illinois' largest donor of immigrants was Kentucky.[52]

War is not necessarily a radicalizing force, it does not have to erode moderation or push it to the fringe. In the Trans-Appalachian country, however, the war with the Indians did just that. Because of their determination to preserve their territorial integrity, and their willingness to leverage direct and indirect violence to further their cause, the Indians exposed a generation of frontier settlers to one of the most intense and long-lasting backcountry wars in North American history. That situation created a type of cultural momentum in the region that transformed the breadth and depth of anti-Indian sentiment in the west, attaching it not just to abstract ideas of *savagery* but a specific narrative of self-realized victimization and the selective identification of wartime atrocities. That narrative was rooted in the region where it came into being; it was fundamentally western and, because of that, it helped to draw a theoretical line along the Appalachian Mountains which served to separate, on that key issue, east from west, backcountry from front country. In the west the American Revolution occurred after its own fashion, but so too did another concurrent—parallel but separate—layer of social revolution. The transformed way in which western Americans conceptualized the Indians was not a complete break with what had gone before (neither was the American Revolution) but it was a radical shift that marked not only a vast increase of the breadth of anti-Indian sentiment but an ideological divergence from the east. Where warfare with the Indians was an abstract notion, it was a distant affair that could be romanticized and forgiven. In the west, where memories were fresh and experience broad, Indian hatred was widely accepted, a celebrated part of the region's culture well into the nineteenth century.

51. Elijah Kilbourn, "Kilbourn's Narrative: A Reminiscence of Black Hawk." in Black Hawk, Antoine LeClair (Translator) and J.B. Patterson, ed., *Autobiography of Ma-Ka-Tai-Me-She-Kia-Kiak or Black Hawk, Embracing the Traditions of his Nations, Various Wars in which he has been Engaged, and his Account of the Cause and General History of the Black Hawk War of 1832, his Surrender and Travel through the United States. Dictated by Himself. Also Life, Death and Burial of the Old Chief, together with A History of the Black Hawk War and Also Life, Death and Burial of the Old Chief, Together with a History of the Black Hawk War, by J. B. Patterson, Oquawka, 1882* (Rock Island: J.B. Patterson, 1882), 162-164.
52. Davis, *Frontier Illinois*, 122-123. For a broader commentary on the dispersal of Kentucky's frontier population throughout the region see Aron, *American Confluence*, 112-113.

Experience, Policies, Failures: President Washington and Native Americans

❀ GEOFF SMOCK ❀

Experience had taught George Washington a great many things. His father had passed away at a young age, denying him the chance for the college education in England that he had been promised. Instead of lecture halls and libraries, his factories of learning were to be the wildernesses of the Virginia frontier, the battlefields of the War for Independence, and the unforgiving campgrounds of Valley Forge. As Joseph J. Ellis succinctly puts it, "Instead of going to college, Washington went to war."[1]

His was an education not in abstract theories, but in gritty realities. Chief among these was Washington's personal experience fighting Native Americans during his first regular military command as colonel of the "Virginia Regiment" from 1755 to 1759. The regiment was a colonial unit tasked with defending the colony's frontier from the French and, more immediately, their Native American allies during the Seven Years' War. At only twenty-three years-old, he had accepted the commission outwardly confident of his prospects for success. "I doubt not but you have heard of the Ravages committed by our inhuman Foes, on the back inhabitants," he boasted to a friend, "I am now upon my march against them, with full hopes, that I shall be able to get Satisfaction for their cruel Barbarities."[2]

It would not be long before this youthful arrogance gave way to chastened experience. "I have been posted . . . upon our cold and Barren Frontiers to perform I think I may say impossibilities," he would soon

1. Joseph J. Ellis, *His Excellency: George Washington* (New York: Alfred A. Knopf, 2004), 11.
2. George Washington to Christopher Gist, October 19, 1755, in John Rhodehamel, ed., *George Washington: Writings* (New York: The Library of America, 1997), 62. I have modernized some of the spelling in Washington's letters for the sake of clarity.

lament, "that is, to protect from the Cruel Incursions of a Crafty Savage Enemy a line of Inhabitants of more than 350 Miles extent with a force inadequate to the task."[3] All too soon and all too often, the young colonel suffered through a painful curricula in the realities of Indian warfare. These lessons would become seared into his memory, to be summoned over thirty years later when he became the United States of America's first chief executive and responsible for its Native American policies.

First among these lessons was that indigenous warriors had a "home field advantage" fighting in the wilderness terrain of the American hinterlands. They were highly mobile and thus notoriously difficult to track, managing to appear as if out of the trees themselves, strike, and disappear as suddenly. "I cannot conceive the best white men to be equal to them in the Woods," Washington asserted to one correspondent.[4] To another, he declared that no "troops in the universe can guard against the cunning and wiles of Indians. No one can tell where they will fall, 'till the mischief is done, and 'tis in vain to pursue."[5] In Washington's mind, they were analogous to wolves: striking in small packs with stealth, quickness, and remorseless tenacity.[6]

Support from European powers complicated matters further, and Washington was not on the job long before he became convinced that fighting was futile so long as the French were present on the frontier to incite and supply the Natives against the Virginia settlements. To his brother he warned, "we must bid adieu to peace and safety whilst the French are allowed to possess the Ohio, and to practice their hellish Arts among the numerous Tribes of Indian Nations that Inhabit those Regions."[7]

Still another lesson was that peace and order on a settled frontier were hopeless daydreams so long as white settlers lived in constant fear of Native American massacre. In an environment where white colonists imagined a blood-thirsty Indian lurking behind every tree, little was needed to send an entire village into a rage of mass hysteria. Washington informed Virginia governor Robert Dinwiddie in one dispatch that "we are told, from all parts, that the woods appear to be alive with In-

3. Washington to Richard Washington, April 15, 1757, Ibid, 88.
4. Washington to Henry Bouquet, July 16, 1758, in W.W. Abbot, ed., *The Papers of George Washington: Colonial Series* (Charlottesville: University Press of Virginia, 1983), V:292.
5. Washington to John Robinson, October 25, 1757, Ibid, V:33.
6. Peter R. Henriques, *Realistic Visionary: A Portrait of George Washington* (Charlottesville: University of Virginia Press, 2006), 19.
7. Washington to Richard Washington, April 15, 1757, in Rhodehamel, ed., *Writings*, 88.

dians, who feast upon the Fat of the Land."[8] Desperate claims of Indian atrocities routinely sent the regiment scurrying back and forth across the countryside in response. On one of these occasions Washington was provided with information that Indian raiders had arrived at a nearby town "and were killing and destroying all before them." Regular firing had been heard, as well as "the Shrieks of the unhappy Murdered." Washington immediately gathered the forces he had and rushed to the troubled spot, "but when we got there, who should we find occasioning all this disturbance, but 3 drunken Soldiers of the Light Horse carousing, firing their Pistols, and uttering the most unheard off Imprecations." Washington used this anecdote to convey to Governor Dinwiddie "what a panic prevails among the People, how much they are alarmed at the most usual and customary Cry's—and yet how impossible it is to get to act in any respect for their common safeties."[9]

After four years, his hopes and overt requests for a regular commission in the British Army had been met with mute indifference, and the futility of fighting against a Native American foe without support or recognition no longer seemed worth it to the ambitious colonel.[10] Having resigned his post and taken his leave, little could he have known what history had in store for him—or that he would have occasion to summon all the agonizing lessons he had learned combating Native American foes.

In September of 1783, nearly twenty-eight years later, Washington was preparing to resign the second independent command of his life: commander-in-chief of the Continental Army. At peace in the naïve belief that his time serving the public was nearing a permanent end, he reflected on the policies the new republic should adopt towards western lands and the indigenous peoples who inhabited them. In so doing, he tapped the deep reservoir of his own experiences fighting them in the Virginia Regiment three decades earlier.

He envisioned a pacific approach, with clearly-delineated boundary lines between tribal territories and white settlements, "beyond which we will endeavor to restrain our People from Hunting or Settling, and within which they shall not come, but for the purposes of Trading, Treating, or other business unexceptionable in its nature." Any and all territory acquired should only be done through negotiation and for fair compensation.

8. Washington to Robert Dinwiddie, April 22, 1756, Ibid, 75.
9. Washington to Dinwiddie, October 11, 1755, Ibid, 65-6.
10. See George to Dinwiddie, March 10, 1757, Ibid, 85-88.

The alternative was perpetual conflict, and Washington's harsh experience in Indian warfare strongly dissuaded him from a bellicose approach. "That it is the cheapest as well as the least distressing way of dealing with them, none who are acquainted with the Nature of Indian warfare, and has ever been at the trouble of estimating the expense of one . . . will hesitate to acknowledge." Negotiation and fair treatment, as befitting one sovereign people treating another, would be the easiest and cheapest way to settle the frontier and profit from its boundless resources. The alternate course would be akin to "driving the Wild Beasts [out] of the Forest which will return [to] us [as] soon as the pursuit is at an end and fall . . . on those that are left there. . . ."[11]

Washington would have a chance to put these words into action by the end of the decade, when his dreams of retirement from "the great theatre of Action" were dashed and he was unanimously elected the country's first president.[12] In that office he would have the opportunity to share the wisdom of his experience with his country and adopt the pacific course he had recommended in September of 1783.

Immediately on Washington's Indian agenda was finding some sort of accommodation with the southwestern tribes, where the potential for bloodshed between Natives and whites seemed most acute. In August of 1789 he proposed a commission designed to settle the differences between the two parties. At the same time, he sought to call the U.S. Senate's attention to the disorder the poor conduct of American settlers there was causing.

Congress as a whole responded by passing a series of statutes regulating American intercourse with the Native Americans. These laws set up a system of licensing to trade with the tribes and declared that the purchase of Indian lands could only be done by a public treaty between them and the United States. They also set up a regime of punishment for homicide and other crimes committed by Americans against the Indians. These laws codified the type of policies Washington had argued for since the end of the Revolution.[13]

Nevertheless, the administration's efforts were almost immediately frustrated. The Southwest Indians were understandably unimpressed by the federal government's promises to protect their lands, or by its promises to make war if necessary. The American army then existed much more in theory than it did in reality, whereas their own military

11. Washington to James Duane, September 7, 1783, Ibid, 535-541.
12. George Washington, "Address to Congress on Resigning Commission," Ibid, 548.
13. Francis Paul Prucha, *American Indian Policy in the Formative Years: The Indian Trade and Intercourse Acts* (Lincoln: University of Nebraska Press, 1962), 45-6.

prowess, buttressed by support from Spain, was quite formidable.[14] Accordingly, early negotiations between the two sides got nowhere.

Trouble was also brewing up north, where military force had to be used to defend American settlers from hostile strikes by tribes of the Six Nations. Though not personally involved in the operations, Washington once again found himself defending panicked settlers from Indian aggression in western borderlands. In his message to Congress in December 1790, Washington lamented that "frequent incursions have been made on our frontier settlements by a certain banditti of Indians from the North West side of the Ohio." Undeterred by "the humane overtures made on the part of the United States," these rogue elements had "renewed their violence with fresh alacrity and greater effect."[15]

Washington kept up his efforts. In a written address to a group of chiefs within the Six Nations, he expressed his hope that in the future "the United States and the six Nations should be truly brothers, promoting each other's prosperity by acts of mutual friendship and justice." He tried to reassure the tribal heads that, "No state nor person can purchase your lands, unless at some public treaty held under the authority of the United States. The general government will never consent to your being defrauded. But it will protect you in all your just rights."[16]

The Washington administration also raised the stakes on relations with the southwestern tribes, seeking to achieve a diplomatic agreement by hosting the tribal leaders at a summit full of pomp, ceremony, and lavish dinners in New York City in the summer of 1790. As Joseph J. Ellis explains, Washington and his subordinates hoped that a breakthrough treaty "that recognized [the southwestern tribes'] legitimate claim to a large slice of land east of the Mississippi . . . would serve as a model for all subsequent negotiations with the eastern tribes."[17]

After nearly a month of intensive negotiations, a treaty was finally produced and ratified by the Senate in August. It stipulated that the United States would preserve and defend an Indian territory encompassing portions of modern-day Georgia, Tennessee, Florida, Alabama, and Mississippi. It was exactly the type of territorial arrangement Washington had envisioned since September of 1783—a separate and extensive Indian territory delineated from American settlements, and any and all trading between Natives and whites could only occur with the approbation of the federal government.

14. Joseph J. Ellis, *American Creation* (New York: Alfred A. Knopf, 2007), 148-9.
15. Washington, "Second Message," in Rhodehamel, *Writings*, 769-70.
16. George Washington, "To the Chiefs of the Seneca Nation," Ibid, 773.
17. Ellis, *Creation*, 153.

This apparent breakthrough on paper was soon undermined by the reality on the ground. As Ellis writes, "The unmanageable problem was demographic. Settlers on the Georgia frontier kept pouring across the newly established Creek borders by the thousands, blissfully oblivious to any geographic line drawn on the maps by some faraway government."[18] Washington and the federal government could make promises, but they had little ability to fulfill them, and the federal government was powerless to thwart, or even manage, western settlement.

In July 1791 Washington despaired that he could not "see much prospect of living in tranquility with [the Indians] so long as a spirit of land jobbing prevails, and our frontier Settlers entertain the opinion that there is not the same crime (or indeed no crime at all) in killing an Indian as in killing a white man."[19] Later that year he told Congress that "the mode of alienating [Indian] lands [is] the main source of discontent and war." He declared that "commerce with them should be promoted under regulations tending to secure an equitable deportment towards them." Finally, he insisted that "efficacious provision should be made for inflicting adequate penalties upon all those who, by violating their rights, shall infringe the Treaties, and endanger the peace of the Union."[20]

Pretty soon a sense of helplessness gave way to despair. All attempts to preserve the integrity of Indian lands by that date had failed, forcing Washington to conclude that "scarcely anything short of a Chinese wall will restrain the Land jobbers and the encroachment of settlers upon the Indian Country."[21] This was rapidly taking the United States in a direction he had expressly wanted to avoid. Over the coming months and years, unrestrained settlement on treaty-protected Indian lands would lead to a perpetual state of asymmetrical warfare between Indians and whites, staining the land with the blood of both. The fecklessness of the federal government, despite the best intentions of its chief executive, was the genesis of a cycle of violence that was spinning out of control.

Impotently watching this cycle unfold, Washington mastered the art of understatement in declaring to Congress in 1792 that he was not able to provide the assembled legislators with "information that the Indian hostilities . . . have terminated." Instead he painted a picture of conflict up and down the western frontier, with fighting occurring with the Iroquois up north and the Cherokee down south, and many locales in be-

18. Ibid, 158.
19. Washington to David Humphreys, July 20, 1791, in Rhodehamel, ed., *Writings*, 779.
20. George Washington, "Third Annual Message to Congress," October 25, 1791, Ibid, 788.
21. Washington to Thomas Jefferson, as quoted in Ellis, *Creation*, 159.

The large silver peace medal presented to Seneca Chief Red Jacket in 1792 by President Washington in Philadelphia.

tween. Washington reiterated once again that it was absolutely necessary that "more adequate provision [be made] for giving energy to the laws throughout our interior frontier, and for restraining the commission of outrages upon the Indians; without which all pacific plans must prove nugatory."[22] What he had not fully realized yet was that no amount of energetic laws could stem the surge of settlement.

He also misunderstood the role foreign powers were playing in his and the United States' frontier troubles. To Thomas Jefferson he claimed that there was "a very clear understanding in all this business between the Courts of London and Madrid; and that it is calculated to check, as far as they can, the rapid increase, extension, and consequence of this country; for there cannot be a doubt of the wishes of the former . . . to impede any eclaircissment [sic] of ours with the Western Indians, and to embarrass our negotiations with them."[23]

Washington was missing the point. The entente between the tribes and European powers was not one of manipulation, but transaction. The United States' inability to prevent the invasion of indigenous lands was driving the Indians into cooperation with the British in the North and Spanish in the south. Foreign interference was not a cause of the

22. George Washington, "Fourth Annual Message to Congress," November 6, 1792, in Rhodehamel, ed., *Writings*, 826-8.
23. Washington to Jefferson, August 23, 1792, Ibid, 817.

problem, it was a symptom. The irrepressible mass of white migration westward was pushing the tribes into the arms of Britain and Spain. Nothing else.

With the cycle of violence rapidly escalating, Washington soon felt compelled to settle matters by force. Thousands of American troops were sent to Iroquoia in 1794 under the command of Revolutionary veteran Anthony Wayne, and in August of that year his forces achieved a conclusive American victory at Fallen Timbers. This triumph not only crushed the Iroquois resistance, but discredited the British, who had failed to follow through on their promise of military support.[24]

Far from having achieved two civilizations living peacefully in isolation from each other, as Washington had sought, Americans had drowned the northern Indians through a migratory flood of settlement consolidated by military conquest. Discussing the matter before Congress, all Washington could do was feebly affirm that "we shall not be unwilling to cement a lasting peace, upon terms of candor, equity, and good neighborhood."[25] This public sentiment aside, Washington finally realized that any relationship with the northern tribes based on "candor, equity, and good neighborhood" was nothing but a pretense by that point.

To prevent something similar from happening to them, the Creeks down south made an alliance with Spain, agreeing to a treaty that recognized their shared desire to expel white Americans from Creek country, which would, in theory, protect Creek sovereignty and preserve a buffer between American and Spanish territories.[26] This alliance (predictably) would be all for naught, as the Spanish and Creeks were no more suited to impede the wave of American settlement than the British and Iroquois had been. The American population was growing at the same rate that the Native one was declining, condemning the latter to being swallowed up by the former. The indigenous peoples of America and their allies could not stop this demographic equation any more than Washington's administration could.[27]

In 1795 Washington told Congress that conflict with the Indians had largely abated, neglecting to mention that this had occurred, not through his preferred route of diplomacy, but through demography and warfare. Still not letting the issue slide though, he declared again that

24. Alan Taylor, *The Divided Ground: Indians, Settlers, and the Northern Borderland of the American Revolution*, (New York: Vintage Books, 2006), 287-8.
25. George Washington, "Sixth Annual Message to Congress," November 19, 1794, in Rhodehamel, ed., *Writings*, 893-4.
26. Ellis, *Creation*, 160.
27. Ibid, 161-2.

to "enforce upon the Indians the observance of Justice, it is indispensable that there shall be competent means of rendering justice to them."[28] As he had nearly forty years earlier, Washington was pleading for more powers to instill discipline and peace on an unsettled frontier. Yet with the Indians up and down the western continent all but completely vanquished, this sentiment was more of a criticism of the settlers and states who had committed grave injustices against the Indians than it was a policy prescription.

History had left Washington and his original intentions behind. He had tried to implement the course of action his experience as a young Indian fighter had taught him was most practical—a course of diplomacy and equity instead of conquest. Much to his consternation, the unyielding momentum of Americans' massive drive towards the West would not permit this, confounding any and all attempts to preserve autonomous lands for the indigenous tribes. As Ellis concludes, his administration had "inherited an Indian policy headed inexorably toward the extermination of Indian Country east of the Mississippi and [had] attempted to turn it around." Washington had "made a heroic effort and had failed, though it is difficult to imagine what [he] might have done differently to change the outcome."[29]

The federal government might have had the military resources to fight a dwindling population of Indians, but it most certainly did not have the resources to stop a growing, determined wave of white Americans. Such an effort would have required multiple forts dotting the frontier with garrisons numbering in the thousands—a dedication of resources the embryonic federal government could not hope to muster for decades.

Washington's inevitable failure was the end of his and the Natives' hopes for extended Native American territories clearly delineated from white American land east of the Mississippi. Most of the Natives' territorial holdings had been wrestled from them at a time when the policy of the federal government was to prevent any such thing from happening. This process would continue in the future, especially under the presidential administrations of Thomas Jefferson and Andrew Jackson, who both instituted deliberate policies of removal to make even more room for American settlement.

The inability of Washington's diplomatic policies to succeed would also lead to what he had predicted it would. Fighting to preserve their

---

28. George Washington, "Seventh Annual Message to Congress," December 8, 1795, in Rhodehamel, ed., *Writings*, 923.
29. Ellis, *Creation*, 161.

ancestral lands, Indian warriors were fierce and unyielding in combat. Defeating them conclusively required immense sums of money, men, and time. Accordingly, Washington would not have been surprised that, in its drive to the Pacific Ocean, the United States would be consumed in Indian Wars nearly a century after he left office. He had learned on the open expanses of the Virginia frontier that you could not try and coercively dispossess Indians of their lands without long, bloody wars. It was a choice of diplomacy and justice towards the Native Americans or year after year of warfare. Experience had taught him this and so he had sought the former. The all-consuming westward mass of migration had opted for the latter—and paid the costs in treasure and blood.

Proposed Alliance of the Knights of Malta and the United States of America

❀❧ BRUCE WARE ALLEN ❧❀

On the face of it, there would seem no greater natural disparity between the two countries, one an ancient aristocratic pan-European (but mostly French) Catholic military theocracy, the other a modern, egalitarian, Anglo-Saxon, Protestant confederation. Nevertheless, during the American Revolution, a healthy number of Order of Knights of the Hospital of Saint John of Jerusalem helped finance and fight for the nation seemingly at odds with all they stood for. The Knights, headquartered in Malta but spread across Europe, were also well represented in the post-war Society of the Cincinnati, a exclusive club open to senior officers who had served the American Revolution. Most notable was Pierre-Andre de Suffren de Saint-Tropez, who resigned his knightly role as General of the Galleys of the Order to serve under Admiral De Grasse. Other members included the Chevalier de Luzerne, first French Minister to the United States, the Count de Colbert-Maulevrier, the Chevalier de Vallongue, the two Counts de Lameth, the Viscount de Noailles, and the Viscount de Mirabeau.

The value of the knights' service (this at a time when the Order, unlike France proper, was technically neutral) was not lost on the Americans. At war's end, Benjamin Franklin as Ambassador to France had a special commemorative medal struck for Grand Master Rohan, which he had delivered with a the following note:

> I have the honour to address to Your Eminent Highness the medal which I have lately had struck. It is an Homage of gratitude, my Lord, which is due to the interest you have taken in our cause; and we no less owe it to your virtues and to your eminent highness wise administration of government.

Permit me, my lord, to demand your protection for such of our citizens as circumstances may lead to your ports. I hope that your eminent highness will be pleased to grant it to them, and kindly receive the assurances of the profound respect etc.[1]

The sentiments were genuine enough, but Franklin was nothing if not practically-minded. The knights' headquarters were on Malta, a small rock of an island smack dab in the middle of the Mediterranean, possessed of a superb deep water harbor and capable of providing shelter from foul weather and Barbary corsairs. With America now independent, the British navy no longer protected American sailors in the Mediterranean and they could use all the help they could get.

All of which Grand Master Rohan would have appreciated when he responded:

I have received with the most lively sensibility, the medal which your excellency sent me, and the value I set upon this acquisition leaves my gratitude unbounded. This monument of American liberty has a distinguished place in my cabinet. Whenever chance or commerce shall lead any of your citizens or their vessels into the ports of my island, I shall receive them with the greatest welcome. They shall experience from me every assistance they may claim, and I shall observe with infinite pleasure any growing connexion between that interesting nation and my subjects, especially if it will tend to convince your excellency of the distinguished sentiments with which I am the grand-master.[2]

The Grand Master was a progressive man, fond of Voltaire and Rousseau, so his support of the new republic comes as less surprising than it might. With the success of the revolution, however, egalitarianism was becoming more than just an intellectual fashion. It began to have teeth. The contradictions between a titled aristocracy and representative rule were not lost on hard-core French revolutionaries, for whom the *Ordre de Cincinnatus* was a step backwards. Honoré, Count de Mirabeau the elder, wrote *Considerations sur l'Ordre Americain de Cincinnatus,* a pamphlet suggesting that the order was the thin end of the wedge of social stratification. All hereditary orders of this sort— and he gave the Knights of St John as an example—were inherently bad and to be abolished lest they bring down the nascent American republic. His younger brother the Viscount de Mirabeau, himself a mem-

1. Benjamin Franklin, *Memoirs of Benjamin Franklin, Volume 1* (Philadelphia: M'Carty & Davis, 1834), 525.
2. Franklin, *Memoirs*, 542.

ber of the Cincinnati, saw value in the Knights of St John, considered them as an unofficial French asset, and not to be alienated.[3]

As to the Society of the Cincinnati, it had no official status or power, nor would it ever. Although ranks and titles were mooted, principally by those who hoped to get them—Margrave was a favorite—they were firmly dismissed when Washington declined the offer of a crown, pointing out the absurdity of trading King George the Third for King George the First. With the Constitutional Convention of 1789, the country was officially free of republic ("if you can keep it," as Benjamin Franklin famously cautioned).[4]

The ratification of the American Constitution coincided with France's own revolution, which played out with less happy results, particularly for the Knights of St. John. Within a year, France had outlawed tithes, the greatest source of the Order's revenue. In 1791, the wearing of the eight pointed Maltese Cross was banned. In 1792, the king was executed and the Order was forced to sell its remaining assets. That same year, the first French armies began to cross into Italy. The Order's holdings on that peninsula cannot have been far from their thoughts, nor the possibility that their days in France, or even on Malta itself, might be numbered.

The knights had been down this road before. In 1291 they were forced from the Holy Land to the Island of Rhodes, a matter of force and skullduggery. In 1520, they were forced from the island of Rhodes off Turkey to the island of Malta. There, in 1565, they had held off the full force of an Ottoman siege in 1565, their finest hour. In 1565, however, they had had the support of patrons from Spain. This time, they were strictly on their own.

Desperate to reverse the forces of revolution that were tearing France apart, the Chevalier D'Estourmel lent King Louis 12,000 francs of the Order's money to fund the abortive flight to Varennes (June 1791), the failure of which led to the king's beheading. By September of 1792, he and the last official representative of the order to France, the aristocratic Bailli de Virieu, departed the Orders' Paris office. The last men standing at the Order's Paris embassy were the very plebeian but very loyal father and son clerks named Jean-François Eleozar Paul de Cibon, the latter "a man of great probity and well known for his attachment to the interests of Malta."[5]

3. For American reaction to the society, see Markus Hünemörder, *The Society of the Cincinnati: Conspiracy and Distrust in Early America* (New York: Berghan Books, 2006).
4. Papers of Dr. James McHenry on the Federal Convention of 1787, *The American Historical Review* vol. 11, (1906), 618.
5. Pierre Marie Louis de Boisgelin de Kerdu, *Ancient and Modern Malta, vol 2, part 2* (London: Richard Phillips, 1805), 35.

With no one to say no, and no one else present to take on any kind of responsibility, the decidedly bourgeois son of necessity styled himself *chargé d'affaires de Malte* and took on the task of maintaining the Order's rapidly diminishing fortunes. He managed to get himself accredited in the *Almanach National* and, to the extent possible, tried to maintain diplomatic relations with any powers willing to talk to him. Through the offices of Pierre Doublet, Head of the French Secretariat and confidant of the Grand Master, he made weekly and bi-weekly reports back to Grand Master Rohan, and attempted to keep lines of communication open between the new French government and Malta, a task made the more difficult by Rohan's refusal to grant him any official status.[6] The knights, officially, demanded four grandparents of unimpeachable aristocratic birth.

Official or not, Cibon was nevertheless a regular at diplomatic affairs and was himself nearly ruined in his attempts to reciprocate hospitality without much in the way of support from Malta other than grudging permission to sell some of the Order's remaining silver plate.

It was, however, Cibon that the American Minister James Monroe (another member of the Cincinnati) addressed to discuss a visit of the American fleet to Malta and a proposed alliance between the Order of Malta and the United States.[7]

With the approval of Grand Master Rohan, who perhaps had gazed into the future and was grasping at straws, Cibon in turn reached out to Monroe in a letter dated October 26, 1794:

> The Chargé d'Affaires of Malta, has the honour to communicate to Mr. Monroe, Minister plenipotentiary of the United States of America, the annexed reflections, and to request that he will be pleased to weigh them in his mind, and give him frankly the result.
>
> Mr. Cibon seizes this occasion to renew to Mr. Monroe an assurance of the respect and attachment with which he is, &c. If there are nations who by their position, their industry, and their courage, become naturally opposed to, and rivals of each other; so there are other nations who with as much courage and industry, feel a motive to esteem, approach and unite together, to increase their mutual prosperity, and to render themselves reciprocally happy by a continual exchange of attentions, regards and services. The United States

---

6. Frederick W. Ryan, *The House of the Temple: A Study of Malta and its Knights in the French Revolution* (London: Burns, Oates and Washbourne, 1930), 238.
7. Pierre Jean Louis Ovide Doublet, *Mémoires historiques sur l'invasion et l'occupation de Malte par une armée Française, en 1798* (Paris: Librairie de Firmin-Didot et Cie, 1883), 387.

of America and the Island of Malta, notwithstanding the distance which separates them, do not appear to be less bound to cultivate a close and friendly union between them, by motives of interest, than they are by those of a benevolent amity.

It is principally towards the Mediterranean that the American sailors, guided by their industry, present themselves in great numbers, forgetting the danger to which they are exposed of becoming a prey to the Algerian corsairs who cover that sea.

The Island of Malta, placed in the centre of the Mediterranean, between Africa and Sicily, offers by its position to all navigators, an asylum, provisions and succor of every kind. Of what importance would it not be for the American commerce to find upon this stormy sea, fine ports, provisions, and even protection against the Algerian pirates.

In exchange for the succours and protection, by means where-of the American vessels might navigate the Mediterranean freely and without inquietude, would the United States consent to grant, in full right, to the Order of Malta some lands in America, in such quantity as might be agreed on between the two governments, placing such lands under the immediate protection and safeguard of the American loyalty?

Thus the commerce of the United States would find, in the Mediterranean, ports to secure it from storms, and vessels of war to protect it against the pirates of Algiers; in exchange for which Malta would possess in America property granted forever, protected by the United States, and guaranteed by them in a manner the most solid.[8]

It was a carefully considered offer, with advantages for both sides. Safety for the new nation, and the prospect of yet another new home for the Order, with an option to grow. Geography did not confine the knights' imagination; as early as the sixteenth century, one of their members had tried and failed to create an outpost in Brazil. The earlier expedition, however, was bravado; Rohan's request was deadly serious.

Monroe took nearly a month to reply, somewhat pointedly addressing him in the fashion of the French revolutionaries:

To the Chargé d'Affaires of Malta. Paris, 22d November, 1794.
 Citizen,-
 I have received with great pleasure the considerations you were pleased to present to me; pointing out the mode by which the United

8. James Monroe, *Writings* of James *Monroe*, vol II, Stanislaus Murray Hamilton, ed. (New York: G. P. Putnam's Sons, 1899), 128.

States of America and the Isle of Malta may be serviceable to each other. It is the duty of nations to cultivate, by every means in their power, these relations subsisting between them, which admit of reciprocal good offices, and I am persuaded the United States will omit no opportunity which may occur to testify that disposition towards the Island of Malta.

The Americans have, it is true, received already great injury from the Algerines, and it is their intention to adopt such measures as shall prevent the like in future. The Island of Malta by its situation and maritime strength possesses the means of yielding that protection, and your suggestion on that subject merits, in my opinion, the serious consideration of our government, to whom I have already transmitted it.

The United States possess at present extensive and very valuable territory. It is their intention to dispose of it by sale; by which however the right of soil only will be conveyed; the jurisdiction still remaining with them. The government too of such territory is already prescribed: It must be elective or republican, and forming a part of the existing national system. I have thought proper to add this information that you may know the powers of our government in relation to this object. Permit me to assure you, that as soon as I shall be instructed thereon, I will immediately communicate the same to you.[9]

The matter seems to have stopped there. From the American point of view, what Cibon was proposing was an impossibility (though they were happy to establish a mission on Malta in 1796).

For the Order, the end game was soon played out. Cibon continued to send status reports to his masters back in Malta and carry on what negotiations he could, reporting honestly and painfully the deteriorating situation in France and struggling to maintain the Order's interests and their archives.[10] When Rohan died in 1797 and the German knight von Hempesich took his seat, it was Cibon, now formally confirmed as *chargé d'affaires*, who was charged with announcing the new Grand Master's elevation and extending that man's rather naive and desperate hopes for good relations and commerce between Malta and France.

It was, alas, too late. Eleven months later Napoleon, one his way to conquer Egypt, invaded Malta, expelled the knights, and made the is-

9. Monroe, *Writings,* 128.
10. Léonce Celier, "L'ambassade de l'ordre de Malte à Paris et ses archives," *Revue d'histoire de l'Église de France,* Tome 22. N 96, (1936): 317-337.

land French. Despite glowing referrals from his fellow bourgeois Doublet, virtually nothing was done for the clerk, and he disappeared without trace into history.[11]

Two years later the British ousted France from Malta, and never quite got around to restoring the power of the Order. In 1834 the wandering knights were forced to a temporal home within the Holy See, which they have retained ever since.[12]

James Monroe by contrast went on to become the fifth president of the United States (1817–1825) and architect of the Monroe Doctrine which posited that America would tolerate no European interference in the western hemisphere—a western hemisphere void of America's friends, the Knights of St. John.

As a practical matter and with the best will in the world, there was little enough that America could have done to help the knights retain power in Malta. Regrettably, the knights' removal from the island meant that they were of no use to America when America needed help against the Barbary corsairs in 1801–1805. Britain, by contrast, was happy to see her former colony struggle without the protection of the Royal Navy; moreover, as masters of Malta they had, by 1800, an important trade in livestock with Tripoli, a trade they were reluctant to jeopardize.[13] In the War of 1812 between America and Britain, again the British looked on with equanimity as the Barbary corsairs harassed their American cousins. As for Malta, it was no longer a refuge for American sailors but rather a holding pen for American prisoners of war.[14]

Could it have happened, could the knights have found a new home in North America? There were, after all, already thirteen self-governing political entities under "American loyalty." More would soon follow. Given the ties of shared sacrifice between the knights and the American

---

11. Doublet himself helped negotiate the terms of surrender of Malta to Napoleon and was made Secretary General to the Commission of Government, later Commissioner during the occupation. With the arrival of the British, he was exiled and lived a thin existence in Rome and Tripoli, only at the end of his life being permitted to return to Malta for good. See Doublet, *Memoires historiques.*

12. Dennis Castillo, "'... The Knights Cannot Be Admitted': Maltese Nationalism, the Knights of St. John, and the French Occupation of 1798-1800," *The Catholic Historical Review*, Vol. 79, No. 3 (July 1993): 434-453; Giovanni Bonello, "The 'Declaration of Rights,' 1802, and William Eton," in Giovanni Bonello, *Histories of Malta - Travesties and Dynasties* (Valletta: Fondazzjoni Patrimonju Malti, 2011), 109-124.

13. Kola Folayan, "Tripoli and the War with the U.S.A., 1801-5," *The Journal of African History* Vol. 13, No. 2 (1972): 261-270.

14. The Library of Congress has a short diary of Obadiah Stevens, one such prisoner. lccn.loc.gov/mm96006327.

revolutionaries and mutual esteem, it must have seemed to Cibon as a more than reasonable suggestion, and indeed, with a few minor tweaks on either or both sides, one can just about see it coming to fruition. Another of history's might-have-beens.

Happily, no ill feelings lingered. The Order of the Knights of St. John today, now entirely devoted to their role as Hospitallers rather than soldiers, provide free health care to American poor, and if the Order has no formal alliance with the United States, they do at least have a Permanent Observer Mission to the United Nations.

Washington's Farewell Advice to the Nation

❦ ERIC STERNER ❧

Every four (or eight) years, Americans observe the peaceful transition of power from one president to another, from one political party to another. Some will point to a tradition that begins with George Washington, who voluntarily stepped down as the first president under the new U.S. Constitution when his second term ended. In fact, the new nation was familiar with peaceful political transitions. As colonists, citizens had experienced such change in English governments. As revolutionaries, their own governors had done the same while at war. Yet, in 1796 all eyes were fixed on Washington, who had dominated the political scene like no other and quite likely could have done so for the remainder of his mortal life.

For his part, the president had tired of public life, which offered constant strife and criticism. Moreover, his wealth and estates had suffered during his absence in the American Revolution, and again during his term as president. In 1792, Washington first considered retiring and invited James Madison to help him draft a farewell address, but tensions overseas, domestic instability, and his sense of duty led him to put off the decision. By the late winter of 1796, Washington was determined to go. In the intervening years, he had drifted away from Madison, who was in Thomas Jefferson's camp as a critic of administration policy, and closer again to Alexander Hamilton, to whom he turned for his latest attempt at a farewell address.

Washington marked up Madison's 1792 draft and forwarded it to Hamilton. The president's notes involved some score settling and spleen venting over the attacks on his administration. Hamilton took Washington's notes and rewrote Madison's draft, but he prepared a second, clean-sheet document that was more statesmanlike, less burdened by the travails of eight years in office, and intended for the ages. Washington, ever with an eye toward posterity, preferred Hamilton's approach and worked with him on a final farewell address over the spring and summer of 1796.[1] Washington wanted to announce his retirement as soon as possible to clear the field for other candidates. Hamilton convinced him to put the announcement off, but without much warning, on September 19, 1796 *Claypoole's American Daily Advertiser* in Philadelphia appeared with an article on page two addressed "To the PEOPLE of the United States." Washington, already rumored to be contemplating retirement, had still surprised both supporters and opponents with the release of his Farewell Address, even as he left Philadelphia bound for Mt. Vernon.[2]

Coming at the end of Washington's public service, the Farewell Address served as a statement of Washington's theory of republican government, which was by no means assured in the nation's future. Europe was already convulsed by the wars of the French Revolution, which itself had contributed mightily to the growing split within his own administration. The Republican faction, led by Jefferson, embraced the French Revolution as patterned on the American Revolution and favored a close alliance with France, which was at war with England (among others). Federalists, on the other hand, retained their kinship to England, recognizing it as a better trading partner with significant interests in the Western Hemisphere. They also favored a stronger central government capable of knitting the country together out of an amalgam of states and emerging economic interests.

The internal split colored Washington's address. He pleaded for unity of government, seeing it as "a main Pillar in the Edifice of your real independence, the support of your tranquility at home; your peace abroad; of your safety; of your prosperity; of that very Liberty which you so highly prize."[3] In truth, Washington's plea was not limited to unity of government, but he sought unity in a nation, which meant identifying as an American: "The name AMERICAN, which belongs to you, in your national capacity, must always exalt the just pride of Patriotism, more than any appellation derived from local discriminations."[4]

---

1. Ron Chernow, *Washington: A Life* (New York: The Penguin Press, 2010), 753; David S. Heidler and Jeanne T. Heidler, *Washington's Circle: The Creation of the President* (New York: Random House, 2015), 385-387.
2. Heidler and Heidler, *Washington's Circle*, 393.
3. George Washington, "Farewell Address," *Selected Writings* (New York: Library of America, 2011), 367. Washington was an eighteenth century writer, fond of run-on sentences and spellings peculiar to modern ears. They have been retained from the original.
4. Washington, "Farewell Address," 367.

He was well aware that America in 1796 was more a collection of states and regions than a country. But, governed by self-interest, he argued that cooperation among regions with unique characteristics would benefit everyone.[5] According to Washington,

> While then every part of our country thus feels an immediate and particular Interest in Union, all the parts combined cannot fail to find in the united mass of means and efforts greater strengths, greater resource, proportionably greater security from external danger, and less frequent interruption of their Peace by foreign Nations; and, what is of inestimable value! they must derive from Union an exemption from those broils and Wars between themselves, which so frequently afflict neighbouring countries, not tied together by the same government' which their own rivalships alone would be sufficient to produce, but which opposite foreign alliances, attachments and intrieugues would stimulate and imbitter.[6]

Thus, Washington's appeal to national unity had both cultural and interest-based aspects.

If unity was the aspiration, Washington saw a myriad of threats to it. First and foremost among these, he was concerned with party or the spirit of party. Disagreements over the meaning of the French Revolution and American obligations to its wartime ally rent his administration deeply, as did debates over the federal government's authority, economic policy, and western policy. In 1792, he felt compelled to write to his Secretary of State, Thomas Jefferson—increasingly recognized as a leader of the pro-French faction—and beg him for greater charity when dealing with cabinet members who held different opinions, arguing, "how much is it to be regretted then, that whilst we are encompassed on all sides with avowed enemies & insidious friends, that internal dissentions should be harrowing & tearing our vitals. The last, to me, is the most serious—the most alarming—and the most afflicting of the two."[7] Within days, he sent a similar letter to Alexander Hamilton, Jefferson's chief antagonist. Unfortunately, the pleas fell on deaf ears.

The split over foreign policy grew particularly divisive. Washington increasingly sided with the Federalists, particularly in his policy of studied neutrality in the wars plaguing Europe. Washington sent Chief Justice John Jay to negotiate a new treaty with England clarifying their relationship after the Revolution. Tensions exploded on the streets after

5. Ibid., 368.
6. Ibid.
7. George Washington to Thomas Jefferson, August 23, 1792, in *Selected Writings*, 321.

the Jay Treaty became public. Federalists viewed it as necessary for American security, but Republicans considered it a betrayal of the principles of liberty, which the French initially claimed to champion, and friendship, which they felt Americans owed France for its contributions to the American Revolution. For their part, Republican attacks grew increasingly strident and personal, the charge being led by *The Philadelphia Aurora* and its publisher, Benjamin Franklin Bache, Benjamin Franklin's grandson. During public discussions, Jay was burned in effigy so widely that he joked he could walk from Georgia to Massachusetts by their light.[8] While Washington was willing to suffer the barbs and arrows of a hostile press for his decisions—he had a clear conscience in his motivations—he was concerned that they would "destroy the confidence which it is necessary for the People to place (until they have unequivocal proof of demerit) in their public Servants."[9]

Complicating things further, protests in western Pennsylvania over the whiskey tax began in Washington's first term, but grew violent as Washington began his second term. Mobs in Pennsylvania had tarred and feathered federal tax collectors over the whiskey tax, eventually leading Washington to raise an army for the suppression of rebellion in western Pennsylvania. Further violence was easy to envision.

In that context, Washington's drift closer to Federal positions, his plea for unity, and his condemnation of party can be easily read as a thinly veiled attack on the Republicans, who had been his worst critics. From anyone else, the words would sound perilously close to the sentiments of a dictator who questioned all opposition or disagreement with his decisions and identified his own wishes as synonymous with those of the popular will. Republican concerns about the ease with which Washington might become a king are easy to understand. Indeed, they were very critical of the address.[10] However, coming with the simultaneous announcement of his retirement from public life and voluntary surrender of power—which Washington had done once at the end of the Revolution after facing mutinous officers—could only force future generations to wrestle with his arguments.

Rather than score settling, Washington's farewell represents his decision to more publicly voice his thoughts about the American form of representative government. Because he saw popularly elected constitu-

8. Thomas Fleming, *The Great Divide: The Conflict between Washington and Jefferson That Defined America, Then and Now* (Boston: Da Capo Press, 2015), 209-210.
9. George Washington to Henry Lee, July 21, 1793, in *Selected Writings*, 332.
10. Richard Norton Smith, *Patriarch: George Washington and the New American Nation* (Boston: Houghton Mifflin Company, 1993), 283-284.

tional government as the ultimate expression of the popular will, opposition to that government's actions constituted a particular danger to it. According to Washington:

> All obstructions to the execution of the Laws, all combinations and Associations, under whatever plausible character, with the real design to direct, control counteract, or awe the regulation deliberation and action of the Constituted authorities are distructive of this fundamental principle and of fatal tendency. They serve to organize faction, to give it an artificial and extraordinary force; to put in the place of the delegated will of the Nation, the will of a party; often a small but artful and enterprising minority of the Community; and, according to the alternate triumphs of different parties, to make the public administration of the Mirror of the ill concerted and incongruous projects of faction, rather than the organ of consistent and wholesome plans digested by common councils and modified by mutual interests.[11]

Today, Washington's plea to avoid parties and factionalism may sound naïve. But, of course he was not new to high-risk politics, political violence and the baser motivations and actions that could affect people. Washington was well aware of what it had taken to achieve independence and build the new country, probably more so than any man alive.

Washington acknowledged that the "spirit of party" was "inseperable from our nature" and had often been controlled, stifled, or repressed in undemocratic societies. But, he also held that it was a most pernicious threat to republican government. Washington expected political parties to alternately succeed and fail in a contest for control of government through manipulation of popular passions and misrepresentation of their own goals and motives, as well as those of their opponents. Victory in these contests would result in acts of revenge against the losers. Eventually, one party would succeed in institutionalizing its success, denying access to the levers of power to any who failed to subscribe to its principles. In short, it would result in a kind of political despotism, in which the interests of the whole nation took a back seat to the interests of the victorious party. Thus, even while acknowledging this outcome was an extreme case, Washington felt it necessary to warn his countrymen about an inherent problem he perceived in popular government.[12] It all began with the kind of factionalism he had experienced as president.

---

11. Washington, "Farewell Address," 370-371.
12. Ibid., 372.

Being a practical man, Washington also left his countrymen with practical advice: minimize debt, avoid a standing army to minimize expenditures, maintain neutrality among nations so as not to go to war either on the behalf of allies or out of emotional animosity towards enemies, ramp up defenses quickly in an emergency to deter aggression, promote the diffusion of knowledge to better inform the public's opinions, recognize that religion and morality are indispensable to political prosperity, and exercise caution in adjusting the Constitution and wielding power under it. Over time, these became maxims. From the Civil War through the 1980s, the address was read routinely in the House of Representatives and the Senate on Washington's birthday.[13]

Washington's Farewell Address is a product of its times, as all presidential farewells must be. But, with a prod from Hamilton, Washington recognized the opportunity to communicate a message larger than a simple announcement of his retirement and response to his critics. Instead, he offered thoughts for citizens of the young republic to consider as they embarked on the grand experiment of representative government. Forty-four presidents and two and a half centuries later they are still worth considering.

13. U.S. Senate Historian's Office, www.senate.gov/artandhistory/history/common/generic/WashingtonFarewell.htm, accessed December 16, 2016; Historical Highlights, U.S. House of Representatives, history.house.gov/HistoricalHighlight/Detail/36742, accessed December 16, 2016. The practice in the House fell off during the 1970s and 1980s. It is still honored in the U.S. Senate.

Thomas Paine, Deism, and the Masonic Fraternity

⁑ SHAI AFSAI ⁑

Thomas Paine's close associations with famous Freemasons in America, England, and France have frequently been taken as evidence that he was a Freemason himself, and have been seen as explaining his sudden rise to literary and political prominence after arriving in the American colonies from England. Likewise, his writing of an essay "On the Origin of Free-Masonry" several years before his death has been interpreted as a confirmation that he was a committed member of the fraternity.

However, a close reading of "On the Origin of Free-Masonry" shows that Paine was not a Freemason at the time of its composition and that the essay's purpose is to attack organized religion as much as to explicate Freemasonry's beginnings. "On the Origin of Free-Masonry," which posits a druid origin to the Masonic fraternity, is of a piece with the confrontational religious approach Paine embraced in his later works, where he denounced revealed religion and endorsed deism. Freemasonry and deism intersected often in revolutionary America and France, and due to Paine's associations with members of the fraternity in both places and sympathy with certain of its beliefs and aims, he devoted an essay to Freemasonry's origins, while simultaneously attacking revealed religion in his exploration of the subject.

Biographer Jack Fruchtman notes that there are no records pointing to Paine's membership in the fraternity: "It has long been questioned whether Paine was a member of the Masons. There is no definitive proof either way. There is no specific date known on which he joined

This article expands upon my prior surveys of the topic, including most recently "Thomas Paine, Freemasonry, and Deism," *Heredom* 22 (2014): 95-106.

nor a specific lodge to which he was attached."[1] Nonetheless, Masonic membership has regularly been ascribed to him. This is seen, for example, in the tendency of some American Masonic Grand Lodges to publish informational brochures that have placed Paine on the roster of famous Freemasons.[2] One such brochure, "The Real Secret of Freemasonry," claims that "the pantheon of Masons holds George Washington, Benjamin Franklin and Thomas Paine, among others."[3] Masonic websites have also continued to make similar assumptions about Paine and Freemasonry,[4] as have articles in Masonic journals.[5]

A chapter of Bernard Vincent's *The Transatlantic Republican: Thomas Paine and the Age of Revolutions* is devoted to Paine and the Masonic Order,[6] and Vincent focuses on a predominant reason for the tendency to consider him a Freemason:

> While working on my Tom Paine biography, I was intrigued from the outset by the fact that all of a sudden, within just a few weeks or months, and as if by magic, Paine leaped from his obscure humdrum existence in England—where he had worked as a corset-maker and Excise officer—onto the American literary and political stage, there to become, at the age of almost forty, one of the leading lights of the Revolutionary movement.
>
> How was it that a man who was little short of a failure in his native country became acquainted so rapidly with the most prominent figures in the Colonies, even becoming a friend of theirs in many cases? How can one account for the quickness of his ascent and the suddenness of his glory?
>
> One way of accounting for this, one hypothesis (which has several times been made), is to consider that Paine became a Freemason and that, as such, he enjoyed, first in America, then in England and

1. Jack Fruchtman, Jr., *Thomas Paine: Apostle of Freedom* (New York: Four Walls Eight Windows, 1994), 491, note 28.

2. See the paragraph on Paine in the list of "Famous Non-Masons" at the website *Anti-Masonry: Points of View*. masonicinfo.com/famousnon.htm.

3. "The Real Secret of Freemasonry," published by authority of the Trustees of The Grand Lodge of A.F. & A.M. of Oregon (U.S.A.: Still Associates, 1990).

4. See, for example, the website of the Scottish Rite Valley of Albany, New York [albanyscottishrite.org], where the opening sentences of Paine's *The American Crisis* are attributed to "Bro. [i.e., Brother] Thomas Paine."

5. See, for example, James W. Beless, "Thomas Jefferson, Freeman," *Scottish Rite Journal* (March 1998), available at srjarchives.tripod.com/1998-03/beless.htm.

6. Bernard Vincent, *The Transatlantic Republican: Thomas Paine and the Age of Revolutions* (Amsterdam: Rodopi, 2005), 35-58, with a selected bibliography on 59-64.

France, the kindly assistance of certain lodges or of certain individual Masons.[7]

Vincent rejects this hypothesis, however, due to a lack of corroborative evidence. While it is certain that George Washington and Benjamin Franklin, for instance, were Freemasons, there is no equivalent support for such a claim about Paine. (Franklin, who provided Paine with a letter of introduction before the latter departed England for the American colonies,[8] is discussed in greater detail below.)

Assertions of Paine's Masonic membership also rest on the fact that between 1803 and 1805, after returning to America from England and France, he penned "On the Origin of Free-Masonry."[9] For some, Paine's curiosity about Freemasonry and his decision to write about it have been, in and of themselves, sufficient proof that he was a Freemason. However, Vincent dismisses this line of reasoning as well:

> Paine's interest in Freemasonry was such that toward the end his life, in 1805, he wrote a lengthy piece entitled *An Essay on the Origin of Freemasonry.* . . . But this does not prove, any more than any other detail or fact that we know of, that Paine was a Mason. There is indeed no formal trace of his initiation or membership in England, none in America, and none in France. Questioned about Paine's membership . . . the United Grand Lodge of England had only this to answer: "In the absence of any record of his initiation, it must, therefore, be assumed he was not a member of the order."[10]

Paine's well-known Masonic associations have also been a source for conjecture about his relationship to the fraternity. It has often been pointed out that Paine had several close friends who were members of the Order, including Nicolas de Bonneville. In his Paine biography, Samuel Edwards depicts Bonneville as an active Freemason who "was convinced that the principles and aims of Masonry, if applied to the world's ailments, would bring peace and prosperity to all nations."[11]

7. Vincent, *Transatlantic Republican*, 35.
8. Dixon Wecter, "Thomas Paine and the Franklins," *American Literature* 12 (1940): 306; and Vincent, *Transatlantic Republican*, 36.
9. Jennifer N. Wunder, *Keats, Hermeticism, and the Secret Societies* (Aldershot: Ashgate, 2008), 37. Vincent (*Transatlantic Republican*, 36) cites 1805 as the year "On the Origin of Free-Masonry" was written, as does Fruchtman (*Thomas Paine*, 491, note 29; and 535). In contrast, William Van der Weyde places its writing in 1803.
10. Vincent, *Transatlantic Republican*, 36.
11. Samuel Edwards, *Rebel! A Biography of Tom Paine* (New York: Praeger Publishers, 1974), 227.

Paine resided at the home of Bonneville and his family while living in France, and Fruchtman proposes that it was Bonneville who introduced Paine to the philosophies of Freemasonry and Theophilanthropism.[12] The bond between the two men was quite strong, with Bonneville's wife—Marguerite—and three sons (one named Thomas Paine Bonneville)[13] eventually following Paine to America.[14]

However, as with Paine's sudden rise to prominence and his composition of an essay on Freemasonry, such friendships do not prove Masonic membership. Rather, as Moncure Daniel Conway contends in an editorial note to *The Writings of Thomas Paine*, "Paine's intimacy in Paris with Nicolas de Bonneville and Charles Francoise Dupuis, whose writings are replete with masonic speculations, sufficiently explains his interest in the subject" of Freemasonry, though he himself was not a Freemason.[15] Similarly, William M. Van der Weyde, in *The Life and Works of Thomas Paine*, mentions Paine's Masonic acquaintances, while at the same time emphasizing that Paine's friendships do not constitute evidence of his belonging to the fraternity: "Paine was the author of an interesting and highly instructive treatise on the *Origin of Freemasonry* . . . but, although many of his circle of friends were undoubtedly members of that order, no conclusive proof has ever been adduced that Paine was a Mason."[16] Vincent offers a long list of Paine's Masonic associates, but his conclusion is similar to that of Conway and Van Der Weyde: they do not prove he was a Freemason.[17]

Marguerite de Bonneville published Paine's "On the Origin of Free-Masonry" in 1810, after his death.[18] She chose, however, to omit certain passages from it that were critical of Christianity.[19] For despite using the Bible to support his arguments in such works as *Common Sense, The American Crisis*, and *Rights of Man*, Paine was in fact strongly opposed to Christianity—and to revealed religion in general—and sought to de-

---

12. Fruchtman, *Thomas Paine*, 275, 379-380. Paine was among the founders of the Society of Theophilanthropists (Friends of God and Man) in Paris. See Harry Harmer, *Tom Paine: The Life of a Revolutionary* (London: Haus Publishing, 2006), 99.

13. Harmer, *Tom Paine*, 99.

14. Fruchtman, *Thomas Paine*, 275, 394-395.

15. Thomas Paine, "Origin of Free-Masonry," in *The Writings of Thomas Paine*, ed. Moncure Daniel Conway (New York: G. P. Putnam's Sons, 1896), vol. 4, 290, note 1.

16. William M. Van der Weyde, *The Life and Works of Thomas Paine* (New York: Thomas Paine National Historical Association, 1925), vol. 1, 171. Most Masonic writers, in contrast, have not shared this high opinion of Paine's essay.

17. Vincent, *Transatlantic Republican*, 36.

18. Fruchtman, *Thomas Paine*, 510.

19. *The Theophilanthropist; Containing Critical, Moral, Theological, and Literary Essays, in Monthly Numbers* (New York: 1810), 370-371.

bunk the Bible in his later writings, including *The Age of Reason*.[20] The removed passages were soon obtained by *The Theophilanthropist*, which supplied them alongside Bonneville's censored version when the essay was reprinted there in 1810.[21] Most of Bonneville's omissions were reincorporated into "On the Origin of Free-Masonry" itself in a subsequent printing of the essay, in 1818,[22] and this version, with an array of editorial notes, is one that readers are likely to encounter today.

Paine's central premise in "On the Origin of Free-Masonry" is that the Order "is derived and is the remains of the religion of the ancient Druids; who, like the Magi of Persia and the Priests of Heliopolis in Egypt, were Priests of the Sun."[23] The idea that Freemasonry developed from druidism did not begin with Paine and has been advanced by others after him. According to Paine, however, this druid origin is the deepest secret of Freemasonry, from which stem its unique fraternal concealments and rituals:

> The natural source of secrecy is fear. When any new religion over-runs a former religion, the professors of the new become the persecutors of the old . . . when the Christian religion over-ran the religion of the Druids. . .the Druids became the subject of persecution. This would naturally and necessarily oblige such of them as remained attached to their original religion to meet in secret, and under the strongest injunctions of secrecy. Their safety depended upon it. A false brother might expose the lives of many of them to destruction; and from the remains of the religion of the Druids, thus preserved, arose the institution which, to avoid the name of Druid, took that of Mason, and practiced under this new name the rites and ceremonies of Druids.[24]

Masonic scholar Albert Gallatin Mackey quips in his 1898 *History of Freemasonry* that Paine "knew, by the way, as little of Masonry as he did of the religion of the Druids."[25] He calls the essay "frivolous" and Paine

20. See Vincent, *Transatlantic Republican*, 10, 89, 99, 145.

21. *Theophilanthropist*, 370-372. Bonneville's earlier published shortened version of Paine's essay appeared in the last thirty pages of the volume.

22. Thomas Paine, *The Theological Works of Thomas Paine* (London: R. Carlile, 1824), 287. The inclusiveness of this 1818 printing is apparently what is intended by Fruchtman when he describes "Origin of Freemasonry" as being "first published in 1818" (*Thomas Paine*, 535), even though he previously states (510) that it was published in 1810.

23. Paine, "Origin of Free-Masonry," 293.

24. Paine, "Origin of Free-Masonry," 303.

25. Albert Gallatin Mackey, *The History of Freemasonry* (New York: The Masonic History Company, 1898), vol. 1, 199.

"a mere sciolist in the subject of what he presumptuously sought to treat."[26] Mackey is only slightly more charitable toward Paine in the entry on him in *An Encyclopedia of Freemasonry and its Kindred Sciences*, allowing that "for one so little acquainted with his subject, he has treated it with considerable ingenuity."[27] Echoing that verdict, Masonic historian Joseph Fort Newton writes in *The Builder Magazine* (1915): "The notion that he was a Mason is probably due to the fact that he wrote an essay on Freemasonry, but the essay, while ingenious in its argument, betrays a vast incomprehension of the Order."[28]

Indeed, it is evident from "On the Origin of Free-Masonry" that Paine was not very knowledgeable of Freemasonry, though this does not in itself prove he was not a Freemason when he wrote it. Paine's general tone, however, discloses him as an outsider trying to assess what is in the Order, rather than a member of it, and indicates that he was not a Freemason when he composed the essay. For instance, after referring to certain statements about Freemasonry in Captain George Smith's *The Use and Abuse of Free-Masonry* (1783), Paine declares:

> It sometimes happens, as well in writing as in conversation, that a person lets slip an expression that serves to unravel what he intends to conceal, and this is the case with Smith, for in the same chapter he says, "The Druids, when they committed any thing to writing, used the Greek alphabet, and I am bold to assert that the most perfect remains of the Druids' rites and ceremonies are preserved in the customs and ceremonies of the Masons that are to be found existing among mankind." "My brethren" says he, "may be able to trace them with greater exactness than I am at liberty to explain to the public."
>
> This is a confession from a Master Mason, without intending it to be so understood by the public, that Masonry is the remains of the religion of the Druids.[29]

Those are not the words of a man who is himself a Master Mason, but rather of one who is guessing at what secrets a Master Mason knows and may be inadvertently revealing. Paine mistakes the conjectures found in Smith's work for an unintended admission on his part about Freemasonry's concealed origins. As it happens, Smith, a Provincial Grand Master of Kent, actually plagiarized the passages that Paine considers his confession. These passages, along with entire sections of

26. Mackey, *History of Freemasonry*, vol. 1, 216.
27. Mackey, *An Encyclopedia of Freemasonry and its Kindred Sciences* (Philadelphia: Moss and Company, 1874), 559.
28. Joseph Fort Newton, "Who's Who," *The Builder Magazine* 1 (1915), 276.
29. Paine, "Origin of Free-Masonry," 294-295.

Smith's chapter on "Antiquity of Free-Masonry in General," are lifted word for word from William Hutchinson's *The Spirit of Masonry in Moral and Elucidatory Lectures* (1775).[30] Smith mentions in *The Use and Abuse of Free-Masonry* that he made it his business "for many years to collect a great number of passages from writers eminent for their learning and probity, where I thought they might serve to illustrate my subject. The propriety of such proceeding is too obvious to need any apology."[31] The propriety of also ascribing these passages to their respective writers, rather than narrating them in the first person, was apparently not as obvious to the unapologetic Smith.

Appropriately, the anonymous author of an 1818 editorial preface to "On the Origin of Free-Masonry"[32] determines that Paine had, despite his best efforts, overreached in attempting to demystify the "abstruse subject"[33] of Freemasonry's beginnings: "Various speculations . . . continue to be made respecting the origin of the society, and its views at the time of its formation; and Mr. Paine, among the rest, with all his sagacity, has suffered himself to be most egregiously deceived by such writings of the masons as had fallen into his hands."[34]

If he was not a Master Mason when he wrote the essay, could Paine have been an Entered Apprentice or a Fellow-Craft? It is difficult to argue—especially given the absence of any records of a Masonic initiation—that Paine was curious enough about Freemasonry's origin and philosophy to write seriously about the fraternity, and also to begin the Masonic degrees, but that he did not wait until completing the first three degrees before concluding his essay. In fact, Paine opens his essay by contending that Master Masons are privy to information on the fraternity's origins that other Freemasons are ignorant about:

> The Society of Masons are distinguished into three classes or degrees. 1st. The Entered Apprentice. 2d. The Fellow Craft. 3d. The Master Mason.
>
> The Entered Apprentice knows but little more of Masonry than the use of signs and tokens, and certain steps and words by which Masons can recognize each other without being discovered by a person who is not a Mason. The Fellow Craft is not much better in-

30. See "Lecture I: The Design" in William Hutchinson, *The Spirit of Masonry in Moral and Elucidatory Lectures* (London: J. Wilkie and W. Goldsmith, 1775), 1-22.
31. George Smith, *The Use and Abuse of Free-Masonry* (London: 1783), 22.
32. Paine, "Origin of Free-Masonry," 290, note 1.
33. "Preface by the Editor to the Origin of Free-Masonry," *Theological Works of Thomas Paine*, 293.
34. "Preface by the Editor to the Origin of Free-Masonry," 287.

structed in Masonry, than the Entered Apprentice. It is only in the
Master Mason's Lodge, that whatever knowledge remains of the origin of Masonry is preserved and concealed.[35]

Had he begun the Masonic degrees, Paine would have likely sought
all the first-hand knowledge they offered, and would have waited until
he had gained access to it before finishing "On the Origin of Free-Masonry." A close reading of "On the Origin of Free-Masonry" makes it
apparent that Paine, although he had companions within the Order,
was not himself a member of the fraternity prior to or during the essay's
composition. While he did have access to texts relating to Freemasonry,
he was prone to misinterpreting them.

In an article on Paine and Freemasonry in the English quarterly
Freemasonry Today, David Harrison speculates that "if Paine did enter
into Freemasonry, it would have been during the period of the American Revolution, his life being at the epicentre of the social elite at that
time, his closeness to Franklin, Washington, Lafayette and Monroe suggesting that he was undoubtedly aware of their Masonic membership."[36]
"On the Origin of Free-Masonry," however, indicates that despite
Paine's closeness to these men, he did not enter into Freemasonry during the period of the American Revolution. Years after the revolution,
he wrote about the fraternity as an outsider and not as an initiate.

Still, facets of Paine's thought may be said to correspond to certain
Masonic principles. In *The Age of Reason*—which Paine may have initially intended "On the Origin of Free-Masonry" to be a part of[37]—he
expounds his religious beliefs: "I believe in one God, and no more; and
I hope for happiness beyond this life. I believe the equality of man; and
I believe that religious duties consist in doing justice, loving mercy, and
endeavoring to make our fellow-creatures happy."[38] Such statements,
which Joseph Fort Newton felt had a Masonic ring to them, prompted
him to write of Paine in *The Builders: A Story and Study of Masonry*:

> Thomas Paine . . . though not a Mason, has left us an essay on The
> Origin of Freemasonry. Few men have ever been more unjustly and
> cruelly maligned than this great patriot, who was the first to utter
> the name "United States," and who, instead of being a sceptic, be-

35. Paine, "Origin of Free-Masonry," 290-291.
36. David Harrison, "Thomas Paine, Freemason?" *Freemasonry Today* 46 (Autumn 2008).
freemasonrytoday.com/46/p11.php.
37. "Preface by the Editor to the Origin of Free-Masonry," 287.
38. Thomas Paine, *The Age of Reason: Being an Investigation of True and Fabulous Theology*
(Boston: Josiah P. Mendum, 1852), part 1, 6.

lieved in "the religion in which all men agree"—that is, in God, Duty, and the immortality of the soul.[39]

Similarly, Vincent maintains in *The Transatlantic Republican* that while Paine "probably never belonged to any specific fraternity, he nevertheless actively sympathized with the Masonic movement and the philosophy it espoused." In Vincent's view, "Masonic thought had much in common with [Paine's] own deistic outlook and his own cult of reason."[40] The movements of deism and Freemasonry often intersected in revolutionary France—where Fruchtman believes Paine was introduced to the fraternity's philosophy—and in revolutionary America, where as Herbert Morais argues, the "growth of deistic speculation was stimulated, not only by the spirit of the times, but also by the development of Freemasonry"[41] and the infiltration of French culture.[42] According to Morais, although "the American Masonic movement was . . . distinctly Christian both in tone and deed . . . nevertheless, its prayers, addresses, and constitutions were written in such a manner that its members were unconsciously familiarized with deistic phraseology . . . [and] with deistic expressions."[43]

Paine's deistic-sounding creed in *The Age of Reason* (and this creed as masonically paraphrased by Joseph Fort Newton) is quite similar to one articulated by Franklin—a self-described deist[44] as well as a prominent Freemason[45]—in his *Autobiography*: "That there is one God who made all things. That he governs the World by his Providence. That he ought to be worshipped by Adoration, Prayer & Thanksgiving. But that the most acceptable Service of God is doing Good to Man. That the Soul is immortal. And that God will certainly reward Virtue and punish

39. Newton, *The Builders: A Story and Study of Masonry* (Iowa: The Torch Press, 1916), 225-226, note 3.

40. Vincent, *Transatlantic Republican*, 35.

41. Herbert M. Morais, "Deism in Revolutionary America (1763-89)," *International Journal of Ethics* 42 (1932): 437.

42. Morais, "Deism in Revolutionary America," 436-437, 442, 452.

43. Morais, "Deism in Revolutionary America," 438-440.

44. David T. Morgan argues in "Benjamin Franklin: Champion of Generic Religion," *The Historian* 62 (2000): 723, that "no one to this very day is quite sure of Franklin's religious beliefs." He suggests that Franklin may be described as a deist, but that his views included "personally tailored modifications of the Deist creed" (728). See also Morais, "Deism in Revolutionary America," 448-449; and Harold E. Taussig, "Deism in Philadelphia During the Age of Franklin," *Pennsylvania History*, 37 (1970): 217-218.

45. See Julius F. Sachse, "The Masonic Chronology of Benjamin Franklin," *The Pennsylvania Magazine of History and Biography* 30 (1906): 238-240.

Vice either here or hereafter."[46] Although, as Robert Falk notes, Paine "nowhere states outright, as Franklin does, that he was a 'thorough Deist,' [he] speaks of the religion always in terms of intimate sympathy,"[47] and "it seems safe to conclude that 'the creed of Paine' was . . . 'the purest deism.'"[48] Indeed, in his conclusion to the second part of *The Age of Reason*, Paine writes:

> If we consider the nature of our condition here, we must see there is no occasion for such a thing as revealed religion. . . .
> [Deism] teaches us, without the possibility of being deceived, all that is necessary or proper to be known. The creation is the Bible of the Deist. He there reads, in the hand-writing of the Creator himself, the certainty of his existence, and the immutability of his power; and all other Bibles and Testaments are to him forgeries. . . .[49]
> The only religion that has not been invented, and that has in it every evidence of divine originality, is pure and simple Deism.[50]

Unlike Franklin, who was usually careful not to offend prevalent eighteenth-century religious sensibilities, focusing instead on what he held to be the beliefs common to all faiths,[51] Paine was not aiming for generic religious doctrine. Forgoing what Vincent terms "the discreet Deism of leaders like Franklin or Jefferson," Paine was vocal in his opposition to organized religion.[52] In *The Age of Reason*, Paine follows his above-quoted statement on his central beliefs with an attack:

> I do not believe in the creed professed by the Jewish church, by the Roman church, by the Greek church, by the Turkish church, by the Protestant church, nor by any church that I know of. My own mind is my own church. . . . All national institutions of churches, whether Jewish, Christian, or Turkish, appear to me no other than human inventions, set up to terrify and enslave mankind, and monopolise power and profit.[53]

---

46. Benjamin Franklin, *The Autobiography and Other Writings*, ed. Kenneth Silverman (New York: Penguin Books, 1986), 104.
47. Robert P. Falk, "Thomas Paine: Deist or Quaker?," *The Pennsylvania Magazine of History and Biography* 62 (1938): 55.
48. Falk, "Thomas Paine: Deist or Quaker?," 60.
49. Paine, *Age of Reason*, part 2, 194.
50. Paine, *Age of Reason*, part 2, 196.
51. Morgan, "Benjamin Franklin: Champion of Generic Religion," 723-729.
52. Vincent, *Transatlantic Republican*, 15.
53. Paine, *Age of Reason*, part 1, 6.

These declarations brought Paine many enemies, including among those who were formerly his friends.[54] The difference in Paine and Franklin's approaches to writing about the sensitive subject of theology can be seen as an extension of the difference in their characters. As Dixon Wecter describes it:

> At his best a Cromwell in the realms of thought, and at his worst a gadfly to Church and State, Paine was a man whose keen though superficial genius included a rare personal gift for irritating all save a minority of kindred souls. Franklin's deeper and more stable character radiated a characteristic serenity; he was a master in the art of mollifying, with a pervasive charm as well as an essential common sense which Paine—despite his nom de plume—conspicuously lacked.[55]

Paine's confrontational religious approach is evident in "On the Origin of Free-Masonry," as well, where he writes that "the christian religion is a parody on the worship of the Sun, in which they put a man whom they call Christ, in the place of the Sun, and pay him the same adoration which was originally paid to the Sun."[56] Further on, he depicts druidism as a "wise, elegant, philosophical religion . . . the faith opposite to the faith of the gloomy Christian church."[57] Such sentiments, which had aroused so much resentment while Paine lived, were what Madame Bonneville sought to remove from "On the Origin of Free-Masonry" when she published it after his death, but as mentioned, she did not succeed in suppressing them for long.

When Augustus Arnold published his *Philosophical History of Free-Masonry and Other Secret Societies* in 1854, he reproduced Paine's entire essay, adding his own notes to it,[58] with the aim of, among other things, correcting what he considered to be Paine's erroneous assertions about the fraternity.[59] As with later Masonic writers, such as Mackey and Newton, Arnold concluded that Paine was not "a member of the brotherhood."[60] Unlike them, he interpreted Paine's essay as a careful attack on both Christianity *and* Freemasonry.[61]

54. Harmer, *Tom Paine*, 92; and Vincent, *Transatlantic Republican*, 16, 90, 153.
55. Wecter, "Thomas Paine and the Franklins," 307.
56. Paine, "Origin of Free-Masonry," 293.
57. Paine, "Origin of Free-Masonry," 296.
58. Augustus C. L. Arnold, *Philosophical History of Free-Masonry and Other Secret Societies* (New York: Clark, Austen, and Smith, 1854), 204-222.
59. Arnold, *Philosophical History of Free-Masonry*, 204, first note.
60. Arnold, *Philosophical History of Free-Masonry*, 204, second note.
61. Arnold, *Philosophical History of Free-Masonry*, 204, first note; 213, second note; and note on 222.

As he evidently was not a Master Mason when he wrote "On the Origin of Free-Masonry"—and as there is no suggestion he joined the fraternity in the interval between composing the essay and his death a few years later, in 1809—it may be concluded that Paine was not a Freemason. Still, though the "pantheon of Masons" does not include Thomas Paine, he remains connected to Freemasonry, if only due to his close friendships with members of the fraternity, to an affinity between his own outlook and deistic aspects of its philosophy, and to his having written an imaginative, if less than accurate, essay on its origin.

Understanding Thomas Jefferson's Reactions to the Rise of the Jacobins

❧ ZACHARY BROWN ❧

Upon the announcement of the convening of the Estates General in 1789, Thomas Jefferson, then the Minister to France, wrote to James Madison with little optimism for the proceedings. In an observation that proved far from prescient, he told his friend on the eve of the country's impending revolution, "France will be quiet this year."[1] The subsequent explosion of revolutionary fervor initially caught Jefferson by surprise. As he would later explain to his Parisian friend Le Comte Diodati in 1807, "I had no apprehension that the tempest, of which I saw the beginning, was to spread over such an extent of space & time."[2] Yet, while Jefferson described the Revolution disparagingly as a "tempest" in 1807, he used very different language in the 1790s. During his time in the Washington administration, Jefferson came to understand both the American and French projects as symbiotic republican experiments. Upon his return to the United States and during his subsequent time as the first Secretary of State, engagement with the French Revolution underpinned the radicalization of Jefferson's political thought, in both domestic and international terms. While Jefferson had certainly celebrated the early and moderate bourgeoisie Revolution led by Mirabeau and his own friend Lafayette, it was the emergence of the violent Jacobin phase between 1792–1793, culminating in the infamous Reign of Terror, which yielded his most enthusiastic and radical support.

1. Thomas Jefferson, "To James Madison, March 15, 1789," in *Thomas Jefferson: Writings: Autobiography, Notes on the State of Virginia, Public and Private Papers, Addresses, Letters*, ed. Merrill D. Peterson (New York: Library of America, 1984), 945.
2. Thomas Jefferson, "To Le Comte Diodati, March 29, 1807," in *The Writings of Thomas Jefferson: Being His Autobiography, Correspondence, Reports, Messages, Addresses, and Other Writings, Official and Private*, ed. H.A. Washington (New York: Cambridge University Press, 2011), 62.

Jefferson's thoughts on this critical period of the Revolution are best voiced in his correspondences with Gouverneur Morris, his successor as the Minister to France, and William Short, the Minister to the Netherlands and Jefferson's friend and former personal secretary. In each case, believing that popular upheaval was a vital mainspring of virtue for a republic, Jefferson's enthusiasm for the Revolution increased as the terror-filled observations of his correspondents became more prominent. Furthermore, as time progressed, he increasingly saw the French Revolution not merely as an extension of the American experiment, but also as an international parallel of his own personal and political struggles with Secretary of the Treasury Alexander Hamilton and the Federalists. Consequently, the rhetoric, language and tone that characterize his letters to Morris and Short suggest that Jefferson's promotion of the French Revolution was intimately connected to a wider project to preserve the spirit of modern republicanism against the vengeful and regressive forces of monarchism, aristocracy, and centralization both abroad and at home. Just as important, his Jacobin panegyrics to Short, and his struggle to act as a detached bureaucrat with Morris, uniquely reveal the extent to which being part of the "republic of letters" was at the same time an intellectual, political, pedagogical, and deeply personal experience for Jefferson, fundamentally tied to cultivating the proper sociability necessary for a republic to succeed.

In January 1792, Jefferson informed Gouverneur Morris that he had been approved by the Senate to serve as Minister Plenipotentiary to France in the midst of transformative change. In the span of just three years, the French revolutionaries had dismantled the Ancien Régime in favor of a constitutional monarchy, which King Louis XVI had accepted in late 1791. Yet this regime was obviously fragile; mob violence and riots dominated the cities, particularly Paris. At the same time, Louis XVI had attempted to flee in his infamous "Flight to Varennes" earlier in the year while, with the king's secret encouragement, Austria and Prussia threatened war. Unlike Jefferson, Morris, a well-known and aristocratic-minded Federalist and friend of Jefferson's archrival Alexander Hamilton, was horrified by the increasing turbulence. While both Morris and Jefferson were in France as the Revolution began, the two men's perspectives could not have been more different. Consider their reactions to the violence that followed the storming of the Bastille in July 1789. In his diary, Morris wrote with horror, "the populace [carries] the mangled fragments [of corpses] with a Savage Joy. Gracious God what a people."[3] In contrast, Jefferson described the same events in a

---

3. Melanie Randolph Miller, *Envoy to Terror: Gouverneur Morris and the French Revolution* (Washington D.C.: Potomac Books, 2005), 26.

Gouverneur Morris, left, Thomas Jefferson's successor as the Minister to France; Jefferson, right, in a 1786 portrait by Mather Brown. (*National Portrait Gallery*)

playful letter to Maria Cosway, telling her, "the cutting off of heads is become so much a la mode, that one is apt to feel whether their own is on their shoulder."[4] While Jefferson did not directly advocate for such violence in his letter to Cosway, he saw it as no serious reason for concern. Morris's anxiety only increased as time progressed, but Jefferson maintained this insouciance towards horrifying violence. This fundamental tension over how they understood the very early upheaval in France would characterize the tone of the two men's correspondence as the French Revolution radicalized further.

Given this difference of opinion, it is unsurprising that Jefferson was apprehensive towards Morris's appointment and made a point to warn against vocalizing anti-revolutionary views in his austere first letter informing Morris of the appointment:

> With respect to their Government, we are under no call to express opinions, which might please or offend any party; and therefore it will be best to avoid them on all occasions, public or private. Could any circumstances require unavoidably such expressions, they would naturally be in conformity with the sentiments of the great mass of our countrymen, who having first, in modern times, taken

4. Thomas Jefferson, "To Maria Cosway, July 25, 1789," in *The Papers of Thomas Jefferson*, vol. 15, *27 March 1789–30 November 1789*, ed. Julian P. Boyd (Princeton: Princeton University Press, 1958), 305–306.

the ground of Government founded on the will of the people, cannot but be delighted on seeing so distinguished and so esteemed a Nation arrive on the same ground, and plant their standard by our side.[5]

In response, Morris acknowledged Jefferson's orders but openly rebuked his superior's idealism, informing the Secretary that he followed his instructions not because France had "plant[ed] their standard by our side," as Jefferson had claimed. Instead, Morris complied because "changes are now so frequent, and Events seem fast ripening to such awful Catastrophe, that no Expressions on the Subject, however moderate, would be received with Indifference."[6] It is not hard to imagine that Jefferson would have bristled at such a sardonic admonishment of his faith in the French Revolution, setting the stage for the subtle hostility, and aloofness on Jefferson's part, that characterized their correspondence until Jefferson resigned his cabinet position in late 1793.

Jefferson gave no similar warning to his friend William Short whom he had informed on the same day of his confirmation as Minister to the Hague. Using a much friendlier tone, he merely told Short, "your past experience . . . renders it unnecessary for me to particularize your duties . . . harmony with our friends being our object, you are sensible how much it will be promoted by attention to the manner, as well as matter of your communications."[7] This dynamic would typify Jefferson's correspondence with the two men for the next two years. A subtle tension characterized Jefferson's letters with Morris as the two clashed and often secretly undermined each other's efforts.[8] In contrast, Short, even as he became disillusioned with the French Revolution, became an audience for many of Jefferson's most personal and radical statements of support for the Jacobins.

It did not take long for Morris and Jefferson to express their dislike for one another directly. In his private notes in March 1792, Jefferson blamed Morris for the President's lack of faith in the Revolution, calling

5. Thomas Jefferson, "To Gouverneur Morris, January 23, 1792," in *The Papers of Thomas Jefferson*, vol. 23, *1 January–31 May 1792*, ed. Charles T. Cullen (Princeton: Princeton University Press, 1990), 56.

6. Gouverneur Morris, "To Thomas Jefferson, April 6, 1792," in *The Papers of Thomas Jefferson*, 23:382.

7. Thomas Jefferson, "To William Short, January 23, 1792," in ibid., 58.

8. For example, Morris actively worked with constitutional monarchists to undermine the National Convention even while Jefferson ordered him to support it. Similarly, he privately sent sensitive diplomatic information to his friend Alexander Hamilton and to President Washington in an attempt to circumvent Jefferson's authority. At the same time, Jefferson actively agitated against Morris's appointment and petitioned Washington against his influence on policy regarding the Revolution.

him "a high flying Monarchy-man, shutting his eyes and his faith to every fact against his wishes, and believing every thing he desires to be true, [his influence] has kept the President's mind constantly poisoned."[9] This devastating assessment of the minister helps to explain why Jefferson engaged so little with the horrifying accounts of violence Morris sent him. Jefferson, already distrustful of the New York aristocrat, had become so committed to supporting the French Revolution that he believed that Morris was nothing more than a monarchical propagandist. Jefferson had legitimate reasons to be suspicious. Morris, without explicit approval from the State Department, had acted as an advisor to the king before his appointment and conspired with constitutional monarchists to devise a plan for the king's escape in the summer of 1792.[10] Nevertheless, at the same time, Morris, clearly wary of Jefferson's domestic influence on the issue of the Revolution, promised his friend Hamilton that he would "apprize [him] of what is doing on this Side of the Water confidentially which I will not do to every Body," and requested that President Washington give him permission to withhold certain information from Jefferson.[11] If Jefferson believed Morris was a monarchist, Morris correspondingly thought that the Secretary of State was a dangerous radical whose utopian ideals promoted the anarchy and mob rule he saw unfolding in Paris first hand.

While neither Jefferson nor Morris fully understood the extent of the profound mutual personal distrust between them, it only grew more apparent as the French Revolution entered its most radical phase in the summer of 1792. Throughout the summer, Morris provided Jefferson with lengthy accounts of recent developments, dominated by his increasing anxiety over urban violence and a clear disdain for the ascendant Jacobin faction within the Legislative Assembly. On June 10 he described the ongoing social upheaval and incompetence of the new government in particularly stark terms, exclaiming, "the best Picture I can give of the French Nation, in this moment, is that of Cattle before

9. Thomas Jefferson, "Memoranda of Consultations with the President, [11 March–9 April 1792]," in *The Papers of Thomas Jefferson*, 23:260.

10. Before his appointment, Morris had advised Louis XVI on the Constitution of 1791. He does briefly mention his participation in the royalist plot to Jefferson through a veiled reference in his July 10, 1792 letter describing the scheme as the King's "New Career."

11. Gouverneur Morris, "To Alexander Hamilton, March 21, 1792," in *The Papers of Alexander Hamilton*, vol. 11, *February 1792–June 1792*, ed. Harold C. Syrett (New York: Columbia University Press, 1966), 162–163. Gouverneur Morris, "To George Washington, April 6, 1792," in *The Papers of George Washington*, Presidential Series, vol. 10, *1 March 1792–15 August 1792*, ed. Robert F. Haggard and Mark A. Mastromarino (Charlottesville: University of Virginia Press, 2002), 224.

a Thunder Storm. And as to the Government, every Member of it is engagd in the Defence of himself or the Attack of his Neighbor." Furthermore, Morris, clearly attacking Jefferson's belief in the Revolution as the "will of the people," described the political system as being on the verge of collapsing into anarchy or military rule as "the great Mass of the French Nation is less solicitous to preserve the present order of Things than to prevent the Return of the antient Oppressions; and of Course would more readily submit to a pure Despotism than to [the present] Monarchy."[12] He was even more despondent on the seventeenth, claiming, in a statement that would have baffled Jefferson, that the Jacobins' desire to "purge" the king's ministers and form a "federal Republic," was evidence they were seeking to destroy "the finest Opportunity which ever presented itself for establishing the Rights of Mankind throughout the civilized World."[13] These reports plainly illustrate a profound divide between Jefferson and Morris. While Jefferson was encouraged that, regardless of the violence, the Revolution was the product of the will of the people and the triumph of republicanism, Morris recoiled at these very same facts with abject horror.

Morris's anxiety reached a fever pitch as his fears became a reality following the journée of August 10, when the revolutionary forces stormed the Tuileries Palace and deposed the king, leading to the September Massacres: a hysteria-fueled wave of prisoner executions committed by enraged mobs of *sans-culottes*. He described the subsequent rise of the new Jacobin dominated republic as a "bloody" second revolution, and claimed that it resulted in "one Week of uncheck'd murders in which some thousands have perished in the City." He consequently refused to recognize the new National Convention, declaring to Jefferson that he "had no Powers to treat with the present Government."[14] In response to this newest wave of concerns, after four months of silence on the issue, Jefferson finally replied in November. He was unfazed by Morris's accounts and provided clear instructions:

> It accords with our principles to acknolege [sic] any government to be rightful which is formed by the will of the nation substantially de-

12. Gouverneur Morris, "To Thomas Jefferson, June 10, 1792," in *The Papers of Thomas Jefferson*, vol. 24, *1 June–31 December 1792*, ed. John Catanzariti (Princeton: Princeton University Press, 1990), 52, 55.
13. Gouverneur Morris, "To Thomas Jefferson, June 17, 1792," in ibid., 93–94.
14. Gouverneur Morris, "To Thomas Jefferson, August 16, 1792," in ibid., 301. Gouverneur Morris, "To Thomas Jefferson, September 10th, 1792," in ibid., 364. Gouverneur Morris, "To Thomas Jefferson, August 30, 1792," in ibid., 332.

clared. The late government was of this kind, and was accordingly acknoleged by all the branches of ours. So any alteration of it which shall be made by the will of the nation substantially declared, will doubtless be acknoleged in like manner. With such a government every kind of business may be done.[15]

As Jefferson would explain in simpler terms on December 30 of that year, upon hearing that the execution of the king seemed likely, "We surely cannot deny to any nation that right whereon our own government is founded . . . the will of the nation is the only thing essential to be regarded."[16] While Morris and Jefferson continued to matter-of-factly discuss the state of France's Revolutionary wars, treaty negotiations, and American, French, and other European political developments, this statement of foreign policy was effectively the final word on the legitimacy of the French Republic and the Revolution. Following his conservative account of the king's trial in December of 1792 and execution in January, until he was recalled in the summer of 1794 just days before the arrest of Robespierre, Morris was conspicuously silent on the escalating Jacobin terror in his letters to Jefferson.[17]

Despite this change in his letters to Jefferson, Morris did not stop discussing the terror entirely as it reached its greatest heights in 1793. Instead, his correspondence with the President became increasingly dire as he reported in February of that year that France's "prospects are [increasingly] dreadful . . . in short the fabric of the present system is erected on a quagmire."[18] Most strikingly, by June he told Washington that while he would continue to follow Jefferson's orders to recognize the National Convention, now entirely controlled by Robespierre's radical Montagnards following the purge of the Girondins, he called these instructions the cause of "embarrassments [which] have arisen from

15. Thomas Jefferson, "To Gouverneur Morris, November 7, 1792," in ibid., 593.
16. Thomas Jefferson, "To Gouverneur Morris, December 30, 1792," in *Thomas Jefferson: Writings*, 1002. Importantly, there are reasons to believe Jefferson never actually sent the December 30 letter to Morris. No record of the letter exists in State Department files, while Jefferson sent a very similar letter to Thomas Pinckney, the Minister to Great Britain, on December 30 that is recorded. Similarly, Jefferson used nearly the exact same language in a March 13, 1793 letter to Morris.
17. In fact, their last correspondence was a letter from Thomas Jefferson to Morris on October 3, 1793, with no further letters exchanged before Jefferson resigned his post in late December.
18. Gouverneur Morris, "To George Washington, February 14, 1793," in *The Papers of George Washington*, Presidential Series, vol. 12, *16 January 1793–31 May 1793*, ed. Christine Sternberg Patrick and John C. Pinheiro (Charlottesville: University of Virginia Press, 2005) 142–143.

inattention to the principles of free government."[19] Collectively, these letters suggest that Morris had given up on both helping to reform the French cause from what he saw as runway radicalism and anarchy or persuading Jefferson to abandon it, realizing that it was in his best interest to simply manage affairs to the best of his abilities until the situation hopefully changed.[20] Meanwhile, Jefferson had effectively ignored Morris's concerns completely and maintained his absolute faith in the Revolution as an extension of the American republican project. If anything, there is reason to believe that Jefferson, who had written only a few years earlier in reaction to Shays' Rebellion that "the tree of liberty must be refreshed from time to time with the blood of patriots & tyrants," saw the popular violence against non-republicans as a sign of the strength and virtue of the French Revolution.[21]

Nevertheless, there is reason to believe that Jefferson was not even reading Morris's accounts very closely. For example, in a letter to James Madison in the summer of 1792 he, in complete contrast to what Morris had told him, claimed that the royal ministry "is of the Jacobin party [and thus] cannot but be favorable to us, as that whole party must be." Yet, he felt completely confident in declaring to Madison, "notwithstanding the very general abuse of the Jacobins, I begin to consider them as representing the true revolutionary-spirit of the whole nation, and

19. Gouverneur Morris, "To George Washington, June 25, 1793," in *The Papers of George Washington*, Presidential Series, vol. 13, *1 June 1793–31 August 1793*, ed. Christine Sternberg Patrick and John C. Pinheiro (Charlottesville: University of Virginia Press, 2005) 146.

20. There is reason to believe that Morris was already arriving at this conclusion independently following the upheaval of August 10, even before he received Jefferson's November response. Consider his August 22, 1792 letter to Jefferson. He remained largely negative in tone lamenting Lafayette's failure to contain the radical Jacobins and his subsequent fall from grace and exile: "He, as you will learn, encamped at Sedan and official Accounts of last Night inform us that he has taken Refuge with the Enemy. Thus his circle is compleated. He has spent his Fortune on a Revolution, and is now crush'd by the wheel which he put in Motion. He lasted longer than I expected." Yet, he now seemed resigned to remaining in Paris, rather than fleeing himself, and accepting the new National Convention as the legitimate government of France, surely anticipating that these would be Jefferson's instructions: "Going hence however would look like taking Part against the late Revolution and I am not only unauthoriz'd in this Respect but I am bound to suppose that if the great Majority of the Nation adhere to the new Form the United States will approve thereof because in the first Place we have no Right to prescribe to this Country the Government they shall adopt and next because the Basis of our own Constitution is the indefeasible Right of the People to establish it." Gouverneur Morris, "To Thomas Jefferson, August 22, 1792," in *The Papers of Thomas Jefferson*, 24:313–314.

21. Thomas Jefferson, "To William S. Smith, November 13, 1787," in *Thomas Jefferson: Writings*, 911.

as carrying the nation with them."[22] That he could confuse the radical Jacobins with the royal ministry they despised suggests that Jefferson cared little about what Morris had to say regarding the horrors unfolding in France and was happy to champion the Revolution based on his faith in the inevitable triumph of republicanism.[23] For Jefferson, learning that the Jacobins had now become radical republicans committed to eliminating royalist opposition by force only enhanced his faith further. In Jefferson's mind, Morris was an aristocratic ally of Hamilton, so, as he had expressed plainly in March, his reports were nothing more than monarchist propaganda meant to support the Federalist agenda in America.

An even more fundamental cause of Jefferson's lack of engagement with Morris was the role he thought the republic of letters played in developing the new nation and republican revolutions both domestically and internationally. While he continued to communicate with Morris periodically as bureaucratic duties demanded, his indifferent tone and infrequent responses suggest that this purely procedural correspondence was always a profoundly unnatural role for Jefferson, particularly on issues he was passionate about, none more so than the French Revolution. As Jefferson would explain to John Hollins in 1809, networks of correspondence were meant to be "a great fraternity spreading over the whole earth" that brought people closer together, a necessity for an ideal republican society, rather than pushing them farther apart.[24]

The intensely personal purpose of letter writing that Jefferson imagined to be essential for cultivating republican sociability and fraternity was thus impossible if not counterproductive with Morris due to the personal and political enmity between them, reaching its zenith as the

22. Thomas Jefferson, "To James Madison, June 29, 1792," in *The Papers of James Madison*, vol. 14, *6 April 1791–16 March 1793*, ed. Robert A. Rutland and Thomas A. Mason (Charlottesville: University Press of Virginia, 1983), 334.

23. To further support this interpretation of Jefferson's unwavering faith in the Revolution consider that he had embraced the Jacobins, even if he misunderstood who they actually were, just weeks after he praised their archrival, and his long time personal friend, Lafayette for "establishing the liberties of your country against a foreign enemy. May heaven favor your cause, and make you the channel thro' which it may pour it's favors. While you are exterminating the monster aristocracy, and pulling out the teeth and fangs of it's associate monarchy." Yet even after hearing of Lafayette's exile from Morris and Jacobin despotism from both Short and Morris, his support for the Revolution only increased. Thomas Jefferson, "To Lafayette, June, 16, 1792," in *The Papers of Thomas Jefferson*, 24:85.

24. Thomas Jefferson, "To John Hollins, February, 19, 1809," in *The Writings of Thomas Jefferson*, 428.

Jacobin Terror intensified in 1792–1793. Jefferson evidently believed that Morris, or any aristocratic Federalist, could never be a true partner in building the new nation as they could not freely communicate and develop the bonds necessary for a republican society to flourish. If anything, Jefferson, already averse to conflict, believed that his unnatural and acrimonious correspondence with Morris alienated him from the sociability natural for a republican order and thus deliberately sought to avoid further communication.

Jefferson's very different and contemporaneous correspondence with his close friend William Short supports this interpretation of the Secretary of State's understanding of the French Revolution and his correspondence with Morris. Short, like his mentor and unlike Morris, had initially been an enthusiastic supporter of the bourgeoisie phase of the Revolution while serving as Jefferson's secretary and then temporary replacement in Paris. Yet, by the time Short had taken up his new position as Minister to the Netherlands, as the Revolution rapidly radicalized, his views began to converge with those expressed by Morris

In August of 1792, Short echoed the very same anxieties that his counterpart in Paris was reporting, telling Jefferson that "arrestations, massacre or flight" had become "friends and supporters of the late constitution." He particularly chastised the Jacobins, claiming, "Robertspierre [sic] . . . and others of that atrocious and cruel caste compose the tribunal . . . we may expect [them to head] proceedings under the cloak of liberty, *egalité* and patriotism as would disgrace any *chambre ardente* that has ever existed."[25] Short's statement amounted to a complete rejection of the radical and violent form that the Revolution had taken under the Jacobins. Short rebuked the fundamental principle of Jacobin republicanism, as Robespierre described it in his infamous *Report on the Principles of Political Morality* (1794):

25. William Short, "To Thomas Jefferson, August 24, 1792," in *The Papers of Thomas Jefferson*, 24:322, 325. The "tribunal" Short mentions is a reference to the Revolutionary Tribunal set up by the National Convention in August 1792 at the encouragement of Robespierre and the Paris Commune. Exactly as Short predicted, the Tribunal quickly became the main organ through which the Jacobins enacted the Reign of Terror, holding what were effectively show trials to justify the purging of royalists and moderates. At the height of the Terror, the Tribunal was entirely dominated by Robespierre and the Committee of Public Safety, which used it to eliminate conservative (Girondins) and moderate (e.g. Danton) Jacobins and those considered too radical (e.g. Hébertists). Short's invoking of the *chambre ardente* is likely a sarcastic reference to the religious courts of the Ancien Régime, where heretics, particularly Huguenots, were subjected to cruel punishments. The implication being that even the absolutist Bourbon regime the republicans deposed would be embarrassed by the new government's despotic tendencies.

> If the mainspring of popular government in peacetime is virtue, amid revolution it is at the same time [both] virtue and terror: virtue, without which terror is fatal; terror, without which virtue is impotent. Terror is nothing but prompt, severe, inflexible justice; it is therefore an emanation of virtue ... a consequence of the general principle of democracy ... subdue liberty's enemies by terror and you will be right, as founders of the Republic.[26]

As his dismissive comments reveal, Short, like many observers to follow, saw Robespierre's argument as nothing more than a pretext for despotism.

Yet, in his remarkable and aggressive response to Short's letter, Jefferson continued to justify the French Revolution on grounds that superficially seem uniquely Jacobin. In his January 1793 reply, he told Short that "the tone of your letters had for some time given me pain, on account of the extreme warmth with which they censured the proceedings of the Jacobins of France. I consider that sect the same with the Republican patriots." He proceeded to describe the Jacobins as virtuous republicans who had realized the failures of constitutional monarchy and agitated for reform with the best interests of the people in mind and the will of the nation behind them. He then turned to the most radical part of his letter:

> In the struggle which was necessary, many guilty persons fell without the forms of trial, and with them some innocent. These I deplore as much as any body, and shall deplore some of them to the day of my death. But I deplore them as I should have done had they fallen in battle ... The liberty of the whole earth was depending on the issue of the contest, and was ever such a prize won with so little innocent blood? My own affections have been deeply wounded by some of the martyrs to this cause, but rather than it should have failed, I would have seen half the earth desolated. Were there but an Adam and an Eve left in every country, and left free, it would be better than as it now is. I have expressed to you my sentiments because they are really those of 99 in an hundred of our citizens.[27]

---

26. Maximilien Robespierre, "Report on the Principles of Political Morality," in *University of Chicago Readings in Western Civilization, Volume 7: The Old Regime and the French Revolution,* ed. Keith M. Baker (Chicago: University of Chicago Press, 1987), 374-375.
27. Thomas Jefferson, "To William Short, January 3, 1793," in *The Papers of Thomas Jefferson,* vol. 25, *1 January-10 May 1793,* ed. John Catanzariti (Princeton: Princeton University Press, 1992), 14.

This striking excerpt suggests that Jefferson had embraced Robespierre's argument that violence and terror were a legitimate means, if not the ideal way, to create a revolutionary republic. While superficially uniquely Jacobin, Jefferson had been developing these very same ideas independently during his time as Minister to France in the late 1780s. As his aforementioned reaction to Shays' Rebellion revealed, he thought popular violence was a sign of republican vigor rather than decay. It was thus, according to Jeffersonian thought, the violence of the Jacobin Terror, rather than the abolition of monarchy or any other political development, that allowed republicanism to prosper. While Jefferson likely did not yet appreciate the despotic tendencies of the Jacobin government, Short's and Morris's attempts to horrify him had only strengthened his faith in the French Revolution as a continuation of, if not an improvement on, the American project.

While certainly a statement in support of the French Revolution, historians often regard this letter as an early example of American exceptionalism. As Annette Gordon-Reed and Peter Onuf argue, while Jefferson believed that "rivers of blood" were required in France before their revolution could equal the American achievement, in contrast, "the American Revolution had succeeded, patriots' blood had stopped flowing and the nation was 'left free.'"[28] However, this perspective is wide of the mark as Jefferson's radical justification for the Revolution clearly connects to his anxieties over both domestic political developments taking place at the height of his inter-cabinet feud with Hamilton and the very foundations of the American Revolution itself.

The importance of this tension in motivating Jefferson's support of the Revolution is most evident in the second half of his January 1793 letter to Short. He justified his enthusiasm for revolutionary France through a veiled, but obvious, attack on Hamilton and the Federalists: "there are in the U.S. some characters of opposite principles . . . hostile to France and fondly looking to England . . . [this] little party . . . [has] espoused [the Constitution] only as a stepping stone to monarchy." He concludes this thought by remarking triumphantly, "the successes of republicanism in France have given the coup de grace to their prospects and I hope to their projects."[29] This statement suggests that the motivations behind Jefferson's support of the French Republic were not primarily a product of his foreign policy ambitions or an attachment to France as has often been supposed. Instead, his thoughts on the Revo-

28. Annette Gordon-Reed and Peter Onuf, *Most Blessed of the Patriarchs: Thomas Jefferson and the Empire of the Imagination* (New York: Liveright, 2016), 193-194.
29. Thomas Jefferson, "To William Short, January 3, 1793," in *The Papers of Thomas Jefferson*, 25:15.

lution were telling projections of his anxieties surrounding American and particularly personal political disputes.

At a time when the anglophilic Hamiltonian economic, social, and political program seemed ascendant, Jefferson championed the "success" of the French Revolution as a vindication of the true principles of republicanism. While the American experiment was at risk of decaying into a British style autocracy under Federalist control, France was making true strides towards creating an ideal republic—a goal for which Jefferson clearly believed bloodshed was a modest cost.[30] Thus, for Jefferson, the American Revolution remained very much alive both at home and abroad, but, at the same time, increasingly in peril as the resurgent forces of British monarchism took on the even more insidious form of pseudo-republicans like Hamilton and his allies. Consequently, redeeming the American project required vigorous opposition to the two foundational tenets of Federalist schemes: Hamilton's financial plan domestically, meant to corrupt the American republic from within, and, just as important, opposition to the French Revolution, meant to slow the inevitable collapse of monarchy and aristocracy internationally. The fact that the most powerful monarchical regimes of Europe - Austria, Prussia, and Britain - sought to crush the Revolution only heightened the importance of the French Republic in Jefferson's mind. Put simply, if the Federalists could convince Americans to abandon their fellow republican patriots in favor of the despotic monarchies of Europe, the American Revolution was over and it had failed.

This interpretation helps to explain the profound difference in tone, language, and subject matter between his correspondences with Morris and Short. According to Jefferson's understanding, while both held official positions under his department, Morris was, unlike Short, a leading member of the monarchical Federalist cabal and thus better left isolated than reasoned with. Like all Federalists, Morris was too blinded by the rapid collapse of ancient and unnatural privileges to realize that the Jacobin Terror was a progressive rather than destructive development, eliminating and purifying the foundations of tyranny by force. Morris's horror at this fact radicalized Jefferson because it illustrated where the American project had failed; fearful of anarchy and mob rule, Americans had become too conservative, imposing the husk of a republic

---

30. An earlier articulation of this idea is evident in the aforementioned June 16, 1792 letter to Lafayette, where Jefferson celebrates French success while lamenting that in America there are "Eastward . . . champions for a king, lords, and commons," and that "Too many of these stock jobbers and king-jobbers have come into our legislature, or rather too many of our legislature have become stock jobbers and king-jobbers."

without completely leveling the social and cultural norms that enabled autocracy in the first place. The Jacobins' comparative success had proven that the unchecked pursuit of the simple egalitarian values of 1789—liberty, equality, and fraternity—rather than the reactionary principles of 1787 was the ideal basis for reviving and fulfilling the republican zeitgeist that Americans had captured in 1776.

As the success of Hamilton's financial plan revealed, as long as these attachments to the old order remained, decay was inevitable as monarchical corruption simply took new forms. The inability of Morris to abandon his sympathies for aristocratic privilege, and embrace the triumphs of republican freedom occurring right in front of him, made it clear to Jefferson that the republican reform pursued thus far was not enough to annihilate these unnatural attachments. Instead, the Revolution had to completely purify society of its old corruptions if it was to succeed. In Jefferson's view, the Jacobins had whole-heartedly pursued this goal, laying the roadmap for the Americans to eventually do the same. If the Federalists succeeded in making the French and American projects appear fundamentally irreconcilable, this opportunity for creating a true republican society would be squandered. This fear is why Jefferson supported the French Revolution with such radical enthusiasm in his January 1793 letter to Short. If Short, a true republican in the Jeffersonian sense, could be tricked by Hamiltonian sophisms and intrigues which had worked to obscure the remarkable achievements of the French Revolution, the Federalists had already succeeded in debasing the fraternity, virtue, and strength of the American republic.[31]

While these ideological and political disputes were a critical impulse for Jefferson's letters to many individuals, his correspondence with Short discussing the French Revolution is uniquely intimate. Unlike his difficulty communicating with Morris, Jefferson's correspondence with his close friend was a far more natural experience, enabling Jefferson to express his enthusiastic support for the French Revolution unabashedly. Jefferson certainly discussed these issues with other friends often with

---

31. For further support of this interpretation of his opinion of both Short and Morris see Jefferson's March 23, 1793 letter to William Short where he wrote: "Be cautious in your letters to the Secretary of the treasury. He sacrifices you. On a late occasion when called on to explain before the Senate his proceedings relative to the loans in Europe, instead of extracting such passages of your letters as might relate to them, he gave in the originals in which I am told were strong expressions against the French republicans: and even gave in a correspondence between G. Morris and yourself which scarcely related to the loans at all, merely that a long letter of Morris's might appear in which he argues as a democrat himself against you as an aristocrat." Thomas Jefferson, "To William Short, March 23, 1793," in *The Papers of Thomas Jefferson*, 25:436.

equal or even greater frequency. However, Short's proximity to the unfolding Revolution made him the ideal individual for Jefferson to articulate his perspectives, likely with hopes of having them confirmed in response.

Beyond his proximity to the Revolution, Short's personal connections to Jefferson exacerbated his importance. While Jefferson and Morris detested one another's political and personal sensibilities, Jefferson's relationship with Short was explicitly and reciprocally described through familial terms. In a 1789 letter to the famous painter John Trumbull, Jefferson called Short his "adoptive son."[32] Similarly, at the height of their disagreement over the French Revolution, Short called Jefferson, while writing to the Duchess de la Rochefoucauld in July of 1794, "my father."[33] It is not hard to imagine that Jefferson took his paternal role in Short's life very seriously and thus sought to educate him through their correspondence. Even though Short held an official position under the State Department, in Jefferson's mind they communicated as father and son rather than as bureaucrats or political enemies. This much friendlier dynamic meant that Jefferson's correspondence with Short was compatible with the purpose he imagined the republic of letters playing in the age of republican revolutions despite their disagreements on the French Revolution. Transcending his petty and counterproductive political disputes with Morris and the Federalists, Jefferson's correspondence with Short, even if typified by intense ideological and political differences, acted as an edifying experience for both parties that reinforced the natural sociability, in this case particularly paternal and fraternal bonds, which undergirded republican societies.

Jefferson's time as Secretary of State coincided with the most explosive phase of the French Revolution. What started as an attempt to dismantle the Ancien Régime and institute a constitutional monarchy blossomed into a radical experiment in creating an entirely new republican society. As his correspondence with Minister to France Gouverneur Morris and Minister to the Netherlands William Short during the emergence of the Jacobin Terror reveals, Jefferson responded to the violent radicalization of the Revolution with enthusiastic support. His advocacy for the French Revolution did not signify his emergence as a disruptive insurrectionist in favor of purposeless violence, anarchy and unbridled populism. Instead, he advocated for recognition and support

32. Thomas Jefferson, "To John Trumbull, June 1, 1789," in *The Papers of Thomas Jefferson,* vol. 15, 27 March 1789–30 November 1789, ed. Julian P. Boyd (Princeton: Princeton University Press, 1958), 164.

33. Marie G. Kimball and Alexandre de Liancourt, "William Short, Jefferson's Only 'Son,'" *North American Review* 223, no. 832 (1926): 481.

of the Jacobin government as a successful international analog to the republican project he wanted to pursue at home at the expense of the "monarchical" aspirations of Hamilton and the Federalists. In practice, the parallels he imagined between the ideal Jeffersonian and Jacobin republics were usually more apparent than real, as Jefferson often ignored the reports of Morris and Short in favor of fanciful idealizing of his French counterparts—a problem Jefferson would only come to grips with in retirement. Despite these dilemmas, Jefferson's impassioned advocacy for the French Revolution proved effective, emerging as a cornerstone of the burgeoning Republican Party's foreign policy and remaining important well into the early nineteenth century, until the Revolution ceased to be an important political issue.

At the same time, his very different letters with Morris and Short reveal the centrality of correspondence in Jefferson's psyche as he sought to promote republican revolutions both abroad and at home. Correspondence was not merely a means to communicate information, but rather a fundamental part of developing the social bonds central to the vigor and virtue of any republic. The mutual ideological and personal distaste that characterized his relationship with Morris made cultivating these links impossible, as factional conflict and intrigue forced Jefferson to take on the unnatural role of an aloof bureaucrat. In contrast, despite their intense disagreement on the Jacobin Terror, his intimate friendship with Short enabled Jefferson to express his most radical statements of support for the French Revolution, hoping that discussion unrestrained by irrational fears and unnatural attachments would cultivate proper republican sociability in both participants. In many ways, his letters with Short are symbolic of the exact kind of discourse Jefferson hoped would predominate in the United States and among republics internationally. Yet, in an ironic twist of fate, it was the faction and intrigue-fueled tensions of his correspondence with Morris, which he detested yet arguably did more than anyone to cultivate, that in many ways won out.

The Tireless Pension Pursuit of Bristol Budd Sampson

ROBERT N. FANELLI

On an October day in 1820, a fourteen-year-old African American boy trudged along a rural lane near the town of Barkhamsted, Connecticut. Two hundred miles from home, in a strange place he had never visited before, the boy tugged at a string trailing behind him. Tagging along at the other end was his father, Bristol Budd, a singular and spirited man, about fifty seven years of age, completely blind, but by no means bowed by infirmity. The pair carried an affidavit from William Taylor, Barkhamsted's Justice of the Peace, which swore that Budd and Taylor had once been brothers in arms, serving together in the 2nd Connecticut Continental Regiment during the Revolutionary War. Now the aging veteran and his son traipsed over rugged, wooded hills toward the town of Canton, ten miles away, following Taylor's suggestion that they visit his kinsman David, also a veteran of the 2nd Connecticut, to obtain another statement that would help the blind man secure a pension, a godsend that could provide him with steady income now that he could no longer work for a living.

Bristol Budd was born sometime between 1756 and 1763, most likely in the southeastern corner of Connecticut.[1] He is described as a black

---

1. Much of the personal information about Budd is from his pension application file in the Revolutionary War Pension and Bounty Land Warrant Application Files, M804, Roll 398, National Archives and Records Administration, Washington, DC (NARA). He is referred to in a variety of ways: Brister Budd, Briston Budd and Bristol Bird. One document, dated December 4, 1820, describes him as "Bristol Budd alias Bristol Sampson (a black man) aged about fifty seven years residing in the Township of Waterford in the County of Susquehanna," suggesting a birth year of 1763. Under the heading "Pensioners for Revolutionary or Military Services," the 1840 Census for Susquehanna County, Pennsylvania, lists Bristol B. Sampson, age eighty-four, which would put his birth about 1756. 1840 United States Census, Brooklyn Township, Susquehanna County, Pennsylvania, 322.

man, and by some as a full blooded African.[2] His name was sometimes given as Bristol Sampson, and this appears to be how he was known in his early days. Later in life he was frequently referred to as Bristol Budd, alias Bristol Sampson, and in his old age his name appears as Bristol Budd Sampson.

He was somewhere between the ages of fourteen and twenty-one when, in March of 1777, he enlisted as a private in the company of Capt. Stephen Betts, of Stamford, Connecticut, part of the 2nd Connecticut Continental Regiment commanded by Col. Charles Webb, also of Stamford. The regiment had been newly formed at Danbury as a result of the reorganization of the Continental Army at the end of 1776. Many of its officers and men had served under Webb in the 7th Connecticut Regiment of 1775 and the 19th Continental Regiment of 1776, which had seen action at White Plains, Trenton and Princeton, and these formed the nucleus of the new organization.[3] It is likely that Budd was a slave when he signed on, though this is not certain. At the time, men were being enlisted either for three years' service or for the duration of the war. Slaves enlisting in the Continental service were frequently promised their freedom if they agreed to serve until the end of the war, and that was how Budd enlisted.

Budd's earlier life had either been spent as a household slave or servant. Because of his skill in cookery and domestic duties, he spent much of his war time working in the entourage of generals and other officers—what Captain Betts referred to as being "attached to the Family" of a high ranking officer. These officers sometimes impressed capable and desirable individuals into their personal service, without regard to the niceties of official orders. As a young private, Budd probably had little say over who might "detain" him on such duties, and this could lead to difficulties when those officers were outside of his normal chain

2. B.H. Mills to Emily Blackman, December 14, 1869, Catalog # 148, Susquehanna County Historical Society. Mills knew Budd through his father, Josiah Mills, a Revolutionary War veteran who met with his fellow veterans twice a year at the Susquehanna County Court House in Montrose, Pennsylvania, when they drew their pensions. B.H. Mills refers to Budd as "one 'Sampson' a full blooded African, who 'had served through the war.'"

3. Fred Anderson Berg, *Encyclopedia of Continental Army Units: Battalions, Regiments and Independent Corps* (Harrisburg, PA: Stackpole Books, 1972), 19-35. Robert K. Wright, Jr., *The Continental Army* (Washington, DC: US Government Printing Office, 1986), 233-239. The 2nd Connecticut Continental Regiment of 1777 was organized in early 1777. It was normally assigned to the Highland Department, but periodically served with the main army. The regiment served as the 2nd Connecticut until January 1, 1781, when most of its remaining personnel went into the 3rd Connecticut Continental Regiment of 1781.

of command. Among others, Lt. James Taylor appears to have appropriated Budd's services as a waiter. It is most likely this practice that caused him to be listed as a deserter on his regiment's rolls in November, 1779.[4]

After the war, Budd told his comrades that he had attended General Washington himself, and he certainly may have waited on the commander in chief during dinners given by the officers under whom he served.[5] These duties did not mean that he was able to spend his time safely behind the lines during an engagement, however. Soldiers who served in various capacities, such as waiters, tailors, or farriers, joined the ranks with the rest of the men when their units were involved in combat. Henry Dearborn, for instance, mentions encountering one of Col. Benedict Arnold's waiters in the thick of the fighting at the assault on Quebec.[6] In his pension application, Budd declared that he "was in the battles of Saratoga, White Marsh, Monmouth & Capture of Stony-Point."[7]

During his first years of service, Budd's regiment was actively involved in a number battles and skirmishes. On the night of June 30, 1777, while the 2nd Connecticut was posted near Peekskill, New York,

4. Bristol Budd, Compiled Service Records, November, 1779, M881, Roll 191, NARA. Budd's former captain, Stephen Betts, in one of his two affidavits in support of Budd's pension, explained, ". . . Budd on account of his remarkable faithfulness and activity, and of his skill in cookery & other duties of a domestic servant, was generally, if not always, while in the revolutionary army, attached to the family of a General, Field, or other officer - that I have no recollection of his having been, at any time during the war of the revolution, returned as a deserter, but if it was so, I think it must have been in consequence of his having been detained by an officer of our army an unusual length of time, without any fault of his; or by some such mistake. I have an impression on my memory, that said Budd was once absent, for a considerable length of time, with a Lieutenant Taylor & of hearing afterwards in the army that he was detained by the said Lieutenant without any fault of the said Budd . . ." Budd, in his pension application, stated that "he was detached . . . for a time to Lieutenant James Taylor in the quarter master department." Document dated December 4, 1820, Pension Application of Bristol Budd. The officer in question may actually have been Lieutenant Augustine Taylor, who served as the Regimental Quartermaster of the 7th Connecticut in 1778. Francis Bernard Heitman, *Historical Register of Officers of the Continental Army during the War of the Revolution, April, 1775 to December, 1773* (Washington, DC: 1914, reprinted Baltimore: Genealogical Publishing Co., 1982), 533.
5. E.A. Weston, *History of Brooklyn, Susquehanna Co., Penn'a, its homes and its people* (Brooklyn, PA: Squier, 1889), 164.
6. Henry Dearborn, "Journal of the Quebec Expedition," in *March to Quebec: Journals of the Members of Arnold's Expedition*, compiled & annotated by Kenneth Roberts (New York: Doubleday & Company, 1938), 149-150.
7. Document dated December 4, 1820, Pension Application of Bristol Budd.

a number of men from the unit were killed, wounded and captured in an encounter with Brig. Gen. Oliver DeLancey's Loyalist Brigade near Kingsbridge. When Washington, facing off against the British who then occupied Philadelphia, called for reinforcements in November, 1777, the 2nd Connecticut was reassigned from the Highlands Department along the Hudson River in New York to the main army. Budd's regiment marched rapidly to Whitemarsh, a few miles north of Philadelphia. There, on December 7, 1777, they participated in an ugly skirmish along the Edge Hill ridge. Facing the vanguard of a substantial British column commanded by Maj. Gen. Charles "No Flint" Grey, the 2nd Connecticut was outflanked, enveloped and caught in a crossfire by an elite force of Hessian jägers, British light infantry, and Queen's Rangers. Here the regiment suffered its heaviest casualties of the war, losing twenty-eight men killed or captured in a matter of minutes, including seven from Budd's own company.[8] Following this, the army shifted its ground to Valley Forge, where the 2nd Connecticut, short on food and clothing, faced a bitter winter.

That Budd was an active and trusted soldier is evident from his reassignment to the light infantry in 1778, when he was detailed, along with some of the likeliest men in the 2nd Connecticut, into a newly formed light infantry company commanded by Capt. Henry Ten Eyck.[9] In the small hours of July 16, 1779, this unit participated in the storming of Stony Point, as part of the main body, which assaulted the fort from the south. Shortly afterward, however, Budd's absence was noted on the light infantry's muster rolls, and he was listed as a deserter. His former captain, Stephen Betts, ascribed Budd's absence to being forced to wait on an officer from another organization, but Budd did not reappear on the rolls of the light infantry or the 2nd Connecticut, and this became an obstacle to his receiving a pension. According to Budd's and Betts's accounts, he continued to serve until discharged at the end of the war in 1783.

Budd's whereabouts between 1783 and 1810 are not recorded, but in 1806, he fathered a son, William, and may also have had two daughters shortly thereafter.[10] By 1810, now a free man as a result of his mil-

8. 2nd Connecticut Continental Regiment Muster and Pay Rolls, December, 1777, M246, Rolls 5-6, NARA.
9. Pension Application of Bristol Budd. However, Budd does not actually appear on Ten Eyck's muster roll till August, 1779.
10. Additional information on Budd's life after the Revolution can be found in these sources: Weston, *History of Brooklyn*, 164-165; Debra Adleman, *Waiting for the Lord: Nineteenth Century Black Communities in Susquehanna County, Pennsylvania* (Rockland, ME: Picton Press, 1997), 10-15.

itary service, he had settled with his son William along the Dry Creek in what is now Brooklyn Township, Susquehanna County, a part of northeastern Pennsylvania then being populated mainly by people from Connecticut. He took up residence near a spring, in a log cabin belonging to the Howard family, earning his living as a day laborer. Sometime in 1814, when Budd was about fifty-one, catastrophe struck: he went suddenly and completely blind. He used to say that his neighbor, Charles Howard, for whom he may have worked, "was the last person or object he ever saw."[11] Following this personal disaster, Budd was no longer able to earn a living. In 1820 he stated, "I have been blind for six years—during that time I have lived entirely on the charity of the people." That he had been reduced to poverty is made clear in the inventory of his possessions that was required as part of the pension application process; Budd's sole possession of any value was "one hen turkey," valued at one dollar. "I live with my father in law a black man, who is as poor as myself . . . The department can judge of our poverty."[12]

In 1818, Congress passed the first Revolutionary War Pension Act, entitling disabled veterans like Budd to a stipend to be paid twice a year.[13] With the aid of several of his neighbors, Budd set about the complex process of applying for a federal pension. For many of the veterans who applied, this proved to be a long and fruitless process. Those who were persistent and could demonstrate the terms of their service were eventually rewarded. Difficulties immediately arose for Budd. He had no record of his service, no discharge papers, and the men he had served with—those still living—were two hundred miles away. In 1818, Rufus Kingsley, Joseph Chapman and Thomas Williams, three Susquehanna County veterans of the Connecticut Line, attested to Budd's serv-

11. Weston, *History of Brooklyn*, 22.

12. Document dated December 4, 1820, Pension Application of Bristol Budd. Prince Perkins, himself a Revolutionary War veteran, moved to Susquehanna County sometime between 1793 and 1795. Weston, *History of Brooklyn*, 186. Family tradition suggests that the two knew each other during the war, and that Perkins may have induced Budd to move there. Private communication, Denise Dennis, June 24, 2017. There is a record for a man named Prince Negro in Captain Jonathan Parker's company of the 2nd Connecticut Regiment. Many African Americans, who are listed in the muster rolls with descriptive names like "Negro," later acquired standard surnames. Budd and Prince enlisted a day apart, March 19th and 20th, 1777. 2nd Connecticut Continental Regiment Muster and Pay Rolls, August and December, 1777.

13. John Resch, *Suffering Soldiers: Revolutionary War Veterans, Moral Sentiment, and Political Culture in the Early Republic* (Amherst: University of Massachusetts Press, 1999), 93-118.

ice in the 2nd Connecticut, but since none of them had actually served with Budd, the Pension Office wanted more proof.[14]

Determined to prove his claim, Budd set out, afoot, on a circuit of Connecticut to seek out his old comrades. A few veterans swore affidavits supporting Budd, saying that they believed his account, based on their own experiences, but they did not personally recall him. Their testimony alone was not likely to carry much weight. Fortunately, he tracked down his former captain from the 2nd Connecticut, Stephen Betts, now living in New Canaan, a well-respected officer who, like Budd, had served through the war. Betts' affidavit, now lost, was a decisive factor in convincing officials of Budd's service. But the Pension Office, checking on Budd's record, came across a muster roll stating that Budd had deserted. Undeterred, in the Spring of 1821, Budd made another trip to Connecticut, again led by his young son, obtaining a second statement from Captain Betts that he had, in fact, served honorably and completed his service.[15]

Once Betts' new statement was submitted to the War Department, the Pension Office finally granted the blind veteran a pension, along with arrears dating back to his first date of eligibility in April 1818. Budd was now to receive $96 a year, payable in semi-annual installments at the county courthouse in Montrose. In addition, the back pay added up to a significant sum. With this money, he purchased property in 1821 and, in 1826, married Phoebe Perkins, a daughter of Prince Perkins, the man described as his father-in-law in 1818.[16]

In June, 1832, pensions were finally granted to all Revolutionary War soldiers who had served six months or more. That September, nearly

14. Budd's neighbor, B.H. Mills said that, in the case of his own father, Josiah, "it was with great difficulty the necessary proofs of identity were secured." B.H. Mills to Emily Blackman, December 14, 1869. Rufus Kingsley had been a drummer serving in Connecticut line from 1775-1778. Joseph Chapman was a lieutenant in the 4th Connecticut. Through conversation, the men were convinced that Budd had also served in the Connecticut line. Weston, *History of Brooklyn*, 165; Pension Application of Rufus Kingsley, Revolutionary War Pension and Bounty Land Warrant Application Files, M804, Roll 1492, NARA.

15. Document dated May 1, 1821, Pension Application of Bristol Budd. Another document, dated June 29, 1821, from the same file, referred to Budd as "A poor old blind Negro, who was led by his son, aged 14, four hundred miles, to obtain the Certificate of his Captain (a respectable Man, of New Canaan, Connecticut) that he did not desert, but served to the end of the War."

16. Weston, *History of Brooklyn*, 164-165. Budd evidently married, or remarried, Phoebe Perkins in 1826 to ensure there was a formal record that would entitle her to receive his pension in the event of his death. Private communication, Denise Dennis, June 24, 2017.

fifty years after the close of hostilities, seventy aged veterans gathered on the courthouse green in Montrose, Pennsylvania and, with fife and drum, drilled before the public with fine precision, to the great admiration of the onlookers. The pensioners subsequently gathered there twice a year, when their pensions were distributed, creating an informal, enlisted man's version of the Society of Cincinnati.[17]

Budd continued to live on his fifty acres, raising a family of several children. He attended the semi-annual pensioners' gatherings, swapping stories and reminiscing with his fellow veterans about the difficult days when they had forged a nation. In the Summer of 1848, then at least eighty-five years of age, Bristol Budd passed away and was buried in the Perkins family graveyard. His widow, Phoebe, eventually moved to Ohio in the 1850's, and claimed bounty land there due her for her husband's service to his country. She continued to draw his pension till the end of her life.[18]

Men who saw long service during the revolution were inured to hardship and full of determination—not the sort easily dissuaded from a cause. Bristol Budd was a remarkable example of that dogged American character, an ex-private who had been through harrowing moments in the fight for independence. Throughout his life, he demonstrated the sort of enterprise, courage and persistence that won the war.

17. Writing of his father, Josiah, B.H. Mills said, "Among my earliest recollections was going with him to Montrose [county seat of Susquehanna County, Pennsylvania] on the fourth days of March & September 'to draw the pension.' Here were gathered a score or more of these war worn heroes. How animated they became as 'they fought their battles over again.' How my young heart was stirred as they talked of Washington, Greene & Gates, of Saratoga & Yorktown . . . On the 4th of Sept. 1832, there was a grand gathering at Montrose of all revolutionary soldiers in the County. About seventy, if memory serves me, were present. They formed on 'the green' under command of Capt. Potter of Gibson. One of their number played the fife, another the drum, & with their canes for arms went through various military evolutions, putting to shame by their perfection the famous 136th Regiment on parade at the same time." B.H. Mills to Emily Blackman, December 14, 1869.

18. The Perkins-Dennis Cemetery, final resting place of Bristol Budd Sampson, is maintained today by the Dennis Farm Charitable Land Trust in Susquehanna County, PA. http://thedennisfarm.org. For Phoebe's bounty land, see document dated June 13, 1855, Pension Application of Bristol Budd.

AUTHOR BIOGRAPHIES

SHAI AFSAI

Shai Afsai is a writer living in Providence, Rhode Island. His articles have appeared in *The Providence Journal, The Jerusalem Post, Rhode Island History, Shofar: An Interdisciplinary Journal of Jewish Studies*, and *Anthropology Today*. His "Jews and Freemasons in Providence: Temple Beth-El and Redwood Lodge" won the Rhode Island Jewish Historical Association's 2013 Horvitz Award.

BRUCE WARE ALLEN

Bruce Ware Allen received a degree in classics from Duke University. He is the author of *The Great Siege of Malta: The Epic Battle between the Ottoman Empire and the Knights of St. John* (ForeEdge, 2015).

BRETT BANNOR

Brett Bannor is manager of animal collections for Goizueta Gardens at the Atlanta History Center (AHC). When not engaged in the daily care of heritage breed livestock or monitoring wildlife on the AHC campus, he studies the historic connections between animals and people. He is author of a book on bighorn sheep for pre-teens and co-author of *Common Gallinule* for the Cornell Lab of Ornithology's Birds of North America database.

ZACHARY BROWN

Zachary Brown is a native of Toronto Ontario, and history student at Stanford University, with a concentration in the United States, under advisor Professor Richard White. His primary research interests are the rhetoric of Anglo-Indian relations along the frontier during the Colonial and Revolutionary periods and the American Civil War as part of the age of nationalism.

ALEXANDER CAIN

Alexander Cain received a degree in economics from Merrimack College and a JD from New England School of Law. He frequently lectures on constitutional and historical issues, and developments in the United States. He has published several research articles relevant to New England militias and loyalists during the American Revolution, and is author of two books, *We Stood Our Ground: Lexington in the First Year of the American Revolution* and *I See Nothing but the Horrors of a Civil War.*

Robert N. Fanelli

Robert N. Fanelli is a founding member of the Washington Crossing Revolutionary War Round Table. He serves as a trustee of the Swan Historical Foundation, which owns the important collection of revolutionary war artifacts on display in the museum of the Washington Crossing State Park in Titusville, New Jersey.

Katie Turner Getty

Katie Turner Getty is a Boston lawyer, writer, and independent researcher. She earned her JD from New England Law Boston, cum laude, holds a BA from Wellesley College with a focus on revolutionary America, and is a graduate of Bunker Hill Community College.

Phillip R. Giffin

Phillip R. Giffin has a BS in Foreign Service from Georgetown University, Captaincy in the US Army Ordnance, 1966-68, and an MAT from George Fox University. He is currently transcribing, researching, and writing a series of essays and a book based on unpublished family papers (the diary and the record book of Sergeant Simon Giffin 1777-1783).

Don N. Hagist

Don N. Hagist, editor of *Journal of the American Revolution*, is an independent researcher specializing in the British Army in the American Revolution. His books include *The Revolution's Last Men: the Soldiers Behind the Photographs* (Westholme Publishing, 2015), *British Soldiers, American War* (Westholme Publishing, 2012), *A British Soldier's Story: Roger Lamb's Narrative of the American Revolution* (Ballindalloch Press, 2004), *General Orders: Rhode Island* (Heritage Books, 2001) and *Wives, Slaves, and Servant Girls* (Westholme Publishing, 2016).

Benjamin L. Huggins

Benjamin L. Huggins is an associate professor and editor at the Papers of George Washington project at the University of Virginia. He received his PhD in history from George Mason University. He is author of *Washington's War, 1779* (Westholme Publishing, 2018), *Willie Mangum and the North Carolina Whigs in the Age of Jackson* (McFarland, 2016), and wrote a chapter in *A Companion to George Washington*, Edward Lengel, ed. (Wiley-Blackwell 2012).

John Knight

John Knight received a joint honours degree in American History/Politics from Warwick University. He was a fine art valuer for a number of London-based auction houses including Christie's and Bonhams before taking up writing and lecturing full time. A confirmed Americanophile, he writes on American culture, society, and history at englishmanlovesamerica.com.

Wayne Lynch

Wayne Lynch is an independent researcher and writer. Since 2010, he has been researching and writing about the Southern campaigns of the American Revolution. He is a certified public accountant and tax attorney in Galveston, Texas.

Louis Arthur Norton

Louis Arthur Norton, a professor emeritus at the University of Connecticut, has published extensively on maritime history topics, including *Joshua Barney: Hero of the Revolutionary War* (Naval Institute, 2000) and *Captains Contentious: The Dysfunctional Sons of the Brine* (University of South Carolina Press, 2009). Two of his articles were awarded the 2002 and 2006 Gerald E. Morris Prize for maritime historiography in the Mystic Seaport Museum's LOG.

Aaron J. Palmer

Aaron J. Palmer earned his PhD at Georgetown University. He is associate professor of history, Wisconsin Lutheran College and co-director of the college's Honors Program. He is author of *A Rule of Law: Elite Political Authority and the Coming of the American Revolution in the South Carolina Lowcountry, 1763-1776* (Leiden: Brill, 2014).

Hershel Parker

Hershel Parker was a 1997 Pulitzer Prize finalist for *Herman Melville: A Biography, 1819-1851* (Johns Hopkins, 1996). That volume and *Herman Melville: A Biography, 1851-1891* (Johns Hopkins, 2002) each won the R. R. Hawkins award from the Association of American Publishers. He is also author of the critically acclaimed *Melville Biography: An Inside Narrative* (Northwestern, 2013).

Jim Piecuch

Jim Piecuch earned his PhD at the College of William and Mary. He is an associate professor of history at Kennesaw State University. He is editor of *Cavalry of the American Revolution* (Westholme Publishing, 2012) and author of *The Battle of Camden: A Documentary History* (History Press, 2006), *Three Peoples, One King: Loyalists, Indians, and Slaves in the Revolutionary South* (University of South Carolina Press, 2008), and *"The Blood Be Upon Your Head": Tarleton and the Myth of Buford's Massacre* (Southern Campaigns of the American Revolution, 2010).

Gene Procknow

Gene Procknow's research includes interpreting the Revolution from a non-American perspective, better understanding the Revolution's global aspects, and Ethan Allen and the creation of Vermont. He is the author of the *Mad River Gazetteer*, which traces the naming of prominent Vermont place names to Revolutionary War patriots.

Ray Raphael

Ray Raphael in an award-winning historian and an associate editor of the *Journal of the American Revolution*. He coauthored with Marie Raphael *The Spirit of '74: How the American Revolution Began* (New Press, 2015), and is author of

Founding Myths: Stories that Hide Our Patriotic Past (New Press, 2004, 2014) and *A People's History of the American Revolution* (New Press, 2001, and Harper Perennial, 2016).

DARREN R. REID

Darren R. Reid is a lecturer in history at Coventry University. His research is concerned in part with the role played by violence in the shaping of early American society. He has presented before the Scottish Association for the Study of America, the British Group of Early American Historians, and the Society for Appalachian Historians.

CONNER RUNYAN

Conner Runyan was a teacher, administrator and professor for forty-one years in Alabama's public schools and universities. Now retired, he lives in Fyffe, Alabama.

BOB RUPPERT

Bob Ruppert is a retired high school administrator from the greater Chicagoland area. He received his undergraduate degree from Loyola University and his graduate degree from the University of Illinois. His interest in history began in 1963 when his parents took the whole family to a small town that was slowly being restored to its eighteenth century prominence—Williamsburg.

IAN SABERTON

Ian Saberton holds a PhD in history from the University of Warwick. He was an adviser on constitutional and political affairs, machinery of government, contingency planning, and devolution in the Northern Ireland Office (NIO) at the height of the Troubles. His service in the NIO has brought to his writing hands-on experience in dealing with a quasi-revolutionary situation.

TOM SHACHTMAN

Tom Shachtman is the author of more than a dozen non-fiction books, including *Gentlemen Scientists and Revolutionaries* (St. Martin's Press, 2014) and *The Phony War, 1939-1940* (Harper & Row, 1982). His most recent award was from the American Institute of Physics for the script of the *Nova* broadcast, *Absolute Zero and the Conquest of Cold*, based on his book of that name. He has lectured at Harvard, New York University, Stanford, Georgia Tech, and the Smithsonian Institution.

JOSHUA SHEPHERD

Joshua Shepherd, a sculptor and freelance writer, has created more than twenty public monuments. His articles, with a special focus on Revolutionary and frontier America, have appeared in publications including *MHQ: The Quarterly Journal of Military History, Military Heritage, Muzzle Blasts,* and *The Artilleryman.*

JOHN L. SMITH, JR.

John L. Smith, Jr. earned a BS degree from the University of South Florida and an MBA from the University of Tampa. He is a Vietnam-era veteran and holds honorable discharges from the U.S. Air Force Reserve and the U.S. Army Reserve. His historical work has been featured by *Knowledge Quest, National Review, CNN,* and *Smithsonian Magazine.*

GEOFF SMOCK

Geoff Smock is a native of western Washington. He received a degree in history from Pacific Lutheran University and a MEd from the University of Washington. He currently teaches eighth grade social studies and literacy near Seattle.

ERIC STERNER

Eric Sterner is a national security and aerospace consultant. He held senior staff positions for the Committees on Armed Services and Science in the House of Representatives and served in the Department of Defense and as NASA's Associate Deputy Administrator for Policy and Planning. He earned a BA from American University and two MAs from George Washington University.

MIKE THOMIN

Mike Thomin is the manager of the Destination Archaeology Resource Center in Pensacola, Florida. He is also a regular writer for the *Unearthing Florida* radio program on NPR. He received a BA in history from the University of West Florida and is finishing his master's degree in public history.

PHILIP D. WEAVER

Philip D. Weaver has been an active living historian for over forty years, mostly with the Brigade of the American Revolution. An original member of the West Point Chapter, Company of Military Historians, he was elected a Fellow of the Company in May 2004. He is the editor and principle author of *The Greatest Hits of The Colonial Chronicle: The Rev-War Collection* (June 2016).

RICHARD J. WERTHER

Richard J. Werther is a retired CPA and history enthusiast living in Novi, Michigan. He studied business management at Bucknell University in Lewisburg, Pennsylvania.

INDEX